The Way It Worked and Why It Won't

The Way It Worked and Why It Won't

*Structural Change
and the Slowdown of
U.S. Economic Growth*

Gordon C. Bjork

Westport, Connecticut
London

Library of Congress Cataloging-in-Publication Data

Bjork, Gordon C.
     The way it worked and why it won't : structural change and the
slowdown of U.S. economic growth / Gordon C. Bjork.
         p.   cm.
     Includes bibliographical references and index.
     ISBN 0–275–96531–7 (alk. paper).—ISBN 0–275–96532–5 (pbk. :
alk. paper)
     1. United States—Economic policy—1993–   2. United States—
Economic policy.   3. United States—Economic conditions.
     4. Structural adjustment (Economic policy)—United States.
     I. Title.
     HC106.82.B58   1999
     338.973—dc21   98–53395

British Library Cataloguing in Publication Data is available.

Library of Congress Catalog Card Number: 98–53395
ISBN: 0–275–96531–7
         0–275–96532–5 (pbk.)

First published in 1999

Praeger Publishers, 88 Post Road West, Westport, CT 06881
An imprint of Greenwood Publishing Group, Inc.
www.praeger.com

Printed in the United States of America

The paper used in this book complies with the
Permanent Paper Standard issued by the National
Information Standards Organization (Z39.48–1984).

10 9 8 7 6 5 4 3 2 1

To Ando, Arjun, Becky, Erin, Hannah, Kate, Matt, and Robert.
And to Ananda, Claire, Elizabeth, Sara, and the rest of the next generation:
With hopes that "you'll figure it out."

Contents

Graphs and Tables

TEXT TABLES

APPENDIX TABLES

Preface

We live life facing forward but understand it looking backward.
　　　　　　　　　　　　　　　　　—Søren Kierkegaard

The decline in the growth rate of the U.S. economy over the past quarter-century is widely recognized by economists. However, the causes of the decline are the subject of extensive speculation by economists and others. Some of the speculation by economists is based on misinformation about the historical record, and misconceptions about the process of economic growth. Some of the misconceptions about economic growth communicated to the public by journalists and politicians are based on misunderstanding of the nature of measurement in economics. These misconceptions lead to assertions that America could reverse the decline in the rate of economic growth and return to higher and increasing rates of growth if we only followed the right policies.

The claims are appealing. Many people yearn for a return to a mythical past when things were better. That theme lies behind part of the title for this book, which is a play on the title of one of my favorite films—"The Way We Were." In the film stars Barbra Streisand and Robert Redford indulge in nostalgic flashbacks to the romance of their college days; but the film ends with their realization that the romance of their adolescence is no longer relevant to their mature years. Similarly contrasting adolescence and maturity, this book explains how measured growth in per capita incomes increased more rapidly in the past than it does in the present—and why it won't increase even that fast in the future.

This book presents and explains the evidence on three related economic phenomena: (1) the acceleration and deceleration over the past century in the observed rate of growth of Gross Domestic Product (GDP) per worker hour resulting from structural changes in the composition of output; (2) the decline in the rate of growth of GDP per capita over the past quarter-century because of the interaction of changes in productivity and changes in the participation of the population in the labor force; and (3) the decline in the proportion of income that the average working American takes home in disposable (after-tax) income—because of the necessary increases in the proportion of national income that go to educate the young and to support and care for the retired population.

My explanation of those phenomena will use the scientific method of observation, disaggregation, and generalization of observed regularities in the evidence. My data all come from standard government sources. To explain diverse technological and organizational change, I use the rhetoric of heuristic examples. In this I rely on the focussed and informed analysis of particular technologies by the engineers and economists who have made the actual observations. If my role here is useful, it is in an attempt to clarify "What oft was thought but ne'er so well expressed," and I am diffident about the extent to which I have been able to achieve that aim in this book.

I want to emphasize, at the outset, that this is not a pessimistic book. The measured rate of growth of GDP per capita and per worker has slowed down and will continue to slow down (measured by the admittedly incomplete and arbitrary national income accounting concepts we use), but the statistically average American will still be better off (by those concepts) as she "crosses the bridge into the twenty-first century" than any of her predecessors in the twentieth century. This book is about the decline in the rate of increase of measured economic output—not the "end of history" (Fukuyama, 1989) or the "end of affluence" (Madrick, 1995) or the end of anything else.

Economic soothsayers with a vision of the future frequently base their arguments on appeals to the past. Positive prophets would have you believe, on the one hand, that the United States is capable of a return to rapid economic growth with a flat tax or investment in infrastructure or some other combination of the "right stuff." They are contradicted by the pessimistic pundits who prophesy inevitable decline.

How can you evaluate these arguments? If you are an intelligent citizen seeking to understand the current economic performance of the United States in terms of an explanation of historical patterns of economic growth and current economic knowledge and data, this book is for you. If you believe you have been working harder and consuming less, this book has an explanation of your experience. You might not want to hear what I have to say, but it may save you from charlatans or politicians or other economists who want to sell you "snake oil" to fix an economy that isn't ailing.

TO THE GENERAL READER

This book is both bumptious and presumptuous. It is bumptious in making an unequivocal prediction about future events—always a dangerous practice in economics, where prudence counsels equivocation and a restricted time frame.

It is presumptuous in attempting to describe and explain an extremely complex subject in simplified terms—always an open invitation to critics to ridicule "simplistic" explanations and point out alternative explanations not considered and data unincorporated into the analysis.

I hasten to add that the book is also substantive—it is evidenced with fairly and consistently presented "hard facts": the national income and demographic statistics collected by agencies of the U.S. government. These are used by choice and by necessity by all economists because of the costs and access necessary for their collection. These statistics are used to explain the slowdown simply by taking them apart. I do not peddle any "theories" (except in the last part of the penultimate chapter); I basically try to present the facts and explain the accounting measurement concepts that lie behind those facts. I have tried to make the explanation simple, but the explanation of a complex subject cannot be very simple.

My primary objective in this volume is to explain the slowdown of the rate of growth of the American economy over the last two decades as a continuation of our experience over the past century. It is important to understand the slower growth of the last two decades in terms of a longer time frame of reference because the rapid growth of the American economy in the quarter-century after recovery from the 1930s Great Depression and World War II was extraordinary in our economic history. We need a longer frame of reference.

Economics is not a dismal science; it is a realistic science that explains how things really happened as a basis for understanding the past and the future. It is only dismal to those who prefer nostalgia or flights of fantasy to the realities of physical and human nature. President Harry S Truman once remarked of his speeches, "I never give them hell. I just tell the truth, and they think it is hell." My explanation of the process of economic growth explains "the way it worked" in the past so you will understand why it doesn't in the present, and "why it won't" in the future.

The English scientist and novelist C.P. Snow lamented the division of the intellectual community into two cultures—the humanistic and the scientific. Things have deteriorated since he made that judgment halfway through the twentieth century. I have tried to bridge that gap in this book in writing for both the intelligent non-economist and my professional colleagues. The chapters in the book are nontechnical discussions of complex issues. "Someone told me that each equation I included in the book would halve the sales," writes Stephen Hawking in *A Brief History of Time*; I have tried to confine the technical material to footnotes and appendixes.

TO THE PROFESSIONAL ECONOMIST

There is nothing "new" in this book for professional economists—no new theories, or models, or data. However, I have addressed this book to you, my fellow economists, as well as ordinary mortals, because you, equally, observe and explain the world through the prism of past experience. Unfortunately for perspective, the working economist's prism is usually an intellectual microscope that allows her to examine, minutely, the structure and behavior of some very small subset of the economy—not the economy as a whole as it changes through time. Progress, in scientific enquiry, is largely made by focussed enquiry that pushes out the sphere of knowledge. But this progress comes with the necessary consequence that economists may have a very good understanding of their own focussed field of enquiry but little knowledge of what has previously occurred in the economy as a whole.

Worst of all, it becomes increasingly difficult for economists to put a total economy, embedded in a particular society at a particular time, in the focus of a telescope rather than a microscope. To further extend the analogy, it is even more difficult if the instrument in question is a radio telescope (where the phenomena are indirectly observed) rather than an optical telescope, where one uses one's eyeball. It is yet more difficult if the objective is to observe changes in acceleration through time rather than the fixing of a position at a moment of time. Declining growth is the deceleration of the rate of change of the (arbitrary measurement construct) GDP of an economy.

This book uses the prism of an historical macroeconomic "telescope" that does look at the economy as a whole and emphasizes the changes in technology, demographics, and social organization that drive "real" and long-term (as opposed to nominal and cyclical) phenomena. My argument depends upon the disaggregation of national income and demographic identities and simulation of changes in those identities rather than time series econometrics. I do think you will find the results of the disaggregation of productivity growth by sector (Text Tables 5.2 and 5.3) very compelling.

Making sense of what is happening to the economy as it changes around us is a perspective problem, a "can't see the forest for the trees" problem for an economist or any other intelligent observer. The likely objection of my fellow economists to my effort to describe the forest is that my preoccupation with the forest has hindered my understanding because I fail to use the specialized knowledge and data on the behavior of the individual cells of the individual trees that make up the forest—and the forest is nothing more than a population of individual trees comprised of cells. I anticipate and accept the criticism. "A little inaccuracy sometimes saves tons of explanation," said H. H. Munro, the Scottish pundit who wrote under the pseudonym "Saki."

Since the positivist methodological revolution of the twentieth century, economics, like other sciences, has become more and more reductionist in the focus of its enquiries. Microeconomics has increasingly asked, "How will an individual behave in response to changes in income, relative prices or other variables?" I believe that this (Marshallian/neoclassical) economic methodology is an appropriate method for analysis of comparative static phenomena. It has little application to the explanation of change that occurs, over time, as the characteristics of individuals change with income, wealth, education, age, and so on, and as technologies change with the advances of science.

Thus, my method of explanation will emphasize change in the composition of aggregates over time—individuals as producers or consumers might not change their behavior much, but as the composition of the populations of individuals changes, the result is aggregate change.   The rate of growth of commodity producing industries may continue at a high rate but their effect on the rate of growth of the economy diminishes as they become a smaller proportion of total output and the slower (measured) growth service economy increases in relative size.   Increases in the participation rate of the population in the labor force increase the rate of growth of total output; but when all the members of the prime working age groups are working, it is self-evident that there can be no further increases in the participation rate!

While I am skeptical of the usefulness of macroeconomic neoclassical growth theory, it is not my purpose to overthrow existing economic theory and create a new intellectual paradigm. My methodological progenitor is the founder of economics, Adam Smith, who modestly entitled his magnum opus *An Inquiry into the Nature and Causes of the Wealth of Nations.* I aim to emulate Smith's perceptive analysis of economic activity and his cautious explanations based on intertemporal and cross-cultural comparison of anecdotal evidence.

Like Adam Smith I am concerned with explaining changes in the rate of growth of the economic output of nations.   His optimistic explanation emphasized "the natural progress toward opulence" that would result from the interaction of self-interest with the spread of market-organized activity.   Like Smith, I also believe there is a natural movement but I believe that, at the current stage of the U.S. economy, it is toward a declining rate of growth of opulence as a result of the opulence, itself.   I believe the historical evidence for my hypothesis is compelling.

ACKNOWLEDGMENTS

The motivation for this book has come from my students' probing questions about how the world works.   My answers aren't finished—they are just published.   Like any author, I am aware of unused and unavailable evidence, unanswered objections, and unpolished argument.   My basis for the answers to the questions addressed   in this book has evolved over many years and has come from many sources and I would like to pay tribute to a few of them: former teachers John Hicks and Douglass North who introduced me to the uses of economic theory and economic history; long-time friend and colleague, Peter Drucker, whose work and conversation has helped me to think creatively about the implications of historical change for economic theory and institutions; the work of Simon Kuznets, whose models and methods of explanation of the process of economic growth are unmistakable in this book; and Richard Easterlin and Nathan Rosenberg, whose research has helped me understand the roles of demography and technology in economic change.

Unlike many modern monographs, this book been developed without the support of foundation or government grants or institutional leaves. For a quarter-century my college—Claremont McKenna—has furnished me with a generous salary for doing a job I enjoy, the amenities of a good office, equipment, support staff, library, and an institutional atmosphere favorable to the pursuit of and reflection on knowledge.   My most important acknowledgment is to my supportive critic, editor, and spouse of forty years, Susan.

CHAPTER 1

The Argument: The Way It Worked and Why It Won't

First...say what the play treats on; then read the names of the actors, and so grow to a point.

—William Shakespeare
A Midsummer Night's Dream

The final decade of the twentieth century has been a prosperous period for the United States. The media have recited statistics of low unemployment, low inflation, rising consumer confidence, and a soaring stock market. Amid all this economic good news about the economy, many working Americans have wondered why their inflation-adjusted take-home paychecks were not increasing very rapidly (or were even declining!). Were they losing out in their share of the American Dream of continuing improvement in their standard of living?[1]

What many have not known is that, even with the excellent economic performance of the American economy, growth in output per worker—the source of paychecks—has risen slowly over the decade. The productivity slowdown of the prosperous 1990s is a continuation of the growth slowdown that began in the 1970s and continued during the 1980s. Further, an increasing share of even this small increase in growth in output has been taken from workers' paychecks to support the younger and older generations that are not in the labor force.

Americans have been told that "something needs to be done" about Social Security, Medicare, and education. What most Americans have not been told is that American economic growth has continued to slow which makes doing something that involves raising taxes more painful—even in the prosperous 1990s—because measured productivity growth is slowing just as it has slowed over the last half of the twentieth century.

The American Dream has always been a hope for continuing improvement in the standard of living. Popular political rhetoric over the past three decades—by both major political parties—has centered on this faith in the possibility of ever improving economic performance by the American economy. This rhetoric plays on the widespread belief that rapid economic growth is the *normal* and *natural* legacy of the American economy and could be regained by appropriate governmental policies and individual economic behavior. There is a strong popular belief that any slowdown in growth could be reversed if only Americans and their government would make the right choices and follow the right policies.

Could the slowdown of growth be reversed? No. Unequivocally, no. The central argument of this book is that the decline in the measured growth rate of U.S. per capita income that we have experienced over the past quarter-century is not temporary, cyclical, or reversible; rather, it is long run, structural, and irreversible.

While the growth rate of the economy might be slightly and temporarily improved by changes in the choices of its participants about working and saving, or changes in government economic policies, it is my contention that the decline in the measured rate of growth in output per capita and per worker cannot be permanently arrested or reversed. The growth rate of the U.S. economy will continue to slow as we move into the twenty-first century. In the pages that follow, I will explain this slowdown in economic growth as the natural and inevitable consequence of the success of the American economy in reaching economic maturity.

THE PLAN OF THE BOOK

Before I present explanation and supporting measurements for the growth slowdown, I will describe how economic growth has occurred in the American past by the consideration of some selected examples. In chapter 2 I will summarize some common features of the historical process of change to stress the once-and-for-all characteristics of change and the limits to further progress posed by the natural world.

Chapter 3 presents measurements of past growth and the components of that growth. It also makes comparisons of U.S. growth with the recorded growth rates of other advanced industrial economies and presents some comparative evidence on the levels of per capita income achieved by the United States and other economies.

Chapter 4 examines the biases and omissions of the accounting systems that are used to measure growth. The methodology of measurement of output and prices may seem tedious to the nonspecialist reader. However, judgments about the decline in growth rates are based on specific measurement conventions for output and prices. The use of different output measures, and the construction of different price indexes, changes the measure of "real" income. This means that one's conclusions about growth depend partly upon the measurement concepts used to measure it, so they need to be understood.

"Economic growth" usually refers to the rate of growth of the ratio of Gross Domestic Product (GDP) to Population. Per capita GDP is also referred to as per capita income. The rate of growth of per capita output (or income) is the sum of the rate of growth of output per worker, and the rate of growth of the proportion of the population that is working (a variant of the participation rate).

Chapters 5 and 6 present the historical record for those two key determinants of growth. In these chapters, as throughout the book, the evidence presented in support of my arguments is official and readily accessible U.S. government measurements of output, population, and labor force. The presentation of the trends and comparisons on which my arguments rest is made in text tables and graphs. The underlying data is presented in greater detail along with its sources and treatment in the chapter appendixes. The data is presented and sourced from readily accessible series and, where transformations have been made, such as price deflation or indexation, the procedures are explained so that any interested reader could reproduce my numbers. My method of argument is simply disaggregation—separating out all the components of growth and noting their relative importance. Trends in the economy result from trends in the behavior of individuals and I have disaggregated those individual behaviors by industries and demographic groups to explain what is happening to output per worker and income per capita.

Chapters 7 and 8 spell out the consequences of economic growth and demographic change for the intergenerational transfer of income from the working population to the dependent school age and retired populations. A primary determinant of the economic success of a society is the "human capital" created by the education of its population. Chapter 7 explains why expenditures on education *necessarily* take a progressively larger share of national income to merely maintain, let alone increase, the level of per capita incomes.

A significant consequence of the economic success of a society is the increase in life expectancy. The increase in life expectancy, however, first accelerates and then decelerates economic growth by changing the proportion of the employed to the retired population. Chapter 8 explains how, and by how much, the increase in life expectancy increases the proportion of income that must be redistributed from the working population to the retired population. In our society this transfer takes place through institutional mechanisms such as Social Security and Medicare and/or is provided for individually by individuals saving a larger proportion of income during a longer working life to provide for a longer retirement. The quantitative magnitude of necessary transfers or saving is exhibited by the use of simulation examples to show the effects of various economic and demographic factors on tax transfer rates and savings.

In chapter 9, I argue that conventional economic theory that explains the growth slowdown as resulting from declining saving or declining marginal productivity doesn't explain our historical experience. The chapter also offers a more speculative explanation of why economic growth does finally lead to a slowdown. Chapter 10 summarizes the main arguments and evidence of the book and briefly explores some of the implications of the decline in growth for our world-view and for economic and political policies.

The Affluence of a Mature Economy and the Growth Slowdown

The deceleration (or slowing) of the growth rate of economic output is the consequence of the success of the economic growth process itself; the high growth rates of the past have created a "mature" economy in which further proportional increases in output will come progressively more slowly.   The American economy is not presently producing less output per capita or per worker than it did in the past.   Output is still increasing—but at a slower rate of increase. The decline in the rate of growth of per capita output does not signal "the end of affluence," as posited by a book entitled with that phrase (Madrick, 1995). It means only the slowing of the growth in affluence.[2]

However, this slowdown in growth necessitates a readjustment in our view of the world we live in and the plans we make. The combination of the decline in growth and the increasing transfers to the young for education and to the retired for pensions and medical care means that personal consumption by the population in their working years will not increase as rapidly as it has over the past century.   For individuals currently making decisions about working and consuming, it means that they cannot postpone working, or postpone saving from current income with the expectation that future incomes will be larger and allow saving to take place more easily.   It will mean that retirement from employment without income reduction will have to come later, and that Medicare and Social Security expenditures per retiree cannot maintain their past rates of increase.

For governments, the growth slowdown means that budgets can't be made on the assumption of higher growth rates in output and tax receipts. For society, it means that dealing with the tensions arising from inequality in income distribution cannot be postponed with promises of future amelioration—"a smaller share in the pie in the present in return for a bigger pie in the future."

Economic Growth and Maturity—a Biological Analogy

Economic knowledge may have helped us learn how to moderate the swings in inflation and unemployment over the business cycle, but economic knowledge will not enable us to reverse the decline in the rate of economic growth—only to understand it. To understand the reasons for the decline in measured economic growth, it may be useful to introduce the analogy of the growth rate of an economy with the growth rate of a climax forest—an "old growth" forest, or a forest that has regrown to maturity after a forest fire or clearcutting.[3]   The growth of the forest begins with grasses, then bushes, then rapidly growing and finally slow-growing trees. At maturity the slower-growing trees finally replace many of the grasses and bushes and faster-growing trees by shading them from sunlight. If we were to measure the growth of the forest as the change in the volume of biomass, the rate of growth would be observed to accelerate, decelerate, and finally reach a constant flow rate.

Analogously, an economy begins with agricultural, handicraft, and household production (the grasses and bushes of the forest). Initial growth in agricultural productivity follows a path of slow growth and then acceleration when the growth allows some capital and labor resources to be devoted to industry and trade (the faster-growing trees in the forest). Finally, the growth in industrial productivity and continuing growth in agricultural productivity leads to the utilization of more and more resources of labor and capital in the service industries (the slow-growing trees in the forest).

We could compare the output of the economy—the accounting concept of GDP—to the annual growth of biomass of the forest. The forest has a "stock" of trees; the economy has a "stock" of accumulated physical, human, knowledge, and natural resource capital. The economy has an annual "flow" of "value added" from its stock of resources; the forest has an annual "flow" of new biomass from its plants.

A complete accounting for the output of the economy would include the household production of goods and services that are not included in the measurement of GDP. A complete accounting for annual growth of biomass of the forest would include the grasses and bushes as well as the trees. For both systems certain flows are conventionally excluded from measurement. In both systems,the excluded flows become less and less important as the economic system and the ecosystem approach maturity.

At maturity both systems have a large stock of resources and at maturity the annual flow of production—biomass or GDP—approaches a maximum. At maturity the climax forest will produce mostly highly valued biomass—old-growth Douglas Fir or White Oak or Teak. At maturity the mature economy will produce mostly highly valued GDP—gourmet food, aesthetically engineered habitation, education, health care, art, and music.

Obviously, economic systems are not ecosystems, but the use of the analogy may help us start thinking about the processes of growth and change and I will return to the biological analogy when I discuss the problems of measurement in economics and in explaining the slowdown in the growth of GDP.

THE AMERICAN EXPERIENCE

The American experience with economic growth is neither smooth nor unidirectional. Text Graph 1.1 exhibits decennial rates of growth in U.S. per capita income over the past century. (An extensive discussion of the definition, components, and determinants of GDP and other NIA concepts is found in chapters 3, 4, 5 and their appendixes.)

The decennial rates of growth in per capita income presented in Text Graph 1.1 are actually the rates of growth in a ratio between census years. GDP—the numerator in the ratio—is the sum of all measured outputs of final products and services in an economy during a year—bushels of wheat and tons of steel, appendectomies and computer software, services of the housing stock and government employees. Output is divided by the total population. Population—the denominator in the ratio—includes workers and nonworkers, infants, retirees, members of the armed forces and residents of asylums and prisons.

A decennial growth rate in the ratio of GDP/Population of 20 percent translates into an annual compounded growth rate of income per capita of just under 2 percent per annum. An initial glance at the decennial growth rates exhibited might lead the casual observer to infer that there were no long-term trends in the rate of growth of per capita income—only deviations around a mean resulting from discrete historical events. However, closer inspection shows a decline in growth of per capita income starting mid-century.

Text Graph 1.1
Decennial Growth Rates in U.S. Real Per Capita GDP:Decades Ending 1900–1990

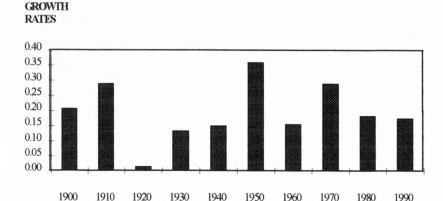

GROWTH
RATES

U.S. per capita growth rates have declined unevenly over the past half century.

Source: Author. See Appendix 3.1.

Movements up and down in the graph of decennial growth rates represent *acceleration* and *deceleration* of growth. The highest decennial rates of growth in per capita income for the American economy in the past century occurred in the decades ending in census years 1910, 1950, and 1970. These three decades witnessed above average growth rates in per capita income primarily because of demographic events that increased the proportion of the population in the labor force between two census years.

The rate of growth of per capita income is the sum of the rate of growth of per worker output, and the rate of change in the participation rate of the population in the labor force. (I discuss and disaggregate these concepts more fully in chapter 3.) The highest growth rate of per capita income in the twentieth century came in the decade of the 1940s—after the ending of the Great Depression and during World War II because the predominantly male labor force returned to work from the abnormally low levels of the Depression 1930s and were joined by a large number of women recruited to fill the labor shortage caused by the war and its aftermath. Interestingly, during this decade ending in 1950, the rate of growth in productivity—output per worker—was actually below trend as a result of the dislocations and waste of a wartime economy and the transition to a peacetime economy. It was not high productivity growth but the large increase in the proportion of the population employed that led to the record increase in income per capita.

The 1960s saw a similarly large increase in the participation rate—but this decade started close to full employment. In the "roaring sixties" it was the labor force entry of the "Baby-Boom" population and their mothers' return to the labor force that brought about rapid increase in per capita income from the increase in the participation rate of the population in the labor force.

Participation Rates and Per Capita Income

Per capita income depends upon output per worker and the proportion of the population that is working—the "participation rate." Growth in per capita income over the past three decades has been increased and sustained by increases in the participation rate of the population. Further increases in the participation rate cannot continue at previous rates because a larger proportion of the population is now working and this diminishes the scope for further increases in participation. Consider: the increase in the participation rate of the population in the labor force from 40 percent to 50 percent is a 25 percent increase. The same absolute increase in the participation rate from 50 percent to 60 percent is only a 20 percent increase. The same absolute increase is measured as a slowdown in growth. And it becomes progressively more difficult to obtain further increases in the participation rate because, in an affluent society, children and the retired population aren't going to be in the labor force. (A detailed presentation of the U.S. data on participation rates is found in chapter 6.)

Output per Worker and Per Capita Income

Because further increases in the participation of the U.S. population in the labor force will be small, further increases in per capita income will have to come primarily from increases in output per worker. However, the rate of

Text Graph 1.2
Decennial Growth Rates in Productivity: Output per Worker and per Worker Hour
GROWTH RATES

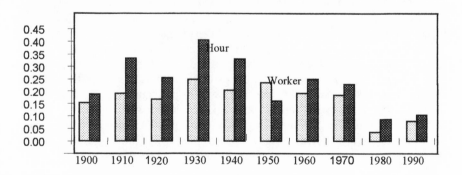

DECADES ENDING

Productivity growth accelerated until the decade ending in 1930 and then decelerated to the present.

Source: Author. See Appendix 3.1.

growth of conventionally measurable output per worker has been declining for a half-century because of the structural changes that accompany economic growth. If this trend in productivity growth continues, the rate of growth in per capita income will continue to decline.

The significant trend to observe in Text Graph 1.2 is the acceleration in the growth of productivity (both output per worker and per worker hour) from the end of the nineteenth century to the "roaring twenties"—the decade ending in 1930—and its subsequent deceleration to the present.

In chapter 5 I will explain acceleration and deceleration in the growth of output per worker hour as a result of structural change in the composition of the output of the economy. Explaining acceleration and deceleration of productivity growth as a necessary consequence of structural change in a maturing economy is the central argument of this book. Apart from the distortions introduced by World War II, growth in output per worker hour has been decelerating for half a century. On the basis of the underlying data, and my understanding of the growth process, I find it difficult to accept arguments that this trend in the growth of labor productivity could be reversed.

THE INEVITABLE DECLINE IN ECONOMIC GROWTH

The misreading of two historical events has distorted public understanding and national policy about economic growth. The first mistake has been in treating the rapid growth in productivity (output per worker hour) of the 1950s and 1960s as a "norm." The second confusion has been failing to recognize that the contribution to per capita growth from high rates of growth in labor force participation over the past two decades is an unsustainable phenomenon.

The maintenance of even the lower growth rates of per capita income in the decades ending in 1980 and 1990 has been possible only because of the increases in the participation rate of the population—and particularly married women—in the labor force.

After taking into account the current level of the participation rate of the American population in the labor force, it becomes clear that growth in per capita income from further increases in the participation rate would be very difficult to secure. If the participation rate of the population in the labor force stabilizes at its current high level, per capita growth will be reduced to the rate of growth in output per worker. (If the participation rate were to fall from its current level—as it could—the rate of growth in per capita income could fall below the rate of growth in output per worker.) Thus, it goes against evidence and logic to argue that U.S. growth rates in per capita income can outperform the levels of the last several decades. Indeed, the growth rates—not levels—of per capita income will inevitably decline further in the twenty-first century.

THE PROBLEM OF DECLINING GROWTH

The decline in the pace of economic growth is not an exclusively American problem—it is widely observed in advanced industrial societies and it is for them a similar natural consequence of modern economic growth. (Detailed international evidence on growth rates and output levels is presented in chapter 3.) However, even if the decline in growth is "natural" and widely shared, the observed slowdown in growth may lead to problems. Specifically, the decline of growth in per capita income will increase the stresses resulting from interpersonal income inequality and from the intergenerational transfer of income from the working generation to the dependent youth and senior populations.

Interpersonal Income Distribution

Members of a society are concerned with their relative as well as absolute incomes. The increase in intergenerational income transfers in a rich society is a consequence of the success of economic growth. In a rich society more must be spent on the education of the young. In a rich society people live longer and more is spent on their maintenance and medical care. Conflict over the interpersonal distribution of income may be intensified by the slowing in the growth of the size of the "pie" to be shared. In the United States over the last two decades there has been an increase in the inequality of incomes. This book does not address issues relative to causes and effects of the increase in interpersonal income inequality. However, the decline in growth in per capita incomes is likely to exacerbate conflict over the interpersonal as well as the intergenerational distribution of income—particularly if the growing retired population attempts to increase or even maintain the relative incomes of retired persons.

There have been three fortunate demographic shifts over the last two decades that will not assist us in the present decade or the twenty-first century: (1) the long-term deceleration of growth in output per worker over the past two decades has been offset by a one-time increase in the participation rate of the population in the labor force; (2) the retired population has increased slowly as a proportion of the total population; (3) the school-age education cohorts temporarily declined as a proportion of the population in the 1970s and 1980s because of the "baby-bust" that followed the baby boom. Together these three trends helped to slow the growth of intergenerational transfers from the working-age cohort to the dependent school-age and retirement-age cohorts in the last quarter of the twentieth century.

However, these favorable trends will not be repeated in the twenty-first century. For the retired population the burden of support will be increased by two separable but multiplicative factors: (1) the increase in the relative size of the retired population to the working population, and (2) the increase in the ratio of retiree income and tax-funded medical expenditures to the average income of the currently employed population. Both of these trends necessitate an increase in the proportion of income to be transferred from the currently employed population to the retired population—largely through Social Security and Medicare taxes. (The changing magnitude and determinants of these transfers are discussed in chapter 7.)

The United States was "lucky" demographically between 1970 and 1990 in that the employed population increased relative to the school-age population.

This allowed an increase in real (inflation-adjusted) educational spending per student without an increase in the proportion of GDP that was transferred from the employed population to the education of the young. After 1990 the "luck" runs out. The school-age population increases faster than the population of workers. Moreover, educational spending necessary to equip the younger generation for the labor force in an advanced economy must continually increase. As a result of these two factors, educational expenditures will have to increase sharply as a proportion of GDP. (The determinants of these expenditures are discussed in chapter 8.)

In the absence of growth in per worker output and/or further increases in the participation rate of women in the market labor force, the tax transfers from the incomes of the employed population for the education of the young and the maintenance of the retired populations will reduce the disposable income of the employed population. How much the reduction of after-tax real income will reduce the extent and intensity of the participation of the population in the labor force is an unresolved empirical and policy question of great importance.[4] In various European countries the high level of transfer payments levied on employment have led to high rates of structural unemployment. The participation rate of older workers has also decreased markedly because of generous retirement programs.

In chapters 7 and 8 I disaggregate the sources of increases in the retirement and education transfer-tax "burdens." This clearly demonstrates the inevitability of their increase. Of course, there are always the options of sending the young to work rather than school, and putting the elderly on rafts and floating them out to sea!

There is no doubt that the slowdown in growth will increase the burden of an increasing national debt.[5] The slowdown of economic growth increases the burden of the national debt of any size simply because of the slower growth of income available to tax to pay the interest or refund the principal.

WHY GROWTH RATES HAVE DECLINED

This book offers a simple, straightforward, two-part explanation of the inevitability of our current situation. First, we have gone through the structural and demographic changes that accelerate growth, and we can't go through the same changes a second time. Second, because of the way we (officially) use NIA concepts to measure economic output, we fail to measure some of the changes in the characteristics of the goods and services we produce and, therefore, fail to record increases in the use-value (as opposed to exchange value) of the goods we produce.

Concepts and Measurement

Before explaining "economic growth" it is important to clarify the concepts and terms used to describe and define it. Over the past century various measures of economic activity have exhibited the economy of the United States growing at varying rates at different times. It is important to understand the differences in some of these varying measures. (They are discussed more fully in chapter 3.)

Extensive growth—variously identified and measured as Gross National Product (GNP), Gross Domestic Product (GDP), Net National Product or Net Domestic Product (NNP or NDP), or National Income—has occurred because of the increase in the population, labor force, stock of capital, and technological and organizational efficiency of the United States. Extensive growth in GDP is often referred to in articles about economic performance and is usually the concept used in political discussions about projected tax revenues. The rate of growth of aggregate GDP is the sum of the rate of growth of the labor force, the rate of growth of output per worker, and the rate of growth of the participation rate (plus their cross-products).

Extensive growth—the rate of growth of aggregate GDP—is usually reported on an annual basis. GDP is also reported on a "real" basis; nominal GDP—GDP in current prices—is "deflated" by a price index to allow a measurement of the change in the quantity of output apart from its price. Part of the growth of aggregate GDP is simply the effect of the increase in the working age population. I do not consider this part of GDP growth in my analysis. Similarly, by measuring growth over decades, I avoid treating short-term variations in the growth rate over the business cycle that are merely changes in the level of utilization of the capacity of the economy. This book is concerned with *intensive* long-term economic growth: the rate of increase in various measures of output per capita, output per labor force member, output per worker, and output per hour of time worked.

Measures of intensive growth can be further refined from output per capita or per worker to yield a variety of different measures of the increase in the productivity of an economy.   Productivity is a concept that compares the measured input of such entities as labor hours and capital stocks with the measured output of such constructs as "gross private sector business output" or such aggregated commodities as tons of steel or kilowatts of electricity and even such services as "education" or "police protection." There are many alternative measures of the extensive and intensive growth of the American economy and these measures have been used to compare the economy's performance at various time periods and to compare the U.S. economy with other economies. Some of these measures are presented and discussed in chapter 3.

THE DECLINE OF GROWTH AND ECONOMIC POLICY

A common response among opinion leaders and economists (not a coterminous set!) to the evidence about U.S. growth declining or lagging other nations over the past four decades and/or to the deceleration to the lower productivity growth rates of the past two decades is an attempt to find the fault in our economic performance with our economic policies and/or institutions. Poor economic performance (a growth rate lower than other nations or declining from previous levels) is variously attributed to "high taxes" or "low saving" or "too much defense spending" or "insufficient educational spending" or declines in the "work ethic" and "family values."

The diagnoses of the reasons for the decline in the growth rate are followed by a variety of policy prescriptions depending on the diagnosis. If the diagnosis is insufficient capital formation, the prescription may be increasing the incentives for private sector savings and decreasing the governmental budget deficit to increase net national savings and, thereby, increase the rate of capital formation. Other strategies, following alternative dissections or hearsay interpretation, (or simple disregard!) of the data include spending more on education or research; removing government regulation of the economy; changing the welfare system; or bringing in school prayer.

Another approach to the evidence is to dispute the applicability of the measurement concepts involved in arriving at measures of per capita income and rates of growth of output per unit of labor input. For example, economists and analysts argue that current statistical measures of output are inappropriate for measuring the current menu of goods and services and their quality differences. It is pointed out that a 1995 computer is considerably more "user-friendly" or powerful than a 1985 computer in terms of its speed and memory, so that it is not enough merely to count the number of computers or what it would cost to produce the 1985 model computer relative to the 1995 computer in creating price indices to arrive at estimates of change in the "real" output of computers. This argument can be extended to a wide range of goods.

Another approach attacks the whole basis of national income measurement. For example, what should be measured—the number and cost of hospital patient days or some estimate of the improvement in health that results from the hospital stay? Improvements in medical technology have increased the "real" (inflation-adjusted) cost of an appendectomy, but if the recovery time is decreased by several days or the mortality rate from the operation is decreased by several percent, it could be argued the "wellness" produced by the operation has increased by much more than the increase in the hours of nurse and physician inputs and medical machinery capital used in the operation.

Should we measure educational expenditures or changes in literacy rates or standardized test scores? There has been an increase in "real" educational expenditures per capita and per student over the past several decades, but it has been accompanied by rising dissatisfaction with the output of our educational system—literacy, numeracy, and the ability of the "product" to participate in labor markets. Our conventional measures of educational output in GDP measure the constant dollars spent, rather than the results achieved.

Expenditures to decrease and clean up air and water pollution end up decreasing the measured productivity of the industries doing the clean-up since the labor and capital required for regulation, inspection, and compliance are counted as costs, but the benefits of improved air and water quality are not counted. Are expenditures on public and private police services to increase domestic tranquility a final good—or an intermediate good?[6]

National income and growth accountants—while agreeing that the measurement conventions used to arrive at output and productivity growth rates can be misleading—argue to preserve them on the basis that the concepts and methods used for collection and estimation are "hard" and "consistent." The measurement controversy is discussed in chapter 4.

Proponents of various diagnoses and policy solutions will probably be disappointed with my failure to directly confront any of their proposed diagnoses of the growth slowdown that emphasize, say, low savings or high taxes or deficient institutions or decline in personal moral standards. My diagnosis of the slowdown in the growth of the economy is that it is simply the manifestation of economic maturity!

ECONOMIC MATURITY AND THE INEVITABLE SLOWDOWN OF ECONOMIC GROWTH

My real (as opposed to measurement) argument stresses the inevitability of the slowdown of intensive growth rates such as output per capita, per worker, or per worker hour. My argument is that the growth rate of an advanced economy will inevitably decelerate and that nations that have led the way in economic growth will inevitably see other nations "catching up" with higher growth rates. My argument about the increasing size of the necessary transfers from the working to the dependent populations depends upon demography as well as the characteristics of education and elder care.

"Inevitable slowdown" arguments are not new to economics.   Thomas Malthus made a form of the argument at the beginning of the nineteenth century on the basis of population growing geometrically while output grew arithmetically because of fixed natural resources. His arguments were extended into a theory of income distribution and the inevitability of the end of growth by the nineteenth century English economist, David Ricardo. Karl Marx predicted that the very success of capitalism would drive down the rate of return on capital while driving real wages to subsistence levels.

In this century neoclassical economics has developed the concept of the "steady state" economy from theorems about the declining marginal productivity of capital pushing the rate of return on capital down to the social time rate of preference. Much of Keynes' General Theory in the Depression-era 1930s assumed the decline of opportunities for investment in Britain and other advanced capitalist countries. At the turn of the twentieth century the head of the U.S. Patent Office advocated closing down the office, on the grounds that "everything useful which could be invented—had been invented!" Modern nay-sayers—such as the Club of Rome—have predicted the slowdown and reversal of economic growth due to the increasing scarcity of natural resources and the finite pollution-carrying capacity of the environment.

Technological Change and Intrasectoral Growth

My inevitable decline arguments are totally different from those of Malthus, Marx, Keynes, and the technological or environmental pessimists. Further, my argument is not that growth will end—only that it will slow down! Unlike the changes in demography or changes in final demand that slow growth, there is no reason why the economic growth from technological change should necessarily and inevitably decelerate in the primary and secondary sectors of the economy (although I am persuaded that it will). I argue in chapter 9 that technological change will eventually slow. My argument is that technological change is largely a matter of specialization that allows exploitation of the economies of scale and scope in commodity production, manufacturing, and distribution. When this has been achieved, the proportional changes remaining to be exploited decline. Further, the increase of specialization in production causes an increase in "transactions costs" that inexorably limits the indefinite increase in specialization.

However, even if the proportional changes in productivity from the exploitation of scale and scope economies were to continue in commodity production, manufacture, and distribution, we would still be left with the critical fact that the decline in the relative size of the labor force in the primary and secondary sectors reduces the scope for productivity gains for the whole economy that originates within those sectors.

What about productivity growth in the "service" sector? Why can't labor-saving technological change be as fast in medicine or education as it is in the airplane industry? Why can't an elementary school class indefinitely increase in size with better technology—a CD-ROM equipped, Internet-connected computer for every pupil? Why can't a range of patient- or computer-operated diagnostic devices indefinitely increase the number of patients served by one physician? Why can't better technology reduce the number of police that we have per population member? My best answer to those questions is that, by and large, we don't observe labor-saving technological change occurring in these sectors and favorably affecting the (measured) rate of economic growth in the personal service tertiary sector.

The Mature Economy Argument

This book makes a different kind of "inevitable slowdown" argument than classical economists or modern nay-sayers. The argument is that the decline of growth of per capita real income is inevitable because the structural changes that accompany growth have occurred and there is diminishing scope for them to occur again. It replaces the Ricardian or Marxian or neoclassical diminishing marginal productivity of capital arguments with a structural change argument. Demographic, structural, and technological changes have been the primary causes and consequences of the measured rates of economic growth that have occurred. These demographic and structural changes can't take place again because they have already taken place!

Structural Change and the Rate of Economic Growth

The central thesis of this book is that structural changes are the primary determinants of changes in the measured rate of growth of per capita real income. By "structural change" I mean two types of changes: (1) changes in the relative size of productive sectors where labor- and capital-saving technology can be used or measured effectively, and (2) changes in the demographic characteristics of the population that change their participation rates in the labor force.

Intersectoral Shifts and Changes in Output per Worker

Changes in the relative size of output sectors accelerate or decelerate the aggregate rate of growth of output per worker for the entire labor force. These changes in the relative size of sectors are the result of the growth process itself. Fast productivity growth within a sector decreases its relative size in the total economy by reducing the relative price of its output and allowing fewer workers to produce the output. Rising incomes produced by growth shift the pattern of final demand first to high-level, high-growth sectors (as from agriculture to manufacturing). In later stages of economic growth, final demand shifts employment from high output manufacturing to lower-output, lower-growth services. It is the shifts in industrial structure that are responsible for the acceleration and deceleration of growth in average output per worker. The evidence on structural change and the rate of change of output per worker is presented in chapter 5.

Demographic Change and the Participation Rate

Over the past century two types of demographic change have affected the participation rate: (1) the age structure of the population, and (2) the shift of women, particularly married women, from household production to market employment. During this period the secular decline in the birth rate (interrupted by the baby boom and complicated by immigration) and the increase in life expectancy have led to continuing changes in the age profile of the population. Until recently those changes in the age profile have been favorable to growth. Demographic change over the past century has usually and gradually increased the proportion of the population in the age group that participates in the labor force (roughly ages 16 to 65). With stable participation by age and sex cohorts, increasing the proportion of the population in the labor force age groups increases average per capita income simply by increasing the proportion of the population that is working.

The secular increase in the participation rate of women—particularly married women—has accelerated the increase in per capita incomes for most of the past century. Married women now participate in the market labor force at a rate close to the rate for men in the same age groups. The shift from household production to labor force participation generates a once-and-for-all acceleration in the growth rate of per capita income. As participation reaches high levels, there is reduced scope for further acceleration. Changes in the participation rate accelerate or decelerate the growth in per capita income resulting from changes in output per worker. (The evidence on participation rates is presented in chapter 6.)

"The Way It Worked"—Acceleration

"The way it worked"—the way in which economic growth increased in the American past—was simple: (1) output per worker increased rapidly with the division of labor, technological advances, and the provision of more and more capital per worker. The rate of growth of output was particularly rapid in commodity production, manufacturing, transportation, and distribution.   (2) Workers shifted from low marginal output industries (like agriculture) to high marginal output industries (like manufacturing).   The bigger the difference between per worker output levels in the two sectors and the higher the proportion of the labor force shifting from one sector to another, the bigger the gain in average worker productivity that resulted from the shift.   (3) Demographic change increased the proportion of the population in the labor force and the shift from household to market production changed the role of women. These interrelated types of demographic change both increased the participation rate and accelerated the growth in per capita incomes.

"Why It Won't"—Deceleration

"Why it won't"—why the rate of growth has decelerated is also simple: (1) output per worker is already at high levels in commodity production and distribution sectors of the economy and, as a consequence, employment in those sectors is a smaller fraction of total employment. Even continued high rates of growth of productivity in the commodity production and distribution sectors (which become more difficult) have a smaller impact on the total economy because the high growth sectors are a smaller proportion of the economy as a whole. (2) The difference in output per worker between sectors of the economy has been equalized, so less can be gained by intersectoral shifts. (3) Most of the population in the working age groups is already working, so there is less scope for further increases in the participation rate of the labor force. Deceleration of the growth in the participation rate reduces the growth rate in per capita incomes toward the underlying rate of growth in output per worker.

STRUCTURAL CHANGE AND THE DECLINE IN ECONOMIC GROWTH

The argument of this book is that there is a natural and inevitable acceleration and then deceleration in the rate of growth in per worker output and per capita real income in an economy. This acceleration and deceleration is the inherent result of the growth process itself. Structural changes alone accelerate and decelerate growth apart from changes in values, policy changes, or scientific breakthroughs that may condition the pace of structural change. Part of the measured slowdown in the rate of economic growth is the effect of measurement conventions themselves. If the society wants to take into account some of the unmeasured changes, the measurement conventions will have to be changed. There is no inherent reason for U.S. per capita economic output to decline from its current high levels and—barring unforeseen events or mismanagement—it will continue to increase. However, output per capita will increase at a slower rate than it has over the past century.

Abstracting from wars, natural catastrophes, and international migration, the rate of economic growth for nations experiencing the transitions from agricultural to industrial to service economies first accelerates and then, inevitably, decelerates when the economy stabilizes at a high level of population participation in the labor force and per worker economic output.   The U.S. economy is asymptotically approaching that level.

An advanced society may lament the slowdown of economic growth and yearn for its return, but the slowdown is the outcome of the successful process of economic growth itself. Just as the volume of the biomass of a climax forest close to maturity cannot grow as rapidly as the biomass of a younger forest—so must a mature economy reconcile itself to a declining growth rate.

NOTES

1. These themes are explored at length in Robert J. Samuelson, *The Good Life and its Discontents: The American Dream in the Age of Entitlement* (New York: Vintage Books, 1995).

2. Much confusion in the discussion of economic growth arises from the terms used. GDP—the measure of economic output per unit of time—is a "flow" concept, a velocity. The increase in the flow or velocity of production is called growth. The slowdown in growth is not a reduction in flow or velocity but a reduction (deceleration) in its rate of increase.

A car maintaining a constant velocity of 50 mph is a counterpart to a GDP of, say, $5 trillion per year. If the car goes from 50 to 60 mph over a time period, we say it has accelerated by 10 mph. If GDP increases from $5 trillion to $6 trillion over a decade, we say the output of the economy has a growth rate of 20 percent per decade. If it grows from $6 trillion to $6.6 trillion over the next decade, we say that the growth rate has slowed or decelerated to 10 percent per decade. But it bears emphasis that the economy is now producing at a higher rate of $6.6 trillion rather than $5 trillion per year.

To express the slowdown in growth in mathematical terms, the rate of growth of output is the first derivative of output with respect to time and the slowing of the growth rate is the second derivative with respect to time. The first derivative remains positive but the second derivative turns negative when there is a slowdown in growth.

3. I hesitate to use a biological metaphor because an economy may have similarities to a forest population but it is also different. In defense of my metaphor, the great economist Alfred Marshall (1890) compared the firms in a mature industry to the trees in the forest—individual firms were created, flourished, matured, declined, and disappeared while the total output of the mature industry stayed constant.

4. "Supply-side economists" have argued that increasing after-tax incomes by reducing marginal tax rates will result in an increase in the participation rate of the population in the labor force. The strength of this effect, based on changes in tax laws in 1982 and 1986, appears to be slight.

5. When the national debt increases relative to national income, the proportion of national income that must be collected in taxes to service the interest on the debt increases. Since the national debt is generally held, directly or indirectly, by wealthier and older segments of the population, income is transferred from the younger and less affluent sections of the population to the older and more affluent. When the debt is held outside the country, income is transferred from tax-paying citizens to debt-holding foreigners.

6. One of the most telling theoretical arguments against the use of national income accounting procedures to measure economic output is that they estimate the wrong measure of "utility." The market prices used to value output measure the marginal utilities of output. Insofar as economic change creates goods and services for which

consumers would be willing to pay considerably more than they actually do—"consumer surplus" is the technical term used by economists—national income accounting is not measuring the "true" benefits of economic growth. The old saw about economists is that they know the price of everything and the value of nothing. A contemporary criticism could be that they measure everything but the right things!

CHAPTER 2

Explanation and Description of Economic Growth and Structural Change

> History—in contrast with the so-called physical sciences—is concerned
> with the description of particular events of the past, rather than with the
> search for general laws which might govern those events.
>
> —Carl G. Hempel
> *Aspects of Scientific Explanation* (1965)

The economic growth measurements discussed in the preceding chapter are intellectual artifacts. What are the historical events those artifacts purport to measure? Observation and description is inherently selective. It is impossible to observe and describe everything that happens over a period of time. Explanation must precede description so the reader knows what to look for.

Historical economics establishes certain categories for observation and then fits the facts into those categories. I have followed that convention in the organization of this chapter. In Part I, I outline six defining characteristics of the process of economic growth. In Part II, I apply those characteristics in my heuristic explanation of how economic growth changed the nature of productive activities in selected areas of the American economy. Part III offers a closer examination of the economic forces driving technological change in the production of capital goods.

PART I: DEFINING CHARACTERISTICS OF ECONOMIC GROWTH[1]

What are the realities underlying the production of bread, steel, cities, and health care? What should we be aware of in our description of economic change? What were the most widespread and critical defining characteristics of economic growth over the past century? Before describing the nature of the changes in the American economy that lie behind our measurements of growth in economic output, I would like to suggest six general characteristics of change:

1. Increasing specialization in production.
2. Technological change.
3. Increasing capitalization of productive processes and human beings.
4. A shift from household to market production of goods and services.
5. An intersectoral shift of the labor force from the production, transportation, and distribution of commodities to the provision of services—particularly education and health care.
6. Organizational change: the substitution of contractual for market or status relationships in all types of economic activity, with a concomitant increase in transactional costs.

Specialization

Specialization in production is a primary cause of economic growth and the analysis of the behavior of specialized individuals and firms is the focus of modern economics.   When Aristotle talked about the economics of ancient Athens, he didn't discuss firms or nations trading with each other, because Greek cities were not organized on that basis.

The first modern economist, Adam Smith, author of *An Inquiry Into the Nature and Causes of the Wealth of Nations* (1776), began his explanation of the historical and international differences in national income by emphasizing effects of specialization in production. Using his famous pin factory example, Smith noted how specialization in the production of a simple item increased output per worker. Specialization increased the physical dexterity of workers in the specialized parts of pin manufacture, eliminated loss of time in moving from one element in the production process to another, and allowed the use of more specialized capital goods.   His insightful analysis has been extended by subsequent economic thinkers to the specialization of firms and regional and national economies.

Specialization increases output per worker. The degree of specialization is limited by the extent of markets. The size of markets limits specialization simply because it is less advantageous to specialize if the specialized producer cannot sell all of the goods and services he is capable of producing by specialization. The American economy was well along with specialization of production by the beginning of the twentieth century and the continuing increase in specialization has contributed to the increasing importance of the other five characteristics of modern economic growth. Specialization of production increases technological change and capital formation. It leads to the shift from household to market production and shifts in the relative importance of increasingly specialized sectors of the economy.   Specialization and increased capitalization lead to increasing transactions costs between individuals and firms, between firms and firms, and between government and firms as the nature of transactions change.

Technological Change

Technology is the knowledge and practice of how to produce things. Cooking over an open fire and cooking in a microwave oven are two alternative cooking technologies. Mud huts and steel beam skyscrapers are alternative housing technologies. Sending a message by runner and by fax are two alternative communications technologies. How does one measure the "quantity" of messages when one is trying to quantify the productivity change in communications?

Building automobiles with individually fashioned components and mass-producing interchangeable parts assembled into automobiles on a continuous assembly line are alternative manufacturing technologies. How does one take into account the qualitative change in automobiles when modern models run twice the miles at half the fuel and maintenance costs of earlier models?

Teaching students with flashcards and with computer software and hardware are alternative learning technologies. Treating an infected leg by cutting if off or curing it with antibiotics are alternative medical technologies. How does one quantify the change in the output of human "wellness" in comparing the results of the two treatments?

Technological change—change in the knowledge of how to make or do things—alters natural physical, chemical, and biological materials and processes and alters the way humans do things. It changes the characteristics as well as the quantity of inputs and outputs. It reorganizes production processes to reduce the amount of labor and natural resource, physical, and human capital necessary for the production of goods and services desired by humans. Behind the increase in the productivity of making bread there is technological change in metallurgy to reduce the cost and increase the durability of tractors and plows, technological change in chemistry to create fertilizer by fixing nitrogen, technological change in genetics to change the characteristics of plants.

Technology is as diverse as production. Nevertheless, there are some main themes in technology and considering them will get us part way in understanding its nature in economic growth. These main themes all involve reducing the amount of human labor, or the amount of physical capital, or natural resource capital, or knowledge capital necessary for the production of a given quantity of output. Because changing technology involves learning how to alter natural materials or biological processes and invent new ways to do things, technology increases the amount of knowledge capital and human capital necessary for production in a modern economy at the same time that it reduces the amount of physical and natural resource capital to produce a given amount of output.

Some Examples of Technology and Technological Change

To start our thinking about technology and the process of technological change, consider some technologies involved in producing goods and services from raw materials. Man has always used technology in the transformation of natural materials into structural materials. Clay is turned into brick, limestone into cement, iron ore into steel, trees into paper or pressure laminated beams, and sand into glass and silicon chips.

All of these examples of transformations of materials by technology involve altering the characteristics of natural materials with heat and/or pressure. The altered materials can then be incorporated into structures for the provision of living and working space that will have a longer life or greater strength or other desirable qualities. Or the new materials can be used to make tools or machines to produce other goods.

The improvement of technology in the transformation of materials typically involves reducing the cost of extracting and transporting raw materials, improving the thermal or mechanical efficiency of energy in production processes, and acquiring knowledge about the physical and chemical changes that occur during processing materials in order to modify their characteristics.

The economic impact of technological change comes through reducing the amount of labor involved directly in the production processes and/or reducing the cost of the capital per unit of output capacity and/or changing the character of the output so that it has greater strength or durability and capacity to provide more consumption goods and services over time.

Consider an example from steelmaking—steel is central to building modern cities, transportation systems, and machinery. Mining technology must decrease the cost of extraction of iron ore, coal, and limestone. The extraction of iron ore and coal progresses from hand shovels and buckets to steam shovels and giant trucks in open-cast mines. Human labor is replaced by mechanical power in loading the furnaces, the mechanical power directed by a single worker is increased, and the cost of producing the mechanical goods that supply and control the power is reduced.

Transportation costs of raw materials from mine to furnace must be lowered by improved transport technology. The iron ore and coal must be conveyed from mine to ore-carrying ships or railroad trains with the capacity and speed to move larger and larger quantities per time period with decreasing costs per ton mile of labor, fuel, and capital. The direct labor in transport must by be reduced by straighter, more level and durable roadbeds capable of bearing bigger, faster trains and concurrently reducing the user cost (depreciation and interest costs on the production costs of the capital equipment) per unit of output capacity of the railroad.

Technological change also modifies production processes. In steelmaking the Bessemer process increases the heat obtained from a given quantity of coal used in changing pig iron to steel by altering its combustion with the injection of oxygen. Small amounts of carbon are also added. This increases the quantity and quality of the output of steel from a given amount of pig iron (and fuel).

By reducing the amount of raw materials necessary to produce a ton of steel, and producing harder steel with more tensile strength (that will last longer, bear greater loads, and withstand greater friction), technology reduces the amount of natural resource capital, physical capital, and labor necessary to produce the quantity of steel necessary for a railroad, an office building, a steel pipe, or an engine of a given size and capacity. The technology of alloying steel increases the tensile strength of the same quantity of steel produced by a given quantity of raw materials by adding alloys of critical types and in critical quantities so that a smaller girder can carry the same weight as a larger one. This also reduces the amount of capital and labor necessary for producing the quantity of steel necessary to bear the weight of the building.

Technology substitutes finished materials in production processes. The natural strength and durability of wood fiber was used in construction as humans advanced from using hand-hewn branches and trunks of trees to dimension lumber in house building.   But more recent technological changes have introduced the lamination of sheets of wood veneer with criss-crossing wood fibers to increase load bearing with less (and inferior) wood.   Plywood and laminated beams are used as alternatives for the load-bearing functions of steel at a lower cost of production and site assembly than steel. Consider another type of technological change—change in design. Architectural and engineering technology change the support structure in the design of a building—the post-and-beam construction of skyscrapers—so that the same amount of useable space can be created with a smaller supporting structure and less labor in construction.

Note that the technology of transforming materials into structural space does not follow any direct route of displacing labor in existing production processes with greater amounts of capital using the same technology. It involves the use of alternative technologies that increase the output capacity of a dollar's worth of expenditure on capital. Technology improves existing processes but, more importantly, develops entirely new ones.

Let us shift our attention from the technology of materials to the technology of machines. Technological change is particularly important in the improvement of machines to make other machines—machine tools. Improvements in metallurgy, cutting technology, and control technology improve the accuracy of drilling and grinding steel so that smaller tolerances can extend the life of moving parts in engines.   Increasing the operating life and decreasing the maintenance of engines reduces the amount of natural resource and physical capital and labor necessary to produce an engine with a given power output capable of operating over a period of use.   Smaller machining tolerances also allow an increase in compression and more thermal and mechanical efficiency in fuel use.   Thus, the effect of technological change in the machine tools that make other machines is to decrease the cost of the capital equipment used in manufacturing or transporting goods.   Technological change decreases the user cost of capital—its cost per unit of output. Technological change increases the output per unit of capital by reducing the initial cost of capital goods with a given output capacity, increasing their durability and working life, and/or by reducing the cost of the operation of those capital goods. The increased output capacity of physical capital made possible by technological change also increases the amount of output possible from the labor that controls the machines.[2]

Technology can change the biology of the natural world as well as the characteristics of matter in the physical world.   Wheat was, originally, a natural grass that grew in a mixed ecology of various plant species.   Early agricultural practice isolated strains of wheat for planting in a monoculture. Increases in output of wheat per acre have subsequently been realized through the application of knowledge developed in genetics and biochemistry and the translation of that knowledge into the development of hybrid seeds that respond well to the use of inorganic fertilizers.   By changing the genetics of seeds and altering soil nutrients, technological change functionally reduces the amount of labor, natural resource, reproducible, and human capital that would otherwise be used in the crop raising stage in the process of food production.

Technology reduced the cost of communication by the invention of the telephone. It progressively substituted mechanical for human, and then electronic for mechanical, switching equipment in telephone system exchanges. It substituted satellites for telephone wires to carry messages. The transmission of the electrical impulses generated by computer and fax machines rather than the human voice further increases the efficiency of communication. The progressive reduction in the cost of communication reduces the costs of organizing production and distribution across the spectrum of economic activity.

To generalize about the nature of technological change, the process of technological change reduces both the direct labor and physical and natural resource capital per unit of output. But the production and use of technologically advanced structures, machines, and processes increases the amount of human and knowledge capital needed for the operation of an advanced economy.

Capitalization

Volumes of economists' prose have been expended on the definition and explanation of "capital." Suffice it to say here that economic growth results from the formation of capital to increase the productivity of human economic activity. In agriculture as the horse replaces the human and the tractor replaces the horse in tilling the earth, the increase in capital per worker—the horse and the tractor—contributes to the increase in the agricultural output one worker can produce. In transportation the railroad replaces the horse cart and, thereby, increases the ton miles of freight that can be transported per worker.

Traditionally, "capital" has been narrowly construed to mean physical capital—factories, roads, equipment, inventories of goods, and so forth. But economists have increasingly realized that capital needs to be construed more broadly to include human, knowledge, and natural resource capital. American economic growth over the past century has depended on capital accumulation—members of the labor force have had more and more physical, human, and knowledge capital to work with. They have used capital to extend their physical strength and control in productive processes and have used physical, human, and knowledge capital to offset any potential limits to growth posed by the stable or declining stocks of reproducible and nonreproducible natural capital (such as forests, soil fertility, mineral deposits, and the waste dissipating capacities of air and water).

For the entire alphabet of physical capital—assembly lines, barns, computers, docks, factories, garbage trucks, houses—it is standard accounting practice to value these additions to the capital stock at their cost of production. The economic logic of this practice derives from the recognition that the production of physical capital is an alternative to producing goods that are consumed during the same period of production. In accordance with several standard assumptions for economic analysis—such as the full employment of resources and competitive factor and product markets—the value of reproducible capital is measured in terms of the cost of production of consumption goods forgone.

Capital formation becomes potentially easier with growth in output since more resources can be allocated to the production of capital goods without unduly reducing consumption in the current time period. On the other hand the increasing stock of capital potentially requires a growing share of national income to be set aside to cover depreciation—increasing saving and investing may be offset by increased depreciation.

The Basis for Expanding the Categories of Capital

Why complicate the analysis of growth by differentiating the types of capital? Because the four types of capital that I have defined have different characteristics in their production and depreciation and ownership. The important analytic function of the expansion of "capital" is to identify the factors that have been important to the formation and utilization of these different types of capital—even if the measurement of their stocks and flows has not been implemented on a consistent basis. (That is an argument for the expansion of our accounting concepts.) Despite the problems in measuring capital stocks and the lack of consistent historical data bases for them, I observe that changes in the rate of growth of output of different sectors of the American economy have been accompanied by changes in four types of capital stocks and by their interaction.

Physical Capital. Physical capital is the kind of capital usually referred to in economic theory. Physical capital is the structures, machines, and inventories produced in one time period for the purpose of producing or providing goods and services in future periods. Private investment expenditures on physical capital are the only investments in capital recognized in firms' financial statements and in the national accounts. Expenditures on research to develop new processes or expenditures on training expenses to develop the capabilities of a firm's employees may be viewed by the firm's management as an "investment" and do more to increase output than adding more machines, but accounting rules classify those activities as a part of the cost of production in the current accounting period. Ironically, the corporate CEO's car may be viewed, by him, as part of his compensation package, but its purchase by the corporation is treated as an investment and its acquisition cost is carried on the firm's balance sheet as a capital asset.

One of the measurement problems for estimating the creation of new physical capital is that it is often built or manufactured rather than purchased by its users. This has, historically, been the case for most improvements to agricultural land and buildings. It is also the case for some industrial plant and equipment and for owner-occupant building and additions to the residential housing stock.[3] Another problem is that the maintenance of capital may be treated as current expense rather than replacement of the capital stock.

A substantial portion of government expenditure goes on the creation or improvement of physical capital—roads, dams, schools. While it is not explicitly segregated from other government expenditures in all government budgets or counted in the output of the government sector, it has recently begun to be accounted for as capital formation. As noted in chapter 7, government expenditures on education form human capital, but that capital formation is not recognized as investment in National Income Accounting (NIA).

Physical capital has received more attention by economists, historically, than other types of capital. I speculate that part of this may have to do with the fact that its cost of production is explicit and it is thereby recorded in accounting transactions (or can be easily imputed by reference to market transactions). Part of the explanation may be that property rights in physical capital are relatively easier to identify and transfer so that there are explicit market transactions that quantify the value of physical capital. The growth of public companies is facilitated by comparable financial statements of income and assets that can be evaluated by investors. The taxation of income has made it necessary to keep accounts of changes in the quantity and value of physical capital because those changes are part of the concept of the "income" that is taxed. Conversely, expenditures on research or employee training are not treated as "investment" in the firm's accounts to lessen the possibility of fraud or tax avoidance.

Unlike physical capital there are limits on the ownership of "human" capital and "knowledge" capital. A firm can't sell an employee to another firm—although it may sell his services.[4] A firm may patent knowledge, but licensing or preventing its unlicensed use may have high costs as the property rights are difficult and costly to enforce.

Available, known, natural resources are not included in the balance sheet of a firm or a national economy. This produces the anomalous convention that if a coal company mines its own coal and stores it above ground, it adds it to inventory on its balance sheet, but there is no recorded offsetting decrease in the valuation of its known coal reserves under ground. (Of course the stock market will value natural resource-based companies like oil, coal, and mineral producers in terms of their known reserves rather than their accounting balance sheets.)

There are substantial cyclical fluctuations in the year-to-year additions (gross investment) to the physical capital stock recorded in the national accounts. Because all of government expenditures on investment in reproducible capital and some of private expenditures on physical capital are not recorded as investment, any generalizations about secular changes in the rate of even gross investment taken from NIA data must be considered incomplete. Ironically, the theory of production emphasizes that it is the stock of capital rather than additions to it that is the determinant of output.[5] Thus, even if we had complete and accurate records of the investment flows into the capital stock, we would not have accurate measurement of the capital stock unless we had reliable and consistent measures of its depreciation.

The structural change from an agricultural to an industrial to a service economy has posed needs for different proportions of complementary capital over the past century. Agriculture, transportation, and urbanization all required large stocks of physical capital that could be formed with relatively limited human and knowledge capital. The United States was advantaged, in its early development, with abundant natural resources that increased the productivity of physical capital and, thereby, required less of it than would be needed by a nation not similarly advantaged.[6] Consider the investments in physical capital necessary to the development of an agricultural economy in Holland below sea level, or in Switzerland on the steep mountainsides!

The U.S. economy in the nineteenth century had greater needs for physical and natural resource capital but had lesser needs for human capital and knowledge capital. In the twentieth century our transportation systems and urban infrastructure are in place and the technological change that has taken place has reduced the relative costs of building roads or structures with given output capacities. The physical capital requirements per dollar of annual output in electronics manufacturing are much less than in steel—and the value of electronics output has risen relative to steel production. At the end of the twentieth century the capital requirements are increasingly for human capital and knowledge capital. High-tech manufacturing and many service industries require increasing amounts of human capital, which, as we will see in chapter 7, has increasing relative costs. As a technological leader in the world economy, we bear the research and development costs of the new knowledge capital even though it may be appropriated by others. Thus, while physical capital has been critical to our early economic development, it is now declining in importance relative to other capital stock categories.

Human Capital. Political theorists, for example, John Locke (Second Treatise on Civil Government) or John Rawls (A Theory of Justice) have often utilized the concept of some "original condition" or "state of nature" as a basis for developing theories about how political arrangements would be formed by groups who have no property rights in existing assets. In the same way economists, implicitly, have often theorized on a similar basis about how productive men would be in the absence of "human capital." Marxian theories of economic development treated labor as "raw labor" and attributed all economic growth to physical capital. Contemporary neoclassical economic theory, on the other hand, makes extensive use of the concept of human capital in the explanation of wage differences in labor markets. Growth accounting or labor market analysis, for example, may take the wages of eighteen-year-old males with a high school education as a benchmark for discussing wage differences based on differential education and experience. Wage differences from this benchmark are attributed to differences in productivity that result from "investment in human capital" through formal education and on-the-job experience and are recognized and compensated by the labor market.

The capital embodied in a labor force by nurture, formal education, and on-the-job training provides the population with a level of productivity far in excess of what would be necessary for social and biological maintenance. Part of the cost of that capital formation is borne by parents in the physical care and informal education of children in the home. The cost is also borne by society in the provision of public education, by individuals themselves in their direct payment for education and the opportunity costs of their education, and by employers who provide on the job training.

The concept of human capital carries with it the idea that human productivity depends upon the investment of one generation in its successors (the same concept inherent in "seed corn"). Child-bearing and child-rearing requires the partial or complete withdrawal of women from the market labor force during a period of their working lives. Feeding and housing children requires resources that could otherwise be consumed by the population or invested in other types of capital formation. The institutional education of the labor force requires a large and increasing expenditure on teachers, buildings, books, and equipment. Further, much human capital is developed on the job—employers pay employees or consultants to train other employees rather than produce goods and services. The time lost from production by the employees while they are being trained is also a cost to the employer and to society in terms of lost current production.[7]

Every member of the labor force has some human capital. The Native Americans who met the pilgrims at Plymouth Rock had an understanding of the cultivation of native plants and hunting native game that they had acquired from their ancestors and that the newly arrived pilgrims did not have. On the other hand, some of the human capital in knowledge about European agriculture and commerce that the pilgrims brought with them was inapplicable to their new environment.The human capital of members of a complex society consists, largely, of its ability to use symbol systems for written and oral communication. The ability to communicate at more abstract and complex levels permits the use of more and more sophisticated physical capital and increasingly specialized production arrangements that are characteristic of high levels of economic activity. The more complex the symbolic systems of a society become, the more human capital will be needed for their operation.

Like many ideas in economics, the importance of human capital in increasing productivity has long been understood. In Adam Smith's explanation of the sources of productivity in his famous pin factory, cited earlier in this chapter, he called attention to the increase in dexterity that came from experience and specialization in production. Smith's pin maker's "dexterity" was acquired by "learning by doing" in making final products. A General Motors engineer's "dexterity" comes from the formal education and on-the-job training that have given her the ability to design capital goods that increase the quality and quantity of the final product produced by workers' labor hours. A modern farmer's "dexterity" has come from an understanding of natural science and the operation of machines and markets that he has acquired in years of schooling and continued study of factors affecting his business. These assets equip him to perform complex management and operational tasks.Historically, there has been an important relationship between the human capital of the American labor force and the level of output per worker. I will note (Text Table 8.1) that the rate of increase in educational accomplishments has slackened— median years of schooling have not increased as much in the last two decades as they did in the previous two decades.

Knowledge Capital. A society's knowledge about how the world works is an integral element in the productivity level of its economy. Treating knowledge as part of the capital stock of a society takes us far from the conventional view of capital as something tangible and secured by property rights. Yet, what is the productivity and multi-billion-dollar market value of Microsoft (computer software), Eli Lilly (pharmaceuticals), or DuPont (chemicals) founded on, if not knowledge? Knowledge has a cost of production—it is created by human (mental) effort and its cost of production could be estimated in terms of the compensation of employees and the equipping of laboratories or in terms of the consumption goods forgone because of the time, labor, and capital devoted to knowledge production.[8]

Microsoft, Lilly, and DuPont invest heavily in knowledge capital because the value of the products that can be produced with the knowledge capital will be highly valued by society. The knowledge capital is a direct counterpart to the physical capital used in producing products—except that its creation is not recorded as investment and its existence is not recorded as capital in Generally Accepted Accounting Principles (GAAP) or NIA.

The market value of DuPont's chemical knowledge for creating synthetic fibres is really a measure of the saving of the labor, physical, and natural capital resources in raising wool or cotton relative to the production of fibers from chemical substances. The knowledge has a cost of production to DuPont (or elsewhere in the economy). While DuPont has substantial physical capital in its plant and equipment, it is the scientific knowledge embedded in its processes and machines, rather than the costs of the physical production of the machines that give the corporation the value reflected in the market price of the stock of the corporation. Costs of knowledge capital, like the costs of human capital, are not accounted for as the costs of physical capital are accounted for in GAAP or NIA.Knowledge is created by human beings. Much of it has been accumulated in the past by the natural curiosity of human beings in the course of working and living. Over the past century knowledge useful for increasing economic output has increasingly been created by the purposeful allocation of knowledge to its creation and expansion. Some of it has been created in universities. The 1864 Federal legislation creating land grant universities in the United States had the specific intent of developing and disseminating knowledge in engineering and agriculture.[9] Current federal programs administered by the Department of Defense, National Science Foundation, or National Institutes of Health have the discovery and diffusion of knowledge as prime objectives.

Increasingly, business corporations have staffed and equipped separate research and development facilities to create new knowledge and technology. Knowledge required to synthesize various plastics and artificial fibers was largely developed by the DuPont chemical company in its own laboratories. Social pressures for protection of the environment have led DuPont to develop methods of recycling artificial materials that will save natural resources as well as environmental quality.

The transistor, which is basic to modern communication and computer technology, was developed in the Bell Laboratories, an operating division of the American Telephone and Telegraph Company that was spun off as the Lucent Technologies Corporation. The Microsoft Corporation developed computer programs to run desktop computers and then built on that knowledge to create the spreadsheet, word processing, and desk top publishing programs that make the computers valuable in so many applications. Microsoft and other software companies are now competing fiercely to develop the programs that will control access to the Internet.

Governments, over history, have fostered the pursuit of knowledge for the expansion of military power.   Since World War II the U.S. government has spent heavily on research for the development of modern weapons systems. This has had the complementary effect of developing knowledge capital available for civilian application—in radar, jet engines, miniaturization, nuclear power, communications satellites, and so on.

Defense and space research expenditures are frequently justified in terms of their spin-off of consumer products.   However, the defense program has also been a competitive employer of scientific manpower that might otherwise have gone into the development of knowledge with more direct civilian applications. Thus, it might be argued that even though defense expenditures on research for the development of new weapons have created knowledge capital, that capital has been created in areas that do not have such a powerful impact in increasing output as they would in other areas of the economy. These expenditures have consequently contributed to the slowdown of growth in knowledge capital and, hence, final output over what it might have been.   The opportunity cost of creating one kind of knowledge is also the forgone knowledge in other areas.

Much human knowledge is contained in the symbol systems of language and mathematics.   Knowledge capital has been accumulated in the disciplines of forestry, chemistry, metallurgy, mechanics, biochemistry, and so on.   This knowledge is recorded and communicated in books, journals, technical manuals, blueprints, and computer programs. Knowledge of how humans behave, individually and in groups, has been developed by the social sciences and the humanities. Some of this knowledge is embodied in constitutions and the common law that are necessary to the formation of all types of capital and the minimization of the transactions costs incurred in the specialization of production.

Because knowledge capital also exists in the minds of the humans who use it, the knowledge capital could be rapidly embodied in a new set of publications if all the old ones were destroyed.   However, if the humans who possessed the knowledge were destroyed as well, those who survived without the knowledge would revert to more primitive times in terms of their productive capabilities.

The quantification of accumulated expenditures to create a stock of knowledge that could be related to output and growth would be arbitrary and incomplete.   Following the convention of valuing additions to capital at cost, one could aggregate expenditures on research by government, independent research organizations, universities,   and business corporations.   But much research does not have the direct increase of recorded market output as an objective or result.   It may be interesting to have learned papers produced by scholars on subjects from astronomy to zoology but most of the expenditures on research sponsored by universities are nearer in character to durable consumption goods that satisfy the curiosity and amusement of their writers and readers than to investment goods that assist in the production of goods counted as part of GDP.

Knowledge capital, unlike physical capital, does not wear out and the use of it by one party does not preclude or diminish its use by another.   This means that there are economies of scale as the same knowledge is used by a larger and larger population.   There is no depreciation-by-use problem with the stock of knowledge. But like physical capital, knowledge capital can quickly become obsolete. One could, theoretically, quantify all expenditures on research to measured additions to the stock of knowledge. However, as with physical and human capital, the quantification of some stock of knowledge by a perpetual inventory method is not going to be useful in developing a quantifiable economic variable capable of explaining temporal variations in the rate of economic growth.

Natural Resource Capital. Any society has some natural resource capital as a result of its sovereignty over a particular geographic area. One immediately thinks of minerals, fossil fuels, forests, and the natural fertility of the soil and climatic conditions. Agricultural and domestic water is a critical natural resource. Convenient lake and river transportation can offer a reduction in transportation costs and a saving in reproducible capital otherwise necessary for roads or canals.[10] Wind and sunlight may be harnessed for the generation of power (although current technology rarely makes it cost-effective by comparison with fossil fuels).

The value and importance of natural resources depends upon other types of capital. Natural resources are important and complementary in economic growth because the availability of natural capital can reduce the need for labor and for other types of capital. The location of natural resources has a direct bearing on economic activity. The agricultural lands of the TransAppalachian west had lower capital and labor requirements per unit of output for the production of wheat or cotton than the lands along the Atlantic littoral. The exploitation of Texas petroleum required less physical capital and labor than West Virginia coal to provide the same BTUs to power generating stations. The utility of the natural capital that a society controls depends upon the other three types of capital. It also depends upon individual owners' ability to control its use through enforceable but flexible property rights and the society's ability to defend its natural resources against other nations. The United States has increased its stock of natural resources by conquest and purchase and their value by the application of knowledge and physical capital to their development. U.S.-based corporations and citizens have also successfully utilized natural resources that are not part of the sovereign territory of the United States to increase the incomes of U.S. citizens and corporations that are counted in GNP (but not always in GDP).

Natural capital has not played a great role in the theory of economic growth (although it has been given appropriate attention in economic theory about the operation of resource markets). It is acknowledged that natural resources may provide a higher *level* of income with a given stock of labor and reproducible capital but the subsequent *growth* of output is attributable to other factors.

I wish to emphasize that the economic value of natural resource capital stocks played a complementary part with other types of capital in the course of U.S. economic development and gave the United States advantages that other nations had to supply with higher rates of growth of other types of capital. With the decline in the relative importance of natural resources and transportation in national output, there is diminished scope for the influence of natural resource capital in the rate of growth. Further, the exhaustion of immediately available resources necessitates the substitution of more reproducible, human, and knowledge capital to maintain production. When a society has cut down its old growth forests, it must increase its output of timber by planting new (and faster growing) trees developed by human capital and knowledge capital and planted, maintained, and harvested with physical capital. Technological improvements must be implemented to make use of dwindling and inferior lumber harvests.

The increasing emphasis on the protection of the environment effectively reduces the stock of natural resource capital available for the market production of goods and services. Prohibiting the discharge of toxic wastes into the environment removes natural capital from production and necessitates the use of physical, knowledge, and human capital to take care of the waste. Prohibiting land use for market oriented activities in order to protect plant and animal populations   necessitates the use of other forms of capital.   The level and composition of the capital stocks that a nation possesses at any point in time are important determinants of its level and rate of growth of economic output. However, the level and composition of the stocks of capital result from a complex of decisions and decision makers that respond to social and cultural forces far more complex than the simple desire to maximize their intertemporal utility and the social rate of return on investment.

Capital Formation and Twentieth-Century U.S. Growth

The rates of growth of individual components of the capital stock and the interaction of those components are, undoubtedly, determinants of changes in the rate of economic growth.   However, current economic concepts and measurement techniques do not make possible the identification and quantification of those relationships. In chapter 5, I will present evidence that the rate of growth of output per worker in the U.S. in the last quarter of the twentieth century has not slowed down *within* sectors—it has slowed down in the aggregate because of intersectoral shifts. Thus, I do not argue that the rate of U.S. growth has been affected by a decline in the rate of growth of the physical capital stock. If there has been a slowdown in the rate of growth of the physical stock, it may be a natural consequence of structural change in the economy that has reduced the relative importance of sectors with high physical capital requirements.

The Shift from Household to Market Production

The decline in the relative size of the agricultural labor force has been a major factor in the decrease in the relative size of the household sector of the U.S. economy. At the turn of the twentieth century, transportation costs of alternative employment and services deterred women and children from working off the farm. The shift from farm to town and the improvement of transportation has steadily increased the share of the labor force participating in the market economy.   Further, the mechanization of household production—food preparation, laundry, cleaning, heating, child-care—has released family labor and domestic servants for production of the consumer durables or market-provided services that replace the goods and services formerly produced in the household sector.

Some of the recorded increase in total output that occurs during economic growth is not really a net increase in the goods and services produced—the real net increase is the market production minus the replaced household production. Thus, there is some overstatement of the increase in output that occurs as production is shifted from unmeasured household production to measured market production. This creates an exaggerated acceleration of output per capita as the shift from home to market employment occurs. It is also important to remember that this is a one-time acceleration of growth that cannot happen again—because it has already happened.

Intersectoral Shift in the Labor Force

A century ago half the labor force was employed in primary production of commodities—agriculture, forestry, fishing, and mining. Basic requirements for food, housing, and energy could only be met with this large proportion of the labor force in commodity production. The increase in productivity in these sectors was critical to growth because it released the labor force to produce other goods and services in sectors with higher levels and rates of growth of productivity. The shift of labor out of commodity production was the combined result of a low income elasticity of demand for food, shelter, and fuel and the high productivity growth rates of these commodity producing sectors.

The first large intersectoral shift in the structure of the labor force was the shift of employment from the production of commodities to the manufacturing sector. The second shift was from manufacture to services. A small proportion of the labor force today is directly employed in the production of food, energy, and manufactures. A declining proportion is employed in transportation. The employees released from the production of food, energy, and transportation have found employment in the service sector. Within the service sector one-third is employed in the development and maintenance of "human capital"—health care and education. Another one-third is involved in regulating and monitoring human activity—in government, law enforcement, law, accounting, finance, and, indeed, in the parts of business management concerned with regulatory authorities or monitoring employees' activities. An increasing proportion of the labor force provides recreation and entertainment services and has nothing to do with providing life's basic needs.

Further, economic growth has been both cause and effect of increasing expenditures on education and health. Increasing the proportion of the labor force involved in the education and training of the labor force was necessary for the development of the human capital required for growth. The increase of scientific knowledge in the health sciences and a rising level of real income and life expectancy has led to a growing proportion of GDP being spent on the provision of medical services.

In observing the change in the sectoral composition of the labor force, it is important to note that the large and growing sector of the labor force that now educates and cares for "human capital" in the market service sector represents a shift and expansion of activities that formerly took place in the household sector.

Children were raised and educated at home for a shorter period of their lives before taking care of themselves. The sick or the elderly were cared for in the household economy for a shorter period of their lives before death.

The large and expanding proportion of the labor force now engaged in regulating and monitoring the activities of the economy is a new phenomenon because household production and the lesser degree of specialization made monitoring less necessary to the coordination of economic activity. There was less to coordinate, monitor, and protect—which brings us to the final characteristic of economic growth.

Organizational Change and Transactions Costs

The process of economic growth leads to increasing specialization and capitalization. As I have noted in the previous section, increasing specialization makes the population more and more interdependent and, as a consequence, an increasing proportion of the labor force must be devoted to the coordination of economic activity and less to "direct" production. The number of workers who manage the work of others increases, as do personnel involved in the purchase of inputs and the sale of outputs in the interdependent economic processes.

Further, the gains from specialization open competition over the distribution of the gains from specialization. Lawyers, accountants, and internal control personnel become increasingly important in the organization of economic activity. Conflicts of interest over the division of the gains from specialization lead to more and more elaborate contracting and monitoring arrangements to protect the interdependent parties. Government gets an increasing role in protecting citizens with regulatory and police powers. I shall argue in chapter 9 that when the increase in transactions costs begins to increase faster than the gains from specialization, this contributes to the slowdown of economic growth.

PART II: HISTORICAL DESCRIPTION OF GROWTH AND CHANGE

How have these changes in the six cited characteristics of the process of economic growth manifested themselves in the United States in the twentieth century? I have already used some examples to illustrate some changes we observe; let us use these characteristics of growth to explain some features of the American economy over the past century. My description and explanation, obviously, must be suggestive, truncated, and simplified. I have chosen to focus on examples of how Americans have changed the way they produce food, habitation, and transportation. I have chosen these examples because of their centrality in the process of economic growth, and because the nature of growth and change in activities discussed in these sectors illustrates the nature of the change in the processes accompanying growth that are important in all sectors of the economy.

Food

Economic growth, in the long sweep of history, could be described as the progression from unspecialized, uncapitalized, hunter-gatherer societies based on extended families, to agricultural societies, to capital-intensive systems in which the production and distribution of food has been specialized, mechanized, and depersonalized. The changes in technology and organization that lead to productivity growth in the provision of food are central to the process of economic growth. Food is a primary human need. Until demands for food can be met, there is no labor available for other activities. And, because the agricultural sector (which includes forestry and fisheries) accounted for half the labor force a century ago, productivity growth in this sector has had enormous quantitative importance in its impact on the total economy.

The rapid growth in productivity in food production has been a major contributor to the overall rate of growth in productivity in the United States over the past century. It is a particularly large contributor to economic growth because the production, processing, transport, and distribution of food required such a large section of the labor force 100 years ago. The changes in this sector released almost half the nation's labor force to work in more productive sectors of the economy.

Over the past century the American economy has moved from a situation where half of the labor force was engaged in feeding the total population to a current system of production where less than 2 percent of the labor force is on the farm. What is more, that 2 percent feeds the entire population as well as exporting substantial output. (Of course, this is possible because part of the rest of the labor force is supplying goods and services like fuel, chemicals, farm machinery, and financial services to the farm sector and is an integral part of its productivity.) The provision of food now occupies a smaller proportion of our labor force than it did a century ago because of the labor-saving changes in technology that have taken place. The essence of economic growth is saving labor—producing more goods with less labor.   This is accomplished by reorganizing production so that each worker and firm is responsible for a more and more specialized part of the productive process, working with more and more capital, with more and more efficient technology, and is contractually organized with other participants in the specialized productive processes that will keep workers and capital utilized near their optimal capacity.

Specialization in Food Production

Specialization, and its accompanying impacts on the production of food, has increased value-added output per agricultural worker about ten-fold—1000 percent—over the past century! How do we know that? Price and wage indices suggest that real wages, per hour, in 1890 were about 10 percent of their 1990 level—approximately a dollar per hour in terms of 1990 purchasing power. The loaf of bread that takes about ten minutes of the average worker's day to earn in 1990 would have cost about 100 minutes' worth of wages to purchase in the local baker's shop in 1890 (except that in 1890, it typically would have been baked at home!). It is the reduction in the number of labor hours necessary to produce the bread from field to table that has led to the decrease in the cost of bread expressed in the number of hours the American worker would have to work to purchase it. The reduction in the number of labor hours necessary to produce the bread is one measure of the change in the cost of a basic standard of living.

How did this occur? In 1890 the wheat for the bread was grown on a farm about one-twenty-fifth of its current average size. An archetypal farmer toiled more than sixty hours a week on a forty-acre mixed farm and, on that farm, grew twenty acres of wheat from seed saved from his previous harvest. He cultivated with a horse-drawn wooden-frame plow with an iron blade. Without the benefit of genetically developed seeds, chemical fertilizers, or herbicides, fungicides, or pesticides, the farmer produced an annual yield of fifty bushels per acre (a total of 1000 bushels from twenty cultivated acres). He hauled it himself in his horse-drawn cart to the local miller.

The nineteenth-century farmer (with help from wife and children) produced those 1000 bushels of wheat, per year, on half his improved land. Because the farmer used horses to plow, disc, harrow, seed, and cut the grain, the remaining acres were used to raise oats, hay, and grass as "fuel" for the horses. (A small area would also have been used for wood lot for domestic fuel and farm-building materials, pasturing a milk cow, and raising vegetables in a kitchen garden.) Because horses were maintained on farm-grown hay and oats, there were no purchased petroleum products or annual costs for tractor and other equipment amortization and repair. There were no purchased input costs for seed, fertilizer, and agricultural chemicals. Note that virtually all of the productive inputs to the production of the wheat originated on the farm rather than being purchased from other suppliers. For the economy as a whole, there was limited specialization in the production of inputs, and limited capitalization. Household production produced a commodity (such as wheat) for sale to others and provided many of its other needs internally. The labor force was concentrated in commodity production, and there were simple and limited contractual relationships involved in production.

In 1990 the grain for bread is grown on the Great Plains on a 1000-acre farm specialized in wheat. The farmer may drive (or hire a worker to drive) a 500-horsepower tractor dragging massive gang-plows made of tempered steel. He relies on sophisticated computer software to continuously analyze the factors determining his optimal inputs of seed, fertilizers, herbicides, fungicides, pesticides, and the timing of their application. He gets twice the wheat yield, per acre, of the 1890 farmer but, of course, has high operating costs for all his purchased inputs of hybrid seed, chemicals, fuels, and the operating costs on his half-million dollars' worth of farm machinery.

Technological Change in Agriculture

Let us consider more closely the nature of some of the technological changes involved in the specialization of production. Every type of economic activity has specific physical problems that must be solved. However, many of the specific problems have similar technical solutions, like the provision of motive power, the reduction of friction, the use of chemical reactions, and so on.

As an example, consider the two basic production problems of agriculture: the competition of other plants with cultivated crops for the moisture and nutrients of the soil, and the competition of animals, insects, and fungi with humans for the consumption of the crops. Agriculture involves displacing other vegetation and stopping the consumption or spoilage of the cultivated crop by pests, insects, or fungi. Technological change in agriculture is mechanical, chemical, and biological.

The first step in displacing other vegetation is cutting down forests or plowing up prairie grasses. The initial clearing can be viewed as a one-time capital cost. Preparing land for crop production can also include the construction of drainage or irrigation systems and fencing.[11]

By the end of the nineteenth century, much of the land needed for agricultural production had been converted from forest and prairie. It had been converted from natural capital into enterprise capital with great amounts of human and animal labor without the benefit of labor saving machines for breaking sod, cutting trees, pulling tree roots, and digging drainage ditches. (At least half the land that was in agricultural use in the United States a century ago is no longer cultivated.) The reduction of the capital costs of land clearing, fencing, or irrigation depends upon the development of machinery to accomplish these tasks. The purchase price and operating costs of the machinery—relative to its capacity to clear and cultivate land—depended on solving various technical problems in its production and maintenance. These will be considered later in this section. The first part of the technological challenge in agriculture is providing motive force to the cutting and breaking of soil. At the end of the nineteenth century, horses, mules, and oxen were the almost universal solution to the provision of motive power and they were still widely in use at the end of World War II. But there was a serious constraint on growth in output per worker here. The amount of power that can be supplied by one animal is, obviously, limited. Teams of animals can be used to pull heavier plows through heavier soils, but there is a limit to the numbers of horses or other animals that can be harnessed and driven by one worker. Prior to the gasoline or diesel tractor, this imposed a limit to the potential number of acres of annual cultivation per worker. Depending on soil type, depth of cultivation, and other factors, the limit of annual cultivation per full time laborer working with draft animals was about fifty acres.[12]

The use of draft animals required that part of the grain that was produced be retained for feeding them, which reduced net farm output. Part of the cleared land that might otherwise have been available for raising food crops had to be kept in pasture for grass and hay, further reducing output. The animals had to be fenced, sheltered, fed, and maintained throughout the year. All of this necessitated additional farm labor that counted into the labor hours necessary for the production of the wheat and bread. Granted, the animals reproduced themselves; they usually did not need to be purchased from an outside supplier and the fuel for their operation could be raised on the farm. The manure produced by horses was recycled as fertilizer. Nevertheless, a considerable part of farm labor, capital, and gross cereal production was devoted to the maintenance of the draft animals used as motive power, and this reduced the crop output available for sale by the farmer.[13]

The technological change that transformed arable farming was the invention and continuing improvement of the internal combustion engine. With relatively low initial cost, and a lower weight-to-power ratio than steam engines, the gasoline-powered tractor spread rapidly in American agriculture after World War I. The tractor's displacement of draft animals increased *net* farm crop production by releasing both land and labor from the support of draft animals to the production of crops. It increased the amount of land under cultivation for grains so rapidly that it contributed to a great increase in output that brought down agricultural prices relative to prices in other sectors of the economy. It plowed so deep and fast that it helped to create the Dust Bowl on the prairies and contributed to the acceleration of soil erosion elsewhere. Its displacement of farm labor led to the decline in the self-sufficiency of the family farm and the urbanization of America. The problem of motive power in agriculture was solved by technological change in the production of tractors and the fuel to run them in the other sectors of the economy.

Technological change replaced horses with tractors and was the most important factor leading to the increase in the number of acres tilled per farmer. Bigger and better tractors increased the value of capital per worker. They also increased agricultural output per unit of capital as their capacity increased more rapidly than their cost. This is the capital saving aspect of technological change that I will discuss in chapter 9.

Consider a second basic technological problem in agriculture. The second part of the physical problem in land cultivation is the effectiveness and durability of the implements used to cut and break the soil—plows, discs, and harrows—that cut the soil as they are dragged through it. The sharper and thinner and smoother the edges, the more effective the cutting action and the less power required to drag them. The cutting edge must be strong and resist abrasion and corrosion.

The technological change in improving cutting implements involved the substitution of steel for iron and continual improvement in the ability of the steel to "hold an edge" and resist the abrasion and corrosion that would reduce its ability to "scour"—the soil that is cut must not cling to the sides of the cutting edge. The capacity of the plow, disc, or harrow was also determined by the power it took to pull it per acre cultivated. The capital cost of cultivating implements was determined by their original purchase price, and their effective working life until they wore out. Their operating costs were determined by the frequency of sharpening relative to work done. Better plows depended upon better steel and better machine tools to cut the steel. Steel and machine tools are the basic technology for the development of cutting tools in a variety of commodity production and manufacturing technologies—plows in agriculture, drill bits in mining, saws in forestry and construction, cutting tools in manufacturing.

At the end of the nineteenth century plows were made of cast iron and bolted or roped to wooden frames. At the end of the twentieth century, cutting instruments made of alloy steel with great tensile strength and resistance to abrasion are welded to steel frames. Coupled with powerful high-speed tractors, the modern gang plows, discs, and harrows enable one agricultural worker to cultivate literally thousands of acres of land per annum.

The cost of operating a tractor includes the amortization of its original cost, maintenance, and fuel. All of these costs have declined per unit of capacity (per acre of ground potentially cultivated per annum). These operating costs have fallen over time as a result of increases in tractor size accompanied by a decrease in purchase cost per unit of capacity because of reductions in the cost of producing the engines, transmissions, and other tractor components.

The fall in purchase costs and maintenance and operating costs per unit of capacity has occurred partly because of reductions in the cost and improvement in the quality of the steel used in the tractors. The fall in the cost has also resulted from more precise machine tools that have reduced the tolerances of moving parts. The increase in the precision of manufacture allows the reduction of friction and the increase of compression. This, in turn, increases power delivered per unit of fuel, increases working life, and reduces maintenance costs. This is one factor that lies behind the reduction in the *operating cost of capital per unit of production capacity* that I will identify as an important factor in economic growth.

What is also observed in the production of tractors and many other types of machinery is a fall in production costs per dollar of output capacity. Better engineering, better and cheaper steel, and better machine tools for cutting and forming it are at the base of much of the increase in the productivity of capital. This is the capital saving characteristic of technological change that I will analyze in chapter 9.

Let me emphasize here an important constraint on technological change: the technological change that increases the output per unit of labor, or capital from using a specialized piece of capital equipment—such as a tractor—cannot go on forever at an increasing or even constant rate because of physical limitations. The tractor is limited in size by the weight to be borne by the soil; the steel cannot last forever as long as it is subject to corrosion and friction; fuel efficiency may be improved but more BTUs cannot be utilized than are present in the fuel; and so on.

The increase in the productive life of a piece of equipment lowers its depreciation cost. Increasing the life of a machine from one year to two years decreases the depreciation rate from 100 percent to 50 percent—a fall of one-half. Increasing the life of the machine from ten years to eleven years decreases the annual depreciation rate from 10 percent to 9 percent. The economic impact of technological change decreases with the extension of physical limits.

Another set of advances in agricultural technology has been in the areas of genetics and biochemistry. The objectives in research and development have been to increase the potential yields of the crops being cultivated and to improve the farmer's capability to eliminate plant, insect, and fungal competitors for the crops.Potential yields have been increased, primarily, by genetically changing the crops being cultivated. Cross-pollination produced hybrid seed. Seeds were hybridized to increase the yield per stalk, or to increase the protein content, or the length of the storage period, or other desirable characteristics for the crop in question.

Only rarely were hybrid seeds developed by farmers on the farm. The improvement of crop varieties depended upon the extension of knowledge in genetics begun by Mendel in Europe in the mid-nineteenth century. The agricultural experiment stations operated by the land grant universities in the United States did not limit their activities to research and development. Their extension agents informed farmers of the availability and use of the new seed varieties and advised on appropriate soil preparation and fertilization. In the twentieth century the improvement in crop varieties has progressed from cross-pollination to cloning. This new technology has depended on the breakthroughs in understanding and manipulating the DNA chromosomes in cells.

The improvement of agricultural yields by genetics was an important contribution to increasing output per acre. Another important biological contribution to the increase in output per acre was the development of manufactured fertilizers. The development of processes to fix nitrogen and to mine, refine, and fabricate other chemicals provided a means to replace and supplement the nutrients that were consumed by cropping methods that did not return the biomass to the earth. Soil exhaustion was an increasing problem on cleared and cultivated land in the United States in the nineteenth century, and without the development of commercial fertilizers, would have greatly reduced crop yields in the twentieth century.

The other biological advances that increased yields in agriculture were herbicides, fungicides, and insecticides. Herbicides have the same objective as the soil preparation by plowing and disking—killing off the plant species that compete with the crop for moisture and nutrients. Fungicides and pesticides are aimed at reducing the loss of the crop to nonhuman competitors for its consumption.[14] Coupled with the mechanical improvements in ground cultivation that increased the annual maximum number of acres per worker, the increase in yield per acre with hybrid seed and manufactured fertilizer further increased output of food per worker. Each worker hour cultivated more acres and each acre produced higher and higher yields.

Technological Change and Further Productivity Gains in Agriculture

Modern agriculture operates like a factory. The soil is merely a place to receive genetically engineered seeds and mechanically produced fertilizers and other chemicals to produce food that is harvested by machines. But once again, a caveat about the necessary limits to continual increases in productivity from the application of biology and chemistry is in order. When all the competitors—plants, insects, fungi, and so forth—have been eliminated from competition for the output, the net output cannot be further increased by the use of chemicals. And we have observed that the chemicals may be evaded by resistant strains or may have unfortunate effects. Genetics may improve yields but they will, inevitably, reach limits that have to do with the nature of biological processes. Hybridization and cloning can only reduce undesirable characteristics and increase desirable characteristics that are present in existing species—they cannot "invent" characteristics that are not present in nature.

The transformation of farms from self-contained units that self-produced almost all of their inputs into highly specialized units that purchase almost all their inputs explains the reduction of the labor force on the American farm from 50 percent to 2 percent of the total labor force over the last century. It is a process far removed from the gathering of the seeds of naturally occurring plant species, which was the origin of agriculture.

Organizational Change

The nineteenth-century farmer hauled his grain to a local water (or steam) mill himself with his own cart. After grinding it with mill stones, the miller dispatched his flour (in his own barrels) by horse-drawn wagon to the local general store where the storekeeper met the needs of fifty local families for general provisions. The households that bought the flour used it to produce their daily bread in their own kitchens. There were many fewer contributors to the production process from field to table.

The modern farmer finds it economic to contract out the harvesting of his grain to combine operators and the transportation to truckers who haul the grain to elevators. That provides for higher utilization of specialized equipment. The 1990 wheat farmer produces 100,000 bushels per year—100 times what the 1890 farmer produced (although his value added is less because of all the purchased inputs). The modern farmer does not supply much physical labor— he provides management of the physical capital and the inputs from all the many suppliers of specialized goods and services.

When it is sold, the modern grain harvest is hauled from the mechanized-loading storage elevator by the railroad 1000 miles to a railside milling corporation that grinds it in computer-controlled, electrically powered milling equipment. The flour is sent another 1000 miles to a baking corporation that has completely mechanized the process of bread baking so that loaves roll through the production line at 100,000 loaves per day. The mixing equipment and ovens produced by specialized manufacturing firms are electrically driven and fired— the electricity is generated 500 miles away in a nuclear-powered generating plant and carried in high voltage power lines to the bakery.

The bread leaves the bakery in large trucks, 5000 loaves at a time, for supermarkets that serve 5,000 families at each store. Store inventories for all the thousands of categories of processed and packaged stocks are continuously maintained by the computerized bar-code readers that check the bread into and out of the store. Our 1990 loaf of bread is picked up by Mary Q. Citizen on her way home from the office after her eight hour workday. It costs her the equivalent of ten minutes' wages rather than the 100 minutes it cost to buy bread a century earlier, even though hundreds of thousands of other workers have been involved in all the specialized inputs to its production.

How did the production and distribution processes involved in the production and distribution of bread from farm to table change from 1890 to 1990? The historical answer is "incrementally." The analytical answer is through specialization, capitalization, and technological change.

There was an increase in physical capital per worker (tractors and plows) that increased output per worker and potential output per dollar of invested capital. There was an increase in knowledge capital (genetics and microbiology) that increased the output per unit of natural capital (land). There was an increase in the knowledge of metallurgy and mechanical engineering that reduced the cost of physical capital (machinery) per unit of output. There was an increase in utilization of the human skills and invested capital.

All of the inputs of fertilizer, fuel, and machinery, as well as the outputs of grain, flour, and bread, have to be transported. Specialization is limited by the extent of the market and, specifically, by transport costs. Output per truck driver and railroad worker rose as bigger, faster trucks and trains, costing less per unit of carrying capacity, increased the quantities of wheat, flour, and bread that could be carried per driver and per dollar of invested capital. Each baker tended faster assembly lines and bigger ovens that produced more bread per worker hour and per dollar of invested capital. Each grocer increased gross sales per foot of building, per dollar of inventory, and per employee hour.

Thus, the story of how the cost of the bread reaching our table has been reduced is the story of specialization, technological change, capitalization, the shift from household to market production, the diversification of the labor force, and the exponential multiplication of contractual relationships.

Habitation

Habitation is more than the visible structures in which we live and work. The story of economic growth in the provision of modern urban and suburban habitation is, in large part, the story of reducing the costs of energy, and cybernetically, the costs of transportation, materials, and construction. Food and energy that have been reduced in their cost of production must be transported cheaply into cities. Water and sewage must be transported by elaborate underground systems of pipes and must be purified before use and treated again afterwards. The transportation of workers must be accomplished by mass transit systems that depend for efficiency on high density apartments and high occupancy office buildings.

A typical turn-of-the-century house stood on an unpaved street in a small town. It had a wooden frame resting on a few well-positioned rocks. The single-wall construction with clapboard exterior was cheaper than a log cabin to erect but equally expensive to heat. Water came from a well or, perhaps, was newly available from a municipal water company, but there was only a single cold-water tap in the kitchen. If there was a flush toilet, the lack of a sewer system necessitated a cess-pit at the bottom of the back yard. Lighting was supplied by kerosene lamps, heating by coal—a stove in the kitchen burned almost continually, and an open hearth in the parlor was used on special occasions and Sundays. The upstairs bedrooms were unheated. City tenements weren't much different in construction and technology.

Coal for cooking and heating was a major item in household expenses. It was mined in underground seams in the Appalachians by miners who worked in miserable and dangerous conditions with picks and hand-drills and hauled the coal to the mine head in small mule-drawn carts. At the mine head the coal was loaded manually onto a short-haul railway and then went to the nearest canal, navigable river, or long-haul railroad. It was then hauled to the local coal merchant, who might serve fifty families. He delivered the coal in sacks by horse-drawn cart to each house's coal shed. On a daily basis the housewife, domestic servants, or children brought it into the kitchen and cleared the stove of slag that had generated from partial combustion. Purchased energy—coal and kerosene—for the average household required ten hours' wages every week.

The modern home's energy requirements have increased in terms of BTUs, but the cost of energy has fallen relative to incomes. Energy no longer comes directly to the house in the form of locally produced wood or coal, even though the electricity that operates the cooking stove may be coal-generated. Nowadays, coal is strip-mined by giant machines rather than miners with picks. It is loaded with enormous shovels, rather than hand shovels, into specialized coal-hauling trains that dump the loads into coal-fired generating equipment. If the central heating is by natural gas, the energy is piped directly from wells into long-distance pipelines for conveyance to local distributing companies. Physical capital has almost completely displaced labor in the delivery of energy and its cost has fallen per unit of energy. Capital costs are nearly 100 percent of total costs and they take a much smaller proportion of consumers' expenditure budgets than they did at the turn of the century.

Specialization and Technological Change in Construction

What about the construction technology for the buildings that we observe in cities above the unseen utility systems and alongside the transportation routes? Here, the story of economic progress is the steady decline in the relative costs per square foot of construction and materials and in the operating costs of the buildings. In the city core tall buildings concentrate population to reduce transportation and utility costs. Vertical cities depend upon steel girders and steel-reinforced concrete and steel pipes. Nineteenth-century cities, which were largely wood and stone, were limited by the stress-bearing capacity of materials to four-story structures. Modern skyscrapers rise over 100 stories.

Modern construction methods include precut and predrilled steel girders that are lifted into place with cranes. Large trucks carry premixed cement to sites where it is pumped into manufactured and site-assembled forms.   Glass windows and external sheeting are hung from the steel skeletons of the buildings. The building interiors are prefabricated wall and ceiling systems. Plumbing, electrical, heating and cooling, and telecommunications systems are installed by subcontractors who assemble the systems from many standardized manufactured components.

Modern residential structures are capital intensive. Houses are located in suburban developments with paved streets and sidewalks served by major arterial roads and freeways.   Municipal water systems deliver purified, pressurized water, and municipal sewer systems carry away waste to treatment plants that restore waste water with biological and chemical treatment to tertiary (drinkable) quality. Electrical, gas, telephone, and cable television systems serve the houses. All of these utility systems are built with powerfule earth-moving equipment and quantities of steel and reinforced concrete.

The houses themselves have steel-reinforced, concrete foundations excavated into the ground.   The hollow-wall construction is insulated with artificial materials and the windows are double-glazed. There is a bedroom and bathroom for every occupant and central heating as well as air conditioning. The houses incorporate appliances for cooking, refrigeration, laundry, and other labor saving devices as a part of their capital. The site value of the land depends upon the considerable capital incorporated into the transportation and public utility systems, which reduce its costs for operation and for the transportation of the inhabitants.

Houses and their mechanical, electrical, and plumbing systems and sub-assemblies are still constructed on-site, as they were a century ago, but all the components have been manufactured and their on-site assembly by the sub-contractors engaged by the developer has all the characteristics of an assembly line. (A substantial proportion of newly constructed inexpensive houses are manufactured and referred to, euphemistically, as "mobile homes.")

A 1990 house is more capital intensive, per square foot of floor space, because of its sophisticated systems, but it substitutes capital equipment for domestic labor and requires fewer hours of wages to pay its operating costs than the 1890 house.   Suburban houses may superficially resemble earlier architectural styles but their construction, once again, has been streamlined by specialized off-site manufacture of components. The foundation is reinforced concrete, as in office buildings. The framing is done with dimensioned lumber that has been precut to standard lengths to avoid wasting materials and economize on the use of on-site labor. Trusses are prefabricated. Doors and windows are pre-hung and pre-framed. Manufactured sheets of plasterboard are more rapidly installed than the old-fashioned lath and hand-troweled wet plaster.

Hollow walls and roof cavities are insulated with artificial materials. Kitchen and bathroom cabinets and fixtures are manufactured on factory assembly lines. Roofs and walls are covered with artificial materials that are cheaper to manufacture and more impervious to insects, fungi, and the elements than wood. Suburban houses are frequently erected in tracts in large numbers to reap the benefit of scope and scale economies in the installation of roads and utility systems and the site assembly of components. The master craftsmen have been replaced with machines.

Consider the reduction in the man-hours involved in the production of dimension lumber, which is only one component of the modern house. The trees are felled in the forest with chain saws rather than hand saws and hauled to the mill on self-loading log trucks rather than being hauled out by oxen or a steam "donkey engine" to a truck or railcar. The costs of constructing logging roads into the forest have been reduced by the use of large bulldozers rather than labor-intensive hand tools. At the lumber mill conveyor belts haul the logs into a computer-guided saw that computes how to get the maximum amount of lumber out of each log and cuts it with a thin blade further designed to reduce wastage.   Sawdust is no longer dumped or burned—it is combined with chemicals and formed under pressure into particleboard.

In place of the longer, larger lumber once used to provide structural strength in buildings, smaller pieces of lumber are laminated into beams to provide greater strength at lower cost. In fact, lamination of beams and the production of plywood and chipboard makes it possible to use the low-density fibers of small, young trees for construction. Genetically cloned stands of southern

Loblolly Pine, which can now be grown to market maturity in thirty years (compared to 100 years for Douglas Fir), are harvested by one worker operating a machine that fells them, trims the branches, and loads them as effortlessly as a combine harvester runs through a stand of wheat and spits out the grain into trucks.

The technology for the production of furnishings has also changed. The rugs, curtains, and upholstery fabrics for houses were formerly woven from cotton, flax, or wool. Now the fibers are artificial and their production requires far less labor and capital to produce than the fabrics they have replaced. Technological change in spinning and weaving likewise has reduced the labor and capital used in manufacture.

Finally, the transactions costs of financing the increased capital costs of housing have been rationalized. Home purchasers borrow money for thirty years on the security of their homes and projected incomes. Appraisals and credit reports are nationally standardized. The local banker who evaluated loan applications on "character" has been replaced by a computerized "expert program" that determines creditworthiness on the basis of computerized inputs of financial data—some of which is furnished by specialized credit-rating agencies. The resulting standardized mortgages are "bundled" into mortgage-backed bonds, insured by governmental or private agencies, and sold into credit markets where they are acquired by mutual funds or pension funds. Standardization of mortgage lending has reduced the transactions costs and risks of lenders. The savings in interest costs accrue to homeowners, who can now borrow at rates of interest only 1 percent higher than the U.S. Treasury.

In habitation, as in food production, the increase in productivity has been accompanied by the six features discussed in Part I of this chapter:

1. *Specialization*:   All of the components of structures are manufactured on a specialized basis rather than being fabricated and assembled on-site.
2. *Technological change*: The materials and methods of modern construction have changed fundamentally.
3. *Capitalization*: Specialized capital for the production of wood, concrete, and steel and specialized capital in earthmoving equipment, materials-moving equipment, logging and milling machinery have increased output per worker while decreasing capital costs per unit of output.
4. *Market, rather than household, production*: Homes are no longer self-produced by members of the household.
5. *Intersectoral shift of the labor force*: Specialization in production has increased the proportion of value added provided by sectors of the labor force other than the construction sector.
6. *Organizational change*: Capital intensity and specialization have given   rise to complex long-term debt and supply contracts with increasing transactions costs for the organization of construction. Part of the economies reaped by specialization and organizational change in house-building has been offset by increasing bureaucratic zoning and planning regulations that increase delay and costs.

In my agricultural example I quantified the results of technological and organizational change in agriculture and food production by talking about a ten-fold fall in the labor hours necessary to produce a loaf of bread. I hesitate to venture any direct comparison of the saving of man-hours of labor involved in providing a cubic foot of living space, in supplying a gallon of water (including energy costs for pumping and material and construction costs for piping) or candlepower of light over the past century. I suspect that the man-hours of work necessary to pay for a cubic foot of house space, a BTU of heat, or the services of an automatic washing machine, refrigerator, or vacuum cleaner have fallen by an even larger magnitude than those of the loaf of bread.

Are further increases in productivity in the provision of habitation possible? Yes, of course. Will they be as rapid as over the past century? How? How many components are not yet produced with specialized and mechanized capital-intensive equipment? Can we continue to see the same rate of growth in the saving of energy in the fabrication and powering of the systems that underlie habitation?

PART III: A CLOSER LOOK AT PRODUCTIVITY, SPECIALIZATION, AND TECHNOLOGICAL CHANGE: DEFINITIONS AND RELATIONSHIPS

Let me begin my argument about the relationship between specialization, technological change, and increasing capitalization and productivity with some definitions: Productivity—the level of output per worker within a firm, industry, or sector—is determined by:

1. *Capitalization*: The total stocks (not just physical capital) of capital per worker.
2. *Capital Productivity*: The ratio of potential output/capital resulting from technology.
3. *Utilization*: The ratio of actual output/potential output resulting from the level of utilization of productive capacity, which is, in turn, determined by the social organization of markets and the management of firms.

Stated formally,

Output/worker $\equiv$ *(Capital/Worker) x (Potential Output/Capital) x (Actual Output/Potential Output)*

The rate of growth of output per worker, in this identity, is the sum of the rates of growth of these three ratios (and their interactive terms).[15] It is these three factors that explain past productivity growth within sectors—particularly commodity producing and distributing (sectors I–VI)—in the American economy.

To understand why, consider how these ratios have worked in the past:

1. The constant dollar value of capital per worker has increased. This has occurred through the substitution of capital for labor as the user cost of capital equipment per dollar of potential output has decreased relative to labor costs.
2. The constant dollar value of potential output per constant dollar of capital has increased. This has occurred as the potential capacity of capital goods, relative to their acquisition cost, has increased, and as their longer productive lives have reduced their annual depreciation cost.

3. I conjecture that the utilization of potential capacity has increased because of improvements in economic organization and the internationalization of the economy that have increased the size of the market. This is even more important for human capital than physical capital.

An Example

Having stated the analytics of productivity change, let me illustrate the operation of the suggested trends in ratios with a simplified example of productivity growth in the production of capital for one sector of the economy—the transportation sector—which could be generalized, with appropriate modifications, to the production of capital goods in other sectors of the economy.

The Southern Pacific Railroad (SPR) is a part of Sector V, transportation, communication, and public utilities. The output of the SPR in transportation services is ton miles of freight. All of the output of the sector ends up as an intermediate input of transportation costs to other sectors of the economy producing final value added output. Capitalization increases when SPR buys a diesel electric locomotive from General Electric (GE) for $1 million: this is an addition to the physical capital stock. It is estimated that the engine has the potential capacity to haul an additional one million miles of freight per year for ten years in conjunction with one additional employee. The capital/labor ratio is $1 million/worker. The potential output/capital ratio is one million ton miles/$1 million or $1 per ton mile per year.

Simplifying, the SPR estimates that the engine will last for 10 years, and that it will borrow the $1,000,000 acquisition price at 10 percent per annum. Thus, the user cost of capital of the engine is $200,000 per year ($100,000 for depreciation and $100,000 for interest) or $.20 per ton mile per year. This figure must be compared with potential revenues (for example, $.50 per ton mile = $500,000) and the other operating costs for labor, fuel, and so on. If the projected total revenues are greater than the projected costs, SPR will decide to increase capital per worker and buy the locomotive.

What determines changes in the capital/worker and output/capital ratios? It is these ratios that drive the output/labor ratio at the heart of the economic growth process. Assuming that the SPR can get full utilization at a constant revenue per mile, the determinants of additions to the capital stock are the user costs of capital, plus the costs of the associated inputs (fuel, labor for operation and maintenance, and other capital equipment costs), relative to the prices received for the projected flow of output. It is these factors that determine the projected net output per unit of capital equipment that will be transformed by management in the investment decision into the ratio of projected net revenue/projected net cost.

What I observe happening in the process of technological change is an increase in the ratio of net output/net cost from a variety of factors: (1) the acquisition cost of capital goods (diesel locomotives) declines relative to their annual flow capacity (ton miles); and (2) their annual user costs per unit of potential capacity decline further because they are longer-lived, cost less to finance, and/or cost less for associated inputs per unit of output (fuel, maintenance, and so on). The result of technological change is a simultaneous increase in the stock of capital per worker and an increase in output/capital ratio. The increase of the two ratios is additive in its effects on output per worker. Productivity growth occurs from the joint operation of these two ratios. It is further enhanced by the increase in the ratio of actual output/potential output—but the continued growth from this ratio is, obviously, limited.

Conventional Versus Empirical Views of Capitalization and Productivity Growth

The conventional economic way of thinking about the growth of productivity has been to postulate diminishing marginal *physical* productivity with the application of increasing amounts of physical capital per unit of labor. This idea (discussed in the Appendix Note 9.1) had its origins in examples like the diminishing marginal productivity of land as more labor was applied to it; or the diminishing yield to seed in terms of seed as more capital (seed) was sown without the increase of other cooperating factors.

A more empirical way to think about the productivity growth process is to note that *increases* in output per unit of capital may be possible when new physical capital goods decline in user cost as a result of technological change. This technological change, in turn, occurs because human capital and knowledge capital is embodied in the physical capital goods. (The GE diesel engine isn't just bigger—it's a better diesel engine made possible by more highly educated engineers operating with more scientific knowledge.) Rather than diminishing returns from increasing the physical capital/labor ratio, there is the possibility of increasing returns from the appropriate combination of increasing stocks of the four categories of capital.

What I observe operating in the historical process of technological change is *increasing* output per unit of capital even though the capital/labor ratio may increase more slowly because of the fall in the price of capital goods resulting from technological change in the capital goods producing sector of the economy.[16] This may seem counterintuitive, but it is because physical capital is frequently thought of in terms of units of machines (like units of labor) rather than the user costs of the machines of a given potential output capacity over their productive life. Both capital stocks and output are expressed in terms of a price-indexed monetary unit, but the capital stocks have the additional dimension of an output flow capacity and user cost. The capital stocks on which the capital/labor and output/capital ratios are based are valued in terms of acquisition cost, which (in competitive markets) is equal to their cost of production. But the projected output flow of the capital stock is compared with the acquisition price and this ratio is increased by technological change that lowers acquisition cost of capital equipment and also increases its output per time unit and its longevity.[17] The relationship between changes in the user cost of the capital stock and potential increases in the flow of output is determined by technology. An investment in the new technology capital stock (a diesel locomotive) that leads to an increase in value added for the new capital stock greater than the older capital stock increases the output/capital ratio.

SPECIALIZATION AND PRODUCTIVITY

The critical question is *how* does GE manage to reduce the cost of production of the diesel locomotives per unit of their output capacity and pass it on to the SPR in the form of a lower acquisition cost? By making more of them! By taking advantage of *specialization* by components suppliers to drive down the production costs of the components of the locomotive. GE itself produces the electric motors that drive the traction wheels. It buys the diesel power plants from General Motors, the alternators from Allis Chalmers, and the computer control systems from Minneapolis Honeywell. GE and its suppliers purchase components from their suppliers and the chain of production goes back to the suppliers of the capital goods used to mine and smelt the raw materials—almost an infinite chain! Specialization in the production of components and the raw materials that go into the components leads to technological change by the specialized suppliers, which is finally passed on in the form of a reduced acquisition cost of the capital good (the diesel locomotive). That leads to the reduction of transportation costs, which leads to further specialization in production in the entire economy.

The efficiencies in the specialized production of the components of the diesel are passed on as lower prices to the purchasers of the diesel locomotives. The lower capital costs, in turn, lead to lower prices of the goods for final consumption produced with the use of the new locomotives, which reduce transportation costs. (The increase in final output, however, is valued in terms of constant prices in the calculation of output change and this is the change in the numerator of the potential output/capital ratio.) The output/capital ratio is increased by the reduction (or slower proportionate increase) in the denominator—the initial cost of the engine and/or the depreciation rate is reduced by the increase in the engine's durability. This, in turn, lowers the necessary gross investment necessary to maintain a given capital stock with a given potential output capacity.

The social benefits of technological change (increased output at lower prices) accrue to society as a whole. The incentive to the final goods' producer for adopting the "cheaper" (lower costs per unit of output) capital good is a temporary return to capital investment above the market return (or cost) of capital. In the longer run failure to adopt the new lower cost production methods made possible by the improved technology (in making the diesel locomotive) will result in higher relative costs of production for the producers who do not adopt the new technology. This reduces their residual returns (profit) from production which must be sold at competitively determined market prices. If they do not make normal profits, the price of their stock falls and they are takeover targets for other firms that do.

Several points deserve emphasis with respect to the relationship between capital formation and economic growth. The fall in the price of capital goods per unit of capacity (made possible by technological change in their production) increases the output/capital ratio. A lower rate of depreciation (or alternatively, lower maintenance expenditures for capital goods) decreases the requirements for gross saving and investment necessary to maintain any given ratio of capital/labor and increases the profit incentive for increased capitalization. Most of the technological change that occurs has the effect of increasing the potential output/capital ratio by reducing the acquisition and depreciation costs of capital equipment per unit of output capacity, as well as reducing the labor requirements per unit of output.[18]

Specialization and the Scope of Capital Goods Production

Technological change usually involves an increase in the specialization of capital goods. There are two reasons for this. First, increases in production allow the specialization of function. To use an old example, a construction worker may dig or carry dirt with a shovel (small-scale unspecialized capital good), but the substitution of a wheelbarrow (larger-scale specialized capital good) for a shovel will increase the foot pounds of earth that can be moved per period of both worker and capital input.

But it only pays to add the wheelbarrow if the excavation is large enough to justify the addition of the more specialized equipment. And it only pays to mass produce wheelbarrows if the market for them is large enough. And so on for the components of the wheelbarrow and the machines involved in making the components and the raw materials.

To return to our modern example, it only pays GE to mass-produce diesel locomotives if there is a market for them, and for GE's suppliers to specialize in the production of components if there is a market, and so on. For example, a particular type of alloy steel may be important in a particular roller bearing used in many different types of machinery, and used in producing many different types of final products. Then having a specialized separate steel producer make that special steel for supply to the specialized roller bearing makers who supply the specialized machine makers who supply the different product makers will increase productivity. This specialization will reduce the cost of the steel that goes into the roller bearings that go into the machinery that is used to make the products that will end up decreasing the cost of the products.

Productivity and the Scale of Physical Capital

The second area of increase in productivity is the increasing size of individual units of capital equipment (as opposed to the number of units of capital equipment produced). There are two separable phenomena involved here: (1) the cost per unit of output capacity of the capital equipment itself and (2) operating economies from increasing the utilization of labor with bigger capacity capital equipment.[19]

Let me illustrate these phenomena with several examples. A freeway or an office building with twice the square feet or vehicles per hour capacity might be built for only 1.5 times the cost; an electric generator or diesel locomotive with twice the power could be built and operated with declining capital costs per kilowatt hour or ton miles of capacity. Static economies of scale from the use of larger capacity capital equipment will often be accompanied with increases in capacity output per unit of labor and capital input. It may also be accompanied by decreases in energy, maintenance, and other costs. The decline in labor costs with the larger capacity of capital equipment comes from workers' unutilized dexterity and monitoring capacities.   One driver can operate a bigger tractor, train, plane, ship, power saw, nuclear reactor, or computer. There are limits to this capacity, although they may be indefinitely extendable—particularly with the availability of sensors and computers to store and process information.

The surprising element in the static economies of scale in capital goods is the economies that come in the construction and operation of the capital goods themselves. Part of the reasons for this have to do with the nature of the capital goods. Both the smaller and larger locomotives can use many of the same control components. There is no increase in the cost of some components for the larger locomotive and a lesser proportional cost for other components.

Some of the reasons for the declining cost of capital goods have to do with the nature of physical objects and processes. Up to the point at which the stress of unsupported spans necessitate stronger materials, the materials used in a larger building provide more cubic space than the materials used in a smaller building. A 4-foot cube has 96 square feet of surface area to 64 cubic feet of space while an 8-foot cube has 384 square surface feet to 512 cubic feet. The ratio of cubic feet of spatial capacity to square feet of surface area increases with the increase in size. If the surface area is the primary determinant of cost and cubic space is the primary determinant of useable capacity, the advantages of scale are readily apparent.

The cubic dimensions of an internal combustion engine block and the steel required to build it increase more slowly than the engine's displacement or horsepower. This reduces material costs of production per unit of power output. Another important reason for the decline in the capital cost per unit of capacity of capital equipment is that within some limits the labor costs of manufacture do not increase proportionately with size. This is a separable characteristic in capital goods from the dynamic reductions in cost that come from making an increased number of capital goods.

Without enquiring further into the examples, it is frequently observed that increases in the scale of capital equipment bring decreasing capital costs per unit of output capacity for the capital equipment.[20] These decreased costs per unit of potential capacity become real decreased user costs of capital if the increased scale capital could be fully utilized.

Consider an elaboration of my heuristic example: The capital cost, per potential freight mile per year at capacity operation of a 1000-horsepower GE Diesel locomotive, series 1000, is a large and powerful engine that can pull twice the load but does not cost twice as much to construct. The operating cost per ton mile of freight, at capacity operation, is also less because there is an engineer and a fireman for both the 1000 and the 500 so the labor costs per ton mile are less for the larger engine. Similar considerations apply for fuel and maintenance costs per unit of potential output capacity.

Why is the capital cost per unit of carrying capacity less for the larger engine? (They are built at the same time by the same company with the same technical knowledge available.) An explanation would have to be made in terms of some costs not increasing on a direct basis with size: for instance, the smaller engine uses the same control systems as the larger engine and the costs of building engines increase less rapidly than additional carrying capacity.

Larger units of capital may also decrease labor operating costs. This is because the labor involved in operating them is capable of a greater span of control. One worker is capable of controlling a larger airplane, ship, locomotive, tractor, computer, and so forth. This increases output per unit of operating labor.

Specialization, Potential Output/Capital, and the Size of the Market

The scope for specialization in a modern economy depends upon the size of the market. The relevant market is not the size of the market for a particular final output (the diesel electric locomotive) but the size of the market for the providers of the chain of inputs for the production of many types of final output (all types of products using the specialized steel roller bearings).

Specialization depends upon the market being large enough to absorb the quantity of output necessary for specialization. Because transportation, communication, and transactions costs are all part of the process of exchanging goods and specializing, these costs are a particularly important part of the specialization process. They are also recursive—the fall in transportation, communication, and transactions costs depends upon specialization in the production of the technology that lowers the cost of those economic activities.

The explanation of economic growth, then, is the explanation of the cybernetic process of specialization leading to technological change leading to increases in the size of the market leading to further specialization leading to further technological change, and so on.

Productivity and Specialization Within and Between Organization

An advanced economy depends upon a high degree of specialization of function in production. This specialization, in turn, requires the coordination of many workers in many different organizations. Productivity increases depend upon cutting down the transactions and coordinating costs that occur when specialized organizations and individuals interface with each other.

To return to our previous example, General Electric (GE) has increased the productive potential of its diesel electric locomotive manufacturing division (and its locomotives to the railroads) by improved coordination between its own individually highly skilled employees, and between its employees and the personnel of other organizations that are customers and suppliers.

GE locomotive designers have progressively improved their understanding of the actual and desired operating characteristics of the diesel electric engines they produce by observing and analyzing the actual and simulated operating experience of the railroads that use the locomotives under a variety of operating conditions. They do this with the active participation of the operating personnel from the railroads.

The GE designers, in turn, take the the operating information they have acquired from the railroads and work with another set of GE engineers to build these operating characteristics into the locomotives. This set of GE engineers, in turn, has learned to work with another set of designers and engineers from

Cincinnati Milling Machines (CCM) to design the machine tools to produce the parts of the locomotives.

This set of CCM engineers, in turn, has learned to work with the GE machinists who actually work with the materials to make the parts. The GE machinists continually improve the procedures they use to make the parts and they, in turn, are given suggestions by the assemblers of the locomotives for changes in the fabrication of parts that would reduce assembly time, and so forth. Information passes up and down the specialized sequence of production processes.

As mentioned earlier, it is a well-known phenomenon in production management that the cost of producing some piece of equipment falls over time because the people involved in producing it keep finding ways to build it better (learning by doing). What is less well known is that the interaction of suppliers and customers progressively improves the operating characteristics of the products that are produced.[21] This might be termed "learning by using," but what is learned is passed back from the users of capital goods to the producers of capital goods. And it is the improvement of these operating characteristics, of course, that is the objective of the production process. This is growth in productivity that comes from the cooperation of the specialized individuals and their organizations.

The consequence of the learning process through the exchange of information with suppliers and customers is the progressive reduction in the costs of production of the specialized capital equipment and improvements in the performance characteristics of the manufactures that increase their value to the user. What is operating here is the creation and development of mutually beneficial knowledge to customers and suppliers from continuing relationships based on market transactions. Companies not only buy and sell items, they also exchange knowledge about the operations of their productive processes in their exchange transactions. This is what lies behind the sort of technological change that reduces the ratio of user cost of reproducible capital/the value of output.

However, the continuing relationships are based on a very different type of transaction than the "arms-length" competitive markets transactions traditionally thought of by economists. There are not many buyers and sellers. The transactions are not single, "one-off" exchanges of goods and services for money alone. The transactions are based on relationships that develop over time and involve the limitation of alternative transactions by both parties.[22]

Specialization and Labor Productivity

The observation that specialization can increase individual labor productivity goes back to Adam Smith's pin factory. It is the basis of Eli Whitney's "American System" of interchangeable parts in manufactured items, Henry Ford's assembly line, Frederick Winslow Taylor's application of time and motion studies, and McDonald's organization of the fast food industry. Individuals can increase their output, and the output of machines can be increased if human activity and machine processes can be concentrated on one stage of a production process that has been broken down into a number of separable steps. As Adam Smith pointed out, the increases in productivity come

from avoiding unnecessary stopping and starting to move from one phase of the production process to another and from increased "dexterity." Specialization of labor entails the entire economy being envisaged as a production line.

One of the explanations of the observed decrease in the cost of building specialized capital such as diesel locomotives, airplanes, computers, or buildings is the phenomenon of learning by doing.[23] GE can project that the number of man hours necessary for producing each component of a diesel locomotive and assembling the same model will decline over time. This occurs as the individual workers on the assembly line, and the teams supplying components to the assembly line, and so on learn better ways of accomplishing their specialized tasks and learn to work better together to avoid the delays arising from simultaneous and sequential tasks. These dynamic efficiencies that reduce costs are additional to the scale economies that come from spreading the initial design and engineering costs of building a diesel locomotive over a large production run.

Scale and Utilization

The complication in our discussion of the reduction of capital and operating costs with similar technology but larger scale is that the technologically similar locomotives are designed for different functions. The GE 500 engine is designed for smaller loads and shorter distances. Operating the 1000 on short-haul routes half full would be much more expensive per freight mile carried for the SPR. Operating costs per unit of potential capacity may decrease with scale but they may increase with unutilized capacity. Which locomotive should SPR buy from GE? Obviously, the bigger one if it has more than enough load on long routes to utilize the larger capacity, but the smaller one if it doesn't.

Productivity Growth, Specialization, and Utilization of Potential Capacity

The productivity growth that depends upon the specialization of individuals and organizations and the scale of capital investments depends upon the extent of effective demand—the size of the market. Acceleration of growth in the American historical experience has, to a large extent, been a result of technological change, which increases the potential economies of scale. Realizing those potential economies through the expansion of output has depended on the expansion of the market through the creation of national and then world markets.

Potential Output and Actual Output

Our discussion, thus far, has emphasized potential output. The larger locomotive or airplane or computer may be cheaper to operate per unit of capacity but the smaller model may be more efficient with smaller loads. This is an issue in considering the effects of *static* economies of scale.

The gains from increases in capacity utilization are obvious and important (but frequently overlooked) sources of increases in productivity. SPR will only get the advantage of lower costs from the bigger locomotive if it operates above a certain capacity.   (It is often noted, cyclically, that gains in reported productivity rise and fall with more or less intensive utilization of existing labor and capital.)

If output can be increased without the increase of capital, costs are going to fall. A railroad or canal not used to capacity can carry more freight with only an increase in operating costs.   The electric generators, transformers, and transmission lines that are operating below capacity can provide additional electricity for only the additional fuel costs of generation and transmission.

Dynamic economies of scale come from volume in the production of capital goods as opposed to their utilization. GE can't benefit from the dynamic fall in the cost of building the same locomotive if they can't sell enough of them, and they may not be able to spread the fixed costs of development and engineering over a long enough production run. These are dynamic economies of scale. The highly specialized producer of roller bearings will be unable to get the economies of scale if there aren't enough firms building machinery to take his output.

The potential gains from fuller capital utilization will be greatest in industries where fixed capital costs are a large percentage of total costs and where capital utilization is lowest.   A railroad operating at 10 percent capacity on its road beds, engines, and rolling stock and with 90 percent of its total costs fixed can get a 45 percent drop in total cost per unit of output with an increase of 10 percent in capacity utilization—a 4.5/1 ratio for cost reduction to capacity increase.   When capital costs are 50 percent of total costs and capacity utilization is 50 percent, an increase from 50 percent to 60 percent in capacity utilization yields only a 10 percent cost reduction—a one-for-one increase. (It is also true, however, that it is generally wise management to have more capacity than needed at the time at which new machines are installed since the additional costs of unused capacity are likely to be smaller than the opportunities forgone if one element in the firm's capacity limits its scale of operation.)

In any industry where capital costs are a large proportion of total costs, and unused capacity is large, there is going to be significant economic pressure for an increase in output. The limitation to this increase in output will be the anticipated responsiveness of increased quantity demanded to the lowering of price.   The reticence of the railroad to cut its freight rates comes from a judgment that relatively large cuts in freight rates will be accompanied with relatively small increases in freight volume. The greater willingness of airlines to cut passenger ticket prices since deregulation—despite having a smaller percentage of fixed costs—is a judgment that passenger demand is highly responsive to reductions in ticket prices.

The most important element for increasing the ratio of actual to potential output, for the economy as a whole, is the utilization of the human capital in the labor force. Workers who are not engaged in productive work during all their working hours are a potential source of growth. Workers who are engaged in tasks that underutilize their human capital are a potential source of growth. Within the firm and within the economy, the rate of growth could be accelerated over a considerable time frame if the firm and the economy could be operated in such as way as to provide full utilization of the labor force and the capital stock.

In a dynamic, full-employment economy, with expansion and contraction of different firms, sectors, and regional economies, an increasing degree of labor mobility is a necessary condition for a fuller utilization of labor. Firms that "downsize" are contributing to economic growth by securing fuller utilization of their existing labor force and releasing underemployed human capital to other places where they can be more fully employed.

Employment practices that discriminate against certain members of the labor force reduce output. In the contemporary United States, the increasing opportunities for women in the labor force have both increased investment in their human capital and secured fuller utilization of the human capital.

Employment practices that restrict or discourage employers from taking on employees because of high expected costs of releasing them from employment will have the short-run effect of reducing the rate of actual/potential production from human capital and, thus of reducing the rate of economic growth. In the longer run these limitations on labor markets may have the further effect of reducing investment in their own human capital by members of the labor force who face limited labor mobility.

The reduction of cyclical fluctuations in an economy can increase the utilization rate of physical and human capital over time. More importantly, by reducing variations in the expected rate of return to investment in physical and human capital, fuller utilization of an economy's capacity can increase the rate of investment, and thus the rate of growth, of an economy over time.

SOCIAL DETERMINANTS OF TECHNOLOGICAL CHANGE

I have discussed how technological change occurs. But another question must also be addressed: Why does technological change occur? I believe that it occurs because of human nature. It results from human effort to understand—and alter—the way the world works. Man—the tool maker, the curious problem solver—is motivated to create new ways of doing things to satisfy human wants with less effort. While this effort may have an altruistic element or be driven by natural curiosity, or be motivated by a desire for the approbation of other humans, it is also strongly motivated by a desire for better personal economic outcomes and outcomes for one's family, firm, community, nation, or all mankind.

But this natural curiosity is also limited by the scarce resources of time and finance. Research and development and technological change cost money. Research and development expenditure to develop new technologies represents an investment in knowledge which is an alternative to investment in physical capital. It must be financed out of the cash flow of the firm or by recourse to investment markets. The stockholders of corporations forgo current dividends on the expectation that the investment of current profits in physical assets or research and development of new products or processes will increase their future incomes. The rate of technological change depends, in part, on the level of investment that the individuals and firms in a society are willing to venture. The uncertain and potential returns are weighed against alternative investments.

Investment in technological innovation depends upon the expectation of uncertain future returns. Individuals and corporations who make investment decisions must be able to make certain judgments about the reliability of their property rights to the uncertain returns from innovation as well as the proportion of those returns they will be able to retain after taxation. Further, tax laws that allow the capitalization of research and development costs improve the ability of firms to finance them internally. So do tax laws that allow the conversion of income from risky investments into capital gains subject to a lower rate of taxation and the balancing of losses against gains.

Economic growth in the United States over the past several decades has benefited from the specialization of some investment bankers in the provision of venture capital. Venture capital firms increase the flow of capital into start-up firms, hoping to capitalize the development and commercialization of new technology by sophisticated screening of applicants and the pooling of risks for investors. They can also add value to their investment allocation function by helping the firms in which they invest by providing guidance at senior management levels to start-up firms.

The Importance of Competition to Technological Change

In competitive markets firms are driven by competition to invent, adopt, and adapt new technology by the search for profit and the fear of loss. These efforts are focussed and intensified by the competitive process. A firm that is only slightly less efficient than its competitors can lose its business, capital, and existence very rapidly if markets are competitive. This occurs when firms have to purchase the inputs of capital, machinery, material inputs, and labor in competitive factor markets and sell their products in competitive product markets.

If firm A buys inputs in competitive factor markets for 100 and combines them to produce an output of 105, it makes a profit and has the resources to grow. If factor markets are competitive, Firm B, like firm A, must also pay 100 for the inputs. If it is only 10 percent less efficient in using them, it will produce an output of 95 while incurring the same cost of 100. Competitive product markets will limit the price it can sell them for to 100 and the loss of 5 will quickly deplete the less efficient firm's capital and drive it out of business. Technological and organizational change drives the ability of the firm to transform labor and capital inputs into output. Thus, competitive factor and product markets are a very powerful influence in motivating the search for new technologies and their rapid adoption.

Internationalization of the Economy

The increased internationalization of markets over the past quarter-century through the reduction in tariff barriers, the reduction in transportation and communication costs, and the shift in production toward higher value/transport cost commodities is well recognized. All of these factors increase competition and hasten adoption of the latest and lowest cost methods of production. It should also be remembered that the same developments in the reduction of transportation costs have been a feature of national markets superseding local markets in the U.S. economy over the past two centuries.

It is sometimes argued that the increasing competition in international markets has stifled economic growth through limiting the profitability of firms and, hence, their ability to finance growth internally. If this were the case, one would expect to observe falling rates of return on capital, but I know of no evidence of an historical trend for the declining profitability of American industry that could be used to evidence this argument.

Technological change in one area may create demands or opportunities in other areas. By creating shortage or surplus imbalances in production, it often stimulates more technological change. Faster weaving looms create a demand for faster spinning machines. Artificial fibers create a demand for new types of spinning and weaving machines. More "user-friendly" software creates a need for faster computer chips.

The increased output per unit of input from dynamic changes in technology creates profits for firms and provides more resources to society to support additional technological effort so that economic growth becomes a positive feedback loop, a "virtuous cycle." Economic growth, then, depends upon continuing specialization and expansion of the market. Does this mean that growth can be continual and never-ending? I think not. Apart from the natural limits to technological change, the limits to the growth process are contained within the specialization process itself.

This long discourse on technological change in the production of capital goods for one sector of the economy is intended to illustrate and explain what lies behind the process of productivity growth. The increase in output per worker in transportation can, once again, be explained in terms of the characteristics of economic growth identified at the start of this chapter. In the production of the capital goods that are at the center of the process, the key elements are specialization, technological change, the increase in capital per worker, and the increase in output per unit of capital by the progressive increase in the ratio of output flows to capital costs and labor inputs.

SUMMARY

There have been enormous changes in technology, the sectoral composition of the labor force, and the organization of the production of goods and services in the American economy over the past century. The changes in the goods and services produced by the economy and the technology and the organization of production used to produce them make it difficult to compare the quantitative changes in the rate of growth of output because the character of the inputs and the outputs have changed so much as part of the process of economic growth.

My description of change has emphasized the importance of specialization, with its concomitant increase in capitalization, the decline of the household sector, and the shift to the service economy. These changes have altered the capital stock, technology, and labor force in ways that would have seemed unfathomable to the observer of a century ago.

It is important to note, in summary, that some of the characteristics of growth that I have observed and emphasized—increasing capitalization and technological change—could continue to spur growth in the twenty-first century. Increasing capital intensity and technological change extend the physical power and control capacity of human beings. But it is important to remember that the improvements in technology that reduce friction or increase thermal efficiency asymptotically approach some maximum where all of the heat is utilized and all friction has been eliminated. There are, similarly, asymptotic limits to biological maximums that will limit the production of food or fiber. In the end it is not economics but nature that is the limit to the potential for growth through technological change. It is impossible for the growth-accelerating shifts of the labor force from household to market production of goods and services and the intersectoral redistribution of the labor force to happen again because those shifts have already occurred.

We have shifted from household production to market production of commodities, and the shift is approaching completion in the human services involved in caring for the dependent generations. When all of the working-age population is in the labor force, there is no possibility of further increases in the participation rate of the population in the labor force. Similarly, when the production and distribution of commodities has been increased by specialization and capitalization, there is ever-diminishing scope for further increases in the aggregate level of output per worker from these sectors because of their declining weight in the aggregate, and because the intersectoral shifts have occurred and can't occur again.

Description and explanation of economic change is inevitably selective. But, after this limited treatment of the nature of the changes that have taken place in our economy over the past century, it is time to leave this chapter's heuristic description of the process of modern economic growth. In the following chapter we turn our attention to some of the quantitative facts about our experience over the past century—mindful of the enormous changes in the character and patterns of economic activity that these artifacts purport to measure.

NOTES

1. These characteristics parallel those presented in Simon Kuznets, *Modern Economic Growth* (New Haven: Yale University Press), 1966.

2. The classic article on the importance of the machine tool industry in the process of economic growth is N. Rosenberg, "Technological Change in the Machine Tool Industry, 1840–1910," *Journal of Economic History*, December (1963).

3. The opportunity cost for a farmer to build his own barn may be fairly low at certain points in the agricultural year, but the value of the labor in the barn will be estimated at its average rather than (lower) opportunity cost. This will increase the estimated value of investment and national product by more than the farmer has given up to produce it.

If an industrial corporation builds its own machinery, its internal accounting could (improperly) show higher costs of production for its reported sales (since the value of the machines produced for inventory is not reported) and there is no reported increase in the value of its equipment. This would not change reported national income (since the expenditures will be included as costs) but the reported output will be classified as consumption goods rather than investment goods and the investment flow and capital stock will be understated.

4. In professional sports one team may sell the exclusive right to contract with a player.

5. An extensive discussion of the problems of identifying and using physical capital as an explanatory variable is presented in the appendix.

6. John Coatesworth, "Obstacles to Economic Growth in Nineteenth Century Mexico," *American Historical Review*, 83.1 (1978) 84–85.

7. It was estimated by one observer that counting the employees' compensated time for training, the expenditures of business for on-the-job training exceeded the expenditures on university education of students.

8. Between 1970 and 1990 the proportion of expenditures on R&D/Physical Capital increased from 40 percent to 60 percent in the U.S. chemical industry. From NSF and American Chemical Mfrs. Assoc.   Quoted in Landau and Rosenberg "Successful Commercialization in the Chemical Process Industries," in *Technology and the Wealth of Nations* ed. N. Rosenberg et al. (Palo Alto, CA: Stanford University Press, 1992), 111.

9. In a classic article Zvi Griliches (1957) estimated that the social rate of return to the investment by the agricultural field stations to the development of hybrid corn was more than 500 percent.

10. Coatesworth, 1978.

11. (It should be noted that estimates of capital formation in the agricultural sector in land clearing, drainage, fencing, barns, and so forth, were a substantial part of gross investment and of measured GNP in the nineteenth century. The value of this capital investment by farm households using their own labor was measured by its imputed labor and material costs. The investment expenditures of the   nineteenth century in land clearing and preparation created part of the capital stock that made possible the higher productivity of the twentieth century.

12. During the second part of the nineteenth century, some steam power was applied to the plowing of agricultural land. Steam tractors and steam stationary engines (which pulled plows on a winched cable) were enormously powerful and made it possible to break and till rich, damp bottomlands with high crop yields. Their disadvantage was their heavy weight-to-power ratio, which made it easy to mire them in damp soils or to use much of their power to ride through the soils, with less left to pull the plow.

13. That ties in with my introductory example of the average forty-acre farm at the end of the nineteenth century, where part of the land was worked to provide feed for the horses and the remainder was sown to wheat to provide 1000 bushels of wheat or corn per year per worker.

14. There is no dispute that these chemical inputs to the agricultural process increase crop yields in the short term. There is considerable criticism of their increasing use along with chemical fertilizers because of their unknown long-term effects in changing the ecology of croplands and their effect on the streams that carry runoff.

15. Mathematically, converting the four terms into logarithmic form and then taking their first derivatives with respect to time, the derivatives of the three right hand variables are additive and equal to the derivative on the left-hand side.

16. This is sometimes referred to as "capital augmenting technical change." The implication of capital augmentation by investment in new capital goods that incorporate technical change is acceleration in the growth of output in the period in which the new capital is incorporated into the economy. M. J. Boskin and L. J. Lau, "Capital, Technology, and Economic Growth," in *Technology and the Wealth of Nations* ed. N. Rosenberg et al., (Palo Alto, CA.: Stanford University Press, 1992), 17–55.

17. The cost of the capital stock is its purchase cost. The cost of a piece of capital equipment with a given output capacity may fall over time as a result of technological

change in the production of capital goods. Thus, one could observe the effect of technological change as reducing the capital/labor ratio (by reducing the purchase cost of the capital goods) and an increase in the potential output/capital ratio resulting from the decline in the cost of the physical capital good per unit of output capacity.

The selection of a particular technology embodied in a particular capital good depends upon the ratio of the value added per dollar of capital/cost of capital. The value added is a flow measure; for example, annual reduction in operating cost or annual net value added by a piece of capital. This is compared with the annual cost; the annual cost is the purchase price multiplied by the sum of the annual depreciation and the annual interest change.

18. The cost of operating a unit of capital equipment with a given output capacity per time unit can be stated as: Annual cost = Acquisition cost (interest rate+depreciation rate). However, producers are not just interested in capital costs and the total advantage of one capital good relative to another must include such associated costs as labor costs, fuel costs, maintenance costs, spoilage rates, and so forth.

19. Edward Denison had made several attempts to quantify the importance of scale economies in U.S. growth over the past century. His estimates, which depend upon a number of assumptions within the framework of growth accounting, attribute from .25 percent to .33 percent in the rate of growth of output to economies of scale. See, inter alia, E. F. Denison, *Trends in American Economic Growth, 1929–1982* (Washington, D.C.: The Brookings Institution, 1985).

20. I confess to being short of evidence on this point. One instance of the relationship between the construction costs per unit of yearly capacity size is in blast furnaces (for iron smelting) which indicates costs savings from increasing scale of enormous magnitude. Bela Gold, *Productivity,Technology, and Capital* (Lexington, MA.: Lexington Books), 128. Another is the continuous process chemical plant where the rule of thumb is that construction costs increase by only 60 percent of the increase in capacity. Cited in Landau and Rosenberg (1992), op. cit., p. 86.

21. For an illustrative discussion of the relationship between the suppliers and users of capital goods, consider the interaction between airframe producers and airlines in the design of new and modification of existing planes. See David C. Mowery, *Alliance Politics and Economics: Multinational Joint Ventures in Commercial Aircraft* (Cambridge, MA.: Ballinger, 1987).

22. For an informed discussion of the relationship between industrial firms, see Alfred Chandler, *Scale and Scope: The Dynamics of Industrial Capitalism* (Cambridge, Mass.: The Belknap Press of Harvard University Press, 1990).

23. The classic article on this phenomenon is Kenneth Arrow (1962), "The economic implications of learning by doing," *Review of Economic Studies* (39): 155–73.

CHAPTER 3

The Quantitative Record of U.S. Economic Growth

> [Per capita GDP] must in every nation be regulated by two different circumstances; first, by the skill, dexterity, and judgement with which its labour is generally applied; and secondly, by the proportion between the number of those who are employed in useful labour, and that of those who are not so employed.
>
> —Adam Smith
> *The Wealth of Nations (1776)*

The previous chapter has described—with a broad brush, and explained—with heuristic simplification, the changes in technology and in the organization of production that are behind measurements of economic growth. This chapter will present some measurements of U.S. economic growth over the past century, contrast recent U.S. growth rates with earlier decades, and compare the American experience with that of other advanced industrial nations. It will also begin the analysis of the relative importance of the factors that have contributed to faster and slower American growth.

"Fast" and "slow" growth are comparative terms. What is the standard of comparison? U.S. per capita incomes have grown faster during the past two decades than some decades in this century but slower than others. American incomes grew more slowly than the incomes of most other industrialized nations over the past quarter-century but the deceleration of those nations' growth rates was greater than the slowdown in the growth of the U.S. economy. And all the other nations started from lower levels of per capita output and, in most cases, were "catching up" from the losses incurred in World War II.

The analysis of comparative growth rates must be undertaken with caution. To use the biological analogy of the first chapter, again, one wouldn't expect an oak forest to grow as fast as a cottonwood forest and one wouldn't expect old oaks to grow at the same proportional rate as young oaks. Economies, like trees, grow at different rates at different stages in their development. Growth rates do vary over time and between nations. With this in mind, let us examine the quantitative records.

As mentioned in chapter 1 (and to be expanded in the appendix to this chapter and subsequent chapters), the measurement of national growth rates is based on national income accounting (NIA) concepts. They quantify the annual flow of output—or value added—of an economy. Accounting concepts are, unavoidably, more arbitrary and complex than the measurement concepts used in the physical or biological sciences to gauge physical quantities such as the weight of solids or the flow of liquids.

The measurement definitions and concepts used in economics structure our understanding of the phenomena observed, classified, counted, and explained. Changes in measurement concepts could produce different measured growth rates for the same economy in the same time period. While using the same NIA measurement concepts over time makes the intertemporal comparison of growth rates more amenable to analysis, it ignores important changes taking place in the characteristics of output that affect the measurement of growth. With these caveats, let's look at the record.

My explanation of changes in the growth rate of the American economy over the past century begins with disaggregation of the output and demographic components that are the first order determinants of the measured levels and rates of change of per capita national income.

MEASUREMENT CONVENTIONS

The use of a decade (rather than the more frequently used annual period) for the measurement of economic performance conceals short-term fluctuations in the capacity utilization of the economy, but the ten-year periods still reveal the impacts of war, depression, and other big "shocks" to the economy.

Growth rates are not constant within decades; measured growth rates would be changed by altering the beginning and ending dates for the periods measured. For example, the decade ending in 1920 coincided with a sharp, temporary downturn in the American economy after World War I. This reduced the measured rate of growth for that decade, and the recovery in the early 1920s from the postwar trough made the decade ending in 1930 look slightly better. The 1920s would have looked still better if the decade had ended in 1929! Similarly, 1960 was near the bottom of a cyclical trough and this made the previous decade look slightly worse and the succeeding decade look slightly better.

I have used decennial years to demarcate the time period of analysis because I wish to emphasize longer-term changes in the structure of the economy—rather than cyclical changes in capacity utilization. Decennial periods are also preferable because the census data available in decennial years is more complete and detailed than annual estimates.

Why Gross Domestic Product (GDP) and GDP Per Capita?

The most widely used measurement of nations' economic performance is Gross Domestic Product.[1] Per capita GDP (also referred to as per capita income). Per Capita GDP is simply the ratio of GDP to Population. Per capita GDP is an important measure of economic performance for an economy for two reasons:

1. GDP per capita is a measure of the total annual output flow of an economy; it can be used as a measure of both the potential capacity and the utilization of the capacity of an economy.
2. GDP is a measure of the total annual flow of production that could (theoretically) be available for consumption by the population if no resources were allocated to replacing the depreciating physical capital of the economy.

Net (as opposed to Gross) Domestic Product (NDP) is an estimate of the annual output that would be available for consumption after allowing for the replacement of the stock of physical capital assets. But the replacement estimates depend upon nonobservable, arbitrary, and variable accounting assumptions about the depreciation rates of physical capital. For this reason GDP, rather than NDP, is a more widely used measure of output for intertemporal or international comparisons of economic performance.

THE HISTORICAL RECORD

Text Table 3.1
GDP Growth Rates for Selected Demographic Aggregates
(Decennial Percentage Rates)

Decade Ending	GDP/ Population	GDP/ Work Age Pop.	GDP/ Labor Force	GDP/ Employment	GDP/FullTime Equiv. Empl.
1900	0.20	0.22	0.17	0.15	0.19
1910	0.29	0.20	0.19	0.19	0.33
1920	0.01	0.01	0.06	0.17	0.26
1930	0.13	0.11	0.13	0.25	0.41
1940	0.15	0.09	0.14	0.20	0.33
1950	0.36	0.42	0.30	0.23	0.16
1960	0.15	0.14	0.22	0.19	0.25
1970	0.29	0.32	0.24	0.18	0.23
1980	0.18	0.15	0.03	0.03	0.09
1990	0.17	0.18	0.11	0.08	0.10

Source: Author. See Appendix 3.1.

Measurements of the rate of growth of GDP per capita and measurements of GDP growth relative to other various demographic sub-groups are presented in Text Table 3.1. The GDP/Population (per capita income) figures for the United States (Col. 1) were presented earlier, in graphic form, in chapter 1 in Text

Graph 1.1. The GDP/FTE (Gross Domestic Product per Full-Time Equivalent worker) figures in Column 5 were presented earlier in Text Graph 1.2.

The decennial growth rates presented in Text Table 3.1 measure the rates at which the ratios of the GDP to total population, and GDP to various other population components, change between census years. As previously discussed in chapter 1, variations in decennial rates of change measure the acceleration or deceleration of the flow of output growth relative to changes in population variables. A decline in the rate of growth of per capita output means that the rate of increase of output, relative to a demographic variable, has slowed—not that the level of output has declined.

Column 1 of Text Table 3.1 is the record of growth in U.S. GDP/Population (per capita income)—the most widely used measure of growth. The remaining columns of Text Table 3.1 show the growth rate of per capita GDP relative to various other demographic aggregates over the past century.

Column 2 shows the growth in output relative to the working-age population (ages 16–64) cohort. This is an important performance measurement of the economy relative to its potential because this is the age group from which the labor force is primarily drawn. Thus, growth in output per member of the working-age or potential labor force is an important measurement of the growth in productivity and utilization of the nation's labor force.

The growth and utilization of the economy's potential is measured in different ways by the data in the remaining columns which consider the growth of GDP relative to the actual rather than the potential labor force (Col. 3), to actual employment rather than defined labor force (Col. 4), and to full-time equivalent (FTE) employment rather than total employment (Col. 5). The rate of growth of GDP/FTE employment is the same as the rate of growth of productivity or output per worker hour previously presented in Text Graph 1.2.

The definition of "labor force" has changed over time. The basic concept of "labor force" is that persons are either working or actively seeking work in the market economy. Some persons younger than sixteen or older than sixty-four are working or actively seeking work. Changes, over time, in the definition of which persons should be considered to be in the labor force depend upon changes in the economy, social attitudes, and legislation that are reflected in the definitions of the labor force by the U.S. Department of Labor. The largest changes in the labor force are brought about by the movement of women from household employment to market employment. Employment differs from labor force by the extent of unemployment—the labor force includes the unemployed.

In Column 5 I have defined Full-Time Equivalent (FTE) employment, arbitrarily, at forty hours per week—2000 hours per year. The secular decrease in average hours worked has meant that FTE employment has increased more slowly than total employment (and that in the early part of the century, when people worked more than forty hours per week, the measurement of FTE employment exceeds the total number of workers employed). Over the last four decades, the average annual hours per worker have decreased substantially. This has occurred, primarily, because many of the women who have shifted from household to market employment have chosen to work less than forty hours per week. There has been little decline in the standard forty-hour work week since mid-century.

Which demographic aggregate is most appropriate to divide GDP to measure the economy's performance? It depends on what factors are being evaluated—worker productivity? worker participation? the output of a population with a predominance of non-working younger or older citizens? In this book I have chosen to explain the behavior of the GDP to population ratio (per capita income) because that is the most widely used and recognized measure of the economic performance of nations.[2]

Observations from Table 3.1

Yes, per capita income grew more slowly in the 1970s and 1980s than in the roaring 1960s but it also grew more rapidly than in the Eisenhower 1950s or the Depression 1930s. The most rapid growth in output per worker or per worker hour in this century took place in the roaring 1920s. Productivity growth was higher in the supposedly low-growth 1950s than in the 1960s. But, ominously, we note that the rate of growth of productivity—output per worker and output per worker hour—was lower in the Reagan 1980s than any decade in the century except the chaotic 1970s! What is behind these numbers?

THE EXPLANATION OF CHANGES IN U.S. GROWTH RATES

Text Table 3.2 allows us to get behind the series in Text Table 3.1 and begin a structured explanation of the changes in decennial growth rates in GDP per capita. More specifically, it puts the decline in the rate of growth of per capita GDP during the decades ending in 1980 and 1990 in historical and analytical perspective. As I have emphasized in chapter 1, the major reason for the decline in the rate of growth of per capita GDP during the decades of the 1970s and 1980s was the continuation of the longer-term decline in the rate of growth of productivity—of output per hour (Col. 1, Text Table 3.2).

Determinants of the Rate of Per Capita Output Growth

My objective is the explanation of the changes in per capita income by the separation of its demographic and productivity components. Column 1 of Text Table 3.2 presents the same series on GDP per capita presented in Text Table 3.1 (and graphically exhibited in chapter 1 as Text Graph 1.1). However, the remaining four columns of Text Table 3.2 present the decennial rates of change for the rates of growth of the component determinants of growth in per capita GDP. The rate of growth of per capita GDP depends upon the sum (and cross-products) of the rates of change of the other four variables presented in Text Table 3.2.

Text Table 3.2
Decennial Growth Rates of Per Capita GDP and Its Determinants

Decade Ending	GDP/ Population	GDP/ Hours	Hours/ Workers	Workers/ Work Age Pop.	Work Age/ Population
	Per Capita GDP 1987$	Productivity 1987$	Intensity	Participation	Demography
1920	0.01	0.26	-0.07	-0.14	0.00
1930	0.13	0.41	-0.11	-0.11	0.02
1940	0.15	0.33	-0.10	-0.09	0.05
1950	0.36	0.16	0.06	0.15	-0.04
1960	0.15	0.25	-0.05	-0.04	0.01
1970	0.29	0.23	-0.04	0.12	-0.03
1980	0.18	0.09	-0.05	0.11	0.02
1990	0.17	0.10	-0.02	0.09	0.00

Source: Author. See Appendix 3.2 and Appendix Table 3.3.

Explanation of Text Table 3.2

The per capita output of an economy depends upon output per hour worked, the number of hours worked, the proportion of the working-age population actually working, and the proportion that the working-age population bears to the total population. Thus, columns 2 through 5 of Text Table 3.2 present the changes in these ratios that are the ratio determinants of GDP per capita:

- Productivity—changes in output per unit of hourly labor input.
- Intensity—changes in average hours worked per worker.
- Participation—changes in the proportion of the working-age population employed in the market economy.
- Demography—changes in the ratio of the working-age population to the total population.

The rate of change of GDP/Population is the sum of the rates of change of these four variables (plus their cross-products).[3] Consider, as an example, the components of the 17 percent growth of GDP per capita (Col. 2) in the decade ending in 1990—the decade of the 1980s:

- Productivity—the growth in output per hour —contributed 10 percent to the overall growth. Intensity—the average hours annual hours worked per worker fell and, thereby, decreased growth by 2 percent.
- Intensity—the average hours annual hours worked per worker fell and, thereby, decreased growth by 2 percent.
- Participation—the increase in the ratio of workers/working-age population—added another 9 percent to overall growth.
- Demography—the ratio of the working-age population to the total population was unchanged during the decade and made no contribution to change.

The sum of the cross-products (not included in the table) was insignificant for the decade.

For the decade ending in 1990, the most important contributor to growth in per capita income was the increase in productivity—output per worker hour increased but the increase in participation added almost as much.

Observations on Text Table 3.2

Is growth in productivity always the most important determinant of growth in per capita GDP? No. In the decade ending in 1980, the gains from increased participation contributed more than productivity to the growth in GDP per capita. But productivity is *usually* the most important determinant and, in the long run, growth in per capita income resulting from productivity growth is the primary reason for growth and is modified by the other factors.

For example, as we noted in the discussion of Text Table 3.1, the decade ending in 1960—the Eisenhower 1950s—witnessed even slower growth for per capita GDP than the decade of the 1980s, even though growth in productivity (GDP per worker hour) was almost three times as rapid in the 1950s as in the 1980s (25 percent versus 9 percent).

Why was per capita growth slow during the Eisenhower postwar "return to normalcy"? While GDP per hour worked grew at a 25 percent rate during the decade ending in 1960, aggregate growth was slowed by the very slow growth in total employment relative to the total population. The 1950s was the decade of the "baby boom," which expanded the proportion of children to the population and, simultaneously, took their mothers out of the labor force. The decrease in participation subtracted 4 percent from growth in per capita income in that decade while it added 9 percent in the decade ending in 1990. Intensity—the annual hours worked, per worker—declined by 5 percent over the decade, while in the later decade hours worked declined by only 2 percent. The sum of these four changes (and their interaction) slowed the growth in per capita GDP in the Eisenhower decade ending in 1960 to one of its lowest rates in the century—despite the highest rate of growth in output per worker hour in the second half of the twentieth century! Disaggregation helps us get behind the factors which determine the rate of growth in per capita income.

The Slowdown in Productivity Growth

The rate of growth of GDP per worker hour from 1970 to 1990 is less than half the rate of the two previous decades. The rates of increase in output per worker hour—less than 1 percent per year over the decades of the 1970s and 1980s—were the lowest in a century!

Text Graph 3.1 is a graphic presentation of the information in Text Table 3.2. It emphasizes the decline in productivity offset by the favorable effects of participation rates and demography on growth during the past two decades, relative to the past.

Text Graph 3.1 emphasizes the importance of the slowdown in productivity growth (presented earlier in chapter 1 in Text Graph 1.2) in the context of the

other factors determining the rate of growth of GDP per capita. The low growth
rates in output per hour of the past two decades exhibit the widely recognized
slowdown in the rate of growth of productivity and pinpoint the reason for the
slowdown in the rate of growth of per capita output and consumption, which is
the focus of our inquiry.

Text Graph 3.1
Components of Growth

% RATES

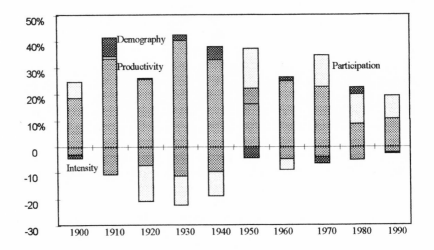

DECADES ENDING

Source: Author. See Text Table 3.2 and Appendix 3.2

However, I will show in chapter 5 (Text Table 5.4) that this slowdown in
productivity growth does not result from a general slowdown in productivity
within sectors in the economy and can be explained almost completely in terms
of the change in the output structure of the economy from a commodity-
producing economy to a service-producing economy.   There is no secular
decline in productivity growth in the commodity-producing and -distributing
sectors of the economy. The decline in overall growth in productivity results
almost entirely from a contraction in the size of the sectors where productivity
growth can be more reliably measured.

This structural change—from commodity production, processing, and
distribution to services—is irreversible. We don't need as many workers to
produce the nation's food and the nation wants to purchase more health care
rather than more food. This is why the economy cannot replicate earlier rates of
growth in output per worker. This structural change in the pattern of output is
the first reason why the decline in U.S. economic growth rates is a long-run,
irreversible phenomenon.

The Importance of Labor Force Participation to Output Growth

As I have mentioned earlier, the slowdown in the growth of productivity during the decades ending in 1980 and 1990 was offset by the increase in the participation rate of the working-age population in the labor force.   The importance of the increases in the participation rate to per capita growth can be clearly seen in the columns in Text Table 3.2 and in the stacked bars of Text Graph 3.1.

It is important to note that in the absence of change in the participation rate of the working-age population in the labor force (and ignoring for the moment interactions with other variables), the growth rate in per capita income would have been reduced from 18 percent to 7 percent in the decade ending in 1980 and from 17 percent to 8 percent in the decade ending in 1990. That would have represented a growth rate in per capita income of less than 1 percent per year over those decades.

In chapter 6 I will present and further disaggregate the dimensions of the demographic changes that have providentially (but temporarily) offset some of the decline in productivity growth in the last two decades. But favorable participation rate changes cannot continue to operate to offset the decline in productivity growth in the present and future decades because—simply stated—participation rates can't increase further when everyone is working! (And, more subtly, as participation rises toward 100 percent, the same absolute increases are smaller relative increases.) Alongside the shift from commodity production to services, this is the second reason why the decline in growth rates is permanent and irreversible.

Differences in Historical Growth Rates

The slow growth of GDP per capita over the past two decades has occurred for fundamentally different causes than the slow growth of the Depression 1930s and the Baby Boom 1950s. In the 1930s output growth slowed because of a fall in employment—annual hours per worker dropped, as did the proportion of the labor force that was employed or even seeking work. Productivity—output per worker hour—for the workers who were employed actually rose by 33 percent during the decade.

Output growth in the 1950s was low because of the decline in the proportion of the working-age population to the total population and the (temporary) reduction of participation in the labor force by women.

The slow growth of per capita income during the decades ending in 1980 and 1990 occurred in spite of the large increases in the participation rate of the working-age population in the labor force. Slower growth occurred because of the decline in measured productivity—the fall in the rate of growth in output per worker hour. This fall in the growth of output per worker hour—the decline in productivity growth—is determinative of our future because, in the long run, it is the only way to secure economic growth.

The quantitative record for the current decade ending in 2000 is not yet complete. However, based on the first six years of the decade, it is safe to say that the trends in the economy are continuing. Extrapolating from the first six years of the decade, per capita GDP will continue to fall. All of the increase in per capita GDP is coming from increase in output per worker. There has been a contiued slowing of output per worker hour—but this has been slightly offset by an increase in the number of hours per worker. The ratios of workers/working-age population and of the working-age population/total population have been stable.

The quantitative record is clear. There is no disputing that the measured rate of growth of per capita and per worker output fell in the decades of the 1970s and 1980s and has continued to fall in the 1990s. This book is an explanation of the nature and causes of the decline and an explanation of why the decline will be permanent.

GROWTH RATES IN INDUSTRIALIZED COUNTRIES

The United States grew more rapidly than most other countries in the first half of the twentieth century. That was the result of differences in the timing of industrialization, different demographic histories, and the effects of two world wars and the disruptions of the interwar years. The United States has grown more slowly than other advanced industrial nations over the last half-century and particularly over the past two decades. Over the past two decades other nations, too, have grown more slowly in comparison to their recent past. (See Text Table 3.3.)

The United States has led the world in the level of per capita real income over the past century. Available historical evidence and measurement techniques generally indicate that the U.S. economy has had a higher level of per capita real income than any other major country in the world since the final quarter of the nineteenth century. (Historical estimates suggest that the United States surpassed Britain, the previous leader, around 1880.)

Modern economic growth started in the United States at a higher level of per capita income and grew more rapidly than most economies in the half-century prior to World War II. Indeed, the U.S. level of output achieved during the war is generally recognized as the predominant reason for the Allies' victory. At the end of the war, the United States was far ahead of other countries in the level of output per capita. As a consequence of our economic maturity (and the lack of war damage to the economy), the United States has grown more slowly than most industrial economies since World War II as other nations have recovered from war and started to close the wide gap in per capita incomes.

Why have all the countries in our comparative tables experienced declining growth rates over the past two decades? The slowdown in growth in the United States over the past quarter-century has been simultaneous with the slowdown in the rate of growth of other advanced industrial nations. There is no reason for growth rates to converge during the same time period when nations are at different stages in their economic development or have been differentially affected by war. However, one would expect that other countries with access to the same technology would approach U.S. levels of per worker output if they adopted that technology and formed the human, physical, and knowledge capital to use it. One would expect convergence in output levels over time. Thus, the fall in growth rates for all industrial countries over the past two decades could be understood as their simultaneous adjustment to economic maturity.

Text Table 3.3 provides some summary evidence on rates of growth in per capita real output for the United States and several other nations with comparable economic histories. It will be noted that for every country (with the marginal exception of Prime Minister "Maggie" Thatcher's Britain, where the one-time windfall of North Sea oil exploitation briefly offset decline, economic growth (growth in per capita GDP) over the past two decades was lower in the 1970s and 1980s than the 1960s. The deceleration of growth over the past two decades was a worldwide phenomenon for modern industrial economies.

Text Table 3.3
Decennial Growth Rates in Real GDP per Capita for a Selected Group of Industrialized Economies for Selected Historical Periods

Country	1870–1913	1913–50	1950–60	1960–70	1970–80	1980–90
United States	0.22	0.17	0.15	0.29	0.17	0.19
Canada	0.22	0.14	0.12	0.42	0.31	0.19
France	0.16	0.10	0.44	0.55	0.30	0.18
Germany	0.17	0.07	0.86	0.39	0.29	0.23
Japan	0.16	0.05	1.07	1.48	0.38	0.41
Sweden	0.23	0.16	0.30	0.46	0.17	0.18
Britain	0.10	0.09	0.24	0.25	0.19	0.28

Source: Author. See Appendix 3.1.

Because of the international simultaneity of deceleration of growth rates in the decade of the 1970s, some economists have attempted, with minimal success, to explain the worldwide slowdown in terms of a variety of causes, such as the increase in oil prices, inflation, the slowdown in the growth of world markets, and so on.

My explanation for the U.S. slowdown during this period is the effect of structural change. I have not done the disaggregation of output sectors or analyzed the changes in participation rates for other economies but I would expect to find that the slowdown observed for all advanced economies is largely explained by the same long-run structural changes with differences in timing and magnitude affected by unique historical events—particularly wars—and by differences in demography that have altered changes in participation rates.

In Text Table 3.3 note that the growth rates in per capita income for all of the countries in the table were lower for the period 1913–50 than the period 1870–1913, preceding World War I. The differences between the two periods can be explained largely by the two world wars and the economic dislocations of the interwar period on the process of economic growth. It will be noted that although their economies were affected by the dislocation of the interwar period, the United States, Canada, and Sweden, which suffered minimal losses of physical and human capital during the two wars, had smaller declines across the interwar period than the combatants had.

A significant part of the high growth rates recorded by France, Germany, and Japan in the decades from 1950 to 1970 can be explained as recovery from the destruction and economic dislocation of World War II. As I noted earlier, the United States had slower economic growth in per capita incomes in the 1950s because of the "baby boom," which added an anomalous number of children to the population and took their mothers out of the labor force.

The relatively low rate of growth in the American economy over the past two decades should not be understood as the decline of the American economy as compared to other nations. It should be seen as the "catching up" or convergence of other industrial nations with American technology.

International Comparisons of Economic Performance

Text Table 3.4 compares the levels (rather than growth rates) of per capita incomes for various nations, including the United States. The standard of comparison is the average income for all OECD countries. The comparisons utilize Purchasing Power Parity (PPP) for three decennial periods rather than prevailing 1990 currency exchange rates for the international comparison of national incomes. This table shows that, in terms of what U.S. per capita incomes would buy domestically, the United States remained substantially ahead of the other six nations in the table, despite lagging growth rates after 1950.

Text Table 3.4
Per Capita GDP for Selected Countries Relative to OECD Average (1990)
Based on Currency Conversions Using Purchasing Power Parity

Country	1970	1980	1990
United States	148	140	138
Canada	108	118	115
France	106	111	109
Germany	93	97	99
Japan	85	95	110
Sweden	115	109	108
Britain	98	95	100
OECD Average	100	100	100

Source: Author. See Appendix 3.1.

While the U.S. lead in economic performance fell relative to the OECD average over two decades, these figures show that the performance of the U.S. economy in the production of goods and services has remained very high in relation to other nations. The United States is not "falling behind" other nations in its standard of living.

CONCLUSION

The growth rate of per capita GDP in the U.S. economy over the past two decades has slowed down relative to the decade of the 1960s. The decline in the growth rate has occurred because of a fall in the rate of growth of productivity— of output per worker hour. This fall in the rate of growth of productivity has been offset by an increase in the participation rate of the population in the labor force. I shall show in subsequent chapters that these changes in productivity growth and participation rates are the natural and inevitable consequences of the economic growth process, coupled with the measurement conventions that are used to measure output in the service sectors of the economy.

The United States started modern economic growth from a higher level and grew faster than most economies until World War II. Since the war other nations have grown more rapidly from a lower base and are now converging in income levels with the United States. But their growth rates, too, are decelerating for the same reasons that the growth of U.S income decelerated. While we should expect convergence of levels of per capita income among modern industrialized countries, when levels of per capita consumption expenditures are compared on a purchasing power parity basis the United States has seen only a small decrease in its lead relative to other advanced nations.

NOTES

1. Statistical departments of international organizations, such as the United Nations (UN) and the Organization for Economic Cooperation and Development (OECD), have adopted uniform national income accounting procedures for measuring Gross Domestic Product (GDP) to increase international comparability.

2. There are many subcategories of GDP and population that change at different rates. See Appendix Table 3.1 for a presentation of growth in various components of GDP and Appendix Table 3.2 for a matrix presentation of the growth of various measures of output and demographic and labor force growth rates for the decade ending in 1990.

3. This method is explained in the appendix to the chapter, and the ratios and index numbers for which rates of change are presented in Table 3.2 are contained in the appendix.

CHAPTER 4

Understanding the Measurement of Economic Activity

> Man the measure of all things—and, himself, the most inconstant measure of all.
>
> —Aristotle

> There are three kinds of lies: lies, damned lies, and statistics.
>
> —Attributed to Benjamin Disraeli in
> Mark Twain's Autobiography

Chapters 1 and 3 have presented and discussed measurements of the economic aggregate called "Gross Domestic Product," or GDP. This book is an explanation of changes in measured levels, rates of change, and changes in rates of change of GDP. But what does GDP measure? And how is it measured? Can we really depend upon the two-decimal-place measures of change in the aggregates of the human behavior that GDP growth measures? We can, but it is important to know what is included and excluded in GDP and what biases to its measurement are imparted by the measurement conventions that are used. In this chapter I will explain how the accounting concepts used to measure GDP have made past growth rates larger and present growth rates smaller, thus distorting the extent of the measured slowdown in growth.

Any empirically based theory, explanation, or measurement of economic growth must be based on some generally accepted accounting conventions for the measurement of economic activity. The conventions must specify which economic activities are included and excluded from measurement and how the activities are to be measured.

Economics uses the concepts and methods of National Income Accounting (NIA) as a basis for inclusion and exclusion. It uses weighted indexes of price and quantity for the valuation of output. The general public is not familiar with NIA concepts and the use of indexes and often draws unwarranted inferences from statements about changes in GDP that are based on NIA concepts.[1] Consequently, I devote considerable discussion in this chapter, and elsewhere in the book, to the explanation of NIA measurement procedures.

There are two characteristics of the measurement of GDP that create biases for inference: (1) Not all economic activity is measured, and the accounting rules for inclusion and exclusion create biases in measurement as the organization of economic activity and the composition of production changes; and (2) GDP is an aggregate of goods and services that are measured in terms of the relative prices of those goods and services rather than some absolute standard of measure (like a meter or a gram.) This chapter will explore and explain the nature and direction of the biases created by these two measurement conventions for GDP.

But first of all I wish to begin by dispelling two misunderstandings: (1) that measurement in economics is not "scientific" and, (2) that changes in the measured rate of growth of GDP are equivalent to changes in the rate of growth of "economic welfare" or "material well-being" or "human happiness" or some abstract standard of value as opposed to quantity of goods and services produced.

ECONOMIC MEASUREMENT AND SCIENTIFIC METHOD

The problems of measurement in economics do not arise because economics is not "scientific." The discipline of economics is "scientific." The characteristics of a scientific discipline are observation, description, classification, measurement, and explanation of observed regularities in the behavior of the phenomena in question. This is what the discipline of economics does. Some of the problems of the measurement of phenomena in economics are similar to the problems of measurement in other scientific disciplines. Some of them are different.

Let me use biological analogy, as with the climax forest referred to in chapter 1, to illustrate the scientific procedures and "problems" that economics shares with other scientific disciplines.

The Design of Data Collection and Explanation

Observation, for the economist, begins with the description and classification of economic activities within a politically defined economic system. The economist includes some activities and excludes others; household production of goods and services are not counted, production or output is recorded at the time of the purchase transaction of final output, and "intermediate" transactions are not counted. The economist tallies the quantities of the annual production of airline travel, appendectomies, apples, and autos, and then aggregates them by measuring the quantities at their relative prices rather than their weights or volumes.

Observation, for the botanist, might begin with the identification of a forest ecological system within a geographic space. The various botanical species are observed, classified, and measured. If the objective is the measurement of the annual rate of growth of the trunk biomass of the trees, some small trees and grasses and shrubs are not counted (the botanist's counterpart to the economist's exclusion of household activity). The root and branch biomass of the trees is not counted, even though it is responsible for the size and growth of the trunk (the botanical analogy to economics' exclusion of "intermediate" transactions). The specified tree trunks are measured at several points in time or the past growth rates may be measured by coring sample trees and measuring the annual growth rings (measurement errors inherent in these methods are paralleled in economics).

The classification and measurement techniques (data collection) in both economics and biology precede the analysis but are based upon an analytic framework that has been created to explain certain observed phenomena that the observing and measuring scientist deems to be important.

The economist may look at variations in annual hours worked or the inflation rate in connection with changes in output per time period. For the biologist, the analysis of variations in annual growth of biomass may start with generalizations about the age and location of the specimens. Are annual hours of sunshine and rain important? Does growth of biomass depend on when sun and rain occur during the year? Are certain minerals associated with variations in growth rates? For both disciplines, decisions must be made about the classifications and measurements for independent (causal) and dependent variables. The investigators in both disciplines must determine whether the relationships are linear or nonlinear, additive or multiplicative, simultaneous or lagged, and so on.

Any technique of measurement depends upon a standard for measurement. Measurement of volume or flow requires the adoption of some arbitrary but invariable specification of a distance between two points, such as a foot or a meter, and it requires a measure of time, such as a minute or year. Measurement of weight depends upon a specific physical standard of measure, such as ounces or grams.

Distances may be measured indirectly, for example with radar, which measures the time for the return of a radio pulse, divides it by the observed speed of radio waves, and presents a reading on an oscilloscope. Temperatures must be measured indirectly with reference to their effect on the height of a column of mercury.

The great Cambridge University chemist, Lord Kelvin, noted that one of the characteristics of science was the measurement of observed phenomena and that science without measurement was a very poor kind of science. The great Cambridge University economist, Lord Keynes, noted in his seminal work, *The General Theory of Employment, Interest, and Money* (1935), that economics could not scientifically analyze and explain the fluctuations in national income without a definition of national income and a means of measuring it. The attempt of economists to follow the measurement practices of the natural sciences was the impetus for the development of NIA measurement conventions. The NIA measurement conventions, in turn, have their roots in the double-entry accounting conventions first developed by Renaissance Italian merchants to quantify the results of their activities.

Economists are notorious for differing among themselves on the explanation of economic activity.   Does an increase in the minimum wage lead to an increase in prices or a decrease in employment?[2]   Different economists investigating such a question might well come up with different data sets and different conclusions for the same economy at the same period of time. But that could also be true for two botanists looking at the relationships between annual sunshine and annual growth of biomass in the same forest.

Would different economists "explaining" variations in the growth of American GDP come up with different explanations? Of course. Would they differ on the measurement of the phenomena to be explained? No—not on the measurement conventions for GDP. They might come up with different measures of the independent (causative) variables. But they would agree that the dependent variable to be measured should be GDP in one of its forms or aggregates. There is a commonly accepted standard of measurement for GDP.

Could another economist collect a different data set than mine and come out with a different set of observations about the decline in the rate of economic growth? Yes. But that economist's data set would have to use different measurement concepts than NIA for her conclusions and those different measurement concepts would cause her work to be noncomparable to the work of other economists. The use of a common set of measurement conventions is important to economics as a science and as a basis for discussing public policy issues.

Are there better ways of measuring economic activity? Possibly. But different methods would be "better" only for a different set of objectives than those for which current procedures were developed.   Current accounting methods were developed with the narrow objective of measuring final output by the relative prices observed in market transactions. I will discuss the direction and magnitude of the biases in the measurement of economic activity introduced by inclusion and aggregation rules later in this chapter.

What Economic Growth Does Not Measure

Before we discuss the biases in the measurement of what NIA does measure, let us be clear about what it does not measure. GDP does not directly measure how "well-off" a nation or an individual is. Many criticisms of the use of GDP as a measure of economic welfare have been made—and deserve to be made if GDP is presented as a measure of something more than an arbitrary measure of output.[3]

Economics measures economic transactions. In measuring GDP, economists record the aggregate market values of certain observed transactions, but economics does not measure some universally recognized human value—nor does it purport to.

Philosophers have agonized over a universal standard of value since Aristotle's epigrammatic statement about "Man the measure of all things." While GDP is measured in money terms, the real purpose of economic activity is not the accumulation of money or even the goods that can be purchased by money but the increase in well-being that humans seek by economic and other forms of human activity.

Economists have tried to distinguish between money and value since Adam Smith made the distinction in *The Wealth of Nations*. In fact, an objective of his eighteenth-century classic was to dispel the misunderstanding promulgated by a group of political philosophers known as "Mercantilists" who argued that the objective of economic activity was the national acquisition of gold and silver. Smith noted that the real objective of economic activity was not the acquisition of gold but of more goods and services. In order to measure the goods and services (rather than the gold), Smith grappled with the problem of value and, in particular, of explaining differences between "value in exchange" and "value in use." To explain exchange value, Smith articulated the theory that the relative prices of goods in observed market transactions would tend toward "natural" prices, which reflected the relative labor content of goods and services. This would allow the aggregation of goods by their relative prices to measure value, which Smith thought had its origin in human labor. Smith wanted to root value theory in the quantity of labor because the creation of value of labor and the source of property rights in the act of creation was the basis of the seventeenth-century English philosopher John Locke's political philsophy.

John Stuart Mill and the neoclassical economists of the nineteenth century pushed Adam Smith's quest for the identification of a standard of value one step further with the concept of "utility." For the Utilitarians the ultimate objective of economic activity was not the production of goods and services but the creation of greater utility. Social arrangements were to be judged on their efficacy in securing "the greatest utility for the greatest number."

The problem of using utility as a basis for the measurement of value is that it cannot be observed directly (like the relative prices recorded in market transactions) and there is no objective measure for a proxy for utility (like the measurement of temperature by proxy with the height of a column of mercury). Economists are very clear (at least in professional discussion) that the ultimate objective of economic activity is not the GDP measured in relative prices but "utility," which cannot be directly observed and measured. The objective of economic activity—increased utility—cannot be measured direcdy with our existing measurement system.[4]

Changes in "real" GDP or national income are frequently used as a proxy for changes in "utility." However, the creation of the NIA variable "real" (constant dollar) national income with index number conventions for price and quantity is, at best, an imperfect proxy for utility. Moreover, discussions of GDP may be further confused by the implicit assumption that "more" is always "better"— which it is not, necessarily, to all persons at all times. More police protection is not better (in my standard of relative worth) than more symphony concerts, but NIA conventions make no distinction about the measurement of their relative value if people pay for both at the relative prices determined by "the market" (or, making a further assumption, relative prices are imputed at the costs paid to the owners of the labor and capital used in production).

The exclusion of many of the facets of economic activity (for example, household or charitable production of goods and services) makes GDP still more arbitrary as a measurement of changes in human welfare. Nevertheless, "real" national income is what we have to work with in economics and the usefulness of the measurement concept is increased if we understand its biases and limitations.

There is no analogous problem of confusing "value" with measurement in natural science because the natural sciences use constant and objective standards of measurement (for example, grams for weight, meters for length) of the phenomena they are studying and they separate questions of measurement from imputations of social value. The biological scientist who measures biomass and the users of the knowledge he generates do not automatically infer that more biomass is "better."   For example, oak grows biomass very slowly while cottonwood grows it very quickly. The silviculturalist who measured the annual growth of biomass of a forest consisting of oaks and cottonwoods would not be under the illusion that the forest was doing "better" if cottonwoods were substituted for oaks to increase the rate of growth of biomass. The "value" or "utility" of a cubic meter of the denser biomass of the more slowly growing oak relative to the equivalent volume of cottonwood would depend upon its use, which is a separate and distinctly different quality than its mass.

The inferred purpose of economic activity is the improvement of human welfare—the improvement of living conditions and, indeed, the extension of life itself. GDP does not measure that. The goods and services measured by NIA techniques are not desired for themselves but for their effects. The standard of living and its rate of change cannot be measured directly. Unfortunately, both economists and generally more sensible individuals frequently do infer changes in the human condition from NIA techniques.

Nonetheless, this confusion between proxy and some idealized value should not discourage us from measuring national income or its growth. We infer the "wellness" of a human being by sticking a glass-clad column of mercury in a patient's mouth and observing its response to body temperature.   Physicians know that the mercury will be relatively higher in the evening, lower in the morning, and reduced with the administration of aspirin. They take these effects into account in monitoring the "wellness" of the patient.

Economists, and those who pay attention to their measurements, should realize the shortcomings of NIA conventions for measuring long-run, structural changes (or cross-cultural comparisons) but will continue to use them as long as they are the only diagnostics available.   Similarly, physicians are aware of a broad range of medical tests that can be used to supplement the inferences of body temperature for gauging a patient's health.

WHAT "ECONOMIC GROWTH" DOES MEASURE

It is important to understand the concepts involved in the measurement of national output in order to evaluate reported differences in growth rates. Economic growth does measure actual, observed phenomena, but those are selected phenomena that are measured with arbitrary and complex accounting concepts. (NIA concepts are discussed at greater length in Appendix 4.A.)

Various accounting conventions necessarily underlie the measurement of economic activity.   As I explain later, the specific conventions used for measurement affect the calculation of rates of growth of national output.

Different measurement conventions applied to the same set of economic activities would change the measurement of the levels and, hence, the reported growth rate of output during that period even though the same economic phenomena were being measured. Different accounting conventions would change comparative rates of growth for different stages of a nation's economic history or comparisons with other nations for the same or different periods. This is why it is important to understand the NIA concepts in order to understand the unavoidable biases they impart to the measurement of changes in economic growth.[5]

"Economic growth" is the measured rate at which national output or income increases. Economic growth is a shorthand term, a biological metaphor for a positive time rate of change in real national product or income. Despite the number of decimal places to which changes in national income are reported, measuring economic output is more complex and arbitrary and less exact than measuring, say, the volume of a physical object or the flow of a liquid from a pipe.

Economic growth measures the time rate of change in national output. National output or its counterpart, national income, is often referred to as a *level* concept but is actually a *flow* concept. It is a measure of the rate at which goods and services are produced by a particular group of humans (usually a nation) with particular skills, capital equipment, technology, and organization during a particular time period (usually a year).

By dividing national output by the number of people or the number of workers, or number of workers actually employed, or the total number of hours worked (paid for!), one obtains national output per capita, or per worker, or per employed worker, or per labor hour. The comparison of these permutations of national product also permit the calculation of rates of change in these variables.

Gross or net, national or domestic, output or income—all of these NIA entities refer to a production rate or flow during a time period. The growth of national output refers to changes in the rate of flow between two points in time. Changes in the "growth rate" represent changes in the rate of change of this production rate or flow level. (Changes in the growth rate are the mathematical equivalent of the second derivative of the level or annual flow of output flow with respect to time.)

Upward Biases in the Measurement of Growth

The NIA convention of excluding household production tends to overstate the rate of increase in net final output that occurs during the process of economic growth and structural change. During periods of structural change, such as the movement from an agricultural to an industrial economy, when the production of goods and services is shifting from household activity to market activity, the rate of growth of national product is increased by the NIA convention of counting only market transactions and excluding household production of goods and services from measurement. This overstated increase in measured output is important in two (overlapping and continuing) processes of economic growth— in the shift of the population and labor force from agriculture to urban activity and in the shift of women from household to market production.

American farms have always been oriented toward producing crops for market, but in the early part of the century farmers also produced substantial food and fuel for their own consumption. In NIA practice this bias was partially offset by the imputation for production of farm-consumed food in the estimation of net farm output. However, this was a partial adjustment that did not capture the full value of all household production.

The increase in recorded output resulting from the movement from home to market production has been particularly important in the United States in the period from 1960 to 1990 as women have moved the locus of their work from home to store, office, or factory. And, when the shift from household to market production slows—because the farm sector has already shrunk to a small size, or because most of the women are already employed in market reported transactions rather than domestic production—the increase in the measured rate of change of national output per person must necessarily decline. (This particular bias is readily handled in "Growth Accounting" discussed in Appendix 4.B.)

Known NIA Biases that Understate GDP Growth

Five measurement conventions tend to understate the quantity and quality increases measured by economic growth:

1. Failure to place a value on natural resources "used up" or diminished in quality in the process of commodity production.
2. Measurement of the quantity of output of certain consumer durables (such as automobiles) and "service durables" (such as education and medical care) as final output during the period in which they are purchased rather than by estimating the quantity of continuing services received from their use during subsequent periods.
3. Assignment of a quantitative equivalent to quality change by imputed changes in the cost of production.
4. Imputation of prices and quantities for services (particularly government services) or owner-occupied housing where there is no market transaction.
5. Use of "current weighted (Paasche) indexes" for valuing GDP at relative prices.

All five areas are acknowledged by economists who deal with national income accounting issues but they are less well recognized by the average citizen reading published estimates of growth rates.

Consumption of Natural Resources and Impairment of Environmental Quality

The first NIA convention to affect the measurement of output levels and growth rates, counterintuitively, understates growth by overstating the earlier levels of output in an economy that was more intensively engaged in the production of commodities—food, coal, lumber, iron, and so on.

Our NIA conventions do not record the "value subtracted" from final GDP by the severance of resources from nature or the diminution of air or water quality by pollution. This subtraction would be required by John Hicks's notion of income (see Appendix 4.A), which is defined with reference to changes in the capital stock.[6] (Natural resources, including water quality, might be considered part of the capital stock of an economy but are not included in NIA.) When an old-growth forest or petroleum pool is "severed," the price paid in a market transaction for the resource is treated as part of "value added" in the measurement of GDP, although it could be argued that there has been an offsetting value subtracted from the stock of the nation's natural resource capital.

The consequence of taking into account all the costs of natural resources consumed or diminished in commodity production would be to reduce the level but increase the rate of growth of GDP. Since the value of natural resource commodities was a larger part of U.S. GDP in the first half of the century, subtracting their value would decrease earlier measurement of GDP levels more than current GDP.

Our current environmental protection laws require the maintenance of water and air quality. Ironically, expenditures on cleaning up air or water pollution increase measured costs and decrease measured net output. Earlier generations that did not incur these costs could record higher net output.   If earlier generations had been subject to the same laws, recently recorded growth rates would be enhanced.

Final Output and Changes in the Flow of Service Output

The second of the five related measurement conventions that tend to understate the growth of economic output is the measurement of purchase transactions only as final output. Consider an example of a consumer durable such as an automobile. The new auto is valued in GDP by its cost of production (equal to its price) when it is purchased by the consumer. However, with a different accounting convention, the auto could be assumed to be an intermediate good with the final good being the miles of transportation services it furnishes in conjunction with fuel, maintenance, and so on during its working life.

Suppose that technological change makes it possible to purchase an auto at the same constant dollar cost that will supply 100,000 miles of transportation rather than 50,000 miles before it is worn out (when the cost of repair is greater than the value of the additional miles made possible by the repair cost). If the quantity of output being measured was potential miles rather than the production cost of the auto, GDP would be increased by the doubling of the quantity of miles at the same price. Now it might be argued here that the miles will be consumed in future time periods so that their production could be counted in future time periods—but they aren't. It is assumed for measurement of GDP that the final demand is the demand for the automobile rather than the miles produced by it.

The real capacity of the auto to produce transportation services has been increased by technological improvements but its price reflects only the labor and capital inputs required to produce the auto, rather than its value to the purchaser in terms of the miles per dollar of operating expenses it will provide over its service life. If the quantity of prospective miles delivered by the auto over its operating life were valued at the time of purchase, there would be an increase in quantity of output (auto transportation miles), which would increase measured GDP.

The increase in the quality and capacity of consumer durables—such as cars, appliances, computers, stereo equipment, and so on—increases the quantity or quality of the flow of services made possible by the purchase of a consumer durable, but this is not measured by the NIA concepts, which measure output only as the final market transaction that takes place when the consumer durable is purchased, rather than as the continuing provision of a stream of services to its purchaser. The increase in the capacity of consumer durables per dollar of cost is not captured by NIA measures and thus, the "real" rate of growth of output is understated by existing accounting conventions.

A dramatic area of recent improvement in the estimation of final output that ought to be included in GDP is not in products but in services. Much is heard about the increase in the cost of medical services relative to other components of national income and the increase in the proportion of national income spent on them. However, the medical services actually measured are different than the health outcomes produced by the services. Medical procedures have recently improved so much that surgical procedures that were once relatively high risk and necessitated days of hospital care can now be conducted on an out-patient basis with a high probability of success.

NIA procedures follow hospital billing procedures in recording as "output" the hospital bed days and operating theater costs along with the charges for the surgery. Further, to gain an estimate of the change in the volume of all health services apart from price changes, NIA procedures proxy them with some standard unit of service output such as a hospital patient days or operating room hours. The quantity and prices of these two "outputs" are measured in 1982 and 1992 for use as an index of price and output increases in medical services. Suppose the hospital patient day costs $100 in 1982 and $300 in 1992. The medical cost index is set at 300 for 1992 and is used to divide through actual hospital costs in 1992 to calculate the increase in their quantity since 1982. This method is used to estimate the "real" output of medical services in the two years from their prices.

However, there have been advances in scientific knowledge and medical technology that increase the measured effectiveness and decrease the measured risks of medical procedures. As a heuristic and hypothetical example, suppose that improved medical procedures reduce the patient's time in hospital and the time lost from work for a standard appendectomy. Suppose, further, that the average mortality from the operation falls from 2 percent to 1 percent. Medical knowledge and technological change in health care have substantially increased the "wellness" made possible by constant dollar expenditure on medical services. Yet, the improvement in "wellness" is not measured—only the costs per hospital day, per operating theater hour, or per surgical procedure is measured!

The valuation of medical services and consumer durables could be valued in terms of the additional quantity of "wellness" they produce.[7] The problem with our current accounting procedures is that the consumers are not recorded as purchasing passenger miles or wellness—the transactions are recorded as the purchase price of an automobile or medical services.

There is a different problem here than is involved in the purchase of investment goods that yield service over future time periods. A manufacturer could purchase a machine tool that has a higher output than one purchased the previous year at the same price. However, in this case the increase in the quantity of the investment good shows up in subsequent years as an increase in the quantity of manufactured goods produced by the machine tool that are counted at their time of purchase. The same is not true of the future output of miles by the automobile or "wellness" by the surgical procedure.[8]

If NIA concepts were altered to measure certain consumer and service "durables" in terms of the provision of a quantity of final services output, any increase in the quantity of services would increase the measured growth of GDP. This becomes increasingly important as a larger part of consumer expenditure goes on consumer durables, medical care, and education.

Estimation of Quantity Equivalent Quality Improvements in Terms of Additional Production Costs

The third bias introduced by NIA techniques is an attempt to deal with the problems discussed earlier for consumer products. This is the method for valuation of new or improved products. The current accounting convention leads to an understatement of increases in the real value of output.

My 1992 386 computer is much faster and has 4MB of RAM and a 100MB hard disk memory compared to my 1982 computer with its 8086 processor, .5MB of RAM, and no hard disk. The 1992 386 costs far less in inflation-adjusted dollars than the old 8086 machine did in 1982. Yet, when the old and new computers are valued for NIA purposes, the estimate of the quantity/quality increase is calculated by taking the current (estimated) cost of production difference between the 1992 model and the old model.

It is estimated that in 1992 the 386 machine would cost only 10 percent more to manufacture than the (obsolete and discontinued) 8088 computer. On this basis it is inferred that the 1992 386 computer has only a 10 percent *quantity* difference with the 1982 8088 computer. Thus, the difference between the output of computers in 1982 and 1992 is the total units sold in both years valued at the 1982 prices for the 1982 models and the 1982 prices plus 10 percent for the 1992 models. While this may capture the value of the capital and labor contained in the computers, it is, obviously, a major understatement of the real capacity or quantity of the 1992 computers, and the measured rate of growth in output in quantity-equivalent quality is substantially understated by the use of this measurement convention.

Valuation by Imputation—Services Without Transactions

An increasing proportion of GNP is measured by imputation rather than market prices. Government services (including public education) are currently nearly a quarter of measured GDP and they are valued at their cost since no price is charged for them. Owner-occupied housing, about 15 percent of GDP, is valued at what home owners would pay for equivalent rental housing (if it existed).

Both of these accounting conventions, which are used to value a large and increasing proportion of GNP, fail to capture increases or decreases in the value of the output of housing, medical, education, or governmental services. Because government services are valued at their cost of production, there is no possibility of measuring any change in output per government worker other than the change in the pay of government workers. Increasing the proportion of government workers in the economy will increase measured economic output if their pay is above average and vice versa if it is below.[9]

If a teacher educates ten students well or twenty students badly, the output is still measured as the cost of the teacher. If a physician paid by a government agency heals ten patients or is unable to heal twenty patients, the value of the output of the government sector of economy is the same. As will be noted in chapter 5, the output per worker in government, education, or medicine is only recorded as changing if there is an increase in the compensation of the workers or if there is an increase in capital costs. Thus, what we measure as productivity change (changes in costs of production per worker in government and the service sector) is not really a measure of productivity at all![10]

Measurement Biases—Alternative Indexes

GDP is measured by the aggregation of output valued at market prices. GDP is measured "looking backward"—we evaluate the past in terms of the present. Current prices are used to value output in past periods. Because consumers (usually) switch toward goods that are falling in relative price, the weight of those items in the current-weighted (Paasche) Index is less than it would be if they were weighted at the higher prices of an earlier year. This results in the value of GDP being estimated at a lower number and, thereby, decreasing recorded growth. Because prices of the goods change at different rates (and change for reasons that systematically bias measurement of growth), the rate of growth of aggregate output will be different if the prices at the beginning or the ending of the period of measurement are used. There is no escaping the problem—it is the classic apples and oranges problem: there is no common unit of measurement for the value of the fruits as there would be if we were measuring, say, their aggregate change of weight or volume (as in natural science) over a time period.[11]   I have discussed the biases introduced by weighting conventions in price indexes in the chapter 3 appendix. The quantitative size of the bias from using one index rather than another is readily determined.

A Bottom Line for NIA

The measurement conventions for estimating changes in the rate of economic growth are arbitrary and imperfect but the effects of their inherent biases on the measurement of unobserved economic welfare are reasonably well known and understood by the economists who work with them. Perhaps their major shortcoming is that while they may be useful for the description of the behavior of aggregates, they are less useful for analysis of the sources of productivity growth by disaggregation. To remedy that deficiency NIA has been supplemented or expanded by "growth accounting." Growth accounting separates the share of income growth attributable to changes in the quantity of capital and the quantity and "quality" of labor and a "residual" that is a measure of "productivity." (See the discussion in Appendix 4. B.)

The most important lesson for the nonprofessional reader of comparisons of economic growth and performance is caution about intertemporal comparisons of the rates of change presented. My intention, in this chapter, has been to suggest that, for the early part of this century, growth rates have been *overstated* by the movement of output from household to market. In the latter half of the century, however, the increasing proportion of consumer durables and medical services in national output and the increasing imputations for Government services have *understated* the measurement of output growth.

If this interpretation is accepted, then the measured slowdown in the rate of growth of the economy is partly a function of our measurement conventions rather than some phenomenon that has to do with a "real" decline in the efficiency with which our economy functions to supply human needs and wants. Earlier growth rates were overstated and later growth rates were understated. Thus, the measured decline in growth rates is less than the *actual* decline in growth rates.

However, measured output levels and growth rates are frequently the basis for public policy debates and demands by various pressure groups. Tax revenues are projected on the basis of accounting income and the failure of accounting income to rise as fast as projected results in tax revenue shortfalls and budget deficits. People compete to maintain a certain accounting income standard through "cost of living" adjustments even though price indices may overstate price increases and the "real" increase in the cost of living and, thereby, overstate the income increases necessary to keep people "even" in real terms.[12] Alas, I do not believe that politicians will cease to raise taxes or that claimants for income shares will reduce their demands even if they come to realize that price and quantity estimates of GDP are systematically biased.

NOTES

1. I observe that many economists do not understand NIA and GAAP concepts as well as they should when they are using the data produced by these measurement conventions. I am tempted to draw an analogy with the physicists who thought they had discovered net energy creation by "cold fusion" because they didn't understand the measurement procedures they were using to analyze physical reactions!

2. There was a serious professional conflict aired at the 1995 convention of the American Economic Association over data used by different economics to analyze the effect of changes in minimum wages on changes in employment in the fast food industry in Pennsylvania and New Jersey.

3. Economists William Nordhaus and Paul Samuelson developed a set of adjustments to measure Gross Domestic Product—such as deducting for environmental degradation

and police services—which they called "net economic welfare." This measurement concept has been extended in Herman Daly and John Cobb in *Toward The Common Good* (Boston, City Press, 1994).

4. Measurement of GDP values all goods in terms of their relative prices. It is assumed that relative prices reflect relative *marginal* costs. It is also assumed that relative prices reflect the *marginal* utilities of goods to consumers. Thus, the change in the quantities of goods produced—valued at their relative prices—is inferred to be equal to the change in total utility; but there is no way to infer the *proportional* change in total utility from the change in the quantity of goods valued and aggregated at their relative prices because total utility is unknown. Further, there is no way of aggregating the utility of individuals, even assuming their individual gains in utility are *proportional* to prices.

5. Business analysts or investors who are evaluating the performance of a corporation start with an analysis of the balance sheet and income statement prepared in accordance with Generally Accepted Accounting Principles (GAAP). However, they interpret the accounts in terms of their understanding of the limitations and shortcomings of the accounts in revealing the "true" condition of the firm. For this reason (and for reasons connected with "expectations" about the future course of the firm), the "book" value of the firm--the value based on GAAP—and "market" value—the value based on the market price of the firm's shares—diverge considerably.

6 John R. Hicks, *Value and Capital* (Oxford: Oxford University Press, 1939), chapter XIV.

7. The State of Oregon has made an interesting and important step in the valuation of the output of medical services to determine which medical procedures will be covered under the State's Medicaid program. More than 700 procedures and treatments have been ranked in terms of their prospective yield of patient quality days per dollar of cost.

8 Education is an interesting intermediate case. Increases in "human capital" formed by education thatincrease productivity in future time periods is captured in the measured GDP of those future time periods as additional output. However, education could also be viewed as a "consumer durable"—for example, the enhancement of enjoyment from reading or listening to music is a nonmeasurable form of consumption in future time periods that the individual could be "purchasing" in the current time period for enjoyment in subsequent time periods.

9. There is an even greater lack of comparability in the accounting treatment of the public and private sectors. In the private sector depreciation and payments to capital are treated as a part of value added, which is the basis for determining output per worker. In the government sector there is no depreciation of capital assets or payments for the use of capital (for instance, buildings and computers), so value added per worker is solely the compensation of employees.

10. The rates of growth in output per capita and output per worker analyzed in this volume are presented to measure growth in output rather than explain it. The growth in output per capita and per worker comes from the growth in the stocks of capital and increasing efficiency in their use. A substantial part of GDP is paid to the owners of capital for their supply of capital services and the rest goes to labor. Consequently, GDP per worker measures not only labor income but the income going to capital as well.

Output per worker in capital intensive areas of the economy—such as public utilities—is very high because the income going to both capital and labor from production in the industry are divided through by the number of workers to obtain output per worker. Measured output per worker in public utilities is higher than output per worker in a service industry like law or accounting because, in the latter, their are virtually no expenditures for capital to be included in the costs of the industry. However, the wages received in law and accounting are higher than the wages received by utility workers because much of the income received for the production of utility services goes to the owners of extensive capital used in the industry.

11.   In a class in "Economics for Engineers" I taught years ago at Columbia University, I spent considerable time on index number theory in explaining the valuation of GDP. Finally, one exasperated young engineer raised his hand and asked, "Why do we have to go through all of these different measures of estimation—let's just measure it."

12. The Boskin Commission proposal (1995) to change the measurement of the consumer price index (CPI) to reflect some of the biases discussed earlier would materially change the size of the transfer payments from the taxpaying to the retired population through Social Security.

CHAPTER 5

Structural Change and the Slowdown of Productivity Growth

The whole is equal to the sum of its parts.
—Euclid

The rate of growth of output per worker in the U.S. economy has been declining for the last half-century. Contrary to popular opinion, however, this decline has *not* occurred because Americans have been investing less or working less efficiently. Practically all of the observed decline in the rate of growth of output per worker in the American economy over the past two decades can be explained by changes in the output structure of the economy. These changes in the structure of output are the natural consequence of the "maturing" of the American economy that has resulted from our successful economic growth.

Of course, Euclid was correct about the "whole," but Euclid's axiom is potentially misleading when one thinks about the growth of the average for the whole economy! The growth rate of average output per worker for the whole economy is equal to the sum of the weighted changes in output per worker in the component sectors of the economy and the changes in the weights of the sectors of the economy. Changes in the relative size of the producing sectors of the U.S. economy—rather than the slowdown of productivity growth rates within sectors—explain most of the slowdown in the growth of productivity in the economy.

As presented in chapter 3 (Text Tables 3.1 and 3.2), the United States is no longer achieving two-digit measured decennial growth in real output per worker and per worker hour. This slowdown is not recent. Aggregate productivity growth—the average growth in output per worker hour for the entire economy—has been slowing for the past half-century. Surprisingly, while the growth rate of average output per worker for the entire economy has declined substantially—from 23 percent in the decade ending in 1950 to 8 percent for the decade ending in 1990 (Text Table 3.1)—productivity growth has not slowed down, on balance, *within* sectors of the economy. For example, growth in output per worker in the manufacturing sector is faster now than it was in the 1950s and 1960s (Text Table 5.2). But, because the manufacturing sector is now a smaller part of the economy in terms of its value added output and employment, its contribution to the increase in the overall average of worker productivity has been diminished.

Additionally, changes in the relative size of sectors resulting from intersectoral shifts of workers from lower productivity to higher productivity sectors (like the earlier shift of workers from agriculture to manufacturing) are now going the other way (from manufacturing to service or government employment). This diminishes the average growth rate of output per worker rather than enhancing it as these shifts did earlier in the century.

This chapter presents the measurements on decennial growth rates in output per worker by sector. These intra-sectoral growth rates are used to explain the slowdown in the growth of aggregate output per worker for the entire economy as the consequence of the changes in the output structure of the economy—namely, changes in the relative size of the productive sectors of the economy. In this chapter I show, through the disaggregation of data on output by sector, why the decline in the measured growth rate can be explained largely as the consequence of structural change in the economy and, thus, why the (measured) slowdown in productivity growth will be permanent and irreversible.

This chapter has five parts and an extensive appendix on data, sources, and methods. Part I identifies nine output sectors and explains the accounting conventions and implications of the accounting rules for the measurement of value added within various output sectors of the economy. Part II presents the evidence on the changing relative size of the sectors of the economy measured both by their share of employment and share of value added output. Part III explains the direct and indirect causal relationships between the process of economic growth and structural change. Part IV explores the consequences of the changing structure of the economy for the rate of growth of output per worker over the past century and—by extension—for the future. Part V emphasizes that it is the lack of appropriate productivity measurement for the expanding service sectors that is pulling down the rate of growth of output per worker rather than any slowing of growth within sectors where productivity growth is conceptually measureable.

PART I: OUTPUT MEASUREMENT BY SECTOR

Measurement Conventions

Before discussing the characteristics of production by sectors, it is important to understand the application of accounting conventions for the calculation of "value added" by sectors. Value added—not gross sales—is the output of each sector in GDP. GDP, which is defined as the value of final output for the total economy, represents the sum of value added by all sectors.

Consider an example: The value of a loaf of bread purchased at the grocery store, including sales tax, is counted in GDP—but only a small part of the price of the bread is represented by the markup of the retail grocer to cover his costs. The value added by the grocery store is its "gross margin"—the difference between the price paid by the grocer for the bread to the wholesale baker and the price for which the store sells the bread to the final consumer (less certain other payments paid to other firms for such intermediate goods and services as electricity, advertising, or accounting services). The value added by the grocery store—its gross margin—is equal to the wages paid to the employees of the grocery store (including employment taxes and fringe benefits) and the payments for the capital used in the grocery business—depreciation, interest to bondholders, and the pre-tax profits.

Every firm involved in the sequence of production and distribution of the bread—from the farmer who grows the wheat to the grocer who retails the bread—contributes "value added."   And so do their suppliers—the seed merchant who supplies the farmer, the oil company that supplies the railroad that hauls the grain, and their suppliers, and so forth.   In each sector it is only the suppliers of the labor and capital services who are the actual sources of the value added in the process of producing the final output—namely, GDP.

This leads us to another important point. Output per worker is not equal to wages or employment cost per worker. Our measure of productivity—output per worker—does not separate the payments going to labor and the payments going to cover the costs of the capital employed in the sector. It is, simply, the result of dividing sectoral output by the number of workers in the sector. This means that in sectors with large amounts of capital per worker a larger proportion of the costs are capital costs and those capital costs, per worker, are added to the wages (and other employment costs) and, thereby, increase reported value added per worker.

The high output per worker in a sector like transportation, communication, and public utilities (Sector V in this discussion) results primarily from the large amount of physical capital employed in this sector. This extensive capital is, in turn, reflected in large annual payments for depreciation, interest, and profits on the invested capital. The workers in this sector receive wages that reflect the value added by the sector after the subtraction of the large capital costs.

To contrast a high-capital sector with a low-capital sector, the incomes received by dentists in the personal and business services sector (VIII) are a large proportion of the costs billed to clients because a dentist's payments for rent and electricity are small relative to his receipts for dental services rendered, and there are few capital goods (for example, dentist drills) to depreciate. The dentist's high income is almost all of the value added in the sector.[1] Thus, the average income of dentists in the personal and business services sector is greater than the average wage of workers in an electric utility even though the measured output per worker employed by the public utility is several times the output per dentist.

Accounting conventions create a further anomaly in the government sector (IX). Government accounting conventions do not include a charge for the physical capital used by the government sector. (Further, no price is charged for the services provided.) The value of the output of the federal, state, and local governments is, therefore, imputed to be equal only to the labor costs incurred in providing government services. Because those costs do not include capital costs, the output—the value added—of the public schools in the government sector, for example, consists almost totally of the wages and other employment costs of the teachers and administrative and support staff even though the school district incurs substantial capital costs for buildings, buses, computers, and other capital equipment. If the school were in the private sector, capital costs would be included in the value-added output.

As we examine differences in output per worker and rates of growth of output per worker by sector, it is important to remember that output per worker and average wages per worker are different concepts. It is the use of large amounts of capital per worker that results in high output per worker, but the use of capital must be paid for. The value added per worker in Sector IX goes for both wages and payments for capital.

Identification of Sectors

Expanding the traditional practice of breaking the economy into primary, secondary, and tertiary output sectors (basically agriculture, manufacturing, and service sectors), I distinguish nine sectors. The basis for my classification (apart from the organization of government statistics on output and employment) is differences between the sectors in their capacity for substituting capital for labor in production, the differential responses of the sectors to changes in final demand, and their amenability to the measurement of changes in the quality and quantity dimensions of output. The sectors are[2]:

I.	Farm Commodity Production
II.	Mineral Commodity Production
III.	Contract Construction
IV.	Manufacturing
V.	Transportation, Communications, and Public Utilities
VI.	Wholesale and Retail Distribution
VII.	Financial Services
VIII.	Personal and Business Services
IX.	Government Services

Sector I: Farm Commodity Production

Sector I comprises agriculture, forestry, and fisheries. Over time the economic activities in Sector I have been transformed from the labor-intensive gathering or harvesting of natural materials to their current capital-intensive culture and mechanized harvesting. Agriculture, silviculture, and aquaculture have applied scientific knowledge to biological growth processes and increasingly specialized capital equipment to cultivation and harvesting.

Value added in Sector I (as in all sectors) is the sum of the factor payments that accrue to the capital and labor employed in the sector. As I have mentioned, the value added within the sector is estimated by the subtraction of the costs of intermediate inputs from other sectors (such as energy, raw materials, or business services) from gross revenues. As an example, the gross revenues of a farm are the sums received by the farm enterprise from the sale of grain to the grain elevator. The farmer pays for intermediate inputs of seed, fertilizer, electricity, and legal and accounting services from other sectors, and the costs of these intermediate inputs are deducted from gross revenues from the sale of grain to calculate the farm's value added. The value added is the difference between receipts for output and expenditures for intermediate inputs and is also the sum of the farm's payments to labor and capital. The portion of value added represented by wages is easy to calculate if the wages have actually been separated out in the farm's accounts. Often, the net income of the farmer has to be broken into a return to the capital assets owned by the farmer and a return to his labor by imputation. A substantial portion of annual value added within the sector is the annual charge for the depreciation of capital equipment. Another part of the value added is explicit interest paid to others or implicit interest on the farmer's own capital used in the enterprise (if the farm reports a profit).

Implicitly, the "value added" by natural resources in this sector—the natural fertility of the soil, the inherited virgin forest, the extant fish stock—are all attributed to the capital and labor involved in harvesting them. Historically, one could argue that the exploitation of the original natural resources in the United States resulted in a high level of output, per worker, in natural resource producing sectors.[3] The progressive exhaustion or diminution of those original natural resources has tended to offset the rate of growth in output per worker made possible, for example, by the substitution of more efficient and specialized capital equipment (tractors and chain saws) for less efficient forms of productive capital (mules and axes).

Measured productivity growth (the rate of change in the ratio of value added/workers) in this sector has been high for a long period of time. This high growth rate has resulted from continuing increases in the purchase of intermediate inputs and increases in capital per worker. This has reduced the proportion of the labor force employed in the sector at the same time that total output and value added per worker by the sector have increased. Specialization and capitalization have increased the total net output of the sector, which is then divided by the diminishing number of workers employed to increase the ratio called "output per worker."[4]

A significant proportion of the reduction in the relative size of Sector I can be attributed to the growth in the importance of intermediate inputs (purchased agricultural chemicals and logging trucks) from other sectors rather than their production within the sector (horse manure and ox-teams tended by employees within the sector).[5] This specialization, and the high rate of depreciation of physical capital in this sector, lies behind the high rates of increase observed in output per worker in this sector.

Sector II: Mineral Commodity Production

The high level of output per worker in mining and its high rate of growth is the combined effect of increasingly capital intensive methods of extraction offsetting the depletion of richer and more accessible natural deposits.

A century ago coal was the primary source of fuel for the U.S. economy and represented a large proportion of the employment and output of the mining sector. Large numbers of miners were employed in digging coal from dangerous underground seams in miserable working conditions. Part of the increase in value added per employee in this sector comes from the modern coal mining technology used in strip-mining coal with huge earth movers; another part comes from the switch from coal to petroleum production, which is even more capital-intensive than coal. In petroleum and natural gas production, increases in output per worker come from improvements in drilling and pumping technology. The relative decline in total output from the mining sector reflects the relative decline in energy requirements per unit of GDP (with the development of service sectors) and the substitution of imported petroleum for domestic coal. Other mineral production—gold, silver, iron, salt, and gravel—is also part of Sector II, which is small but has very high levels of output per worker.[6]

Sector III: Contract Construction

Construction has conventionally been linked with manufacturing in the sectoral division of output. Modern construction methods increasingly resemble the production line assembly of prefabricated components. The construction industry assembles manufactured components to reduce the on-site labor costs that are the major component of the value added for the construction industry. As an example, "ready-made" cabinets produced by the manufacturing sector have replaced on-site cabinetmakers whose employment is now reflected in the manufacturing rather than the construction industry. This reduces the relative size of value added and employment in the construction industry. Further, as skilled craftsmen are replaced with "assemblers," average wages in the construction sector are depressed.

Specialization reduces the size of this sector in other ways. If a contracting firm owns its own capital equipment, the depreciation and capital costs of that equipment will be part of the value added of the construction sector. However, when a construction firm rents heavy equipment, say bulldozers, from an equipment-leasing firm, the payment for the use of the capital goods is reflected in Sector VIII (Business and Personal Services) or Sector VII (Financial Services) if the equipment is leased from a bank and the value-added output of the contract construction sector is diminished.

The construction industry produces (and repairs) structural capital goods such as houses, offices, factories, roads, bridges, and pipelines. Reductions in the real cost per square foot of buildings, or in the measurable performance characteristics (for example, flow capacity per time unit) of other structures (factories, roads, bridges, dams, pipelines), do not show up as increases in productivity of the construction industry, but rather in the sectors of the economy that purchase capital goods from the construction sector.   A significant proportion of the reductions in the real cost of buildings or other structures produced by the construction sector (roads, bridges, pipelines, and so on) results from increased productivity in the other sectors that supply intermediate inputs (lumber, steel, excavation services) to the construction industry. Thus, to take an example, cheaper lumber or prefabricated plumbing might reduce the cost of construction per square foot of housing, but this decrease in cost would not show up as an increase in value-added per worker in the construction sector.

It is also important to note that reductions in the capital costs of production of services from buildings, pipelines, and so on produced by the construction industry increase the output/capital ratio of the capital-using industries and are reflected in increased productivity in the sectors that purchase the structures from the construction sector rather than as measured productivity within the construction sector. Along with the earlier-mentioned increase in the purchase of components produced off-site, this explains why productivity in this sector appears to be so small and slow growing.[7]

The benefits of cost reduction in the construction sector go to other sectors by reducing the capital costs per unit of production. The amortization of the capital goods is a component of the value added in the production of goods and services by other sectors. For example, the amortization of rental housing shows up in Sector VII, financial services. Or increased productivity in the building of natural gas pipelines shows up in increasing the productivity of Sector V, transportation, communication, and public utilities. The lower cost of transporting natural gas will be reflected in lower costs to consumers and greater value per worker (in constant dollars) in Sector V.

Sector IV: Manufacturing

Sector IV, manufacturing, creates value by changing the physical characteristics of materials produced in Sectors I and II and utilizing services produced in all the other sectors. Manufacturing is broken down into many major and minor sub-classifications with varying levels and rates of growth of output per worker. Nondurables include such items as processed foods, textiles and clothing, chemicals, electricity, and fuels. Durables include such consumer goods as furniture and appliances, automobiles, and television sets, and such producer goods as airplanes, electrical generators, and computers. Technological change and the substitution of capital for labor, traditionally, have made manufacturing a sector of rapid productivity growth. However, the changing performance characteristics of both consumer durables and capital goods create measurement problems for determining the level and rate of growth of value added in this sector. (As discussed in chapter 4, what is the appropriate way to measure the output of cars or computers with improving performance capabilities?) Our accounting conventions may very well understate the rate of growth of productivity in this sector.

Sector V: Transportation, Communications, and Public Utilities

Sector V creates value by the transportation of commodities (including water, sewage, and garbage), people, and information. Road, rail, air, sea, telephone and pipeline transportation systems and foot-messenger, wire, fiber-optic, and satellite communications systems are all part of this sector, so are radio and television broadcasting stations that produce and transport entertainment rather than information.

Most of the production in this sector is done by privately owned but publicly regulated utilities that operate water, gas, sewer, electricity, and telephone systems.   When these utilities are publicly owned, for example, by the Tennessee Valley Authority or Los Angeles Department of Water and Power, they are in Sector IX, Government. Rapid technological change and high ratios of capital to labor and capital to output are responsible for high levels and rates of growth in measured output per worker in this sector as they are in Sector IV, manufacturing.

Increases in output per worker (and per unit of capital) in this sector also occur when there is more complete utilization of existing systems (for example, fuller utilization of a railroad right-of-way or communications satellite); or productivity increases may come from economies of scale due to the creation of larger systems of transportation (railroads, electricity generation and distribution, sewer systems, telephone systems, television networks, and so on).

High and growing output per worker in this sector reflects the additional output possible from (1) higher ratios of capital/labor, (2) increases in the output/capital ratio, (3) increased capacity utilization, and (4) falling prices of capital equipment per unit of output capacity. This can also be reversed when electric generating equipment is underutilized or when nuclear generating facilities stand idle.

My figures show that this is a sector where growth "slowed down" over the past two decades. I think (but have not done the disaggregation to prove my hypothesis) that slowing productivity growth within this sector—from 47 percent per decade in the 1950s and 1960s to 22 percent in the 1980s—can be substantially explained as the result of the shift in the relative importance from more capital intensive to less capital intensive industries within the sector. That is, less capital intensive trucking has grown relative to more capital intensive railways, and less capital intensive communications has grown relative to more capital intensive electrical and water utilities.   Thus, I conjecture that the observed decline in output per worker within the sector is not due to any decline in productivity growth within specific industries, (railroads, trucking, telecommunications, or electrical distribution) but the shift in employment from more to less capital intensive sectors where value added, per worker, is less because of the smaller capital costs per worker. In 1990, for example, 61 percent of employment in this sector was in transportation. Within the transportation sector, employment was shifting from more heavily capitalized rail to less heavily capitalized truck transport. (The government furnishes the capital for roads, and capital costs are not included in output in the sector, unlike the capital costs for railroad tracks.) The communications sector—primarily telephones and secondarily, broadcasting—had the highest rate of growth in productivity (more than 50 percent for the decade of the 1980s) but shrank in relative share of employment from 26 percent to 21 percent of the sector.[8]   At the same time employment in public utilities (electricity, gas, water, and sanitary services—sewer and garbage) increased, and measured productivity growth was very low (7 percent) in this sector.

Sector VI: Wholesale and Retail Distribution

Value added in wholesale and retail trade is the gross margin between the cost of goods sold and sales revenues (less some costs that accrue to other suppliers). NIA concepts do not capture much of the productivity gain that has occurred in this sector. In grocery retailing the constant dollar volume of sales per employee and per dollar of inventory has increased because of a variety of organizational and technological innovations.   For example, the bar-code scanner speeds goods through checkout lanes, reduces pricing costs, and increases the ratio of sales/workers and sales/inventory.   However, the decreased costs resulting from the increase in sales per worker and per dollar of capital are passed on to customers in the form of reduced markups on groceries. In general, merchandising corporations like Wal-Mart, and in mail-order retailing, Lands' End, have also greatly increased sales per employee and per dollar of inventory and physical plant capital relative to traditional retailers. Similar considerations apply to a "fast food" firm such as McDonald's. A higher volume of food is produced with smaller markups over the cost of materials, labor, and capital than one would observe in a more traditional restaurant. In all of these enterprises in the trade sector, savings resulting from increases in efficiency have been passed on to customers in the form of lower markups over the cost of goods sold.

Ironically, from an accounting vantage point, this reduction in markup margin offsets the increases in physical volume and the increase in value of sales from increasing turnover/capital and output/labor—in other words, increased productivity. The reduction in markup offsets the increased volume and, thereby, decreases value added per unit of sales. Because the increase in productivity per employee and per dollar of capital (measured as the constant dollar value of goods) is accompanied by a reduction in the margin on sales (forced by competition), the increase in value added, per employee (the product of increased volume and reduced margins on that volume) is reduced. Thus, the real increase in output of this sector is understated and accounting and price deflation conventions do not adequately measure much of the actual productivity change in the distribution sector.[9]

Sector VII: Financial Services

Sector VII encompasses financial services, insurance, and real estate brokerage and real property management. In such financial services as banking, value added is primarily the gross margin between the interest costs of deposits and the interest revenues on loans and customer service charges. Value added is created, as in other financial intermediaries, including insurance, by the bearing of risks and by the management of assets.

Increases in the dollar value of assets managed, per employee, increase the volume of value added, but, like wholesale and retail distribution, increases in assets managed per employee made possible by productivity change (for example, computers, automatic teller machines, "smart" software programs for credit analysis) are offset by reductions in the margins charged on managed assets that diminish value added per employee. Once again the measurement of output and productivity is distorted by quantity and quality considerations. If my mutual fund manages $1 million for a 1 percent fee or $2 million for a 1/2 percent fee, it collects the same management fee. If one employee is involved, the "value added" is measured as $10,000 per employee and there is no increase in value added when the volume is doubled and the fee is halved.

The largest financial service industry within this sector is real estate management. The high output per employee in this sector primarily reflects the returns to the rental value of real estate, which has high value, added per employee because most of the revenues are due to the large values of real estate under management. This is particularly true for the imputed rent on owner-occupied residences, where there is no corresponding report of employee (owner) compensation for the management of assets.[10] Thus, the high output per worker levels and their declining growth over time is misleading. In financial services (such as banking and portfolio management) there has been enormous growth in assets managed per employee. In the management of real property, levels and rates of growth of income per worker are a function of changes in the mix of property income and accounting conventions.

Sector VIII: Personal and Business Services

The services sector includes economic activities with disparate reproducible capital/worker and educational capital/worker ratios and is fraught with measurement problems regarding output. At one end of the service sector are low-skilled domestic workers while at the other end of the sector are doctors, lawyers, and accountants. Because the services rendered in this sector are measured in terms of their labor costs of production, changes in value added per worker in this sector reflect changes in the composition of activities and labor force. Further, because there is relatively less physical capital employed in this sector, per worker output may appear low with respect to other sectors even when wages are considerably higher. The high incomes of professionals like doctors and lawyers reflect the considerable investment in the human capital that they bring to employment.

The largest growth area in the service sector is privately provided health services. (Public hospitals are in the government sector.) The measured decline in productivity in health services during the decade of the 1980s was 20 percent—an unlikely outcome in a period in which medical advances were increasing health and health maintenance organizations (HMOs) were increasing efficiency.

Another rapidly growing area in the services sector is business services. When agriculture (I), or petroleum (II) or construction (III) or manufacturing (IV) or transportation (V) or distribution (VI) or financial services (VII) sector firms purchase accounting or legal or consulting or maintenance or temporary personnel services from Sector VIII service firms, they decrease the employment and value added reported in their own sector and transfer them to Sector VIII. Temporary personnel services are one of the most rapidly growing employers in the economy. When they "rent" workers to a manufacturer, the rental revenues are recorded in the service sector, and in the manufacturing sector the number of employees is decreased. But both employees of the firm and rented workers are producing with the capital equipment supplied by the firm and the smaller number of permanent employees of the manufacturing sector is recorded as having an increase in output per worker.

Sector IX: Government Services

Output in the government sector includes federal, state, and local government expenditures on the provision of services—national defense and local police, the administration of Social Security and welfare offices, judiciary and prisons, public schools and public hospitals. Output—value added—as in other sectors subtracts government purchases of goods and services (paper and electricity) from other sectors, but excludes capital costs and includes only the compensation (including benefits) of government employees.   Since the accounting conventions for government agencies do not account for capital services, the value added per government employee is not increased by the capital costs of government agencies. This tends to reduce the size of output per worker in this sector. As in other sectors it is not an indication of relative wages. Government employees tend to have wages reflecting their education levels and years of experience.

Contrary to popular myth, federal employment has been declining as a share of the labor force over the past half-century. The increase in the share of government employment in the labor force has been at the state and local level. The primary sources of the increase in the ratio of government employment/total employment in the labor force until 1980 were from public employees in education and health services. Government employment declined as a proportion of the labor force between 1980 and 1990.

Since value added per employee in the public sector reflects only wage and benefit costs, changes in the relative wages of government employees primarily reflect changes in their occupational distribution; the lack of any measured growth in output per employee reflects the measurement convention, which equates unobserved value-added output with employee costs. It may or may not be true that government is less efficient than the private sector, but the figures presented reflect only expenditures and do not reveal any information about "real" changes (services rendered per employee) as opposed to the measured changes in output per worker.

PART II: CHANGING SHARES OF GDP AND EMPLOYMENT

The evidence on the changing relative importance of the nine sectors in the economy is presented in graphic form in Text Graphs 5.1 and 5.2 (and in tabular form in Appendix Tables 5.1 and 5.2).

Text Graph 5.1
Sectoral Shares of GDP

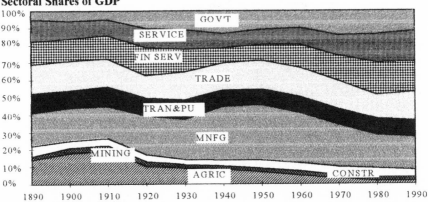

Sectoral shares of GDP change over time; agriculture decreased after World War I; manufacturing peaked after World War II; services have been increasing as a share of the economy.

Source: Author. See Appendix Table 5.1

Changes in the Structure of Output

Text Graph 5.1 exhibits the changes that have occurred in the sectoral structure of output (the proportion of value-added GDP in each sector) over the past century. It should be noted that, in addition to changes in relative size of sectors exhibited in the graph, all of the sectors have undergone enormous changes in their internal composition. For example, mining started out dominated by coal and ends up being dominated by petroleum. The manufacturing sector started out with lumber and ended up with computers. The service sector started out with household domestics and ends up with accountants, doctors, and lawyers.

The decline in relative size of the agricultural sector has been occurring since the eighteenth century. At the end of the nineteenth century and the beginning of the twentieth century, the relative decline was temporarily delayed by the enormous expansion of agricultural exports. The contraction of the agricultural sector resumed with the loss of international markets at the beginning of World War I and, by the end of the twentieth century, accounted for less than 2 percent of the value-added in GDP. As noted earlier, part of the decline in its relative size is a result of the increasing use of purchased inputs from other sectors.

Manufacturing grew in relative size from the beginning of the century, peaked in 1950, and declined to its present size of just under a quarter of the economy's output. It is important to realize that productivity change has been so rapid in the manufacturing sector that relative prices have fallen and reduced the relative size of this sector in the value of total output.[11] Mining and construction have always been relatively small sectors. The decline in the relative importance of mining is explained by the relative (and absolute) decline, first of coal mining and then of domestic petroleum production.

The transportation, communication, and public utilities sector includes road, rail, air, and ocean transportation and privately owned telephone, electricity, water, and natural gas distribution systems. The relative share of output in this sector has stayed fairly constant, despite large changes in the composition of output within the sector. Trade is both wholesale and retail. Specialization and the decline of household production have both increased the volume of trade. However, in both wholesale and retail trade, technological and organizational change have reduced the relative prices charged for intermediate input services and kept the relative GDP output of the sectors relatively constant.

The financial services sector includes such obvious categories as banking, insurance, real estate and stock brokerage. Less obviously, it includes the management of real property, including the imputed rental value of owner-occupied dwellings. The share of financial services fell in the first half of this century and then its relative share of output more than doubled between 1940 and 1990.

The service sector accounts for the value of services provided by domestic servants, barbers, and beauticians. But it also includes the services of hospitals and physicians, lawyers, accountants, and educators who are not employed in the government sector. Its initial decline in relative size was due to the decline in (reported) domestic employment. It has more than doubled in relative size over the past half-century. Its increase in size, particularly since 1970, reflects both the changing pattern of household expenditure and the increase in transactions costs (lawyers and accountants) and "outsourcing" (temporary worker and equipment leasing firms) by the other sectors of the economy.

The government sector has been expanding throughout most of the century. As noted earlier, however, most of the relative expansion has been state and local government employmen—police and fire, water and sanitation, and increasingly educators and health service employees in government schools and health care institutions. The government sector reached a peak in relative size in 1970 and has been declining since then. That makes it difficult to blame the decreasing rate of growth in output per worker on government—at least in its effect on the purchase of services!

Text Graph 5.2
Sectoral Shares of Employment

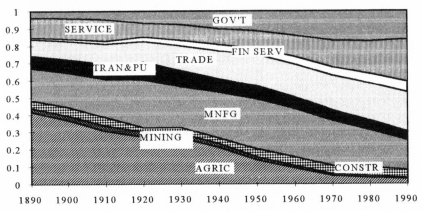

Sectoral shares of employment have changed; the share of employment in manufacturing and agriculture has declined while employment in government, services, and trade has increased.

Source: Author. See Appendix 5.2

Changes in Employment Shares

Changes in the relative share of employment (Text Graph 5.2) reflect the changing shares of GDP displayed and discussed earlier, but they also reflect the differential growth in labor productivity between sectors. For example, in 1890, agricultural employment accounted for 42 percent of employment but only 14 percent of GDP. By 1990 it accounted for 3 percent of employment and 2 percent of GDP.

The big movement in relative employment shares during the first half of the century was from agriculture to manufacturing and distribution. In agriculture rapid productivity growth was accompanied by the loss of foreign markets, a relative decline in the domestic demand for unprocessed food and fiber, and the increased use of inputs from other sectors. In manufacturing, on the other hand, productivity increased rapidly, but demand continued to grow to increase the relative share of employment in the sector. Manufacturing employment grew from 19 percent to 29 percent of the labor force between 1890 and 1950 but then shrank back to 17 percent by 1990.

In the second half of the century, the relative share of agricultural employment continued to decrease, but so did the relative share of employment in manufacturing. In the case of manufacturing, demand made a relative shift from manufactured goods to services. Trade and services both doubled their relative shares of employmen, but in both sectors the increase in part-time workers increased the number of workers more than hours worked. Employment share in the government sector continued to increase in relative size until the decade ending in 1980.

PART III: SOURCES OF CHANGE IN OUTPUT AND EMPLOYMENT STRUCTURE

There are six sources of change in the output and employment structure of the economy that accompany and are a necessary part of economic growth:

1. Differential productivity growth increases output per worker faster in some sectors than others; for example, rapid growth in agricultural productivity has reduced the proportion of the U.S. labor force employed in agriculture.
2. Differences in productivity growth between sectors result in changes in relative prices between sectors. These changes in relative prices, in turn, can further change the relative size of sectors measured in dollars of final output. The fall in relative prices reduces the value of GDP measured in current prices. As remarked earlier, much of the relative decline in the size of the manufacturing sector represents a decrease in relative prices rather than a decrease in the volume of output. On the other hand, the government sector increases in relative size as the wages of government employees keep up with wages in the rest of the economy; but there is no change in the volume of inflation-adjusted output.
3. Changes in final demand accompany economic growth as people spend their increasing incomes in different sectors. As people grow richer, they don't eat more food; they eat a smaller volume of food, which is processed outside the household. Their expenditures on food shrink as a proportion of their expenditures as their incomes increase and the proportion of these expenditures going to the processors and preparers of food increases. A similar change occurs with clothing. Rising incomes bring about a relative decline in expenditures on goods and an increase in expenditures on services. The importance of changes in the pattern of household consumption for the sectoral composition of GDP is presented in Text Graph 5.3. The increasing role of government as a purchaser and supplier of goods and services has also changed the pattern of final demand. In the decades ending in 1950 and 1960, government purchases of weapons expanded the manufacturing sector. Over

the subsequent three decades, governments taxed an increasing share of rising household incomes to provide more education and health care and, thereby, shifted final output from manufacturing to services.

4. The increase in the international flows of goods and services are an important cause and effect of economic growth. For example, the domestic mining sector has declined in relative importance because of massive importation of petroleum. On the other hand, the agricultural sector would have declined even more had it not been for massive exports of American agricultural products. Within the manufacturing sector, the United States produces fewer cars and clothes than are consumed by the population because of imports. On the other hand, we export more airplanes and pharmaceuticals. International trade is also an important contributor to exports of financial services (commercial and investment banking, insurance) and business services (accounting, consulting, and law).

5. Changes in the age structure of the population that accompany economic growth have affected the sectoral patterns of final demand. To cite the obvious, the elderly spend more of their incomes on health care and the young spend more on education.

6. Technological and organizational change, interacting with changes in the pattern of final demand, further change the relative size of various sectors of the economy. Technological change in agriculture, for example, leads to fewer farmers producing more food because they don't need to produce the inputs that are now purchased from other sectors. This, of course, increases the size of the other sectors. Organizational change in manufacturing means that companies contract out their janitorial, food service, and legal services. They even contract out employment by hiring temporary workers from firms in the service sector and, thereby, reduce the labor force reported in their own industries.

Changes in the Pattern of Final Demand

One characteristic of economic growth is the increase in specialization of production. This means that final demand ends up as output in several sectors. As an illustration, household consumption of food has declined from 26 percent in 1910 to 16 percent of household "final" expenditure in 1990 (Text Graph 5.3). An intuitive response to changes in the pattern of consumer demand is to think that changes in demand are reflected in the sectors that seem to correspond. Thus, most of the demand for food might be expected to end up in Sector I, which includes agriculture. Farmers and fishermen actually produce (and receive) a very small part of that 16 percent of household expenditure. The farm-gate cost of the wheat in the loaf of bread is a small part of the bread's cost on the retailer's shelf. It is an even smaller part of the prepared dinner in the food retailer's freezer or in a restaurant meal.

Only a small part of the price paid by the consumer for the wheat in the loaf of bread actually goes to the value added by the farmer in Sector I. Further, as discussed earlier, "value added" within the agricultural sector comprises primarily the labor and capital costs of producing the wheat that are incurred by the farm enterprise. The farmers' costs for intermediate inputs, such as the current capital cost—interest and depreciation—of tractors, and agricultural chemicals from Sector IV, payments to distributive Sector V for transportation and communications services, to Sector VI wholesalers and retailers, Sector VII bankers and insurance providers, and Sector VIII accountants, lawyers, and other business services are all subtracted to obtain value added within the sector.

Increases in per capita real income and changes in relative prices change the pattern of household final demand. The changing pattern of consumer final expenditures on various goods and services are exhibited in Text Graph 5.3.

Text Graph 5.3
Changing Patterns of Household Consumption

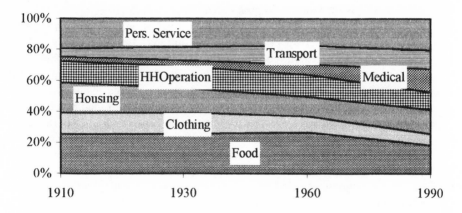

Household consumption patterns have changed over time. Decreases in the proportion of consumer expenditures on food, clothing, and household operation have been accompanied by increases in the proportion of expenditures on transportation and medical services.

Sources: Personal Consumption Expenditures for 1910 and 1930 come from U.S. Bureau of the Census, *Historical Statistics of the United States: Colonial Times to 1970* (Washington D.C.: Government Printing Office, 1975). Series G41, G470. Estimates for 1960 and 1990 come from U.S. Department of Commerce, *Survey of Current Business* (July 1961) Table 15 and (July 1991) Table 2.4.

Two factors are operational in determining changes in the pattern of consumer final expenditure: the price elasticity of demand and the income elasticity of demand. Price elasticity is a measure of the proportional change in consumption of a good that accompanies a change in its price relative to other goods. Income elasticity is a measure of the proportional change in the demand for a good or service when consumers' incomes change. To illustrate both factors, food and fuel have a relatively low price elasticity of demand. While consumers may switch from beef to chicken, or coal to natural gas because of changes in the relative prices of chicken and beef, or of coal and natural gas, the proportion of consumer expenditures going to food and fuel will not increase much over time because the relative price of all food and fuel alternatives falls as a result of productivity growth in the sectors participating in the production of these commodities. The low price elasticity of demand for these goods reflects the fact that while different types of foods and fuels may be substituted easily for other types of foods or fuels, there are virtually no substitutes for food or for energy in the consumer's needs and preferences.

Further, the income elasticity of demand for food and fuel is low— consumers do not eat significantly more food or burn more fuel as their incomes increase. They may eat better food, or more highly prepared food, or live in bigger houses that require more heat, but final consumption demand for the quantity of the food and fuel output of Sectors I and II does not increase commensurately with income growth. This is one major reason for the relative declines in the size of Sectors I and II over time. The other major contributor to the decline is the more rapid productivity growth in these sectors.

In connection with household demand for food, it is interesting to note the change in the characteristics of expenditures on food. Between 1960 and 1990 household expenditures on food consumed at restaurants (including "fast food" outlets) increased from 20 percent to 30 percent of total food expenditures. Of these expenditures, probably less than a third represented the actual cost of food (as opposed to its preparation). Further, most of the price of food purchased by restaurants or households in supermarkets would be accounted for by the value added in sectors other than agriculture. Food purchases (including alcohol and tobacco) by consumers at restaurants and supermarkets and all other vendors accounted for 16 percent of consumer expenditures in 1990 while (value added) output of the agricultural sector (including forestry and fishing) was less than 2 percent of GDP.

The biggest increase in relative consumption demand resulting from economic growth is in the demand for services. This is particularly true for medical services. Price elasticity is low (particularly because of the growing predominance of third-party payment systems), and income elasticity is high. The growth of consumer final expenditure on medical services is particularly striking after 1970. In addition to rising incomes, the increasing age of the population increased the demand for medical services. The household expenditures represented in this instance do not include the value of medical services provided by government hospitals or health-care workers.

A substantial increase took place in household consumption of transportation during the last century—from 5 percent to 12 percent of household spending. At the beginning of the century, most of the expenditures were on public transportation. At the end of the period, 90 percent of transportation expenditures by the household were on the purchase, operation, and maintenance of automobiles. (Once again, freight costs show up as part of the cost of production of commodities in all sectors.)

There is a remarkable constancy in the relative proportion of expenditure on other services. What is even more remarkable is a reasonable consistency in the distribution of expenditures within this category. In 1990, as in 1910, about 50 percent of household expenditures on services were on bank, brokerage, legal, insurance, and other services of that kind. About 10 percent were for private education, 10 percent were for barbers and beauticians, and almost 20 percent of the expenditures for "services" represented gifts to churches and charities. Households have not been increasing the proportion of their income that is directly spent on services. The increase in the size of the service sector is more attributable to the growth in the purchase of inputs from the service sector by other sectors (the purchase of banking, legal, insurance, or janitorial or equipment leasing, for example).

Households currently spend about 15 percent of disposable income on housing services—the portion of GDP is valued as actual rent paid or imputed rent for the owner-occupants of housing. Expenditures on housing first rose and then fell as a proportion of consumer expenditure. Americans currently spend a smaller proportion of their larger incomes for more and better housing than they did a century ago. The pattern of private final consumption demand does not include the services provided by public, rather than private, expenditure. Prominent in the former is the increased proportion of government expenditure on public health and public education (considered separately in chapters 7 and 8).

PART IV: THE CONSEQUENCES OF STRUCTURAL CHANGE

The changing relative sizes of the various sectors of the economy—with their different measured levels and growth rates of output per worker—would change the aggregate rate of growth of the economy even if there were no changes in intra-sector growth (the rate of growth of productivity within sectors). As mentioned in the introductory chapter, the rate of growth of output per worker within sectors, such as manufacturing, is not slowing down. But, partly because productivity growth in manufacturing has reduced the proportion of workers in manufacturing, and partly because consumers (and governments) are buying services rather than manufactures, the manufacturing sector has less overall effect on the economy. Further, the movement of workers from sectors with lower average output per worker to sectors with higher output per worker adds to—or subtracts from—the growth that results from intra-sectoral change. In the first half of the century, when farmers left cotton hoeing in Alabama to work on assembly lines in Detroit, they enjoyed large increases in their incomes. The national average income per worker also increased because workers were withdrawn from lower output sectors and added to higher output sectors. In the second half of the century, the intersectoral shifts in the labor force were more likely to represent moves out of higher output sectors and into lower output sectors.

Differences in relative output per worker, by sector, are presented in Text Table 5.1. The ratio values in the table represent the value of output per worker by sector relative to average aggregate output per worker in decennial years.

In the first half of the century, many of the intersectoral shifts in employment were from lower productivity to higher productivity sectors and this tended to equalize differences in output per worker between sectors. For example, in the decade ending in 1900, the movement of a worker from agriculture to manufacturing was from an industry where output was 49 percent of the average to another, where output was 95 percent of average.

As mentioned earlier, in the second half of the century, the shift is likely to be in the other direction. In the decade ending in 1990, the movement from manufacturing to service would entail a movement from an industry where relative output per worker was 109 percent to one where relative output was 76 percent.[12]

Text Table 5.1
Relative Output per Worker (Current $)

	I	II	III	IV	V	VI	VII	VIII	IX
Year	Agri	Min	Cons	Mnfg	T,PU	Trad	FiSer	Serv	Gov't
1900	0.49	1.20	0.82	0.95	1.30	1.57	9.50	0.84	1.46
1910	0.63	0.97	0.80	0.81	1.25	1.36	8.13	0.72	1.04
1920	0.37	0.92	1.76	0.79	0.95	1.11	6.09	1.67	1.46
1930	0.34	0.79	0.86	0.96	1.19	1.10	4.32	1.21	1.39
1940	0.40	0.88	1.09	1.14	1.24	0.96	2.37	0.94	1.28
1950	0.54	1.82	1.00	1.01	1.22	1.01	3.09	0.82	0.73
1960	0.45	2.12	0.95	1.00	1.36	0.88	3.23	0.82	0.77
1970	0.64	2.24	1.05	0.96	1.43	0.83	2.93	0.76	0.78
1980	0.69	3.81	1.03	1.00	1.63	0.74	2.81	0.73	0.69
1990	0.71	2.95	0.95	1.09	1.69	0.69	2.97	0.76	0.75

Source: Author. See Appendix Table 5.2.

Still another factor is at work here. By decreasing the differences, equalization of output per worker reduces the scope for increasing average output by shifting workers between sectors. For example, relative output in agriculture—a diminishing sector—moves toward the average while gaining sectors, such as trade, service, and government, move down. Equalization reduces the scope for further measured gains.

Intersectoral shifts in employment can also decelerate aggregate growth when workers shift from higher to lower per worker output sectors. In the last half-century, high output per worker sectors like IV (manufacturing) and V (transportation and public utilities) have declined in relative employment and the work force has shifted toward sectors with lower output per worker, such as VI (trade), VIII (service) and IX (government).

Consider how this occurs. Recorded output per worker may decrease when a worker in the manufacturing sector retires (and is not replaced) and his daughter increases the ranks of the teaching profession. Even if the daughter's wage were higher than his, the value added output of the education sector is treated largely as being equal to the teachers' salaries, whereas, in manufacturing, the computation of value added includes workers' compensation and substantial payments for the use of physical capital in the sector.

PART V: THE IMPORTANCE OF SECTORAL SHIFTS IN THE MEASURED RATE OF GROWTH OF VALUE ADDED PER WORKER IN THE ECONOMY

The rate of growth of aggregate output per worker for the economy as a whole can be attributed, conceptually, to three factors: (1) the rate of growth of output per worker within sectors—"intra-sectoral" growth, (2) changes in the relative size of employment within output sectors—"intersectoral weight shift," and (3) the shift of workers from lower to higher output sectors—"intersectoral level shift."

Decline in Relative Size of High Growth Sectors

The four sectors of the economy with high measured growth rates of output per worker (see Text Table 5.2) are sectors I, II, IV, and V, agriculture, mining, manufacturing, and transport and public utilities. In the 1950s (Appendix Table II) these four sectors accounted for half of all employment in the economy. By 1990 they account for only a quarter of the nation's labor force.

The sectors of the economy with the slowest (or negative) measured growth in per worker output are sectors VIII and IX, services and government. Growth in measured output per worker in these sectors is close to zero because the value-added output of the sectors is equal to employee compensation and any capital costs that are small in the private sector and zero—for accounting reasons—in the public sector. In 1950 these two sectors accounted for 22 percent of the labor force. By 1990 they account for 41 percent of the labor force—their relative share has doubled.

The measured growth rate of output per worker is negative in the service sector (VIII) for every decade after 1960. This measures a shift in the mix of employment (rather than productivity-based changes in output per worker) in the service sector toward part-time employees and lower-paid employees. The growth rate of output for Sector IX, government employment, is negative for every decade except for that ending in 1990, where it is 1.5 percent—presumably reflecting a change in the composition of government employment toward more highly compensated employees.

In 1950 sectors VIII and IX accounted for just less than 22 percent of the labor force. By 1970 that proportion has risen to almost a third of the labor force and by 1990 it is more than 40 percent of the labor force—it almost doubles in terms of its relative share in employment over four decades.

The diminished share of the high-productivity growth sectors in overall employment accounts for their declining contributions to the overall rate of growth in output per worker. There is no slowdown in growth within these sectors.

Sectoral Determinants of Aggregate Productivity Growth

To restate my argument, measured growth in output per worker from intra-sector growth depends upon (1) the relative size of output sectors, (2) the relative output per worker in the various output sectors, and (3) the rate of growth of output per worker within sectors. The decennial rate of growth of output per worker within the various sectors (intra-sectoral growth) and the share of total growth accounted for by intersectoral shifts is shown in Text Table 5.2. The contribution of weighted intra-sector growth by each sector to the aggregate growth rate of output per worker is shown in Text Table 5.3.

Text Table 5.2
Decennial Rates of Change in Output per Worker by Sector

Decade Ending	1960	1970	1980	1990
Deflator	58$	72$	72$	87$
Sector				
Agriculture	48	67	21	61
Mining	55	61	-30	67
Construction	8	-5	-20	-4
Manufacturing	22	32	28	36
Trans., Com.,& Pub. Util.	47	47	29	22
Wholesale. & Retail Trade	13	14	4	23
Financial Services	12	9	7	-4
Services	3	-3	-4	-9
Government	-2	-6	-11	2
Total Intra-Sector	17	18	9	13
Inter Sector Shift	4	0	-1	-5
Total	21	18	8	8

Source: Author. See Appendix 5.4.

Referring to these tables, it will be noted in Table 5.2 (bottom line) that the aggregate rate of growth in output per worker declined from 21 percent in the decade ending in 1960 to 8 percent for the decade ended in 1990. *This is the decline in output per worker that I seek to explain by structural change.*[13] Intra-sector growth in output per worker has continued to increase over the last four decades in most sectors where it can be meaningfully measured. The rate of growth of output per worker in Sector I (agriculture, forestry, and fisheries) increased from a decennial rate of 48 percent in the decade ending in 1960 to 61 percent for the decade ending in 1990. A similar record is observable for

Sector IV (manufacturing); the rate of growth of output per worker accelerates from 22 percent to 36 percent.

Total weighted intra-sector growth—even burdened by measured negative growth in heavily weighted services and government—declines by only 4 percent over four decades (third line from bottom). On the other hand, intersectoral shifts increase growth in the 1950s by 4 percent and decrease it in the 1980s by 5 percent (second line from bottom)!

Text Table 5.3
Contribution of Intra-Sector Growth to Aggregate Growth in Output per Worker

Decade Ending	1960	1970	1980	1990
Sector				
Agriculture	1.9	1.6	0.6	1.2
Mining	1.1	1.1	-0.7	1.2
Construction	0	-0.2	-0.6	-0.2
Manufacturing	6.3	8.4	7.1	6.9
Trans., Com.. & Pub. Util.	3.5	3.9	2.8	2.1
Wholesale & Retail Trade	2.1	2.3	0.6	3.6
Financial Services.	1.4	1.2	0.9	-0.6
Services	0	0	-0.4	-1.3
Government	0	0	-1	0.2
Total Intra-Sector	16.9	17.6	9.3	13.2

Source: Author: See Appendix Table 5.5.

The effect of the decline in the relative size of the high growth sectors (which affects the weighted contributions of each sector on total growth) can be seen in the changes in the contributions by each sector to aggregate growth between decades (Table 5.3). Note that a slower intra-sectoral rate of growth in Sector I (Table 5.2) contributed 1.9 percent to the aggregate growth of output per worker in the earlier decade (1960), but a faster rate of intra-sector growth in the same Sector I contributed only 1.2 percent in the later decade (1990).

For Sector IV (manufacturing) the acceleration of growth from 22 percent to 36 percent was accompanied by a contribution to total output change from 6.3 percent to only 6.9 percent—this is 6.9 percent out of the total decennial growth of 8 percent! Why? Simply because the relative size of manufacturing (and other high-measured growth output sectors of the economy) had fallen and, thereby, decreased its contribution to aggregate growth.

The Importance of Sectoral Change—A Counterfactual

Another way to think about the decline in the growth rate of aggregate labor productivity resulting from the change in the relative size of sectors is to ask what measured growth in aggregate output for the highest recent productivity growth decade (the decade ending 1960) would have been with the same intra-sectoral growth rates in each sector, but with the economic structure of the decade that ended in 1990—and vice versa.

In order to make this calculation, I substitute one decade's labor force distribution and per worker output levels for the other decade and leave the intra-sector growth rates the same. Thus, if the 1950s structure of relative output levels and employment were combined with the intra-sector growth rates of the decade ending in 1990, the aggregate intra-sector growth rate would have been 19 percent as opposed to the 13.2 percent it actually was in the decade ending 1990. If the slow-growth decade of the 1980s had had the same output structure as the high-growth 1950s, it would have had higher growth rates than the high-growth 1950s. Conversely, if the 1990 structure had been in effect in the 1950s, the intra-sectoral growth rate for the decade would have been only 11 percent, rather than its actual 17 percent. These two examples of the effect of output structure on average growth rates illustrate the importance of structural change in determining aggregate rates of growth in per worker output by changing the relative size of sectors.[14]

Productivity in the Service Sector

Text Table 5.3 exhibits the low measured rate of growth of output per worker in Sector VII (financial services), Sector VIII (services), and Sector IX (government). Text Table 5.4 demonstrates how these sectors have dragged down the growth rate of average output per worker for the economy—particularly in the decades ending in 1980 and 1990. In chapter 4, I have explained why our accounting concepts produce these measurements and why they are misleading.

The growth in productivity in the service sector is impossible to measure appropriately because the unit of personal service input and output is often the same. The inputs for an hour of legal services and the output is the same for the primary determinant, the lawyer herself. The other inputs for office space, secretaries, and computers are likely to be a small and relatively constant proportion.

What is the value or usefulness of an hour of legal services? The client doesn't value the services in terms of the number of hours billed, but NIA practices assume the value of the legal services to be equal to the cost of the services. Thus, our accounting conventions make it impossible to measure increases in the productivity of the lawyers in the service sector. Similar considerations apply to the services of physicians, accountants, and government employees. The three largest employers of the service sector are government, health care, and education. (Most employees in education and many of the employees in health care are government employees.) The proportion of government employees in the labor force has increased steadily during this century, but it reached a peak in 1980 and declined slightly thereafter (see Text Table 5.2). Most of the increase came in state and local government rather than federal employment. This largely reflects the increase in the ratio of education and health-care employment to the population as a whole.

It will be seen in chapter 8 that the ratio of students to teachers has fallen over the past century and that other expenditures per student have also risen. Coupled with the increase in the proportion of the population enrolled in school at every level, there has been a ten-fold increase in the proportion of national income going to education.

Does this mean that productivity growth in education has been negative? Yes, definitely, if the output is measured in terms of student years taught per teacher; or constant dollar expenditures per student on facilities and equipment. But not necessarily, if the output is measured in terms of the human capital necessary to maintain a high-level economy. Neither answer alleviates the fact that increased sums spent on investment in human capital through education leave a smaller proportion of income available for consumption or for other types of capital formation. It cannot be ascertained from existing accounting concepts and measures of value added in education whether there has been productivity growth in education. Further, the increased employment in the education sector reduces the labor available for potential output in other sectors.

Over the past century we have progressed from the one-room schoolhouse to the computerized classroom of the modern urban or suburban school with thousands of students and specialization by the teachers and administrative and support staff. It is technologically possible to increase the ratio of students to teachers enormously with televised lectures or computerized instruction. However, it is not clear that this application of potentially labor-saving technology will positively affect the educational outcomes of literacy, numeracy, and problem-solving skills that education is expected to develop. An apposite analogy for education of increasing capitalization and students per teacher is that of building a bigger and better bridge in the wrong place so it carries fewer vehicles where people need to go.

The workforce in health care is large and growing rapidly. Advances in scientific knowledge accompanied by technological changes in diagnostics, equipment for treatment, and pharmaceuticals have greatly increased the potential of health care to produce "wellness." The 1890 physician treating pneumonia could do little more than prescribe rest in a warm bed. The 1990 physician can administer antibiotics and cure the infection. In both cases the treatment is valued at its cost of production—the charge made for the physician's services. If output were to be valued in terms of, say, the increase in the number of quality days of life for the patient, medical services might be observed to have had a very high rate of increase in productivity.[15]

Perversely, the success of medicine in prolonging life creates a population that requires more and more medical care as older and weaker humans survive to older and older ages. As a consequence, the ratio of the health services labor force and the ratio of reproducible capital to output in health care have both increased enormously.

Does this mean a decline in productivity in this area? Maybe not, in terms of the increase in health per unit of capital and labor, but the continuing increase in the proportion of GDP spent on health care results in the transfer of income from the healthy and employed population to the sick and retired population and that legitimately contributes to the judgment of many Americans that they are working harder and enjoying less real disposable income than they did in the past.

What is the output of government employees? The value of the output of the city administrator or the state government planner or the Federal Social Security administration clerical worker are all valued in terms of the salary and benefits paid to the employee. Has the value of their output increased in real terms over time? NIA concepts do not make it possible to judge.

The service sectors have experienced similar trends to those that have marked the changes in other sectors of the economy: specialization, technological change, capitalization, the movement from household to market production, the intersectoral shift of workers—largely to the service sector— and the increase in transactions costs. But the increasing size and importance of the service sector has not been accompanied with changes in accounting conventions that would allow an estimation of the rate of change of value-added output per worker. Until new measurement concepts are developed, we do not know whether there is any real growth in output in this sector. And until we have appropriate measurement concepts, the average level of output per worker will be pulled down as the proportion of the labor force with zero or negative measured productivity growth becomes larger and larger.

SUMMARY: STRUCTURAL CHANGE AND THE DECLINE IN GROWTH

To summarize and emphasize, the rate of growth in aggregate output per worker has slowed over the past two decades because (1) the high-growth sectors were larger before 1970;and (2) because the intersectoral shifts were larger, on balance, from lower to higher output per worker sectors before 1970 and from higher to lower output per worker sectors after 1970.

For the decade ending in 1960, the 22 percent decennial growth rate in per worker output in the manufacturing sector (Table 5.2) contributed 6.3 percent—less than a third—of the total growth of labor output, 22 percent for the decade (Text Table 5.3). In the decade ending in 1990, the higher 36 percent labor output growth rate in the manufacturing sector accounts for 6.9 percent of the 8 percent growth in labor productivity for the whole labor force—almost all of it! To reiterate, the growth rate of output per worker in high measurable productivity sectors, for example, manufacturing is higher in the two decades after 1970 than before. In fact, the decennial rate of growth in output per worker in manufacturing in the decade ending in 1990 is higher than in any previous decade (Text Table 5.2). Yet, because of the diminished share of manufacturing employment and other high measured growth sectors in the total labor force, their contribution to the overall growth rate falls in absolute terms even as it rises in relative terms. It is as though we had decided to calculate the batting average of the entire team by a smaller and smaller proportion of the team and counted the rest as zeros in computing the average!

Why has there been a slowdown in growth? Growth has slowed down because of contraction in the relative size of sectors of the economy where growth is high and measurable and the increase in the relative size of the sectors of the economy where growth is inevitably slow or unmeasurable with current accounting methods or both. The slowdown in growth in output per worker can be completely explained by changes in the structure of the economy.

Why isn't "it" working? Why has the measured growth rate of the American economy slowed down? It has slowed down because of the effects of growth on changing the output and consumption structure of the economy. Explanations of the slowdown in growth that talk about decline in capital formation,or a fall in labor force quality or other factors are hard to reconcile with the facts about intra-sector productivity growth that show no decline—indeed, which show increase within sectors! I will return to these facts in chapter 9.

NOTES

1. It is useful to remember in this connection that the high salaries received by the dentist accrue to him, in part, as a result of his many years of education—a large part of the compensation is payment for the use of his "human capital."

2. Abbreviations are noted because they are employed in some tables and graphs.

3. This point has been explored in chapter 4.

4. The large number of seasonal part-time workers in agriculture, forestry, and fisheries is a partial explanation of the relatively low average output per worker in this sector.

5. Value added in this sector would be even lower if services provided below cost or at no cost by government (subsidized water for agriculture, fire-protection for forestry, Coast Guard protection for the fisheries) were attributed and subtracted from gross output for this sector.

6. The drop below trend in value added in agriculture in 1980 (reflected in 1987 prices) reflected the decline in agricultural prices in 1987 used to deflate it. The temporary upward blip above trend in mining output and employment in 1980 reflected the effects of the Iranian oil shortage in 1979–80 on drilling activity and petroleum production.

7. Low measured productivity growth in this sector is frequently cited as an example of an erroneous measurement. The measurement is not erroneous—it is misunderstood. The increase in purchased inputs from other industries reduces value added in the industry by more than the increases in capital and labor employed in the industry and the result is the slow (or no) growth in measured labor productivity in the construction industry—even though there is a fall in the relative price of such physical entities as cost per square foot of building or cost per unit of road capacity.

8. Information on the relative size and productivity growth rates in this sector is drawn from the detailed accounts of output and employment by sector in various issues of the *Survey of Current Business*.

9. The problem of determining "value added" in retailing is carried over into the construction of the consumer price index (CPI). The reduction in the retail prices of goods from a "full service" by a "discounter" are not reflected in the CPI since the assumption is made that there is a reduction of distributional services to the consumer.

10. In 1990 roughly half of the output of Sector VII, financial services, was the rental value of buildings, and half of that was the imputed rent on owner-occupied residences. If this were subtracted from the output of this sector, it would reduce output per worker in this sector by a half if all real estate management were excluded or by a quarter if the imputed rent on owner-occupied residences were excluded.

11. The magnitude of this phenomenon can be inferred from the differences in the relative value of output in this sector when expressed in prices of different years. In Appendix Table 5.3, it will be noted, for example, that the output of the manufacturing sector was 19% of GDP when expressed in 1987 prices but 24% of GDP when expressed in 1972 prices. For 1960 the relative output of the sector was 29% of GDP when expressed in 1958 prices as compared to 23% when expressed in 1972 prices.

12. The shift example should not be taken literally. It is the marginal output rather than the average output that is important.

13. The value for the decade ending in 1960 in Text Table 5.2 (21%) differs from the value presented in Text Table 3.1 (19%) because they are based on different price indexes.

14. Preliminary data on employment and output for the first six years of the decade of the 1990s indicate the continuance of the trends noted in Text Table 5.2. Output per worker in Sectors IV, V, VI, and VII actually increases over the previous decade but is, once again, dropped down by negative measured growth in services and no growth in Government.

15. The State of Oregon recently began ranking medical procedures in terms of their anticipated effects in increasing patient quality days per dollar of expenditure.

CHAPTER 6

Structural Change and the Participation Rate

> Adult women are the only demographic group whose paid labor outside
> the home advanced continually over this century.
>
> —Claudia Goldin
> *Understanding the Gender Gap* (1990)

This chapter explores and explains how the increase in the participation rate of
the population in the labor force has increased U.S. economic growth. I have
already shown (Text Table 3.2 and Text Graph 3.1) the relative importance of
the increase in the participation rate of the working-age population (16–64
years old) to the rate of growth in U.S. per capita incomes over the past half-
century. In the decades of the 1960s, 1970s, and 1980s, increases in the
participation rate of the population in the labor force accounted for about half
of the growth in per capita incomes. Indeed, on the basis of (unrealistic) *ceteris
paribus* assumptions, it could be shown that U.S. GDP in 1990 would have
been 20 percent lower than it was, had it not been for the very substantial
increase between 1950 and 1990 in the proportion of the working-age
population actually employed.[1]

However, the United States will soon not be able to enjoy the benefits of
growth in per capita incomes resulting from increasing participation rate of the
population in the labor force for the simple reason that there will be no
possibility of further increase in participation when everyone is participating!
More subtly, as the proportion of the population employed reaches
progressively higher levels, the same absolute increases in participation are
measured as smaller percentage increases. For example, the ratio of workers
to working-age population increased from .51 to .57 between 1960 and 1970
and from .64 to .70 between 1980 and 1990—the absolute increase was the
identical .06 for both decades (Appendix Table 3.3). Because of the larger base

against which the same absolute increases are compared, however, the same absolute increase in the proportion of the working-age population at work increased participation and aggregate growth in output per capita by 12 percent in the earlier decade but only 9 percent in the later decade.

CHANGES IN LABOR FORCE PARTICIPATION AND U.S. GROWTH

The participation rate—the ratio of employment/working-age population— increased from 47 percent to 70 percent between 1940 and 1990 (Appendix Table 3.3). The most important contributor to the rate of growth of the aggregate participation rate (and, consequently, the rate of growth of per capita GDP) over the past half-century has been the change in the participation rate of working-age married women in the labor force. Their participation rate has doubled, bringing about a marked increase in the growth in the labor force and, as a consequence, a much higher rate of growth of per capita output than would have been possible simply from increases in output per worker.

The enormous change in the participation rate of married women in the labor force over the past century has resulted primarily from changes in the organization of the economy—structural changes—that have been both cause and effect of economic growth. The determinants of GDP per capita (Appendix Table 3.3) show that the proportion of the working-age population to the total population has been roughly stable from 1950 to 1990. Changes within the age structure of the working-age population—an increase in the younger age groups with higher participation rates—have been slightly favorable to growth during the last quarter-century. But changes within the age structure of the working-age population will become less favorable to continued high participation rates after the turn of the twenty-first century as the population ages and the working-age population moves into older age cohorts with lower participation rates. Changes in age structure are relatively insignificant in comparison with changes in participation rates.

This chapter is organized into three main parts and a data appendix. Part I discusses the effects of the change from household to market production on measured GDP levels and growth rates. Part II presents the decennial changes in the participation rate of the population in the labor force disaggregated by age, sex, and marital status, and explains some of the economic and social forces behind the changes. Part III discusses the changes in the age structure of the population and their impact on employment.

PART I: THE NECESSARY RELATIONSHIP BETWEEN INCREASES IN PARTICIPATION IN THE LABOR FORCE AND GDP GROWTH

GDP, the measured output of goods and services, is produced by the members of the population who are employed in the market labor force. Household activities (as noted in chapter 4, and with some minor exceptions) are not included as a part of GDP for accounting reasons. The reason for the exclusion of household production from GDP is that there are no reported market transactions to provide a basis for valuation of household production.

One cause and effect of economic growth has been to shift a larger and larger proportion of every age group of the population to employment in productive activities outside the household. As examples, the farm youth gives up splitting farm-grown wood for household fuel—his family buys coal and the youth works on the production of market crops or works for wages, perhaps for a coal merchant. The urban housewife reduces time spent on food preparation and laundry at home, buys prepared foods and an automatic washer/dryer, and is employed part- or full-time in an office. Even more significantly, she sends her children to daycare and her aged parents to a retirement home so that the care of both generations of dependent populations is shifted from the household to the market economy.

The changes in the patterns of economic activity that accompany economic growth result in measured changes in output greater than the actual changes in output that occur in the production of goods and services. Workers who were formerly not counted as employed or part of the labor force are now counted as employed and part of the labor force since they are working at recorded market activities rather than household production. Laundry and eldercare are no longer done at home—where these activities were previously uncounted in production for GDP. These functions are sent out to a commercial laundry and a retirement home, and their "processing" is, therefore, counted in GDP. Further, governments can tax the wages of the persons and profits of the firms doing the laundry and retirement care!   The movement from household production to market production primarily changes the production patterns and participation rates of married women. It results in an overstatement of the real increase in GDP and output per capita because some of the increased GDP results from not measuring production that is done in households and measuring it when it is done by firms.

The acceleration of measured GDP growth from the shift from household to market production is a transitional consequence of changing economic organization and the changing economic role of women.   The acceleration of economic growth resulting from the movement from household to market production cannot happen more than once. After a car has accelerated from 40 to 50 mph, no further acceleration occurs as long as it maintains that speed. The increase in the participation rate of married women has the same effect— the growth rate of per capita income is accelerated until the new participation rate is stabilized, but then it cannot happen again.

The movement of workers from household to market production increases measured output and simultaneously increases the market labor force. The simultaneous increase of both measured output and labor force will invariably increase GDP per capita. However, the growth of average GDP per worker is also slowed by the transition, because the shift of population from household to market employment initially increases the proportion of workers with less market employment experience—and, consequently, lower productivity and wages. The immediate effect of the shift of women from household to market production reduces the rate of growth of aggregate output per worker because less experienced workers produce less, on average, than the more experienced workers who are already in the labor force. The market value of the services formerly done by households—laundry and retiree care—also tends to be lower market-valued production.

The expansion of the labor force after the "baby boom" during the decade of the 1960s by the delayed entry or re-entry of married women who were shifting from household to labor force employment simultaneously increased the participation rate and slowed the increase in the rate of growth of output per worker. The 1960s also witnessed an increase in the proportion of younger workers in the labor force that had the same effect on the change in output per worker.

Younger and less experienced workers receive lower relative wages than older and more experienced workers, whatever their education level. It is assumed, in economic analysis, that these lower relative wages reflect relative productivity. Operating on the basis of these facts about relative wages and this theoretical assumption, the increase in the proportion of younger workers and housewives returning to the labor force is an explanation of the simultaneous increase in the participation rate of the population in the labor force and the decrease in the rate of growth of output per worker.

An additional explanatory factor that is not captured by the presentation of participation rates is that part-time workers are treated the same as full-time workers as far as participation statistics are concerned. Married females are far more likely than males to work part-time rather than full-time. Thus, the increase in married female participation in the labor force has contributed to the reduction in the average hours worked, per worker, which, in turn, has the effect of reducing the rate of growth in output per worker (rather than per worker hour).

For the last four decades, the growth in output per worker hour has been greater than the growth in output per worker, reflecting the fall in the average number of hours worked (Text Tables 3.1 and 3.2 and Text Graph 1.2). The primary reason for that fall has been the increase in the proportion of part-time workers—who are disproportionately married females.

PART II: BEHIND THE AGGREGATES—UNDERSTANDING THE CHANGE IN PARTICIPATION

The aggregate participation rate of the population in the labor force has risen fairly steadily over the past century (Text Graph 6.1). There was a two-decade slackening in the increasing rate, between 1950 and 1970, coincident with the "baby boom." However, the rise in the aggregate participation ratio of the population in the labor force over the last quarter-century has been the combined result of a continuing rise in the participation rate of women, offset by a fall in the participation rate of men.

Detailed information on the changes in labor force participation rates by age, sex, and ethnicity are presented in Appendix Table 6.1, and by age, sex, and marital status in Appendix Table 6.2. Participation rates for sub-groups within these categories and in Text Graph 6.1 are presented as the proportion of an age- and sex-defined cohort of the population that is participating in the labr force (rather than employed).[2]

Text Graph 6.1
Aggregate Labor Force Participation Rates

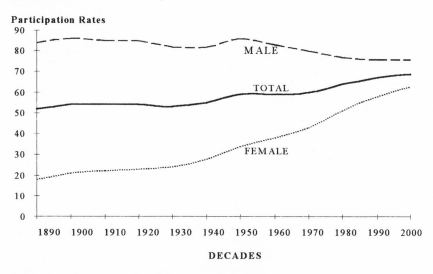

The total participation rate of the population in the labor force has risen because of rising participation by women offsetting the decline in participation by men after 1950.

Source: Author. See Appendix Table 6.1 and Appendix Note 6.1.

The rise in the aggregate participation rate for women seen in Text Graph 6.1 is the result of large increases in participation by all female age cohorts (except the sixty-five-plus age cohort). A close examination of participation rates disaggregated by age, sex, and marital status (Appendix Table 6.3), however, reveals that virtually all of the change in female participation rates has resulted from changes in the participation rates of married women, and formerly married but currently single women listed as widowed, divorced, or separated.

Text Graph 6.2 emphasizes the importance of the changing role for married women in the market labor force changing the participation rate of the total population. It presents the participation rates only for the prime working-age (25–34 years old) cohort by sex and marital status, but this age cohort is representative of the experience of other working-age cohorts. (Data for all cohorts are contained in Appendix Table 6.2.) It will be noted that the participation rates for married males are the highest, closely followed by single males and single females, and that all three groups are relatively constant during the period. All three groups have maintained high and steady participation rates over the past four decades. However, married females (and the 25–34 age group is representative of all age groups) have exhibited a huge increase in labor force participation relative to men and single women.

Text Graph 6.2
Labor Force Participation Rates of 25–34 Age Cohort by Sex and Marital Status

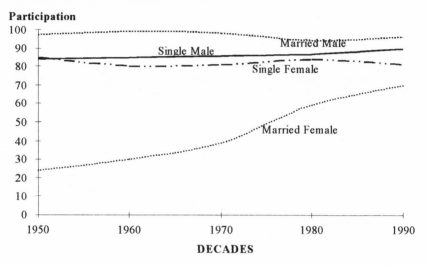

All age cohorts of married females (except sixty-five+) have increased their participation rates in the labor force.

Source: *Author*. See Appendix Table 6.2.

The increase in the participation rate of married females explains the increase in the overall partipation rate. The recent rapid rise in the participation rate of married women exhibited for one age cohort in Text Graph 6.2 is exhibited for all age cohorts of married women in Text Graph 6.3 Between 1950 and 1990 the participation rate for every age cohort of married women (except the sixty-five-plus cohort) more than doubles! (There is also a more modest increase in participation for previously married single women who are currently separated, divorced, or widowed—not shown in the graph but evident in Appendix Table 6.2.)

Text Graph 6.3
Labor Force Participation Rates of Married Females by Age Cohort

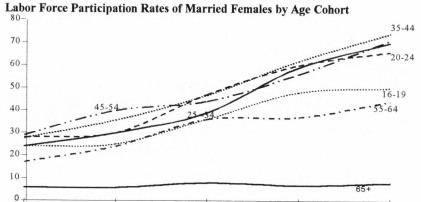

All age cohorts of married females (except sixty-five-plus) have increased their participation rates in the labor force.

Source: Author. See Appendix Table 6.2.

Text Graph 6.4
Married Male Participation Rates by Age Cohort

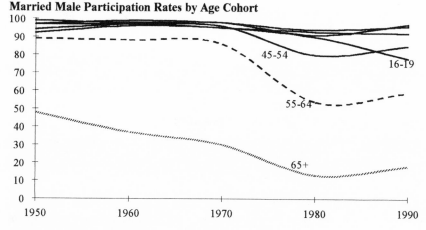

Older married males have decreased their participation in the labor force.

Source: Author. See Appendix Table 6.2.

While the increase in the participation rate of females is due to the increase in participation by married females in all age cohorts, the decline in the participation rate of men is due overwhelmingly to the drop in participation by all marital categories of men over the age of forty-five. Text Graph 6.4 (and Appendix Table 6.2) reveal that the drop in participation rates for men is greatest for married males over forty-five. (There has also been a drop in the participation rate for married males aged 16–19—a very small group.)

Changes in Marital Status and Changes in Participation

In addition to the changes in the participation rates of married men and married women in the labor force over the past several decades, there have been substantial changes in the proportion of the population that is married. The reduction in the married proportion of the female population has further contributed to the increase in the overall participation rate for women because single women are more likely to participate in the labor force than married women in the same age cohort. The proportion of the married female population in various age cohorts is shown below in Text Graph 6.5.

Text Graph 6.5
Proportion of Married Females by Age Cohort

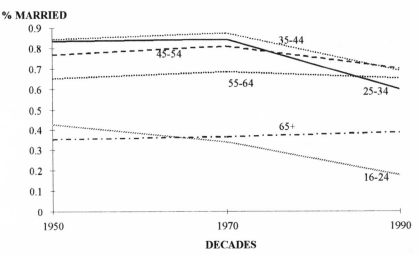

The proportion of married females in age cohorts younger than 45 has decreased over the past two decades.

Source: Author. See Appendix Note 6.1.

It will be noted that the steepest declines in the proportion of married females come in the younger age cohorts. Married males participate in the labor force at only a slightly higher rate than unmarried males, so the decline in the proportion of the married male population (not shown in Graph 6.4) has tended to depress male participation rates only slightly. (The proportion of married males over age sixty-five has increased—there are fewer widows and widowers—but members of this group are not major participators in the labor force.)

To summarize the disaggregated evidence on changes in participation rates, increases in the participation rates of married women, and changes in the marital status of the female population have been very substantial over the past century. The large increases in the participation rates of married women and the increase in the proportion of unmarried women have offset the substantial reduction in the participation rates of older men to enable the aggregate participation to continue to increase.

Explanations of Changes in Labor Force Participation

What has caused the substantial changes in the participation rates of married women and older men in the labor force over the past century? My explanation emphasizes economic changes but, of course, these economic changes are both cause and effect of changing social values.

The Economic Explanation

Let us begin with a purely economic explanation of the huge increase in the participation of married women in the labor force. The economic explanation for the shift of married women from household production of services to market employment emphasizes changes in the comparative advantage of market production versus household production. For married women the alternative of market employment, rather than housekeeping and care of dependent children and the elderly, can be explained by changes in relative costs and wages for employment outside the household relative to the value of home production and "personal time."[3]

The farm wife of a century ago worked from dawn to dusk—but was not recognized in national income statistics as a contributor to GDP. She cared for small children and elderly parents, baked bread and preserved homegrown vegetables and fruits, cleaned the house with broom and mop, and did the laundry on a washboard. The urban housewife of today works eight hours in an office and is recorded as a participant in the labor force and a producer of GDP. She takes her children to daycare and her elderly parent is in a retirement home. She buys prepared foods, uses power equipment to do the housework and laundry, or employs a cleaning service and commercial laundry. She makes these choices for the use of her time because they are economically advantageous and socially acceptable Both of those reasons are important and they are interdependent.

It must be economically attractive for married women to leave household production to participate in the market labor force. The process of economic growth—specialization in, and capitalization of housekeeping and care of dependents—changes the economics of household versus market production of services. It should be noted, at the outset, that a married woman who runs a household rather than working for an outside employer supplies several kinds of services—household operation and the care of the dependent young or elderly. For household operation economic change reduces the cost of the capital goods—washing machines, vacuum cleaners, refrigerators, and furnaces—necessary for running a household relative to the cost of her labor services, which are the alternative. It is important to note the relative costs, because it pays to substitute capital for labor only if the cost of capital is less than the opportunity cost of the labor.

Suppose the capital costs (interest and depreciation on the purchase price of a washing machine) amount to $1 per hour of operation. It pays to use the washing machine only if it saves an hour of work and the work is worth at least $1 per hour. Economic growth promotes the substitution of capital for labor both by reducing the capital costs of labor-saving machinery and by increasing the opportunity cost of the labor saved by the substitution of capital. The household will buy the washer only if the time saved is worth $1 per hour in other activities and, critically, if the household worker (usually a married woman) could earn more than $1 per hour from employment outside the household.[4]   Alternatively, the household will send out the washing to a commercial laundry if the cost of having the laundry do it is less than the opportunity cost of having a household worker do it. This will occur when the laundry lowers costs as a result of specialization, fuller utilization, and capitalization, and when the opportunity cost of the household worker rises.

Thus, as a first order of explanation, the shift of production from household production to market production is the consequence of both the increase in the wages of women outside the household and the relative reduction in costs in the market sector for the provision of goods and services formerly produced by the household.

It bears emphasis that urbanization and the reduction in transportation costs plays an important part in the shift from household to market production. A farm wife can't work for wages off the farm if the transportation costs to employment are high. A commercial laundry can only lower its costs if it reaps the benefits of specialization, full utilization, and capitalization by having a large market and low transportation costs borne by the laundry, directly, or by the customers who bring in the laundry and then pick it up.

The second important element of household production of services is the changing economics of the care of young children and the elderly. For both the care of children and the elderly. there are two separate economic reasons that shift care from the home to market institutions—time utilization and third-party payment.

One woman can care for more than one child or elderly dependent along with household management—particularly if capital goods have reduced the labor time necessary for food preparation, laundry, cleaning, and so on. However, for children to be sent to daycare or elderly dependents to be sent for outside care, the working mother must be able to earn more in wages (after taxes and employment related costs for travel, clothing, and so forth) than the cost of daycare or eldercare for it to be economically advantageous to work rather than caring for dependents at home. Leaving aside the issue of capital costs of the daycare or eldercare facility, the woman who sends her children or elder dependents to outside care must earn more than the per-child or per-elder cost of the caregiver at the commercial daycare or eldercare facility, multiplied by the number of dependents sent to daycare or eldercare. It needs to be borne in mind that the rise in real wages for women that accompanies economic growth raises the cost of caregivers at the same time that it raises the wages of working mothers.

The advantage of specialization in market employment rather than home care of children must also be great enough to cover the transportation costs and the taxes subtracted from the incomes of the mother and the daycare worker.[5] There is little, if any, immediate economic advantage for low-paid women to work and send their children to daycare. (There may be a longer run social advantage if the work increases their earning capacity in the future.) Women's choice to participate in the market labor force rather than caring for children at home depends upon both the increase in female wages and the reduction in the number of children and elderly dependents cared for per woman.

However, there is an additional factor, here—third-party payment. The "Great Society" programs of 1965 instituted Medicare and Medicaid to pay for the care of the elderly and removed some of the economic necessity for their care at home. Further, the subsidized care of the elderly is available outside the home but not in households. Thus, a change in social policy has reinforced the incentives for market rather than household provision of services for the care of the elderly dependent, and contributed to an increase in the participation rate of females in the labor force. There have been lesser changes in social policy in the subsidization of daycare outside the home that have had a similar effect in increasing the economic advantages for women to work outside the home rather than in caring for children within the household.

A popular explanation for increased female participation in the labor force is that it has become "necessary" for married women to work in order to maintain an acceptable standard of living (because of the slow or negative growth in disposable incomes for married males during the last two decades). An alternative way of explaining the change in participation, however, is that women are expressing a preference for more income. The choice could be also be interpreted as a preference for more income rather than more personal time—meaning that married women have revealed their preference for more money income rather than the increased personal time available to them from the mechanization of household activities. It can be interpreted as the "substitution effect" resulting from the decreased comparative advantage from household production of goods and services (because of the declining price of market provision relative to household production of prepared foods, fast food, laundry, child care, and so on).

Many contemporary women complain that the cost of attaining their desired (material) standard of living is the sacrifice of personal time at home. The evidence indicates that working women have sacrificed personal time by continuing to devote a number of hours to household maintenance in addition to the time spent in market employment.[6] Some survey data has shown that women working full-time continue to spend twenty or more hours per week on housework.

The growth in productivity per worker hour allows for the benefits of growth to be enjoyed in terms of more personal time or more goods. For the labor force as a whole, a substantial part of the gains in output per worker hour over the last century have been used to shorten the number of hours worked. The benefits of growth in output per worker have been taken as greater personal time—the "wealth effect" has played an important part in decisions about how to use one's time.

As household managers women have also had a choice about how to allocate the gains in household efficiency between employment and personal time. They have chosen to work more hours outside the home for more goods rather than opting for more personal time. To use economic terminology, the "substitution effect"—the higher opportunity cost of personal time relative to labor force wages—has led women to work more hours.

The increase in the relative value of market wages to household employment is an economist's explanation of the increased participation of women in employment outside the home. The change in relative financial returns from household and market employment has been accompanied by a steady increase in the proportion of women in the working-age cohorts working outside the home.

This process was accelerated by the decrease in the relative size of the farm population, where women played an integral part in market production but were not counted as part of the labor force. The urbanization of the population has decreased time and transportation costs relative to wages for working outside the home or farm. Sectoral change in employment has increased the proportion of employment involving manual dexterity or mental activity—areas of employment in which women have a comparative advantage.

Cultural Values

Social values have also changed. There is increased social recognition and approval of women's activities outside the home relative to activities within the household. In fact, most women now feel that they have higher social status from having a career in the market labor force than they have as a "homemaker."

Divorced and single mothers are no longer socially stigmatized. These changes in social attitudes "reduce the cost" to women of working outside the home or choosing to forgo a marital relationship in which they are financially supported. There is a continuing difference of opinion among economists about the causes and extent of the "gender gap"—the difference in female/male employment and compensation.[7] The distribution of the gains from economic growth brought about, in part, by increases in female participation in the labor force is not a topic I am prepared to address in this chapter. I am confining my attention to the explanation of changes in the rate of aggregate economic growth rather than its distribution.

Future Gains in Female Participation

Can participation rates of the population in the female market labor force continue to increase and, thereby, increase the rate of growth of per capita income? Yes, but at a decreasing rate and within limits. The participation rate for any demographic group can't exceed 100 percent!   But for women of childbearing age, the participation rate can't be that high if they are to have time for childbearing and child rearing.

Between 1970 and 1980 the participation rate for twenty-five- to thirty-four-year-old married women increased from 39 percent to 59 percent—a decennial rate of increase of 51 percent (Appendix Table 6.2).   If the rate were to increase from 59 percent to 79 percent in the decade ending in 2000 (maintaining the same absolute percentage change as in the previous decade), the rate of increase would have decreased to 34 percent rather than 51 percent because of the larger base.

Suppose the participation of females were to increase from 79 percent to 100 percent, with every twenty-five- to thirty-four-year-old married woman at work—that would, indeed, give an increase of 27 percent in the participation rate—but that 27 percent is only about half the increase recorded between 1970 and 1980!   When an economy has once experienced acceleration in growth rates due to an increase in participation rates, it can't have them again!

What is an upper limit for participation rates for married women?   That depends upon demographic choices and social policy.   To maintain a population at a steady state in the long run requires 2.1 births per woman. For illustrative purposes, assume that our demographic choice was a steady-state population and our social policy encouraged mothers to take one year out of the labor force when a child was born.   Carrying out these assumptions, assume, further, that all women (not just married women) between the ages of twenty-five and thirty-four produce two children and leave the labor force for one year to bear and care for each infant, but otherwise participate in the labor force at the same rate as males.

What would be the consequences of these assumptions for participation rates? Leaving the labor force for childbearing for two years out of ten would reduce the participation rate for women by 20 percent—their rate of participation would then drop 20 percent below the rate for males of the same age cohort.

The rate for twenty-five- to thirty-four-year-old married males was 96 percent in 1990, as opposed to 70 percent for married females and 81 percent for single females in the same age cohort (Appendix Table 6.2). My example would make possible an "upper limit" of 76 percent on participation of married women—only 6 percent greater than it actually was in 1990! For single mothers in that age cohort, participation would be 101 percent—an obvious impossibility and a striking way to think about the high participation rates of single mothers!

Of course some women would choose to lower participation between the ages of sixteen and twenty-four and thirty-five and forty-four, but I think the upper limits are evident for female participation in the labor force if the population is to reproduce itself and mothers and children receive minimal pre- and post-natal care.

A primary effect of "supply side" of reduction in marginal tax rates is assumed to be an increase in the incentive to substitute work for personal time. The Reagan tax cuts of the 1980s substantially decreased the marginal tax rates on market employment. Married women's participation rates did increase in the 1980s when marginal tax rates on married couples were lowered—but so had they for previous decades when marginal tax rates were high for married women. So it is difficult to say that lower taxes increased female participation. It is ironic that the same political group that favors tax-rate cuts to increase labor force participation by married women also emphasizes "family values" and making it possible for married women to stay home and raise their families!

Interestingly, participation rates for married males in older age brackets did reverse in the 1980s relative to their fall in the higher marginal tax 1970s. Thus, one could say that supply-side economics did have an effect in increasing participation rates and, thereby, economic growth in the 1980s.[8]

The Participation Rate of Older Males

If it were a matter of public policy to increase the participation rate of the population in the labor force, future increases would probably have to come from the category of older married males. Between 1950 and 1990, the participation rate for married males, ages fifty-five to sixty-four, fell from 89 percent to 59 percent. For married males sixty-five years and older, it fell from 30 percent to 18 percent (Appendix Table 6.2).

Early retirement has not come about because the physical demands of work are becoming greater—during this period the male labor force shifted from field, factory, and mine to offices and other less physically taxing employment. The earlier retirement of men has been the result of more generous private and public retirement provisions. (Part of these have been subsidized by the increased participation rate of females.)

The participation rate decision by older males can be economically explained by the retiree's choice between the net benefits from continued work or retirement. The older worker makes a choice between the net benefit of continued employment—the after-tax and after-employment-related expense net income and the after-tax income from a private pension and Social Security.[9]

Increases in pension benefits and Social Security and the guarantee of medical coverage in retirement by Medicare have decreased the anticipated net benefits for continuing to work until age sixty-five for many older workers. At the same time, private sector employers consider the higher pay and benefits of older workers relative to their perceived productivity and decide that they could get the job done more cheaply by younger workers. The decrease in participation rates by the older population is an inevitable consequence of decreasing the gap between what are perceived to be the net benefits from employment and what will be received by public or private transfer of funds from the employed to the retired population.

There is an equity choice for every society concerning the level of income and public medical expenditures for the retired population. I do not intend to prescribe what that level should be. However, it is a matter of arithmetic to recognize that the level and rate of growth of a society's income are affected by the participation rates of the population in the labor force. Over the past two decades, the participation rates of the older male population have been falling in response to changes in social provisions for the retired population that are paid for by the working generation. I will return to some of these questions in chapter 7.

PART III: PARTICIPATION RATES AND THE AGE STRUCTURE OF THE POPULATION

Participation rates in the labor force are closely related to age, and, consequently, changes in the relative size of working-age cohorts have had a small positive effect over the past two decades on overall participation rates. As noted in the preceding section, participation rates within age cohorts are strongly affected by changing social roles for women and by changing trends in education and retirement. These changes in work and retirement patterns, in turn, are the effects of economic growth on lifetime patterns. Thus, economic growth has cybernetic (feedback) effects on economic growth through changes in the age structure and participation rates of the population.

Text Graph 6.6
The Changing Age Structure of the Population

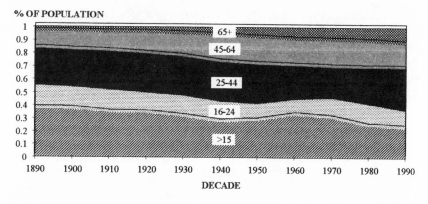

The older population has increased steadily during the twentieth century while the "baby boom" temporarily increased the younger population between 1940 and 1970.

Source: Author. See Appendix Note 6.1.

Text Graph 6.6 exhibits the changes in the age structure of the population over the past century. I have broken the working-age population into three age groups. The group aged from sixteen to twenty-four years is in the labor force but has tended to have lower and part-time participation while staying in school.   The twenty-five- to forty-four-year age group has the highest participation rates.   The forty-five- to sixty-five-year age group has witnessed declining participation rates for men over the last two decades.

Two basic factors have determined the age structure of the American population over the past century: (1) the secular fall in the birth rate (with a temporary contrary movement in the post–World War II baby boom), and (2) the secular increase in the life expectancy of the population. The effects of these two factors can be seen in Text Graph 6.6.

The decline in the birth rate—an effect of economic growth—has increased the average age of the population and the proportion of the population in working-age cohorts. Its effect in decreasing the relative size of the ages zero-to-fifteen pre-labor force population cohort (except during the post–World War II baby boom) is shown in the graph. The combined effects of the decline in the birth rate and death rate can be seen in the steady increase of the aged sixty-five-plus post-labor-force age cohorts.

Over the course of the past century, there has been a steady increase in the relative size of the age cohorts with the highest labor force participation rate—the twenty-five to sixty-five-year age groups—except for the decades ending in 1960 and 1970. Over the past two decades, there has been a dramatic increase in the proportion of the sixteen- to forty-five-year age cohort in the full-time labor force.

The U.S. birth rate fell throughout the nineteenth century and up until the 1940 census. The effect of this fall was to steadily decrease the relative size of the younger age groups and increase the relative size of the older age groups (Text Graph 6.5).   The effect of the falling birth rate on age structure was further augmented by the fall in the mortality rate that increased the number of survivors from each age group into the next.

A full explanation of the secular decline in the birth rate is outside the scope of this enquiry.[10] An economic explanation of the fall in the birth rate would emphasize the improved opportunities and increased wages for female employment outside the home that increases the opportunity cost for women to bear and raise children. This is inferred to produce a conscious decision by women to restrict births in order to increase labor force participation.

The falling birth rate is also a rational societal response to a falling infant mortality rate, since fewer births are needed to ensure that a desired number of children survives into adulthood. (The infant mortality rate has fallen from more than 10 percent to 1 percent over the past century.) The falling infant mortality rate, in turn, may be attributed to improved nutrition, sanitation, and medical care—all of which are effects of economic growth on demography.

The increase in the relative size of the labor force population cohort has also been increased at the start and end of the century by immigration which has tended to be concentrated among working-age immigrants.

Immigration into the United States is the combined effect of "push" factors in countries of provenience and "pull" factors in the United States. Pre–World War I immigration came largely from Europe and was restricted after 1922 by the McCarran Act. Post–1970 immigration resulted from liberalized immigration laws in the 1960s, together with a huge surge in illegal immigration, and has come largely from Central America and Asia. In the last two decades, immigration has swelled the working-age population and labor force. The higher birth rates of immigrants has also raised the aggregate birth rate. Immigration laws and their enforcement are policy variables that powerfully affect the age structure of the population and the growth of the labor force with consequences for economic growth.

The declines in mortality and morbidity, which increase life expectancy, and the proportion of the population in older age groups are also consequences of the improved nutrition, sanitation, and medical care that are attributable to economic growth (Robert Fogel, 1986).

RETROSPECT AND PROSPECT

Over the past century economic growth has shifted economic activity from the household to the market. The labor market counterpart of this shift has been the shift of married women from the household economy to the market economy. This has accelerated the rate of growth of measured GDP/population—or per capita income. We cannot sustain the increase in the ratio of the labor force/population of the last century that has come primarily from the changing role of women in a changing economy. The shift of married women from the household economy to the market economy increased growth rates on a one-time basis. We cannot see that fortunate contribution to economic growth continue unless women choose to give even less time to bear and care for children or the birth rate of the resident population falls below the rate necessary to maintain a zero-growth population. (That, of course could happen, as it has in several European countries.) But after two decades of favorable effects on income through a further small rise in the participation rate of women, the consequence of declining population would have severe adverse effects on participation rates as the population aged after several decades.

We have also had the once-and-for-all benefits of the demographic transition on the age structure of the population. As a first approximation, it is useful to think of the population between ages twenty-five and fifty-four as the prime working-age population. The effects of economic growth on the birth and death rates initially increase the relative size of this age cohort relative to the total population. As the proportion of population between these ages increases, it has the effect of increasing the participation rate of the labor force. The increase in the relative size of this age cohort prior to 1950, and again from 1970 to 1999, had a one-time effect in increasing the participation rate of the population in the labor force. We will not have the benefit of that increase again. Rather, as the population ages the proportion of the population in the prime working-age will diminish and, as a result, decrease the participation rate of the population in the labor force. We have reached the stage in our economic history where demographic changes will work against—rather than in favor of—further growth in participation rate and per capita incomes.

NOTES

1. This contrast is based on taking the actual age structure of the population in 1990 and asking what proportion of the working-age population would be employed in 1990 if the 1990 population participated in employment at the participation rates that prevailed in 1950. Of course, this contrast assumes everything else remains constant, which it never is in the real world!

2. (The concept of *participation—labor force/population*—is different from the concept of employed population/working-age population presented in Appendix Table 3.3. Here it is labor force, rather than actual employment, which is in the numerator and the population sixteen-plus (rather than the population 16–64), which is in the denominator.

Thus, in Appendix Table 6.1 the participation rate for both sexes rises from 59 percent to 67 percent between 1950 and 1990, while the employment/working-age ratio rises from 54 percent to 70 percent in Appendix Table III.3. Both the numerator and denominator concepts are different. I used employment in chapter 3 rather than labor force—because the former can be observed, while the latter is a matter of definition from changing questionnaires. I am using the Labor Department's changing definitions of labor force in this chapter because those are the data available.

3. The conventional economic term is not personal time but "leisure." Leisure seems a particularly inappropriate term for farm or household labor so I have substituted another term.

4. There is also a utilization constraint on the substitution of capital for labor. It is economically advantageous to substitute the capital for labor only when the capital is used to a certain proportion of its capacity.

5. There is substantial evidence that the physical affection and emotional stimulation given to young children is a significant element in their development. Thus, to the extent that home care gives more and better human attention to young children than daycare, daycare may reduce the development of human capital.

6. Juliet Schor, *The Overworked American: The Unexpected Decline of Leisure.* New York: Basic Books, 1991.

7. The arguments and evidence are assayed in Claudia Goldin, *Understanding the Gender Gap: An Economic History of American Women.* (New York: Oxford University Press. 1990).

8. The big increase in participation rates for males, during the 1980s relative to the 1970s, was for black males whose participation rates rose from 59.9 percent to 71.6 percent, while the corresponding rates for white males fell from 80 percent to 77 percent. (See Appendix Table 6.1). Whether this represented a change in employment behavior or a change in the definition of "participation" or "seeking employment" in response to unemployment benefits or welfare eligibility, I cannot say.

9.   The economic incentives for early retirement and their relationship to participation rates by older males are forcefully presented in Jonathan Gruber and David Wise (1998).

10. The foremost economic demographer of American economic history, Richard Easterlin (1968,1980), has explored and explained the effect of immigration on the United States in the 1870–1940 period. From 1870 to 1914 immigration increased the relative size of the working-age population and employment/working-age population because immigrants were largely concentrated in the sixteen- to thirty-five-age group and there was a disproportionate number of males in the immigrant population.

The sharp reduction of immigration in the interwar years tended to reduce the ratio of working-age population/total population. The decline in the proportion of the foreign born population, coupled with the movement of population from farm to city, the depression of the 1930s and World War II lowered the birth rate from 1925 to 1945. The reaction to this, according to Easterlin, was the compensatory increase in the birth rate during the "baby boom" from 1945 to 1965. The birth rate declined from 25.1 per thousand population in 1925 to 18.8 in 1938 before rising to a high of 25.3 in 1957. By 1968 it had declined below its 1938 low.

CHAPTER 7

Transfers to the Older Generation: Taxes and Saving

> Government is not the problem, and government is not the solution. We, the American people...are the solution. (We want) a nation where our grandparents have secure retirement and health care, and our grandchildren know we have made the reforms necessary to sustain those benefits for their time.
>
> —William Jefferson Clinton, Second Inaugural Address (1997)

> For every complex problem there is a simple solution—and it is wrong.
>
> —Anonymous

As we "cross the bridge into the twenty-first century" (to quote Democratic Party campaign rhetoric in 1996), the effects of successful economic growth have brought intergenerational equity issues to the fore. Because successful economic growth has increased life expectancy, the share of national income allocated to the quality of life of the larger and longer-lived retired population must expand. Because the creation of a post-industrial, knowledge-based society has increased the human capital requirements of the population, expenditures on education must increase. These increased demands from dependent generations can only be satisfied by the transfer of income from the working population to the generations being educated in their youth and maintained in their retirement.

As a consequence, the employed generation will be subject to rising transfer requirements from both the younger and older generations. Coupled with the projected decline in growth in per capita GDP, explained in chapters 5 and 6, that will reduce the rate of growth if not absolute consumption level of the working population in the first decade of the twenty-first century. Grandchildren and grandparents are going to be competing for transfers from the employed population.

Transferring incomes from working generations to the younger and older generations without stress between generations has never been simple; but it was easier in earlier decades of the twentieth century because of more rapid economic growth and more favorable demographic factors than we will experience in the future. The simultaneous slowdown in growth in per capita income and the increase in the proportion of national income that will need to be transferred from the working population to the dependent populations of young and old in the twenty-first century will mean that the disposable incomes of working taxpayers are going to be stagnant at best and declining at worst. Understanding the causes of the phenomenon will not change it, but understanding how structural changes have affected "the way it worked, and why it doesn't" with respect to increasing intergenerational transfers may make them easier to accept.

WHY IT WAS EASIER IN THE TWENTIETH CENTURY

In the twentieth century rapid growth in per worker incomes eased the transfer problem because it was easier to raise taxes on rising real incomes—to cut smaller shares of a rapidly expanding pie. In the twenty-first century, however, cutting smaller shares from the same size pie will make it more difficult to accept some of the intergenerational choices we made more readily in the past—when growth in income was more rapid and demographic trends were beneficent.

The favorable phase of economic growth is over and done. During the first half of the twentieth century, growth in output per worker was accelerated by structural change in the composition of output. During the second half of the century, productivity growth was decelerated by structural change, but the effects of the productivity slowdown were offset by the increase in the participation rate of the population in the labor force.

The deceleration of productivity growth due to structural change will continue and, as argued in chapter 5, measured growth in output per worker will asymptotically approach a steady state. Throughout the twentieth century the increase in the participation rate of the population of the labor force leveraged increases in output per worker to sustain the growth in output per capita. But, as shown in chapter 6, at the end of the twentieth century, we cannot expect further increases in participation rates when almost the entire working–age population is engaged in the workforce.

Further, we no longer have favorable demographic shifts to postpone the problem. The long-run decline in birth and death rates that shifted a higher proportion of the population into working-age cohorts with favorable effects on growth and reductions on demographic transfers has already occurred. The next stage of demographic change will be the decrease in the size of the working population relative to the retired population. Besides further decelerating growth in per capita income by decreasing the participation rate of the population in the labor force, this change will increase the proportion of income that must be transferred from the working population to the retired population.

In addition to adjustment problems created by the fundamental changes in productivity and demography, the tensions over intergenerational distribution of income in the United States have been exacerbated by past legislative actions. The Social Security computation of individual income based on a rising covered wage and the "indexing" of benefits to an upwardly biased Consumer Price Index (CPI) in 1972 has had the effect of substantially increasing the incomes of the retired population relative to, and at the expense of, the rest of the population. Further, the governmental provision of medical treatment as an entitlement for the retired population has also burgeoned transfer spending. Past legislation has increased Social Security and Medicare/Medicaid benefits, per retiree, faster than the after-tax incomes of the working population—increasing the ratio of retiree benefits /worker incomes. This has accelerated the increase in tax rates necessary to pay for those benefits.

These are the complicating political issues that exacerbate the fundamental demographic factors that lie behind the debates on the future of the Social Security System and Medicare and Medicaid programs.[1] This is why tax rates on payroll income for Social Security and Medicare have increased rapidly over the last two decades and, if changes are not made, will approach 25 percent of payroll income by 2020 merely to maintain current ratios of average retiree benefits to average worker incomes.

It is irresponsible to frighten the population by claiming, as some "conservatives" have, that the Social Security System will be bankrupt by the time the current thirty-year-old workers are ready for retirement. But it is also irresponsible to call even a slowdown in the rate of increase in retiree benefits from Social Security and Medicare/Medicaid "cuts," as some "liberals" have done.

We have, indeed, lived through a "golden age," we have seen the luster of that age diminish over the past two decades. It is natural to regret the passage into a more difficult period in our nation's economic history. For a society with a retired population that is increasing in relative size and relative age, and a school age population that needs more years and more educational spending to merely maintain the stock of human capital necessary for high levels of production, there are no acceptable alternatives to educating the young and caring for the elderly. And there is no simple solution for balancing the wants and needs of the dependent age cohorts that are in competition for a share of the current output of the economy. But there are complex solutions.

In this chapter I will discuss transfers to the retired population and in the following one I will treat the rise in educational costs. In Part I of this chapter, I discuss the recent historical development of the social institutions for intergenerational transfers from the working to the retired population. In Part II, I discuss the nature of intergenerational transfers and some of the ethical issues that are inherent in the conflicts over the magnitude of those transfers.

In Part III, I will explain and illustrate by simulation the quantitative determinants of intergenerational transfers. I will analyze the necessary rates of transfer taxes—such as Social Security and Medicare taxes—to fund a universal pension and health-care system similar to our current Social Security/Medicare arrangements. I will also explain the social mechanisms and rates of individual saving that would be necessary to provide for "independent" retirement through individual saving and investment and the creation of private retirement annuities.

PART I: AN HISTORICAL PERSPECTIVE ON INSTITUTIONAL ALTERNATIVES FOR INTERGENERATIONAL TRANSFERS

Intergenerational transfers from the working population to the dependent young and old are inevitable in any society; however, the social institutions to accomplish the transfers vary and are shaped by social values and by the specialization of labor that accompanies economic growth. Consider the alternative social arrangements that could be used to accomplish the same economic functions in intergenerational transfers: (1) they could be personalized within a multigenerational family, (2) they could be individualized through accumulation and liquidation of claims to assets over a lifetime, or (3) they could be socialized by state support of children and the retired population through taxes levied on the incomes of the employed population for transfer to the dependent generations.

In traditional societies raising children is partially motivated by the anticipated need of the parents to have a source of income support and care in retirement. The "investment" in children has a prospective return in the children's support of their parents in the parents' dependent old age. The relatively small retired population is cared for, directly and personally, by their adult children.

It is a recent development for the retired generation of Americans to be wholly or substantially financially independent of their children. Only a small minority of the retired population is substantially or completely financially independent because of private savings. For the majority the largest part of retirement income and medical care in old age has come from governmental transfers.

The socialization of income transfers for the retired population has largely occurred during the past two decades. The great majority of retirees currently relies heavily on governmental transfers, Social Security and Medicare and Medicaid, in addition to the personal savings that have gone into pensions or other retirement assets accumulated during their working lifetimes.

In an individualized society, organized on the basis of individual private property rights in productive assets (titles to real estate, stocks, bonds, or the pension funds or insurance policies that invest in those assets), individuals would be able to maintain themselves, independent of family and government support in old age, by living on investment income and liquidating accumulated claims to income-producing assets.

In nineteenth- and early twentieth-century America, much of the saving (and simultaneous investment) that took place resulted from the purchase and building of houses, the improvement of farms, and the buildup of the value of business enterprises. On retirement, these assets could be rented or sold to provide retirement income from the proceeds. One variant of intergenerational transfers occurs when parents are partially or fully maintained by their children during their retirement years on the explicit or implicit promise of inheritance of their parents' accumulated stock of capital assets when their parents die.

Another current variant for intergenerational transfers is unfunded or underfunded pensions or medical insurance for retirees. But private or public pension systems that are underfunded must use current income to finance the pensions or costs of medical care of retirees. This reduces income available for current employees. For example, USX (formerly U.S. Steel) currently has five retirees drawing medical benefits for every active employee of the corporation. Current employees (or customers or shareholders) implicitly finance former employees who are drawing current benefits from underfunded pension systems.

Private or public employee defined-benefit pensions that are not fully funded on the basis of their actuarial liabilities lead to nongovernmental intergenerational transfers. Underfunded pension systems place a burden on the current generation of workers, taxpayers, and/or stockholders in a particular private firm or public employer for the support of the previous generation of employees who are the current generation of retirees. The benefits of underfunding the current generation of retirees also accrued to the previous generation of employees, taxpayers, and/or stockholders.[2]

The United States is presently organized to provide intergenerational transfers from current output to the retired population through all of the three modes mentioned—through intergenerational family transfers, through individual and independent saving and dis-saving, and through governmental transfers. Intergenerational transfers to the young and old have always occurred in every society. What is new, in our time, are the changes in the institutional arrangements for those transfers and the increase in their magnitude.

When Social Security was introduced in the United States in 1935 as part of the "New Deal," only 7 percent of the population lived beyond the Social Security retirement age of sixty-five. And for those who did live past sixty-five, their Social Security pension was a smaller percentage of the pre-retirement average wage than it is currently.[3]

A half-century ago more than twenty workers paid into the Social Security fund for every worker drawing out funds. Currently there are five. Equally important in determining the magnitude of Social Security taxes necessary to fund Social Security payments, the average Social Security benefits have increased relative to the average wages that are taxed to support the system. As a consequence, FICA contributions have risen from 1 percent at the inception of the program to over 12 percent of base wages by 1995.[4]

Only three decades ago there was no Medicare to pay the medical bills of the retired population. Medicare was instituted in 1965 as a part of Lyndon Johnson's "Great Society Program" with a 1 percent payroll tax to support it. Over three decades the Medicare tax rate has trebled to 2.9 percent while the proportion of copayments from retirees has remained constant, despite the contentious budget debates of the last decade.

The historical growth of combined payroll tax rates for Social Security and Medicare is presented in Text Graph 7.1.

Text Graph 7.1
Social Security/Medicare Tax Rates

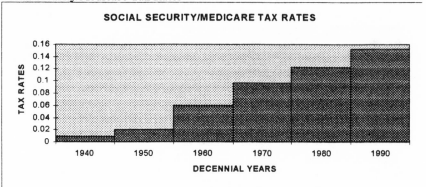

Source: Author. See Appendix 7.1

Until 1986 Social Security was basically a "pay-as-you-go" system in that taxes were periodically raised to fund current benefits. Part of the tax rate increases were due to increases resulting from demographic factors; most of the increases resulted from the increase in the ratio of benefit levels to worker wages. Text Graph 7.2 presents the trends in the factors that have determined the change in the transfer tax burden of the retired population on the working population.

Several trends are evident in Text Graph 7.2:

1. There has been a steady increase in the ratio of the retired population (aged 65-plus) to the adult population (aged 16-plus). The other way of representing this is the steady decrease in the ratio of the working-age population (aged 16 to 64) to the retired age population (aged 65-plus).
2. Because of the substantial increase in the ratio of employment to the working-age population, the ratio of employed population to the retired population has actually increased since 1960. In 1990 there was actually a higher ratio of workers paying into Social Security/Medicare than there were beneficiaries collecting benefits.

Text Graph 7.2
Historical Determinants of Transfer Burden of Retired Population

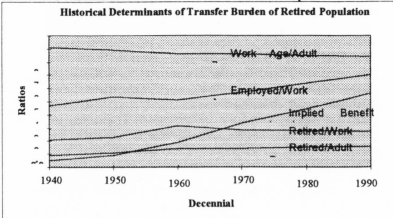

Source: Author. See Appendix 7.2.

3. The "implied benefit level" is the ratio of average Social Security and Medicare benefits relative to average worker incomes that could have been paid by Social Security and Medicare tax rates that were in effect in the various decennial years.[5] This ratio is included to emphasize that it has been increases in benefits relative to wages that have driven increases in Social Security and Medicare tax rates over the past three decades.

However, we face a new demographic situation in the current and succeeding decades. The increase in the ratio of the retired/working population, coupled with the stability or decline in the participation rate, will increase the transfer tax rate even without any increase in the ratio of retiree benefits/worker income. If the increase in the ratio of retiree benefits from Social Security/Medicare/Medicaid benefits is not halted—the necessary transfer tax rate to fund those benefits must rise even more.

The Origins of Social Security

The initial level and coverage of Social Security pensions was designed to be supplemental to private and family support of retiree dependency. The eligibility age for Social Security was set at what was then the current life expectancy level. The logic of the system, at its founding, was that participants collected benefits only if they outlived the average life expectancy—it was, implicitly, insurance against survival beyond one's assets. It was assumed that individuals would continue to save enough to support themselves for a normal life span and the state supplement would be available only to those who lived beyond it. The extension of Social Security to provide survivors' benefits to widows and orphans of those covered by Social Security was an extension of the idea of government-provided insurance that had its roots in Federal coverage of the widows and orphans of men who served in the armed services. The provision, increase, and extension of benefits until the 1960s were justified to the public as extensions and supplements to intergenerational family transfers and individual saving for old age.

Enlargement and Extension

The proportion of the labor force covered by Social Security was increased in the 1940s and 1950s and the level of benefits was substantially increased as part of the "War on Poverty" of the Great Society programs of the 1960s. The increase in benefits per retiree in the program was implemented after two decades of rapid growth in productivity and income per worker that were optimistically projected to continue indefinitely. The increase in benefit levels also coincided with the large increase in the participation rate of the population in the labor force, which markedly increased the ratio of workers to retirees.

The Medicare legislation of the Great Society was accompanied by Medicaid—a public assistance program to provide medical coverage for the poor who were not covered by private health plans. Ironically, one of the effects of the extension of Medicaid coverage was the reduction in private medical coverage by employers of lower-paid workers.   Another unforeseen consequence of the extension of governmentally provided health insurance was that by 1995 two-thirds of the expenditures under Medicaid were going to provide nursing-home care for the retired population.

Both Medicare and Medicaid have taken increasing proportions of the Federal budget over the past two decades. States and municipalities also bear a large and increasing level of expenses in their general budgets for medical care and general assistance for the elderly.

The Indexing of Social Security

In 1972 Social Security benefits were indexed to the CPI so that inflation would not reduce the absolute level of the "real" Social Security benefits received by retirees. It was a "no-lose" guarantee that the real value of Social Security benefits could never fall below their level at retirement.

However, during the late 1970s and early 1980s, the CPI rose more rapidly than nominal wages, resulting in a decrease in "real" wages. This increased the "real" income of retirees relative to workers in before-tax terms. Additionally, the increase in Social Security and Medicare taxes to fund the increase in benefits further reduced the after-tax income of workers.[6]

As Social Security benefits became increasingly accepted as a matter of social and political policy over the past half-century, increases in the rate of payroll taxes imposed for the operation of the program could be postponed or their incidence could be "finessed" because increased tax rates only slightly diminished the rise in worker incomes.   After 1965 the rapid increase in participation rates by married females and the increase in the ratio of the working-age population to the retired population diminished the necessary increases in rates to support rising benefit levels.

Further, in the 1960s and 1970s, because the retired population was small relative to the employed population, the retired population's share of national income was very small. Even large percentage increases in this very small share of the national income going to the retired population required only a very small percentage tax increase on the large share of national income going to the employed population. So, since per worker income was rising rapidly, all that was entailed and observed by employees during the period from 1935 to 1970 was a slight reduction in the rate of growth of the disposable incomes of the working-age populations.

In the 1970s the increasing burden of social security transfers was initially lessened by the increase in the ratio of the labor force to the retired population as the "baby boomers" and their mothers increased participation rates and swelled payrolls. But then the effect of the rise in Social Security benefits through indexation and the increase in the ratio of the retired population began to make it more difficult to fund the Social Security transfers without an increase in the FICA payroll tax. The rising FICA contributions were deducted from paychecks that were stagnating, so that for some workers take-home pay was actually reduced.[7]

In the last decade of the twentieth century, it has been increasingly difficult to finesse the questions about the intergenerational distribution of income because transfer payments to the retired generation have become a larger proportion of a more slowly growing national income. In 1997 the intergenerational transfers accomplished by taxation of the employed generation through Social Security and Medicare taxes amounted to more than 15 percent (12.4% FICA plus 2.9% Medicare) of employment income. The Old Age Survivors Insurance (OASI) component of Social Security taxes has produced a surplus since 1986 that goes into the Social Security Trust Fund. Medicare taxes are partially matched by beneficiary copayments. Medicaid is financed from the general budget.

These transfer taxes have already reduced the rate of growth of disposable income for the employed population and they have contributed to the reduction of the disposable incomes of a proportion of the employed population over the last two decades of slow growth—even with a labor force that was growing relative to the retired population. In the forthcoming century the labor force will shrink relative to the retired population and this will necessitate further increases in Social Security and Medicare tax rates even without any increase in benefit levels.

Non-Federal Income Transfers

In addition to rising Social Security and Medicare tax rates on the payroll, contributions by employers to under-funded pension plans and payments of medical program premiums for both current and former employees are now shrinking the funds available to employers to meet the payroll. In discussions of the stagnation of take-home pay for the labor force, it is frequently overlooked that the payments by employers to Social Security and Medicare, and the payments by employers to pension funds and medical plans are treated as a part of employee compensation in the national accounts. But they are a part of worker compensation that does not go to the currently employed labor force. The take-home wages of the employed population are diminished by the private transfers of national income to the retired population before they are further diminished by rising Social Security and Medicare taxes!

Institutional Change

Of course, in the past, when take-home pay was a larger proportion of worker compensation and national income, the working generation helped—personally—to care for the dependent older generation. In traditional working- and middle-class families, the male worker's paycheck paid the grocery bills and medical bills for aging parents. The female caregiver's home care of the elderly prevented her working outside the home. As a result, the working class household's ability to spend on the personal consumption of the working-age population was correspondingly lower. In upper income families domestic servants cared for the elderly at the expense of the family and, frequently, without report in national income statistics.

A half-century ago the population that survived to retirement age was largely looked after by married women who raised their children for the first two decades of their marriages and then cared for surviving parents in their own homes for the next two decades before they, themselves, became dependent. Today, those women are in the market labor force—increasing GDP—but their wages, and those of their husbands, are being taxed to support the institutional care of aging parents.

Since per capita GDP has risen through increased output per worker and increased labor force participation, many workers (and social observers) want to know where the increased incomes have gone. Part of the answer is that they have gone to pay for services that were formerly provided in the home by women who now participate in the market labor force instead of devoting their labor to the household production of services for the dependent young and old.[8]

In earlier societies transfer arrangements took place between multigenerational families. The take-home paychecks of one-earner families—their after-tax income—represented a larger proportion of national income, but the proportion of that amount that the wage earners had to spend on themselves was reduced by inter-family transfers for the care of the dependent generations and by personal saving to build up a capital stock for income maintenance during an uncertain future.

Expenditures for the care of the dependent old have always reduced the income that was potentially available for personal consumption by wage earners. What has changed is the amount of the transfers and the role of the state. Today, intergenerational transfers are accomplished increasingly by the tax mechanisms of the state rather than the intergenerational family or individual saving. Further, the incentives for saving by individuals to maintain a particular income level during periods of unemployment or after retirement are diminished by the entitlement to such tax-transfers as unemployment and disability benefits, Social Security pensions, and Medicare payments for health care.

PART II: INDIVIDUALISM, DEPENDENCY, AND INTERGENERATIONAL TRANSFERS

American social and political philosophy has traditionally emphasized individual liberty and self-reliance. A fundamental premise of our system of social and economic organization, based on individual liberty and private property,[9] has been the link between individuals' production and consumption shares.

However, this theory of human behavior is incomplete because all human beings spend part of their lives dependent upon others—traditionally their parents or their children or, currently—the welfare state. Economic theories of production and distribution that emphasize workers having "property rights" in the value of what they produce ignore the problems of how much workers receive as children through transfers before they enter the workforce and how much they should receive when they have retired from the labor force. An economic theory of distribution must deal with issues of lifetime production and consumption rather than merely production and distribution within a limited time period.

Further, as a matter of intergenerational ethics, it needs to be realized that an individual who consumes more than he produces over his lifetime diminishes the share of other members of his own generation and/or the members of the next generation. In terms of reciprocity, if I, as part of the employed generation, fail to support the retired generation from my current income, I am failing to repay them for the consumption they transferred from their incomes for my support and education when I was in the dependent youth population. If I fail to support the current youth generation during their period of dependency and education, will they have the means, obligation, or the inclination to support me during my period of retired dependency?

A necessary intergenerational dependency underlies intergenerational transfers. All human lives begin in a protracted stage of dependency and, in civilized societies, most end in an extended period of dependency. By "dependency" I mean simply that dependent children and the dependent elderly rely on income support from their immediate family, or on transfer payments for their maintenance from the larger society to which they belong.

Human lives go through three definable economic periods: the dependency of youth, a period of income production and wealth formation in maturity, and the dependency and wealth consumption of retirement years. The nature of dependency is that dependents consume current economic output without currently contributing to it. As I shall explain, even retired people living on their past savings are dependent on abstention from consumption—saving—by the currently employed population.

Youth Dependency

The U.S. labor force is conventionally defined as starting at age sixteen, but few youths are fully employed and independent at that age in contemporary American society. Youth dependency typically continues until about age eighteen and may continue partially or fully into the mid-twenties if the youths continue with their education. The length of the period of youth dependency has increased markedly over the past century as child labor laws have been implemented, labor-force entry for adolescents has been postponed, and the length and intensity of education has increased.

The period of youth dependency has been lengthened by deliberate individual and societal decisions to increase the development of human capital through education. The period of dependency in the contemporary American economy has also been prolonged inadvertently by social failure to develop well-functioning institutions to integrate young people who have minimal human capital into the labor force by providing on-the-job education and training.

During the period of youth dependency, the young are supported by "transfers" from the rest of society. Their support comes either from their families or it comes from transfer payments from taxpayers. Most welfare programs—Aid For Dependent Children (AFDC), food stamps, public housing subsidies, Medicaid, and many state and local programs—are designed for dependent children and their single, care-giving mothers who are dependent on society while raising the children.

Dependent youth consume current output of the economy. They limit the potential market output of society by taking their mothers out of the labor force. Their nonparticipation in the labor force reduces the potential output that would otherwise be available for consumption by others, or for investment in physical or other kinds of capital. Even if college students take out loans to finance their tuition and living expenses to be repaid out of future personal saving from future output, the college students are socially dependent—they are currently consuming and not producing current output. The working or retired generations must reduce their own current consumption to provide the source of the loans.

Youths also receive the benefit of substantial public and private expenditures on education to increase their human capital. By consuming goods, receiving education, and not working to produce goods and services, dependent youths reduce the potential output that would otherwise be available for investment or consumption by the remainder of the population. The youth population "competes" with the retired population for transfers of income from the working generation. (The implications of the increasing proportion of national income devoted to education are considered in chapter 8.)

Retirement Dependency

In the contemporary United States, retirement is conventionally demarcated at age sixty-five. Persons are defined as part of the labor force during the age span from sixteen to sixty-four; however, labor force participation rates have been decreasing for individuals on both ends of that span extending beyond those years with diminishing frequency. Appendix Table 6.2 shows the dramatic decline over the past four decades in the participation rate of older men in the labor force.

Women typically retire earlier and participate in the labor force—working outside the home—for a shorter period of their working lives than men because they are involved in bearing and caring for children and/or personally caring for their elderly dependents. During their period of care-giving and consequent nonparticipation in the market labor force, women are economically supported by their spouses, or by the rest of society through transfer payments. While "dependent" nonparticipants in the market labor force, they are "productive." In addition to the economic value of housework, they contribute to the creation of the human capital of the young and, by caring for the elderly at home, they spare the market economy from the allocation of resources and market-recorded expense that would otherwise occur for the institutional care of the elderly.[10]

The last quarter of the twentieth century has witnessed a major change in the social and economic condition of the elderly population. They have increased in number and age and the arrangements for their maintenance have shifted from the intergenerational family to the welfare state.

Social Security and Intergenerational Transfers

Many retired Americans believe that their monthly checks from the Social Security Administration represent the repayment of the contributions they have put into the Social Security Trust Fund during their working lives. They believe that they are entitled to the benefits they take out because the source of the funds is what they put in—they regard the Social Security Trust Fund that administers the system like a savings account at a bank.

Similarly, many of the current criticisms of the operation of the system by younger working Americans stem from a belief that the benefits they receive in their old age should be based on their contributions and the interest on those contributions. Like the retirees, they believe that they should get out what they put in; however, most of them believe that their contributions will not be repaid with interest because the present recipients are getting part of their contributions and receiving more than they should.

The beliefs of both groups are at odds with reality. The present Social Security system is a simple system for the intergenerational transfer of income from the working to the retired population. It is not based on the creation of capital assets by one generation of workers to pay themselves an income in retirement from the increased income made possible by capital formation.

The current U.S. Social Security system is a straightforward intergenerational transfer. The small current surpluses of the Social Security system are not invested in claims to income-increasing capital stocks. They are invested in U.S. Government Bonds which, in turn, have been issued to fund the deficits resulting from government spending and transfer payments in the general budget that exceed tax revenues.[11]   The current surpluses are not primarily intended to fund future payments for retirement and to avoid taxes on future generations. For any surpluses in the Social Security Trust Fund held in government bonds, interest paid to retirees will have to be collected from future taxpayers. As the bonds mature the funds for the repayment of principal will have to be collected from taxpayers. There is no way to relieve future taxpayers of the costs of Social Security payments.

Intergenerational transfers are unavoidable when production is being carried out by one age cohort of the population to provide for consumption by all three cohorts. However, their increasing size relative to worker incomes and the recent shift of institutional mechanisms for transfer from the intergenerational family and individual saving to a system of governmental tax collection and distribution increases the need for wider and deeper understanding of the bases of intergenerational equity.

It is economically important for the members of a society to agree on equity issues. Agreement will increase the time and energy that members of the society devote to increasing the size of national income rather than redistributing it. It will reduce the amount of transactions, monitoring, and enforcement costs devoted to the regulation of social and economic activities. It will also stimulate productive employment and saving and investment—what Adam Smith called "frugality"—if people have greater confidence that they will personally reap the benefits of their work and saving and taxpaying in their own retirement years.

Intergenerational Equity

Intergenerational equity ranks along with murder and robbery in the Biblical Ten Commandments. The Fifth Commandment lays down the active obligation to "Honor thy father and mother that thy days may be long upon the land that the Lord thy God giveth thee."[12] This is a classic statement of the bonds between generations. I construe the modern meaning of this moral categorical imperative as being "Support your own parents in their dependent years so your children will do the same for you."[13]

The Fifth Commandment does not address the question of how, or how much, children should contribute, nor does it deal with the question of the responsibility of parents for the education and support of children. In a traditional society, however, the support and education of children is a prudential obligation if the children are to be able physically and economically to support the parents in their dependent old age.

The same ancient Biblical injunction raises even more critical questions for intergenerational income distribution in our modern age. There are several reasons for this: First, the stock of assets held by our society has been accumulated from the work and saving of many previous generations, and the flow of income available from them can be increased or diminished for subsequent generations by the actions of the current working and retired generations. This is also true for natural resources.

Second, the traditional structure of the intergenerational family, that the Fifth Commandment presumed, has been altered. Many children do not live with, and are not supported by, their biological or adoptive parents. Most retirees do not live with, and most are not financially dependent on, their biological or adopted children. In the United States over the past century, the modal intergenerational family gave way to the nuclear family and the modal nuclear family has given way, increasingly, to single-parent families and many unattached individuals. Lacking the emotional ties of an intergenerational family, who will pay attention to the Fifth Commandment?[14]

As both cause and effect of the change in the structure of households, the welfare state has, increasingly, assumed economic responsibility for the care and education of children and the income support and medical care of the retired population. The assumption of the support of the dependent young and old by the state necessitates large and increasing transfers by taxation of the incomes of the employed generation.

Third, the increase in the proportion of the population reaching retirement age and the increase in the ratio of retirement years to working years are steadily increasing the proportion of national income that must go to support the dependent elderly population. A larger share of national income for the retired population entails a smaller share for the working population and/or the dependent youth population. What ethical principle will prevent the socialization of intergenerational transfers by the welfare state from ending the process of capital accumulation? Or, what will stop an individualist ethic that minimizes the claims of one generation on another from consuming the capital that one generation bequeaths to the next?

Demographic Shifts and Intergenerational Transfers

Until the last few decades, decisions about intergenerational income distribution were decided within families. As noted in the previous section, the United States was a relative latecomer in the provision of a compulsory state pension system. Coupled with substantial institutional changes in intergenerational transfers are large changes in the size of those transfers. Increasing transfers through Social Security/Medicare-Medicaid and through the operation of employer-sponsored pension funds have already checked the rise in disposable income for the employed population. In the twenty-first century the reduction of disposable incomes from employment will have to increase still further even if Social Security payments per retiree and Medicare expenditures per patient at each age group could be held constant. The increases in Social Security and Medicare taxes—even with constant benefits per person in each age group—are inevitable because of changes in the age structure of the population and the increasing cost of medical care, per person, for an aging population.

Given that we can no longer finesse the questions of intergenerational income distribution, the subsequent sections of this chapter are addressed to the creation of a framework for understanding the parameters that structure fundamental principles and quantitative answers to questions raised by the Fifth Commandment.

BASES FOR INTERGENERATIONAL EQUITY

Intergenerational transfers might be more simply rationalized[15] in terms of intergenerational equity in a society with static incomes and a static demographic structure. In such a hypothetical society, the working generation supports the older generation in return for their past support and supports the younger generation in terms of their prospective support of the current working generation in their retirement. The rationalization of intergenerational transfers is more complex in a society like our own with incomes growing as a result of capital formation and/or age structure changing as a result of declining birth and death rates.

Growth in Income

Consider, first, the situation of growth in incomes: One generation (A) adds to the per person capital stock through saving. (This saving reduces generation A's consumption during their working years.) The additional capital stock permits a higher level of output for the next generation (B). Some or all of the higher income from the larger capital stock goes to the owners (or creators) of the capital stock of the previous (A) generation. This could support the retired generation A of capital creators with the incremental income resulting from their work and saving without reducing the income that would have been available to the current B generation in the absence of generation A's addition to the capital stock.

Only in a society in which the capital creation of generation A increases the incomes of workers in generation B is it possible to effect an intergenerational transfer that does not reduce the income of generation B below what it would have been in the absence of the capital formation of generation A. The additional income provided by the additional capital stock formed by the workers in generation A can be paid to them during their retirement dependency years without reducing the income that would have accrued to the workers in generation B in the absence of the additions to the capital stock by generation A.

The property rights in the ownership of capital created by saving are an inducement for the saving of the first generation (A). The second generation (B) has an incentive to purchase those property rights from generation (A), and to create additional property rights (by net social saving) in new capital assets in order to maintain themselves in their retirement from returns on capital and the sale of property rights to capital to the next generation (C), and so on from generation to generation.

Should a prior generation be able to consume the additional capital it created earlier, as well as the income from it? The only way that the capital stock can increase from generation to generation is for earlier generations to "bequeath"—and not consume—some of the capital stock that they have created to subsequent generations. But then the question arises: Why should a poorer prior generation accumulate capital and pass it on to the richer generation that follows?   The following generation is richer because the previous generation reduced its own consumption. I know of no ethical answer to that question. But, factually, each generation "stands on the shoulders" of the preceding generation and a generation that consumes its own net capital formation (let alone consuming what it inherited) breaks that process.

A fully capitalized retirement system need not burden one generation at the expense of the succeeding generation—but only if the capital stock has been increased sufficiently and has a high enough rate of return to pay for all of the consumption of the retired population. As Part III demonstrates, the amount of saving and the rate of return necessary to accomplish the nonburdensome transfer is high relative to recent experience.[16]

Demographic Growth

Next, consider demographic change: The "burden" of the retired population on the working population can be temporarily diminished by a growing population that increases the ratio of the working to the retired population. Or it can be offset by a labor force that is growing through increases in participation rates. Both of these demographic trends reduce the burden of the retired population on the working population by increasing the ratio of workers to retirees to a higher level than it would be for a stable population with a stable age structure and stable ratio of retirees to workers. The increases in cost of the Social Security system to the working population of the United States over the past half-century have been diminished by the growing participation rates of the labor force and the increase in the ratio of the working-age to retirement age population. But, when this comes to an end, further increases in transfer rates cannot be accomplished without reducing the incomes of the working population that is stable (or declining) relative to the retired population.

Equity and Incentives

Ethical questions about intergenerational transfers are unavoidable, but there is also an unavoidable incentive problem joined to the equity problem. While changes in the intergenerational distribution of national income at a particular point in time are largely a zero-sum game, over longer periods the distribution of the consumption of national product between generations emphatically is not a zero-sum game. Increasing the current rate of net social saving (with a consequent reduction in current consumption) builds up the stock of physical capital and other forms of expenditures that are not counted as saving in accounting terms; for instance, investments in research charged to current expense may increase the stock of knowledge capital or lead to new technologies that preserve natural resource capital. Increasing the share of national resources going to the education of youth builds up the stock of human capital available for use in the next generation.

A key premise of neoclassical or "supply-side economics" is that the individual incentives for production and saving provided by economic systems organized on the basis of private property are an important determinant of the magnitude of capital stocks. Increasing transfer payments via the tax system reduces incentives for individual work and saving. From the vantage point of "supply side economics," the critical long-term social problem with increasing the proportion of current consumption transferred to the retired population through taxation is that it may decrease incentives for work and saving. There is substantial comparative evidence (Gruber and Wise, 1998) that the current structure of retirement benefit systems in industrial nations, including the United States, reduces participation by older workers in the labor force.

The level of work effort and saving by the employed population may be reduced if it is not directly and individually linked to its own higher current and future consumption. According to supply-side economics, cutting transfer taxes and reducing the prospective size of transfer payments may motivate a higher level of labor force participation and production. It may also motivate a higher level of saving from a larger volume of production if the current producers know that they will not be able to count on a high level of socialized income transfers during their years of retirement dependency.

Critically, keeping the current and prospective future transfer levels down may stimulate a higher level of additions to the stocks of human, physical, and knowledge capital. Increasing the share of income going to the retired population through taxing the employed population may be inimical to building up the stocks of capital if high rates of tax and the security of future socialized transfers reduce incentives for work and savings. This is the incentive argument for individualizing decisions about the levels of lifetime labor force participation and consumption.

Individual Saving, Aggregate Saving, and Net Capital Formation

Could intergenerational transfers be handled by each generation individually—without dependency on the next? Counterintuitively: No! The retired generation cannot live on its assets without the reduction of consumption by the current working generation. Members of the retired population may have saved sufficient proportions of income during their working years to finance their own periods of retirement; however, their reliance on their personal savings and accumulated capital for their maintenance during old age still increases the proportion of current national income going to the retired population. This is because the retired population's amortization of its accumulated claims to capital assets through their sale must be matched by purchases by the employed population of stocks, bonds, and/or real estate from the retired population.

These purchases of titles to existing assets from the retired and dis-saving generation entail a consequent reduction in the consumption of current earners from their current income. The reduction in consumption to buy the titles to assets transfers purchasing power to the retired class. If current producers did not reduce consumption below production and save part of their income to buy the stocks and bonds being liquidated to finance retirement by the retired population, the value of the stocks and bonds would fall until the effective increase in the rate of return from the assets balanced the offsetting demands of the earning and retired populations for current consumption.

During their period of labor force participation, society members produce goods and services and receive income for their labor. They individually consume and share the consumption of the largest part of this income with family members. Part of personal income is taxed by governments to provide government services. Another part is transferred by government to dependent-age cohorts by other forms of taxation (Social Security, Medicare, taxes for schools, and the portions of general expenditures going on welfare programs). An additional part of income is transferred by personal saving to offset the dis-saving of the retired population.

From an aggregate point of view, most of the income that is individually "saved" by households is really transferred—it goes to purchase claims to existing assets such as real estate, bonds, or equities. These financial assets represent claims to income from corporations or other households that own reproducible capital. Purchases of the ownership claims to income-producing assets from other holders of those claims thereby allow an increase in the consumption by the dis-savers of the retired population during their period of dependency. The working population that saves to purchase the assets reduces its current consumption to accommodate the consumption of others.

From a social point of view, individuals go through a life cycle of saving and dis-saving: they dis-save during their dependent youth, save through their working years, and then dis-save in their retirement years. A primary motivation for household saving is the deferral of consumption to the future and particularly for retirement. Much of the saving in today's economy is done automatically through employer and individual (tax-deferred) contributions into pension plans, increases in the cash values of life insurance policies, and the amortization of home mortgages. The liquidation of the assets of pension funds to pay pensioners or of the assets behind insurance policies or the sale of homes by the retired population depends upon offsetting purchases. The underlying debt or equity instruments or titles to real estate can only be purchased by the currently working population through their curtailment of current consumption to do the saving. If there were no purchasers of the securities or real estate sold to finance retirement, there could be no sellers and the retired population would have to reduce their consumption.[17]

Net social saving occurs only when consumption by all generations is reduced sufficiently to create net new assets. At any given period, the distribution of the output from current resources between consumption and investment accounts for all production. The distribution of the current consumption output is a zero-sum game between all individuals and generations. If either the retired or working generations were to attempt to increase their consumption, the effect would be a fall in asset prices and a rise in interest rates. This fall in asset prices and consequent rise in rates of return would discourage the production of net new capital in order allocate resources to the increase in consumption.

For national income accounting, "saving" is the difference between production and consumption during a particular time period. Saving is done by both workers and the owners of capital. When part of national income is not consumed privately or collectively—it is saved. Saving makes it possible to use part of the labor and capital resources of society to produce more capital goods and, thereby, increase the stock of capital.

I will argue in chapter 9 that the size of the capital stock is a determinant of the level of output and that additions to the capital stock permit further increases in output—namely, economic growth. It is the decisions of all the population in any one time period to increase production and reduce consumption to create net social saving that increase the capital stock and, thus, allow the increase of future output. This increase in future output, in turn, allows the current working generation to consume in the future without reducing the consumption of generations to follow. Ultimately, the ethical principle that allows each generation to stand on the shoulders of its predecessor is a necessary condition for economic growth.

At the time of their retirement from the labor force, some people have accumulated a personal stock of capital from saving during their working lives. The size of their stock of capital is determined by how much they may have inherited, by the amount and time of the saving during their working lives, and by the rate of interest earned on their accumulated capital during its period of accumulation. (The personal stock of capital may be negative if people have borrowed.)

During their period of retirement, people continue to consume without producing as members of the labor force. The amount they consume reduces the amount of production left for the working population and the dependent youth population.

The size of aggregate national income and per capita national income at any particular time is overwhelmingly determined by the past. As I will explain in chapter 9, a nation's wealth and income in the present depends upon the past accumulation of the stocks of reproducible, human, knowledge, and conservation of natural resource capital. It also depends upon the technology developed in the past to harness those stocks for the production of national income.

It is possible to make the equity argument for taxing the current generation of taxpayers to support the current generation of Social Security recipients on the basis that the current Social Security recipients increased the current capital stock during their lifetimes by net national saving.

But, if higher levels of Social Security taxes may reduce the work effort and saving and, thereby, the capital formation of the current generation they will, in turn, have the effect of reducing the amount of capital bequeathed to the next generation. Because the consumption of every generation depends upon the production and saving of past generations and will, in turn, determine the possibilities for future generations, the intergenerational equity problem cannot be escaped by making an individual's work, consumption, and saving decisions a personal matter on the grounds that they do not affect others. I shall return to this issue in chapter 9 in my explanation of the process of economic growth in the United States.

PART III: DETERMINANTS OF INTERGENERATIONAL TRANSFERS

How much income should be transferred from the working generation to the retired generation? Should it be 50 percent of pre-retirement income at age sixty-five? Or 70 percent at age seventy? Should it depend on prior earnings? Should Medicare cover organ transplants or indefinite maintenance on mechanical systems?

Economics and economists, qua economists, cannot answer those questions, but it is possible to estimate what will be the magnitude of the first order effects of economic decisions based on moral choices.

Economics can address such questions as:

1. What are the determinants of the proportions of income that must be transferred from the employed population to sustain particular levels of retirement income and medical care for the retired population ?
2. What levels of Social Security and Medicare taxes would be necessary to finance particular levels of benefits from the employed population to the retired population ?
3. What levels of savings and rates of return on capital would be necessary to finance retirement on an privatized basis?
4. What are the implications for Social Security and   Medicare/Medicaid of the slowdown in the rate of economic growth and the projected changes in the age

structure of the labor force? Specifically, what are the tax and transfer implications of the increase in both the youth and retired populations relative to the labor force?

5. What are the implications of low productivity growth in the provision of medical services and education for the proportion of national income allocated to those areas?

These are pressing questions and to understand the nature of the answers to them we need to model the magnitude and interaction of alternative arrangements for intergenerational and interpersonal flows in a modern society.

Associated with the question of the sources of the income transfers to the retired population is the question of the level of income and consumption of the retired population relative to their pre-retirement income and to the disposable income of the working population, and the maintenance of and educational expenditures on the youth population.

The proportion of national income that the working population will have available from take-home wages for their personal consumption expenditure or saving depends critically upon the proportion of income the employed population will have to transfer for the maintenance of the retired population and the support and education of the dependent youth population. This chapter deals with the determinants of payments for support of the retired population and the following chapter deals with the increasing proportion of national income necessarily allocated to the education of the young.

Let us now turn from the description of issues and institutions involved in intergenerational transfers to the identification of the factors determining the quantitative size of intergenerational flows.

In a traditional system the intergenerational distribution of income in the family is determined by the family itself (the situation for which the Fifth Commandment was explicitly intended). I will not analyze this system. I will model the necessary flows for a simplified redistributional system (similar to Social Security/Medicare/Medicaid) and a simplified system of individual saving, capital formation, and capital consumption (similar to some proposals for the privatization of Social Security).

INTERGENERATIONAL TRANSFER BY TAXATION

To begin our thinking about the magnitude of intergenerational income flows through social transfer by taxation, consider a simplified society in which half the population works and pays taxes to support the other half; the rate of taxation of the working class would have to be 50 percent of working-class pre-tax incomes to support the leisured class at the same level of after-tax income as the working class, or 25 percent to support the leisured class at one-third of the after-tax income of the working class. (If the tax rate is 25%, the after-tax income of the working class is 75%.)

The tax transfer rate necessary to finance the dependence of one class of the population on another depends on (1) the relative proportions of the dependent and producing populations, and (2) the desired ratio of the levels of income of the dependent population to the income of the producing population.

The number of workers depends upon the relative size of the working-age population and its participation rate in the labor force. The number of retirees relative to the working population depends upon the ages of entry and exit into and out of the labor force and the demographic history of the population.[18]

Text Table 7.1
Transfer Tax Rates Required for Various Retirement Income Ratios with Illustrative Employment and Demographic Ratios

Employment Ratios	Retired Ratios	Income Ratios			
		0.4	0.5	0.6	0.7
0.5	0.1	0.09	0.11	0.13	0.16
	0.12	0.11	0.14	0.16	0.19
	0.14	0.13	0.16	0.20	0.23
	0.16	0.15	0.19	0.23	0.27
	0.18	0.18	0.22	0.26	0.31
	0.2	0.20	0.25	0.30	0.35
	0.22	0.23	0.28	0.34	0.39
	0.24	0.25	0.32	0.38	0.44
0.6	0.1	0.07	0.09	0.11	0.13
	0.12	0.09	0.11	0.14	0.16
	0.14	0.11	0.14	0.16	0.19
	0.16	0.13	0.16	0.19	0.22
	0.18	0.15	0.18	0.22	0.26
	0.2	0.17	0.21	**0.25**	*.29
	0.22	0.19	0.24	0.28	0.33
	0.24	0.21	0.26	0.32	0.37
0.7	0.1	0.06	0.08	0.09	0.11
	0.12	0.08	0.10	0.11	0.14
	0.14	0.09	0.12	0.13	0.16
	0.16	0.11	0.14	_0.15_	0.19
	0.18	0.13	0.16	0.18	0.22
	0.2	0.14	_0.18_	0.20	0.25
	0.22	0.16	0.20	0.22	0.28
	0.24	0.18	0.23	0.25	0.32

Employment ratio: Employment/Working-age Population (16–64). Retired ratio: Retired Population (65+)/Adult Population (16+). Income ratio: Retiree Income/Worker Income. (Underlined figures are referenced in the text.)

Source: Author. See Appendix 8.

The tax transfer rates necessary for the support of the retired population at various relative income levels, with differing population and employment ratios are shown in the body of Text Table 7.1. For example, reading from the upper left-hand corner, with a 50 percent employment ratio and a ratio of retired/total adult population of 10 percent, and a policy-determined income ratio of 40 percent for average worker income/average retiree income, a tax rate of 9 percent (underlined) of worker income would be necessary to support the retired population at this ratio. To make a historical comparison, in 1990 the employment ratio (workers/working-age population) was close to 70 percent. (See Appendix Tables 3.3 and 7.2.)[19] The population ratio (retired-age/adult-age population) in the 1990 Census was approximately .16. If Social Security pensions and Medicare/Medicaid expenditures per retired person were equal to 60 percent of per worker income (an approximation to the ratio in 1990), the table shows that the necessary tax transfer rate to accomplish this transfer by payroll taxes would be 15 percent (italicized and underlined in Text Table 7.1). In 1990 Social Security taxes were 12.4 percent of payroll up to $51,380 and Medicare taxes were 2.9 percent on all payroll income, for a total tax rate of 15.3 percent.[20]

Social Security/Medicare type transfer tax ratios were lower in the past because the retired population was a smaller fraction of the working population and they were supported at a lower level of expenditures per retiree through the Social Security system. (There was no Medicare/Medicaid until 1965.) Appendix Table 7.1 details historical ratios of retirees and workers and payroll taxes.

What will happen in the future? The ratio of the retired/adult population is projected to be approximately stable at about 16 percent until after 2005, but then the ratio will start to rise. Meanwhile, the ratio of workers/working population will probably decline as the population shifts into older (working-age) cohorts.[21] If this happens, thereby reducing the employment ratio, transfer tax rates will have to rise. Or, if Social Security and Medicare expenditures rise relative to average income per worker, the necessary transfer tax rate will have to move up.

For example, what will happen when the ratio of the retired population/adult population reaches 20 percent, if the ratio of workers/working-age population drops to 60 percent? If we were to maintain the current ratio of retirement benefits and Medicare expenditures per retiree/average payroll income per worker, the combined Social Security/Medicare payroll tax rate would have to rise from its current 15.3 percent to 25 percent (underlined and bold in Text Table 7.1). If Social Security and Medicare benefits were to continue to rise relative to worker incomes—say to 70 percent—the increase in the transfer tax rate would have to rise to 29 percent (* in table).

These examples show the importance of the participation rate in keeping the tax rate down. Yet, higher payroll taxes discourage participation. Payroll taxes at these levels in European countries have led simultaneously to high reported nonparticipation and unemployment (Gruber and Wise, 1998) and a large underground economy that pays no taxes.

The important determinants of the size of intergenerational "pay-as-you-go" tax transfers through a system such as Social Security/Medicare are:

1. The age structure of the population.
2. The participation of the working-age population in the labor force.
3. The level of retiree benefits relative to the incomes of the working population.

The United States benefited during the last quarter-century from the offsetting increases in the employment ratio (workers/working-age population) and the retirement ratio (retired/adult population). This allowed more modest increases in Social Security/ Medicare taxes than would otherwise have been possible to fund the increases in the levels of benefits per retiree. After 2005 the retirement ratio will rise and the employment ratio is projected to fall as the labor force ages (if workers continue their present level of labor force participation at different ages).

As I have said, the ratio of spending on the elderly to the income of the working population is basically a moral and political question. However, it must be remembered that the ratio that is chosen for the support level of the retired population legislatively will involve an offsetting tax transfer that depends on the benefit level, the ratio of the working/retired population, and the employment ratio. That cannot be escaped. The entitlements of the retired generations are the tax obligations for the working generation. Text Table 7.1 presents those ratios.[22]

Policy Choices

What do I personally think should be done?

1. Slow, stabilize, or reverse the increase in the ratio of retiree benefits/worker incomes. This increase (without original Congressional intention) has resulted from the use of the upwardly biased CPI. Change the basis of CPI calculation in the first instance, and consider the possibility of increasing benefits by less than the CPI for a few years to correct the past mistakes in constructing the CPI (probably politically impossible).
2. Reducing Medicare expenditures per retiree by increasing copayments for financially able retirees and by shifting control of costs to managed care rather than fee-for-service medicine.
3. Reduce Medicaid expenditures per retiree on nursing home care by increasing the amounts paid by the retiree's estate.
4. Slow the growth in the ratio of retired/adult population by extending the age for retirement. (This policy change has already been made for Social Security after 2000, but the rate of increase in the retirement age could be accelerated.)
5. Increase the participation rate of the working population by measures that discourage early retirement and encourage working after eligibility for Social Security benefits by increasing benefits for those who continue to work.

If we do not stop the increase in Social Security benefits/worker incomes that results from the use of the upwardly biased CPI and the increase in Medicare-financed medical spending per retiree, we will move from the current ratio of 60 percent inexorably toward 70 percent in the retiree benefit/worker income ratio. Keeping it at 60 percent along with participation rates at 70 percent and a retired/adult population of 20 percent would allow the United States to balance the Social Security/Medicare program at an 18 percent employment transfer tax ratio (underlined, bold and italicized in Text Table 7.1)—less than 3 percent above our current level.

FINANCING RETIREMENT BY PERSONAL SAVING

Concerns about the capacity of the Social Security system to provide an adequate level of retirement benefits without an excessive level of payroll taxes has been one element contributing to current discussions about the privatization of retirement pensions and/or the partial privatization of Medicare through Medical Savings Accounts.

Estimating the amount of personal saving during a working lifetime that would be necessary to finance a particular level of consumption in retirement through a private retirement annuity is a more complex analytical problem than figuring the tax rate necessary to transfer a particular level of income from one generation to another. However, in discussion of the possible "privatization" of Social Security it is important to be realistic about the magnitude of saving and the compounded "real" rate of return on savings necessary to provide a particular level of income through an annuity.

Once again, let us start by simplification with a concrete example. Assume:

1. A two-year life span.
2. In the first year the individual works.
3. In the second year, the individual is retired and living on saving from the first year.
4. No interest is earned on the first year's savings.

To live at the same level during one's retired year as during one's working year, it would be necessary to save 50 percent of income during the working year. If one worked for thirty years and was retired for thirty years (without interest on the savings and annuity), the same requirements would obtain. The amount one must save depends critically upon the length of retirement relative to the length of one's working life. The Biblical parable of saving during seven fat years followed by consumption during seven lean years is apropos.

If one worked for forty years and was retired for twenty, it would be necessary to save (once again, without the complications of inflation or a return on savings) only 25 percent of income during working years to provide for retirement at 50 percent of working income. (.25Q x forty years = .5Q x 20 years).[23] The basic determinants of the level of savings necessary to provide for retirement are the multiplicative ratios of (1) retired to working years, and (2) retirement income to working income. The larger the ratio of retirement years/working years and the higher the ratio of retirement income/working income, the greater the necessary saving ratio.

The real world is more complex than our simplified example, however. Savers can earn a positive "real" rate of interest on their savings that compounds to a capital sum until retirement. At retirement the accumulated and continuously reinvested savings can be converted into an annuity to provide a stream of income over a retirement period. The principal sum of the annuity depends both on the rate of savings and the rate of return on the savings. The level of the flow of income that can be paid on the annuity includes both amortization of the annuity principal and projected interest earned on the unamortized balance of the annuity. The higher the rate of return on investment, the larger the annuity that can be provided by a particular level of saving during a lifetime and the larger the annual payment from the annuity.

The second complication to our model arises from the fact that most incomes are not constant during a working lifetime. Incomes grow as a result of general economic growth and most workers earn more as they age and accumulate more experience, so that ending income is greater than starting income. This means that any given saving rate on a rising income yields less savings during early years when the savings have more years to compound. And, to remind of the related difficulty arising from the growth in incomes over a lifetime, incomes at retirement—on which retirement consumption levels are based—are generally higher than average incomes over a working lifetime.

There is a multitude of factors that determines the savings rates necessary to provide for a secure retirement. However, a privatized pension system would depend on the following basic determinants of the level of employment income/retirement income and consumption during worker years/consumption during retirement years:

1. The length of working life.
2. The employment ratio—the ratio of employed years/working life—the combined effect of the participation rate in the labor force and the unemployment rate for labor force participants during various periods of working life.
3. The rate of growth of income during working life accruing from general economic growth.
4. The wage gradient during working life.
5. The rate of saving during working life.
6. The rate of interest on accumulating savings.
7. The rate of interest on the retirement annuity.
8. The length of retirement.

Let us briefly consider these eight factors:

1. Length of working life: The longer the working life, the greater the accumulated earnings and savings and the longer the period for interest to accumulate and compound on the capital formed by savings.
2. The participation rate: Persons do not work continuously during their entire working lives. Women, particularly, withdraw from the labor force during childbearing years. Voluntary and involuntary unemployment reduces income available for saving for retirement (and consumes part of that saving).
3. Rate of increase of income during working life: Counterintuitively, more rapid growth of worker income creates a problem for the retiree. (It is assumed that average incomes increase at the same rate as national income over the worker's lifetime.) If levels of retirement income are based on income at the age of

retirement, and average incomes have grown rapidly during the worker's lifetime, this means that income levels at retirement are considerably higher than during the early period of earning and saving. This reduces the relative importance of savings during early years that have had a longer period to accumulate with compound interest.

4. Wage gradient during working life: The wage gradient is the relationship between income and age for a cross-section of the population. This has the same effect as the rate of growth of average incomes and interacts with it to determine the amount of savings during early working years that have a longer period to accumulate and compound.

5. Ratio of saving/income: Obviously, the higher the rate of saving (and the lower the rate of consumption) during a working lifetime, the higher the rate of consumption possible during retirement.   (Further, my table will consider the ratio of consumption during working years to retirement years, rather than income. Saving during working years lowers consumption and, consequently, the consumption necessary during retirement years to sustain a given ratio of consumption in the two life periods.)

6. Rate of interest earned on savings: Clearly, the higher the rate of interest earned on saving, the greater the compounded value of accumulated savings that form an annuity at the time of retirement.

7. Rate of interest on annuity: Evidently, the higher the rate of interest earned on the annuity, the higher the level of the retirement income funded by it.

8. Length of retirement years: Plainly, the longer the period of retirement the smaller the annuity payment and the consequent level of consumption in retirement relative to consumption during the working life.

These eight factors vary widely between retirees, and the factors are going to vary over lifetimes. We can consider only a limited number of simplified cases, but I hope they will make clear the importance and interaction of the identified variables to a retirement based on individual saving for capital accumulation and decumulation.

A Simple Model

Let us begin our analysis of the magnitude of necessary saving rates with an extremely simple case. Assuming:

1. A working life of forty years and retirement life of twenty years. The person begins work at twenty, works continuously until sixty, and lives until eighty.

2. A saving rate of 20 percent.

3. A "real" (inflation adjusted), compounded rate of return of 2 percent on accumulated savings and 2 percent on the annuity created by forty years of saving.

Other assumptions that improve the ratio of retirement years consumption/working years consumption are: (a) no growth in income, (b) zero wage gradient, (c) employment for forty years.   Under these favorable assumptions, the worker who has worked for forty years, and saved 20 percent of her income that has been invested with a real, compounded return of 2 percent per annum could retire with an annuity that yielded 49 percent of income during working years or 61 percent of consumption during working years. (The percentage of pre-retirement consumption is the correct figure for comparison.)   Notice how favorable the assumptions are: forty years of continuous work with a 20 percent saving rate!

How do changes in the simple model change the ratio of retirement consumption/pre-retirement consumption? A reduction of the saving rate from 20 percent to 10 percent saving reduces retirement consumption from 61 percent to 27 percent of pre-retirement consumption, while an increase to a 30 percent saving rate increases retirement consumption to 104 percent of pre-retirement consumption. The saving rate is obviously very important.

Reducing the real rate of return on savings by half from 2 percent to a 1 percent decreases relative consumption only from 61 percent to 55 percent while increasing it to a 3 percent real return increases it only 61 percent to 68 percent. The compounded rate of return does not make such a large difference as one might think because most of the retirement annuity is funded by the consumption of capital rather than the returns earned on it.

Changing the ratio of working life to the retirement period from forty/20 to 45/15 increases retirement consumption income to 87 percent of pre-retirement consumption. Reducing the ratio of work years/retirement years to 35/25 reduces consumption to 44 percent. The ratio of working/retirement years is important because one more year to save also means one less year to live on the savings.

The relative strength of the assumptions is clear—the saving rate and work/retirement ratio have strong effects, with changes in the interest rate having a weaker effect.   Nevertheless, it bears emphasis that favorable assumptions—a 20 percent saving rate, a 2 percent real return on investment, and forty years of uninterrupted work to twenty years of retirement are necessary to produce the oft-quoted ratio of retirement income of 60 percent of pre-retirement expenditures/post-retirement expenditure.

A More Realistic Model

What would constitute more realistic assumptions about a normal working life? The following assumptions increase the realism of the example, although they are still more optimistic than a typical work experience:

1. Annual growth of real worker incomes of 1 percent—less than our historical experience (see Text Table 3.1)—more than we have experienced over the last two decades.
2. A wage gradient that increases by 3 percent per year for the first decade of employment, and 2 percent, 1 percent, and .5 percent per year for successive decades of employment. This approximates the recent wage gradient for male college graduates. It means, for illustration, that within a particular occupation, the starting salary of $15,000 for an entry level worker compares to $45,000 for a worker with forty years of experience.
3. Employment is continuous—a highly optimistic assumption. There are no periods of nonparticipation or unemployment during the employee's working years. This is

a critical assumption. Most workers do not work for thirty or forty years continuously after beginning employment. While married males have participation rates of 90 percent between ages twenty-five and forty-five, participation rates drop during later years and are lower for women in the same age cohorts. (See Appendix Table 6.1.) Further, over the last two decades the level of unemployment has averaged over 6 percent.

4. During periods of nonparticipation and/or unemployment in the labor force, workers not only cannot save but they must use prior savings to maintain consumption. The effect of the continuous employment assumption can be allowed for by modification of the various ratio assumptions; if, for example, a person were not working for five of the thirty years in the labor force, they might be working (and saving) for twenty-five years, nonemployed and dis-saving for five years, and retired and dis-saving for thirty years. Thus, one could refer to the 25/35 working years/retirement years in the table for an approximation of the effect of discontinuous employment.

5. Compounded real rates of return of 2 percent, 4 percent, and 8 percent. Rates of returns on savings and investments are generally quoted in nominal rather than real terms. Short-term, risk-free investments have a real rate of return close to zero. Over the past seventy years, the average pre-tax, "real" rate of return on the S&P 500 stocks has been estimated at 7.6 percent, while the average return on long-term Treasury Bonds has been estimated at 2 percent.[24]

Example

Inspecting Table 7.2 (top left corner), a worker who worked for forty years and was retired for ten, saved 5 percent of income, and earned 2 percent real return on her savings accumulation and retirement annuity would be able to replace only 25 percent (underlined in table) of pre-retirement consumption income!

A Modal Case

There really is no "modal" case to analyze—different people have very different lifetime work and consumption patterns.   But, for the sake of argument, let us consider two possible cases. Consider one thrifty examplar in the forty work years to twenty retirement years group. He starts work at twenty and works for forty years without ever missing a paycheck and retires at 60. He saves 15 percent of income every year, never dips into his savings, earns a favorable 4 percent real return on his savings, and gets an insurance company to write a twenty-year level payment annuity with a real interest rate of 4 percent.   This modal worker is able to retire on a pension that allows consumption of 1.07 percent (italicized and underlined in Text Table 7.2) of pre-retirement consumption—that is, there is no change in consumption after retirement.[25] However, realistically, the majority of American workers are unlikely to be able to save 15 percent of their incomes for an uninterrupted forty years and earn a compounded real return of 4 percent.

Text Table 7.2
Income Replacement Possibilities with Privatized Retirement:Replacement Ratios with Various Assumptions on Ratio of Working/Retirement Years, Savings Rates and Rates of Return on Investment

Working Years/ Retirement Years	Savings Rates	Rates of Return		
		0.02	0.04	0.08
40/10	0.05	<u>0.25</u>	0.41	1.2
	0.15	1.09	1.79	5.3
	0.25	3.35	5.5	16.4
40/20	0.05	0.14	0.24	0.83
	0.15	0.59	*1.07*	3.6
	0.25	1.8	3.3	11.2
30/30	0.05	0.07	0.12	0.35
	0.15	0.29	0.49	1.42
	0.25	0.75	1.29	3.7
25/35	0.05	0.05	0.09	0.23
	0.15	0.2	***0.35***	0.9
	0.25	0.49	0.82	2.2

Underlined figures, or those in boldface or italics, are referenced in the text.

Source: Author. See Appendix 7.2

Consider a typical female who is in the labor force from twenty to fifty, takes some full and some part time off for children, and lives until eighty; she has twenty-five years of full-time employment during a thirty-year working life followed by thirty years of retirement. She saves 15 percent of her income, and earns a 4 percent real return on her savings and annuity. However, during her periods of nonemployment, the family draws down savings to maintain consumption so her position approximates the example of the twenty-five working years/thirty-five retirement years. She retires with only 35 percent of her pre-retirement consumption (italicized and boldface in Text Table 7.2). The average American cannot retire without assistance on that amount.

I would like to emphasize that the problem is not caused by the average American family saving a smaller proportion of their incomes than they did in the past. The problem arises because the average American is entering the labor force later, retiring sooner, and living too long! When a fortunate American of the first half of the twentieth century worked for forty years from sixteen to fifty-six, and was retired for ten years before dying at sixty-six, a continuous 15 percent savings rate and a 4 percent real rate of return on capital would have provided an annuity that yielded 1.79 times his pre-retirement consumption level. He and his widow would have left a sizable estate relative to their lifetime income to their heirs!

An American who lived in the second half of the century might start work at twenty-five, work continuously to fifty-five, and be retired for thirty years to age eighty-five. If he saved the same 15 percent and earned the same real 4 percent as his earlier counterpart, his retirement annuity would yield a sum less than 30 percent (.29) of his pre-retirement consumption level—one sixth of his counterpart in an earlier age!

THE "BOTTOM LINE" FOR THE CONSUMPTION LEVELS OF A MATURE ECONOMY

The high rate of consumption growth of American society in the two decades after World War II was possible because of the concurrence of two favorable growth factors—growth in per capita incomes due to the rapid increase in per worker productivity and the increase in the participation of the population in the labor force—and one demographic factor—a small retired population.

But the world has changed! The rate of growth in per worker income is declining. The participation rate of the population in the labor force is approaching a maximum. The retired population is growing in relative size. The ratio of retiree/worker relative income transfers is growing. That is why transfers for Social Security have increased steadily and could approach 25 percent of income by 2020.

It is irresponsible to say that there won't be any Social Security by the time that the current thirty-year-old gets around to collect it. It is also irresponsible to say, however, that the rate of increase in Medicare can't be cut or, on the other hand, that we could shift from a nearly universal Social Security system to a voluntary private pension system.

It is often said that private savings must be increased to fund retirement. While private savings are important, the simulation models of this chapter show why the rates of private saving necessary to maintain the retired population at reasonable proportions of the income of the active population are beyond our historical experience if the retirement age continues to drop at the same time that life expectancies increase.

It is not possible to make social policy on the basis of the average citizen working without interruption for forty years and saving 15 percent of after-tax income in every one of those years and never touching savings. It is unrealistic to assume that people will not be paying off their own educational debts during their early lives and paying part of their children's educational costs during their middle years. It is unrealistic to think that people will average 4 percent compounded real returns after administrative costs on their investments. And half of all Americans will outlive a twenty-year retirement period in the twenty-first century if their retirement begins at age sixty.

Some Americans could retire on their savings, but the observed participation rates of the population in the labor force and the continuing extension of years of education and life expectancy doesn't make it possible for most Americans. And as one considers the average American, it must be realized that people currently earning less than the average income are not going to be able to save 15 percent of that income to fund a private retirement annuity and, even if they could, they are not going to be able to live above the poverty level if they are trying to live on, say, 50 percent of their pre-retirement consumption levels.[26]

NOTES

1. The increasing public belief in Medicare as a comprehensive medical entitlement and the political strength of the retired population is reflected in the inability of the Congress to deal with the increasing share of national income and the federal budget going to Medicare funding. Proposed increases in Medicare copayments and premiums to be paid by retirees have not been passed the Congress because it is politically impossible to challenge increases (let alone the current, high level) in the proportion of national income that is transferred from the working generation to the retired generation.

2. If we are considering an underfunded pension fund for private employees, the current retirees had larger "take-home" pay during their previous period of employment than they would have had if sufficient deductions had been made from their paychecks to fund their pensions. It is also possible that stockholders or even customers during the period of underfunding benefited from the underfunding. If the underfunding is compensated for in the current time period, current employees, stockholders, or possibly customers will carry the burden.

Similar considerations hold for underfunded pensions for federal, state, or local public employees. The "customers" of the public employers are the recipients of public services. Previous taxpayers paid less (or received more public services) while current taxpayers pay more or receive a lower standard of services for the taxes they do pay.

3. When Social Security was established in 1935, the age for eligibility for retirement benefits was set at sixty-five—the life expectancy for male workers at that time. The philosophic basis for the arbitrary age of eligibility might have been support for those who outlived their normal life expectancy. The (apocryphal?) story is told that when Bismarck instituted the first national pension scheme in Germany in 1880, he set the eligibility age five years *after* average male life expectancy!

4. See Appendix Table 7.1. In 1995, 6.2 percent of the employees' gross pay is allocated to the employer's contribution to Social Security before the worker's paycheck is cut. This amount is never seen by the employee. Another 6.2 percent is then subtracted from the employee's gross pay before additional deductions for fringe benefits. The worker even has to pay income tax on the 6.2 percent deduction from the paycheck that he never sees! (But the taxation of the gross income is used as the

justification for nontaxation of Social Security benefits.) There has also been a steady increase in the level of income subject to Social Security tax.

5. A number of simplifications have been made in the calculation of this ratio. The assumptions and derivation are explained in Appendix 7.2.

6. In 1995 the Boskin Commission estimated that the current CPI has an upward bias of 1.1 percent. In the late 1970s an earlier version of the CPI had an even greater bias because of its treatment of housing costs. This bias was eliminated in 1982 but there was no correction of the level of the CPI or the Social Security benefits that had been indexed to it. Thus, it could be argued that Social Security benefits are probably 25 percent higher in real terms than they were in 1972. The upward bias in the CPI is responsible for part of the reported decline in real wages but the fact that nominal wages have not risen as rapidly as the CPI (while Social Security has) means that the real incomes of Social Security recipients have risen relative to the real incomes of the average wage earner. For a discussion of CPI bias issues (see Boskin et al., 1998).

7. During the decade of the 1970s, GDP per worker hour—not wages—increased by 9 percent during the decade (Text Table 3.2). During the same decade Social Security and Medicare tax rates increased by 2.7 percent. During the decade of the 1980s, GDP per worker hour increased by 10 percent and the combined Social Security and Medicare tax rates increased by 3 percent. In both decades maximum taxable earnings also increased faster than worker incomes, and worker incomes increased more slowly than GDP so that the increase in transfer taxes in both decades took more than one-third of the increase in the (modest) increases in output per worker.

8. The decades of the 1970s and 1980s witnessed the rise of the "Yuppie" generation—Young Urban Professionals. One of the defining characteristics of this group was their high personal consumption patterns made possible by two-earner households without dependent children or parents.

9. What C. B. Macpherson (1960) has referred to as "possessive individualism."

10. In 1995 the national average cost for the care of elderly in nursing homes—exclusive of physician or skilled nursing services or medicines—was more than $100 per day.

11. There is a good deal of confusion about government deficits and the "burden" on future generations created by the investment of Social Security trust funds in government debt. For an explanation of the issues, see Appendix Note 7.1

12. From Exodus, XX 12, King James Version of The Bible.

13. The Fifth Commandment also notes that the source of support for the society is the land given by God. In a hunter-gatherer society (the Jews were wandering in the wilderness en route from Egypt to Palestine when they received the Ten Commandments) the land is the only asset available for food, water, and shelter. To put another modern cast on the commandment, the resources available to a society for production and consumption are not personally owned—they are to be socially shared in an intergenerational trust.

14. There is also the argument of sociobiology that the support of the younger generation by the older is genetically driven.

15. I take the position that ethics are involved when resources are divided among individuals.

16. When growth ceases the ethical problem returns to its simpler original dimension: one generation supports the succeeding generation in their youth so that they may, in turn, be supported in their retirement.

17. The prices of stocks, bonds, and real estate are determined by the flows of funds into and out of their ownership. The run-up in asset prices in the 1980s and 1990s reflected, in part, the net purchases of pension funds. The change in the balance between purchasers and sellers with changes in the age distribution of the population will continue to affect the changes in asset prices in present and future decades. Increased consumption by a growing retired population financed by the sale of assets will tend to reduce asset prices unless there is a corresponding increase in saving by the working population.

18. See Appendix Note 7.2 for the formal derivation of the formula.

19. See Appendix Table 7.1 for historical data on ratios

20. Not all employed workers are covered by Social Security—some are covered by governmental pensions systems. Not all retirees draw Social Security. Social Security also provides other benefits than pensions. The ratios presented are meant to be illustrative of magnitudes.

21. There is an additional important complication in the computation of the ratio of employment/working population. Part-time workers are counted the same as full-time workers and earn less income on which Social Security/Medicare taxes are levied.

22. It also needs to be pointed out that if Social Security and Medicare taxes in 2020 were, say, 25 percent to provide a retiree income ratio of 60 percent, the ratio of retiree income to worker after-transfer tax income would be 80 percent. This is before the payment of all other taxes for the support of government functions and transfer taxes for education!

23. Of course, the saving of 25 percent of income would leave 75 percent of that income left for consumption. Thus, the ratio of consumption during working years/consumption during retired years would be 2/3.

24. A listing for returns on various assets is contained in Appendix Table 7.2. These real rates of return do not allow for transactions costs or management fees by investment advisors. There is substantial variance of returns over various periods. The problem for the investor nearing retirement with a large sum to compound is that prudence counsels moving toward shorter-term, risk-free bonds with less asset value and interest rate risk at the time when the rate of return on the portfolio has the greatest effect in determining the principal sum of the annuity to fund retirement.

During the last two decades, the stock market has produced compounded rates of return in excess of those that I have used in my simulation. In the long run the valuation of stocks depends upon three factors: (1) the stock's current cash flow (dividend), (2) the expected growth rate of the cash flow, and (3) the discount rate used to present value expected future cash flows. If the dividend rate and the discount rate were stable, the rate of growth of the stock's value would be equal to the rate of growth of expected earnings.

In the long run the expected rate of growth of earnings of all stocks combined would be equal to the rate of growth of the economy unless profits were changing as a proportion of GDP. If profits were increasing faster than the rate of growth of GDP, it would mean that the wages being paid to the working generation were increasing more slowly than GDP. Thus, under some restrictive assumptions, the rate of growth in the stock market is equal to the rate of growth of the economy, unless the share of income going to the current labor force is changing. In the short run one could increase the rate of return on stocks to increase the share of GDP going to the retired population, but the gain would result from a change in relative shares.

25. To put the percentages and proportions into some illustrative real figures—the sixty-year-old making $40,000 per year pre-tax, and $32,000 per year after tax in the year 2000 retires with a pension fund of $284,000. His pre-retirement spending was $27,200 per year, and the retirement annuity is $29,104 per year.

An enquiring reader will ask: Why did you use 4 percent return on savings and the annuity? That seems historically low and way below what portfolio managers or annuity makers would offer. The important thing to remember is that the interest rates are "real" (inflation adjusted) rates. After twenty years of inflation at 4 percent (the average rate over the past half century), the purchasing power of the initial pension has been halved. If the purchasing power of the annuity fund is to be maintained, a real return of 4 percent can be paid out and 4 percent of the rest of the nominal return of, say 8 percent, must be plowed back into investments to maintain the real income from the fund for the next twenty years.

26. A person working full-time at the minimum wage earns $10,000 per year. Does anyone seriously propose that they would save 15 percent before retirement, and live on $8,500 per year before retirement, and $5,000 per year during retirement?

CHAPTER 8

Transfers to the Younger Generation: Economic Growth and the Increasing Burden of Educational Costs

> The good Education of Youth has been esteemed by wise Men in all Ages, as the surest Foundation of the Happiness both of private Families and of Commonwealths. Almost all Governments have therefore made it a principal Object of their Attention, to establish and endow with proper Revenues, such (institutions) as might supply the succeeding Age with Men qualified to serve the Publick with Honour to themselves, and to their Country.
>
> —Benjamin Franklin (1743)

A necessary foundation and inevitable consequence of living in an advanced society is allocating a large *and increasing* proportion of national income to education. While the citizens of an advanced economy might choose to spend a smaller proportion of income on, say, food or recreation, they must spend a larger proportion of their national income, even as it increases, on education if they wish to maintain or increase the "human capital" on which their level of income depends. Spending a greater proportion of income on education is not optional—it is a necessary condition for maintaining an advanced economy and society.

Just as an individual has to spend a larger proportion of a lifetime acquiring an education in order to participate in the labor force of an advanced society, the society as a whole has to allocate an increasing proportion of its productive resources to provide the teachers, buildings, libraries, laboratories, computer software and hardware, and support staff and services to "produce" human capital citizen.

Most of the costs of education at all levels are financed by state income and sales taxes and local property taxes.[1] Most citizens are unaware of the proportion of their state and local taxes that goes to the support of education unless they carefully analyze their local property tax bill or read in detail about education budgets in the battles in state legislatures or between school boards and teachers' unions over school contracts. They are mostly unaware of the large and increasing proportion of their incomes that is paid in taxes to finance the educational expenditure to create the human capital on which a high level economy depends.

We read about the "saving rate"—the proportion of national income that is allocated to pay for investment in physical capital. We almost never hear discussion about the proportion of national income "invested" in the creation of human capital. But, just as saving reduces the proportion of national income available for consumption, increasing the proportion of national income taken by taxation for educational expenditures decreases the household disposable income available for consumption expenditures (or saving).

Some students—and their parents—become aware of the magnitude of the costs of a year of higher education when they pay private college tuition bills. However, these tuition payments cover only a fraction of total educational costs—even in private institutions. Privately borne expenditures—primarily for college tuition costs but increasingly for elementary and secondary education— also reduce the disposable income available for private consumption. Families save to finance higher education for their children, and college graduates repay the interest and principal on debt that they personally borrow to finance their post-secondary education.[2]

The oft-quoted adage, "If you think education is expensive, try ignorance!", is a flippant statement of an important truth. Ignorance is not a viable alternative for a post-industrial society. Also, regretfully, the providers of educational services in the United States have not been very successful, to date, in improving organizational efficiency or using new technology to reduce the cost of creating human capital through institutional education. Our seeming inability to increase productivity in education is and will be a factor in further reducing the rate of economic growth and growth in personal consumption as the educational sector continues to grow in relative size in the economy.[3]

THE HISTORICAL RECORD

Education costs necessarily increase as a proportion of national income. This economic necessity was temporarily obscured in the United States. between 1970 and 1990 by a demographic anomaly. The "baby boom" that followed World War II was followed by a "baby bust" after 1965 that reduced the school-age population cohorts during the decades of the 1970s and 1980s at the same time that the "baby boomers" joined and their mothers rejoined the labor force. As a consequence, in those decades the number of income-producing and taxpaying workers increased relative to the number of non-income-producing and tax-supported students. This temporarily stabilized the proportion of educational costs to national income and educational cost per taxpayer.

This was a temporary phenomenon. In the current decade and into the next, the ratio of educational expenditures to national income will increase—even without increases in real expenditures per student—because the number of students is increasing relative to the number of workers.

Over the past century the proportion of U.S. national income allocated to institutional expenditures on education has increased ten-fold.

Text Graph 8.1
The Ratio of Educational Expenditures to National Income

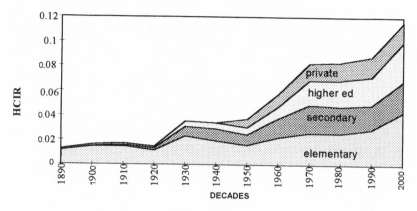

Source: Author: See Appendix Table 8.3

There is no counterpart to "saving" and "investment" rates for physical capital for human capital formation flows in the national income accounts. To emphasize the parallel nature of the flows for physical and human capital formation, I present a counterpart to saving and investment flows for physical capital for measuring expenditure flows on education as a proportion of national income. I call it the "human capital investment ratio," (HCIR)—the ratio of institutional education expenditures to national income is the HCIR.[4] This chapter analyzes the major determinants of the proportion of educational expenditures/national income—the counterpart of the saving ratio for physical capital.

The proportion of educational expenditures to national income shown on the vertical axis in Text Graph 8.1 and labeled the "Human Capital Investment Ratio (HCIR)" has increased from 1 percent to 10 percent of national income over the past century. (The Ratio for 2000 is projected from 1995 cost and enrollment data and their extrapolation to 2000.) The HCIR, the proportion of national income allocated to education, has increased because:

1. Educational expenditures per student, at every level of education, have increased faster than national income.
2. A larger proportion of the population has been educated in every educational level age cohort.
3. Higher levels of education cost more per student year and higher educational levels have witnessed the greatest increases in enrollment.

Several striking features are to be noted in Text Graph 8.1. One is the large proportion of educational costs committed to elementary and secondary education. The quantitative importance of higher education expenditures—

public and private—becomes significant only after World War II. (Prior to 1940 private and public institutional expenditures on all levels of education are not separated in the graph. In Appendix Table 8.3, however, they are.)

Another feature of the graph is the discontinuities (slightly distorted by the use of decennial benchmarks) in the large jumps in the ratio of educational expenditures to national income in the 1920s, again between 1950 and 1970, and projected for the 1990s. There is stability in the educational cost ratio between 1930 and 1950 and then again between 1970 and 1990. The huge increase projected and currently taking place during the decade of the 1990s is due, primarily, to the "baby boom" currently surging through our elementary schools and, secondarily, to an increase in college enrollments. Because of another "baby boom" that started in the mid-1980s, elementary enrollments rose 8 percent between the 1990 and 1995 school years and are projected to rise an additional 5 percent by the year 2000. Higher education enrollments are on track to rise by a projected 12 percent over the decade.[5]

Economic Growth and the Level of Education

Investment in education and an increase in the proportion of national income going to education are both quantifiable causes (Denison, 1962; Romer, 1986) and benefits of economic development. As noted in chapter 2, human capital—the level of educational investment embodied in the knowledge and skills of a society's labor force—is as necessary as physical capital for a society operating at an advanced level of production. And that human capital is created by educational expenditure.

The proportion of educational expenditure to national income depends primarily on the years of education necessary for citizens and workers to participate in a society at a particular level of technological and organizational development, and by the costs of producing those years of education relative to other goods and services.

The increase in levels of educational attainment parallels the level of economic output. The relative cost of producing education rises as productivity rises elsewhere in the economy and reduces the relative costs of other goods and services while it is stable, or increasing, in the educational sector.

Two measures of educational attainment—median years of education and the proportion of the adult population with a high school diploma—are presented in Text Table 8.1. A striking trend to be noted in Text Table 8.1 is the rapid increase in median years of school completed for the adult population between 1940 and 1970 and their slower subsequent growth. It will be noted that the proportion of the population completing high school actually declines after 1970. Apart from judgments about the quality of education, these figures on recent changes in the level of educational attainment for the U.S. population are alarming. High school "drop-outs" are unlikely to be significant contributors to the U.S. labor force in a "post-industrial" society.[6]

TEXT TABLE 8.1
Education Completion Levels

	Median Years of School Completed for Pop. > Age 25	High School Graduates as % of Population > Age 17
1890	n.a.	4%
1900	n.a.	6%
1910	8.1	9%
1920	8.2	17%
1930	8.4	29%
1940	8.6	51%
1950	9.3	59%
1960	10.5	70%
1970	12.2	77%
1980	12.5	71%
1991	12.7	74%

Source: National Center for Educational Statistics. U.S. Department of Education. Office of Educational Research and Improvement, *Digest of Educational Statistics, 1991.* (Washington, D.C. 1991), Tables 8,95.

Economic Growth and the Necessary Increase in the HCIR

During the course of the development of the American economy, an ever-increasing proportion of the population has been educated to progressively higher educational levels. Maintaining and increasing the "human capital" embodied by education has been accompanied by allocating an increasing proportion of national income being allocated to educational expenditure.[7]

We are familiar with the use of the term "investment" in connection with the production of physical capital. Like physical capital, human capital has a cost of production. Allocating resources to the creation of human capital through education reduces the resources available for the production of consumption goods in the period during which the human capital is formed. The members of the labor force who are forming human capital by teaching, and the physical capital embodied in schools rather than factories is not available to grow food or build houses.[8] The "gross" investment in human capital, like investment in physical capital, is accomplished by the allocation of productive resources from producing goods and services for current consumption to the maintenance of existing human capital levels and the creation of "net" new human capital. The human capital of citizens and workers who leave the labor force or retire is lost for the productive capacity of the society—just like physical capital, which is depreciated.

For physical capital, the transfer of resources from current production to capital formation is called "saving"; distinctions are made between "gross" and "net" saving and investment. For physical capital, aggregate flows of saving are compared to national income flows to obtain "saving" rates.

By definition, the HCIR is the ratio of educational expenditure to national income. The component determinants of the HCIR can be derived through the disaggregation of an educational cost identity into six demographic and economic ratios. These determinants, in turn, can be identified at three educational levels—elementary, secondary, and higher education. The disaggregation of economic and demographic ratios allows us to understand why the HCIR has increased over the past century and why it will necessarily continue to increase even more over the current and succeeding decades if educational levels rise parallel with national income levels.

The allocation of an increasing proportion of national income to create and maintain increasing levels of human capital per person is analogous to increasing the allocation of national income to saving to maintain or increase the level of physical capital per population or labor force member.[9] The higher the level of physical capital per worker, the higher the gross saving ratio necessary to just maintain it at any given depreciation (or amortization) rate. (New entrants to the labor force must be educated to replace the retirees—accounting for this replacement cost is the counterpart to the amortization of physical capital.)

Also, analogously for human capital, an increase in the level of educational capital (years of school) per labor force member, labor force growth, or a decrease in the average number of years of participation in the labor force (which increases the amortization rate) all necessitate an increase in the HCIR, the counterpart to the saving ratio. Additionally, the HCIR is raised when cost per student year is augmented by increases in such "quality" factors as the teacher/student ratio, the ratio of average teacher compensation/average worker income, and/or the ratio of indirect educational expenditures/teacher compensation.[10]

I present a heuristic and simplified explanation of the ratio determinants of the HCIR later in this chapter.[11] The determining components of the HCIR are:

1. Enrollment ratios—the proportion of school-age population cohorts enrolled in school.
2. Demographic structure ratios—the proportion of school-age cohorts to the total population.
3. Staffing ratios—teacher/student ratios (the reciprocal of student/teacher ratios).
4. Overhead ratios—total educational costs/teacher compensation ratios (actually, "markup" ratios).
5. Compensation ratios—average teacher compensation/ national income per worker ratios.
6. Population/labor force ratios (the reciprocal of participation ratios).[12]

Part I of this chapter presents and discusses the demographic, enrollment, and expenditure data comprising the ratios and the historical determinants of the behavior of the ratios. Part II develops indices of the ratio variables and explains the relative importance of various factors in the recent increase of educational costs relative to national income. Part III uses the ratios variably to quantify the relative importance of the determinants of increases in the HCIR over the past half-century.

Investment in education has benefits as well as costs, so Part IV introduces some *ex ante* estimates for the projected social returns from incremental investment in education using 1990 data on educational costs and income differentials. The final section of the chapter summarizes major points and policy issues.

In the appendix to this chapter, I present the ratios that determine the HCIR for the United States for census years from 1890 to 1990 with demographic projections extended to the census year 2000. These ratios show the changing relative importance of the factors that determine the level and increase in the ratio of educational expenditures to national income.

PART I: DETERMINANTS OF THE HUMAN CAPITAL INVESTMENT RATIO

Text Graph 8.1 has exhibited the ten-fold increase in the HCIR—the proportion of national income allocated to educational expenditures over the past century. How did it happen? What is the relative importance of the factors that have determined the increase in that proportion? Why is an increase in the HCIR an inevitable consequence of economic growth?

The economic and demographic determinants of the HCIR—the ratio of educational costs to national income—can be disaggregated from an identity that specifies the relationships of demographic and economic factors:

1. Total educational expenditures are, by definition, the product of the total number of students and the cost per student; let E represent total annual institutional expenditure on education, c represent costs per student, and S represent the total number of students: $E \equiv cS$.
2. Let Y represent national income, y represent national income per worker,[13] and N represent the total number of workers: $Y \equiv yN$.
3. HCIR, the Human Capital Investment Ratio, is defined as the ratio of Educational Expenditure to National Income: E/Y or, by expansion: $HCIR \equiv E/Y \equiv cS/yN$.
4. By regrouping of elements: $HCIR \equiv c/y \times S/N$.

Thus, the HCIR—the ratio of educational expenditures to national income—is equal to the product of the demographic ratio of students to workers (S/N), and the economic ratio of annual educational cost per student to annual income per worker (c/y).

The HCIR is completely analogous to the transfer rate from workers to retirees discussed in the previous chapter. Thus, for example, if the ratio of students to workers were 1/5, and the ratio of annual cost per student to annual income per worker were also 1/5 , the HCIR would be 1/25 or 4 percent.

To put numbers to the ratios, say that $4000 is the yearly cost per student and $20,000 is the yearly income per worker; the HCIR—which could also be thought of as a "school tax" rate—would be $4000 for each student to be paid for from the incomes of 5 workers collectively earning $100,000 or a tax rate of 4 percent.[14]

The Student/Worker Ratio

The ratio of students to workers (S/N), is the multiplicative product of three demographic ratios:

1. Enrollment: the enrollment rates of age cohorts in the various levels of education.
2. Relative cohort size: the ratio of various educational age cohort to the total population.
3. Labor force participation: the participation rate of the population in the labor forcereciprocal of the ratio of workers to the population.

The interaction of these factors in the American experience of the last century has produced the ratio of students to workers that is presented in Text Graph 8.2.

Text Graph 8.2
Ratio of Students/Workers

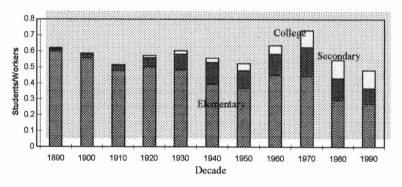

Source: Author. See Appendix Table 8.3.

Text Graph 8.2 details the changes in the ratio of students to workers by educational level. It shows the recent effects of the post–World War II "baby boom" on increasing the ratio of students to workers between 1950 and 1970 and the fall in the student-to-worker ratio after 1970, despite the increase in the proportion of the population enrolled in college. It also emphasizes the relative importance of elementary education—elementary education takes in nine years per student (grades K-8) and is virtually universal.

The Relative Cost—Student Cost/Worker Income Ratio

The ratio of cost per student/income per worker (c/y) depends upon the "production function" for education—specifically, the product of three factors:

1. The staffing ratio: the teacher/student ratio, or reciprocal of the student/teacher ratio.
2. The compensation ratio: the ratio of teacher compensation/average worker income.
3. The "overhead ratio": the ratio of total education expenditures/teacher compensation.

The level and changes in the cost per student year relative to national income per worker year for three educational levels are presented in Text Graph 8.3.

Text Graph 8.3
Cost per Student Relative to Income per Worker:
Student Costs by Educational Level

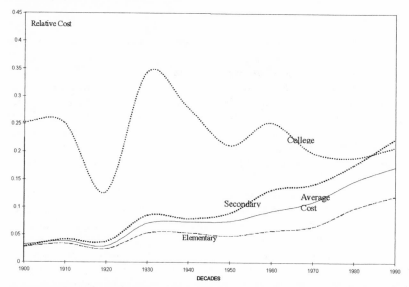

Source: Author. See Appendix 8.3.

Text Graph 8.3 shows the relative costs—student cost per year relative to average annual worker income—of the three levels of education. The ratio of average cost per student to average national income per worker of .17 in 1990 is the same ratio explained with historical data in endnote 14. The cost numerator represents the weighted average of the larger number of elementary students and smaller number of secondary and college students. Its rise over time is a combination both of rising costs at all levels and the increase in the proportion of students in more expensive higher levels of education. Because costs per student (the numerator) are rising more rapidly than incomes per worker (the denominator), there would be a secular increase in the HCIR without any increase in the ratio of students to workers. However, both the demographic and cost factors contribute to the increase in the burden of educational costs—the human capital investment ratio—as costs rise more rapidly than national income.

Inevitability of the Rise in the HCIR

It is important to understand the long-run inevitability of a rise in the HCIR as a consequence of economic growth.[15] There are two reasons why the relative share of output of one section of an economy grows relative to the rest of the economy: either the relative demand for the good produced by the sector increases, or the relative price of the good produced by the sector increases because of slower productivity growth in that sector than the rest of the economy. Usually, fast-growing sectors of the economy are those with falling relative prices. The HCIR increases necessarily with economic growth because both its share of real output increases and its relative price increases.

The Student/Worker Ratio

Abstracting from demographic factors (such as changes in the birth rate and death rate, which change the age structure of a society over time), economic growth increases the ratio of the human years spent in education relative to worker years spent in the labor force. As an example, consider first a society in which the average person goes to school for ten years (ages 6 to 15) and then works for fifty years (ages 16 to 65); then consider the effect of economic growth in extending education from ten years to fifteen years (ages 6 to 20) while working life is shortened to forty-five years (ages 21 to 65). The student years/working years ratio is increased from 10/50 to 15/45—from 20 percent to 33 percent.

What will be noted, in the American experience, is that the growth in the ratio of student years/worker years with the rise in average level of education was held down by two factors: (1) In the last half of the nineteenth and first half of the twentieth centuries, working lives were extended relative to student years by increasing life spans. This trend didn't continue when life expectancy passed normal retirement age and it is now diminishing as workers retire earlier. (2) The increase in the participation rate of married women has increased the ratio of workers to population.

However, if economic growth were to occur with increases in output per worker accompanied by an increasing period of education years in a population with a stable demographic structure and no changes in the participation rate of the population in the labor force, the ratio of students to workers would necessarily increase with economic growth.

Student Cost/Worker Income

There are two reasons why the ratio of cost per year of education rises relative to annual income per worker: (1) productivity (output per worker) is growing more slowly in the educational sector than it is in the rest of the economy; (2) educational costs rise with educational level—secondary education is more expensive than elementary, college is more expensive than secondary school, graduate and professional education is more expensive than undergraduate education.

There is nothing inevitable about the slower growth of productivity in education than elsewhere in the economy. However, as I shall argue in chapter 9, productivity growth in the commodity production and distribution sectors of economy has occurred because of productivity growth in the capital goods producing sectors of the economy; it becomes cheaper to produce cars because the robotic machines used to produce the goods are produced more cheaply—

per unit of output capacity. In education, human capital (teachers) is used to produce the next generation of human capital (students). (If only we could produce teachers, like cars, with robotic machine tools!) If there is no productivity growth in the production of teachers and no substitution of physical capital for teachers, even constant productivity in education, coupled with rising productivity elsewhere in the economy, will increase the cost of education relative to costs in the rest of the economy.

The problem is compounded by the increase in education costs per student at higher levels of education basically because the faculty/student ratio is higher and teachers at higher educational levels must have more education themselves. It should also be noted that in the American experience there has been a very substantial increase in staffing ratios, teachers' compensation relative to average income per worker, and a rising proportion of expenditures on overhead. These expenditures increase costs per student.

To summarize, in the long run the HCIR inevitably increases with economic growth because the students to workers ratio (S/N) rises and the ratio of student cost to worker incomes (c/y) rises. If (S/N) rises from 1/5 to 1/4 (a relative increase of 25%), and (c/y) increase by the same amount from 1/5 to 1/4 (also a 25% increase), the HCIR rises from (1/5 x 1/5 = 4 percent) to (1/4 x 1/4 = 6.67%). A rise in both of the constituent ratios by 25 percent doesn't just lead to an additive 50 percent increase in the HCIR. It increases the HCIR by 67 percent—the ratios are multiplicative!

PART II: EXPLAINING RELATIVE IMPORTANCE OF FACTORS BEHIND THE RISE OF THE HCIR WITH THE RATIOS

My explanation of the historical rise in the observed HCIR utilizes the six ratio determinants discussed in Part I for each of the three levels of public education—(elementary, grades K-8; secondary, grades 9-12; higher education, grades 13+).[16]

Ratio Determinant 1: Demographic Structure

A society experiencing economic growth undergoes a demographic transition. The falling birth and death rates and the increasing participation rates that accompany economic growth increase the ratio of working adults to student children and consequently offset the increasing costs of education.

However, the demographic transition is affected by discrete events. The United States, like every society, has a unique demographic profile that has changed over time. From the beginning of the nineteenth century until World War II, the United States had an initially high but secularly decreasing birth rate that steadily decreased the size of the school-age population cohorts relative to the total population. In the four decades prior to World War I, a large flow of immigrants with a higher male/female ratio concentrated in age groups that had higher labor force participation rates marginally lowered the student/worker ratio. However, the new immigrants also had a higher birth rate than the native born population and, thus, slowed the decline of the aggregate birth rate in the pre-World War I era (Easterlin, 1968).

In the twentieth century U.S. demographic structure was radically altered, first by a sharp decline in the birth rate in the inter-war period and then by the "baby boom" that followed World War II. This resulted in temporary increases in the ratio of school-age cohorts to the population between 1950 and 1970 for elementary and secondary education and between 1960 and 1980 for higher education. (The impact of the baby boom and bust on educational enrollments has been noted in Text Graph 8.2.)

In the 1990 census the elementary school-age cohort (ages 5-14) had fallen to some 15 percent of the population in contrast to the 20 percent that it represented in 1970 after the end of the "baby boom." However, the five-to-fourteen age cohort is currently growing rapidly in relative size and is on track to increase back to 18 percent of population by the census year 2000. This is a 20 percent increase in the cohort from which elementary students come and is the most powerful factor in increasing the burden of educational costs in the decade of the 1990s. It is as big a "bulge" as the baby boom of the 1950s.

The twenty to twenty-four age cohort, from which most of higher education enrollments are drawn, rose from 6 percent to 9.5 percent of the population between 1960 and 1980 before dropping back to 7.5 percent in 1990.[17]

Ratio Determinant 2: Enrollment Ratios

It is a useful generalization to say that, during most of the last century, the decline in the relative size of the elementary-age cohorts was offset by an increase in the proportion of the cohorts enrolled. For secondary and higher education, where the increase in enrollment ratios was far greater than the decline in relative cohort size the ratio of students to the total population increased.[18]

The large increase in the enrollment ratio in public higher education over the past five decades has been a large contributor to the increase in the HCIR. Its projected increase during the current decade is the second most important reason for the projected increase in the HCIR during the decade. (See Appendix Table 8.2 for actual enrollment data.)

Ratio Determinant 3: Teacher/Student Ratios

The rise in teacher/student ratios over the past century in elementary and secondary schools is impressive and an important economic contributor to the increase in the HCIR. This ratio rose sharply for secondary education after 1940, and for elementary education only after 1960. (A teacher/student ratio of .05 is a student/teacher ratio of 20/1.)

Teacher/student ratios in higher education were much higher than for elementary or secondary education prior to World War II. Faculty/student ratios in higher education actually reached an abnormal peak in 1960 after the subsidence of the enrollment "bulge" from the GI bill and coincident with the small college-age population cohort resulting from the low birth rate of the

1930s. In the 1960s the teacher/student ratio in higher education declined precipitously, coincident with the trebling of college enrollments. It moved back up again slowly in the 1970s and 1980s as enrollment growth slackened and higher education budgets grew. Thus, the decline of the teacher/student ratio in higher education in the 1960s had the effect of delaying the rising cost burden from the rapid growth in higher education enrollments in the 1960s until the 1970s and 1980s.

The post-1970 increase in the elementary teacher/student ratio coincided with the demographically caused decline in elementary enrollments in the period up to 1990. The secondary teacher/student ratio rose sharply between 1980 and 1990 for the same reason. One might interpret the increase in teacher/student ratios in public elementary and secondary education from 1970 to 1990 as a deliberate policy to increase the quality of education; however, it might also be partly explained as a consequence of a policy of maintaining teaching staffs in districts with declining enrollments and the maintenance of teacher/student ratios in districts with expanding enrollments.

It will be noted that increasing teacher/student ratios—particularly for elementary and secondary education—are a major reason for the increasing HCIR. Are increasing teacher/student ratios inevitable?

The teacher/student ratio in education is, in some ways, analogous to the capital/output ratio for the economy as a whole. I will argue in chapter 9 that technological change has decreased the physical capital/output ratio—by decreasing the cost of production of physical capital per unit of production capacity—and, thereby, reducing the necessity for higher physical capital/labor and higher saving ratios. But the cost of teacher capital in education increases rather than decreases—because the cost of educating teachers is rising. Thus, our inability to decrease the cost of capital in teachers' education will progressively increase the relative size and cost of the educational sector in the national economy.

Why not offset the increase in the cost of human capital (the teachers) with an increase in the (student/teacher) output/capital in education? We can observe that it is possible to substitute physical capital for (teacher) human capital in some parts of education. There is no reason why a university lecture can't be broadcast on TV screens to really large audiences. This technology increases the ratio of students/teachers in lectures. There is no reason why students can't use interactive software for rote learning to augment the student/teacher ratio with the use of physical capital.

However, the operative constraints for decreasing teacher/student ratios are inherent in the process of producing human capital by education. For elementary grades the constraints come from the need for human discipline and motivation. For high school and college students, the constraints on increasing student/teacher ratios grow out of the nature of education.

There are (at least) five levels of understanding in learning: (1) recognition, (2) memorization, (3) application, (4) explanation, and (5) evaluation. Students can be taught to recognize or memorize patterns or definitions with educational technology; for example, a computer program is an efficient substitute for a human being teaching vocabulary or multiplication tables with "flash cards."

Students may check their ability to find the area of a circle with a formula with a computer program that validates their answers (although research indicates that students are likely to iterate rather than learn to apply principles to obtain answers).

However, "higher education" involves students learning why certain formulas or principles are the right ones to apply in particular circumstances but not in others—not just learning the right answers but learning why answers are right. The highest level of education involves learning the bases for evaluating alternative explanations of phenomena, and, at this point, there is no substitute for the teacher reasoning through alternative explanations or methods with the student individually. High-level societies require more people with these kinds of reasoning skills and there are limited ways to extend this kind of teacher/student interaction. As a consequence I do not foresee large potential gains through substituting technology for teachers.

Ratio Determinant 4: Relative Teacher Compensation (Teacher Compensation/National Income per Worker)

In the long run, relative teacher compensation will increase relative to worker incomes because of the increase in the human capital of teachers relative to the average human capital level in the rest of the labor force. In the nineteenth century, teachers' compensation in elementary and secondary education was less than half of average income per worker, but this was partly determined by the limited scope of education. Schools operated for half the year and average daily attendance was considerably smaller than enrollment. The labor force during this period was predominantly male and full-time, while teachers were predominantly female and part-time. These factors were contributing determinants to the lower relative pay ratio of teachers.

Increases in the length of the school year, in average daily attendance, and in the male percentage of the teaching staff all accompanied the rise in average teacher compensation relative to average income per labor force member until 1940.[19] Teachers' compensation figures, post-1950, include employer-paid fringe benefits for retirement and medical insurance. For reference, national average salary and benefits for public elementary and secondary teachers were taken as $32,448 and $33,701 respectively in 1990 reports on educational expenditure, while National Income per Labor Force Member was calculated as $35,737 for the same year.[20] After falling relative to average income per labor force member in the 1970s for all three levels of education, relative teacher compensation rose again in the 1980s.[21]

It is unwarranted to draw equity inferences from the increase in the 1980s in the ratio of average teacher compensation/national income per labor force member, I have introduced the ratio of teacher compensation to national income per worker to show that the rising "burden" of educational costs to the taxpayer is due, in part, to teachers' compensation rising more rapidly than the incomes of the labor force that comprise the tax base.

Ratio Determinant 5: "Overhead Cost" Ratios

"Overhead" is a slightly misleading term—the ratio presented is actually a "markup" factor.[22] It represents the ratio of total educational expenditures to teacher compensation; thus, an "overhead" factor of two implies that teacher compensation is 50 percent of total educational expense. The substantial rise in the overhead ratio over time reflects better facilities and maintenance, more books and classroom materials, more busing expense, and more educational administration. (It also arises from the lack of distinction in institutional budgets in earlier years between teaching and administrative activity in school budgets and personnel assignments in earlier years.)

The decline in the overhead ratio for all levels of education in the 1930s and 1980s is mostly explainable in terms of the decline of capital expenditures—particularly on buildings—during those decades. While school districts do run capital budgets, both capital and operating expenditures are included in national figures on educational expenditures.

Teaching-compensation expense and overhead expense in higher education include expenses for research.   They exclude expenditures for auxiliary enterprises such as dormitories, dining facilities, and extracurricular athletics. Expenditures for teaching assistants in universities are not included in faculty compensation but are included in overhead.[23]

Ratio Determinant 6: Population/Labor Force

As remarked in the introduction to this chapter, and illustrated in Text Graph 8.3, the most significant factor between 1970 and 1990 in offsetting the increase in the relative per student cost of education (c/y) has been the decline in the demographic ratio of students/labor force (S/N). This has resulted from the simultaneous demographic decrease in the proportion of elementary and secondary students to the population and the increase in the participation rate of the population (which is represented as a decline in the population/labor force ratio).

The same factors are operative here as in the previous chapter with regard to the retired population. The increase in the size of the labor force relative to the student population increases the total income available to support the dependent student population. With the exception of the 1950 to 1970 decades, when the "baby boomers" went to school and their mothers stayed out of the labor force, the ratio of students/labor force has declined secularly.   The labor force participation rate (reciprocal of population/labor force ratio) has risen faster than the ratio of students to population. In the decades of the 1970s and 1980s, this caused national income to grow at a similar rate to total educational expenditures and, thereby, temporarily stabilized the HCIR which would otherwise have increased because per student expenditures rose faster than worker incomes.

This favorable trend, as noted in chapter 6, is an unrepeatable historical anomaly resulting from the entry of married women into the labor force. In the current decade the increase in the participation rate of the population in the labor force has stabilized with the smaller increase in married female participation being offset by the decreased participation rate of older males. The recent "baby boom" and the projected increase in enrollment rates in higher education is behind the current increase in this ratio of students/workers.

A critical consideration for projections of the burden of education costs over the current decade and in the future are the limits to further increases in labor-force participation by women of working age (since most of them are working), and the aging of the population. Population aging will not only reduce the proportion of the population of working age but, as we noted in the preceding chapter, will increase the rate of growth of demand for transfer payments from the employed population to a dependent population for retirement and medical care. This increases the competition for tax revenues between the dependent young and old generations.

PART III: THE PRIMARY DETERMINANTS OF RECENT INCREASES IN THE BURDEN RATIO OF EDUCATIONAL COSTS

What has been the relative importance of various factors in increasing the HCIR? Table 8.2 presents the relative importance of various factors over the past half-century.

Text Table 8.2
Relative Importance of Factors Determining Increase in Human Capital Investment Ratio (HCIR) (Public Institutions Only)

Ratio Determinants	Elementary	Secondary	Higher Ed
1950–1990			
Enrollment	1%	19%	395%
Age Cohort	-9%	-1%	-3%
Teacher/Student Ratio	59%	53%	-35%
Teacher Comp.	22%	27%	29%
Overhead	29%	29%	17%
Pop/Labor Force Ratio	-20%	-20%	-20%
Interactive Factors	2%	29%	-104%
Total Change In HCIR	84%	136%	279%
1980–1990			
Enrollment	1%	3%	33%
Age Cohort	-4%	-25%	-22%
Teacher/Student Ratio	14%	19%	4%
Teacher Comp.	20%	18%	16%
Overhead	-10%	-10%	-11%
Pop/Labor Force Ratio	-5%	-5%	-5%

Text Table 8.2 continued			
Interactive Factors	-3%	-7%	-9%
Total Change In HCIR	12%	-8%	6%
1990–2000 projection			
Enrollment	4%	10%	16%
Age Cohort	23%	0%	-2%
Teacher/Student Ratio*	0%	0%	0%
Teacher Comp.*	0%	0%	0%
Overhead*	0%	0%	0%
Pop/Labor Force Ratio	10%	10%	10%
Interactive Factors	12%	1%	1%
Total Change In HCIR	50%	21%	25%

Source: Author: See Appendix Table 8.3.

It was shown in Text Graph 8.1 that the HCIR for all levels of education (including private) rose from less than 4 percent to more than 8 percent of national income between 1950 and 1990. If an increase of this proportion—a doubling—in the national saving rate were to take place, it would be hailed as an enormous achievement in national thrift! This doubling in the HCIR is the combined and weighted result of the rates of increase for the three levels of education for the 1950 to 1990 period.

What were the most important factors in this large increase in the HCIR—the human capital investment ratio? Text Table 8.2 (based on the ratios of Appendix Table 8.3 and the indexation of these ratios in Appendix Table 8.4) displays the components of the cost increases for all three levels of education. I have shown the overall determinants between 1950 and 1990 because these four decades illustrate the influences of "baby boom" and "baby bust." I have also presented information on the "unusual" decade of the 1980s, when demographic factors were instrumental in restraining the growth of the HCIR. I have also included projections for the 1990s based solely on demographic factors with the ratios of cost per student relative to income per worker frozen at their 1990 level.

Discussion of Recent Changes in Determinants of the HCIR

Elementary Education

As displayed in Text Table 8.2, the HCIR for public elementary education increased by 84 percent (from 1.6% to 2.9%) between 1950 and 1990. The table shows that the increase was primarily attributable to increases in real resources per student—the teacher/student ratio (59%), relative teacher compensation

(22%), and increases in the overhead ratio (29%). The expense of increases in real resources per student was offset by a decline in the relative size of the elementary age cohort and the increase in the participation rate of the population in the labor force (shown as a decline in the the Pop/Labor Force in the Table).

At the other extreme, over the shorter period of the 1980s decade, there was only a 12 percent increase in the education cost burden ratio for elementary education with virtually all of the increase attributable to increases in the teacher/student and relative teacher compensation ratios. Both in short (decade) and longer periods, decline in the relative size of the elementary-age cohort and the increase in the participation rate of the population assisted in keeping total costs from rising, even though there were substantial increases in real expenditures per student.

Secondary Education

The HCIR ratio for secondary education increased by 136 percent during the 1950 to 1990 period from less than 1 percent to more than 2 percent of national income. An increase in the enrollment ratio, as well as increases in the ratios determining per student cost, were largely responsible for the overall increase. Interestingly, the secondary education cost burden ratio actually declined in the 1980s due to the shrinking of the relative size of the secondary-school-population cohort, and the small increase in the enrollment ratio. The result was an absolute decline in enrollment and a decline in the HCIR for Secondary Education.

Higher Education

Higher education represents a very diverse spectrum of institutions ranging from community colleges through research universities and professional schools of law and medicine. The primary determinant of the near trebling of the HCIR ratio in this sector from 1950 to 1990 was enrollment increase.

Increases in relative teacher compensation in higher education were offset by a decline in teacher/student ratios; overhead increases were smaller than in elementary and secondary education. The more modest rise in per student costs in higher education during the period was partially a consequence of an increase in the ratio of students in relatively lower-cost community college programs to students in research universities and liberal arts colleges. Between 1970 and 1990, the proportion of FTE students enrolled in community colleges rose from 27 percent to 38 percent of total enrollments.

The Current Decade

Three factors have led to increases in the HCIR in the decade of the 1990s: (1) The ratio of population/labor force (the inverse of the participation rate) did not decrease as it did over the past four decades to offset the increase in students and cost per student; (2) elementary education, the largest enrollment sector (because of near-universal enrollment and a nine-year, K-8 enrollment span) shows a substantial increase in students because of the rise in the birth rate in the mid-1980s; and (3) an increase in enrollment rates for post-secondary education. (The "starred" teacher/student, relative teacher compensation, and overhead ratios have been assumed constant for the decade.)

These demographic factors would lead to an increase in the HCIR even without any change in the other factors that have contributed to the large increases in the educational cost burden over the last four decades.

Using the census projections for population in the year 2000 and the Department of Education projections for enrollment in the same year, the combination of an increase in enrollment and decline in the work force relative to population would lead to an increase from 8.56 percent to 11.62 percent in the HCIR between the 1990 and 2000 census years. This projection assumes no increase in the determinants of cost per student and no decline in the age-specific participation rates of the labor force.[24]

The teacher/student, teacher compensation/worker income, and overhead cost factors are the educational policy variables that were primarily responsible for the increase in the education cost burden ratio between 1950 and 1990. In my projections I have frozen them at their 1990 levels. While it might be possible to freeze them at their 1990 levels in the real world, this would conflict with the declared national objective to increase educational quality over the next decade.

It needs to be emphasized, however, that even if the determinants of real expenditures per student are frozen at 1990 levels, the projected increase in the ratio of students/labor force between 1990 and 2000 will increase the education cost burden ratio by an additional 3 percent of National Income—the largest absolute one-decade increase in the education cost burden ratio the United States has ever experienced! The implication of this projected increase in the HCIR needs to be understood: If growth in GDP per worker grows at the same 8 to 9 percent rate as the last two decades, one third of it would have to go to maintaining human capital formation at the same level—even with no increases in the real expenditures per student at any level! This is the startling implication of the slowdown of growth and the maturation of the population and the economy.

PART IV: RETURNS TO INVESMENT IN EDUCATION

When and at what level will the HCIR stabilize? The rise in the HCIR would slow if the ratio of students to workers (S/N) were to stabilize (as in the 1970 to 1990 period). But, paradoxically, an increase in productivity growth elsewhere in the economy would increase the HCIR as the ratio of costs per student year of education rose more rapidly relative to the costs in other sectors. Of course, the high productivity growth in the rest of the economy is due in no small part to the increase in human capital produced by the education sector.

How much education should the economy produce? From a strictly economic point of view that measures education in terms of its capacity to increase the production of market valued goods and services, a national policy to increase the educational level of the population will increase economic growth as long as the allocation of resources to create human capital for education has a higher rate of return on investment than the allocation of resources to produce other kinds of capital. Therefore, it is important to estimate the returns to investment in education as well as the cost reflected in the HCIR. Economists must measure benefits as well as costs!

In a neoclassical growth model, the physical capital stock/output ratio increases until the return on capital stock per worker is driven down by diminishing projected returns to an interest rate equal to the social rate of time preference (Barro, 1990).

Acknowledging that the expected social returns from investment in education are subject to conceptual complexity (Blaug,1976), the cost data in this chapter, together with some earnings data, may be used to provide some "order of magnitude" estimates for a limited concept of the societal returns to investment in education that may then be compared with returns on private investment.

To estimate the incremental "social return" to investment in human capital through education, make the following assumptions:

1. The total public and private costs of education are the sum of institutional educational expenditures and the opportunity costs of forgone employment and output of enrolled students. "Opportunity costs," in this context, are a measure of the social output lost when students are enrolled full time in education rather than producing goods and services as members of the labor force.
2. The opportunity cost of high school education for high school students is full-time work at the minimum wage.
3. The opportunity cost of college students is the average wage of full-time workers with twelve years of education in the 25 to 34 years-old age cohort.
4. The social return to additional education is equal to the current absolute earnings differences for males and females in different age cohorts with different levels of education.[25]
5. Earnings differentials are taken as the averages for ten-year-age cohorts, by sex, for 1990.

For my calculations I assume that high school graduates leave school at eighteen years of age and work, continuously and full time, until age sixty-two, and that their earnings differentials with same-sex workers in the same age cohort are an accurate indicator of their incremental contribution to social output made possible by the incremental investment in their four years of secondary education. A similar calculation is made for college graduates, except that it is assumed that they graduate at age twenty-two and work continuously and full-time until age sixty-two.[26]

Parallel to the calculations on private saving to fund retirement, I have made the assumption that workers work uninterruptedly for forty years. Reduction from the forty-year, full-time participation assumption significantly reduces return calculations. These participation assumptions are extremely optimistic because the labor force participation rates for males and females over these periods are near to 80 percent for males and 60 percent for females. (See Appendix Table 6.1.) On the other hand, the assumption of full-time labor force participation of high school or college students arguably overstates the estimated opportunity cost of education and, thereby, reduces the internal rate of return calculation. Still, the effect of my assumptions is to increase the calculated social rate of return on investment in education.

To illustrate the effect of different assumptions about labor-force participation on rates of return, I have included an estimate of the internal rate of return on investment for a college-educated male who retires at fifty-two rather than sixty-two. I have also shown the calculation for a female college graduatewho withdraws from labor-force participation between age twenty-five and thirty-four but then returns to the labor force at thirty-five with the same relative wage as a woman who has not interrupted labor force participation.

Rate of return calculations are shown in Text Table 8.3.

Text Table 8.3
Social Rates of Return on Incremental Investment in Education

Demographic Group	Rate of Return
High School, Males	11%
High School, Females	7.00%
Public Higher Education, Males	8.70%
Public Higher Education, Females	8.10%
Higher Education Males, Retire at 52	7.20%
Hi Ed., Females, Out of Labor Force, 25–34	2.60%

Source: Author. Earnings differentials and opportunity costs calculated from National Center for Educational Statistics. U.S. Department of Education. Office of Educational Research and Improvement. *Digest of Educational Statistics, 1991* (Washington D.C., 1991), Table 358. Educational costs taken from Author, Appendix Table 8.3. Rates of return on higher education are based on public higher education only.[27] Calculations are based on the internal rate of return concept.

What inferences might be drawn from these "order of magnitude" calculations on the internal social rate of return on investment in education? First of all, they are all above the estimate of the long-term, risk-free "real" rate of interest of 2 to 3 percent. (See Appendix Table 7.6 for the real rate on government bonds.) On the other hand, they are in the same range as the long-run after-corporate-tax rate of return on corporate capital. This would indicate that the social rate of return on investment in the physical capital of private corporations is greater than the social return to education.

However, recent work on the relationship between physical and human capital in the aggregate production function (Lucas, 1988; Romer, 1986) would indicate that the comparison of marginal rates of return on either human capital or physical capital do not capture the social returns to investment in education because they fail to account for the impact of additional education of other workers and on the rate of return to investment in physical capital.[28] What is involved here is a social production function for GDP in which the simultaneous investment in physical, human, and knowledge capital is complementary and provides increasing returns.

SUMMARY

Economic development increases the necessary size of the educational investment flow relative to national income—the education cost burden ratio (HCIR) I have discussed in this chapter. It does this both by increasing the cost per student year of education relative to national income per worker and by increasing the proportion of a lifetime spent in student years relative to labor force years of the average population member.

The HCIR necessarily increases for a society with a high level of educational capital per worker, just as the gross saving ratio must increase for a society with a high level of physical capital per worker. The temporary increase in the ratio of students to workers due to unusual demographic changes during the decades from 1970 to 1990—the large increase in the participation rate of women and the reduction in school-age children from the baby bust—may well have concealed this economic necessity from public (and professional) notice.

While there are striking analytic similarities between the saving rate for physical capital formation and the HCIR for human capital formation through educational expenditures, there are marked differences in the incentive structure for the decision makers who determine the ratios. Unlike individual saving for physical capital formation to earn a rate of return on the investment, individuals in one generation do not pay for their own entire educational costs or amortize them or directly receive a return from investment in their own education. They pay for the education of the next generation—largely through taxes.

The significant difference between saving to purchase an expected earnings stream from the ownership of a financial asset, and paying taxes for the support of schools or children's tuitions to create human capital by educational expenditure is that the investors have no individual property rights to the return on investment, at least for the earlier years of their education.

Besides recognizing it as an investment, therefore, expenditure on education needs to be understood as an intergenerational transfer from the employed population cohort to student population cohorts. In this respect it resembles the operation of the Social Security system. Through the tax mechanism the current bearers of the educational tax burden do tap the future incomes of the generation they pay to educate for the provision of their own retirement incomes and medical expenses.

I believe it is insufficiently understood in debates about educational policy and election rhetoric urging "no new taxes" that the current cohorts being educated at the expense of tax-paying cohorts will in turn be supporting the cohorts who have paid for their education. Another set of intergenerational transfers for Social Security and Medicare will support the latter cohort through their retirement years.

The United States was lucky to temporarily escape the rising burden of educational costs in the 1970s and 1980s. The current decade has experienced significant increases in the "burden" of educational costs on the tax- and tuition-paying population. The size of these burdens is currently increasing rapidly for reasons connected with demography, the increasing demands for higher educational accomplishment to compete in a more complex international economy, and the likely trend for productivity to increase more slowly in the educational service sector than elsewhere in the economy.

This chapter provides evidence that real expenditures, per student, have increased substantially over the last three decades of this century and, based on the disaggregation of that evidence, that the HCIR—the proportion of national income devoted to human capital formation—will have to increase in the current and forthcoming decades if we are to maintain our advanced society.

All the estimates in this chapter are estimates of costs. There is no direct evidence on the quality of educational attainment. It is widely reported that educational outcomes have deteriorated. The American public no longer believes that increasing per student educational expenditure, by itself, will result in improved educational outcomes and they regard the educational establishment's claims to the contrary to be self-serving.

In this context it is important to understand why the burden of educational costs is increasing, why the costs are taking an increasing portion of a more slowly growing national income, and why they are a necessary component of future growth in incomes.

While legislators and voters could stabilize or lower the growth in the transfers from the working population to the population being educated by reducing the extent or quality of education, the long-run consequences would be as detrimental as allowing the stock of physical capital to wear out, or the stock of natural resource capital to be exhausted to enable the current generation to have a temporarily lower level of taxes and higher level of consumption.

NOTES

1. While federal expenditures on education are a relatively small proportion of total expenditures, the exclusion of state and local taxes from taxable income for taxpayers who itemize constitutes a considerable federal "tax subsidy."

2. In current discussions of the increase in the share of disposable income going to the top quartile of the population it is frequently overlooked that the high incomes accruing to these households are partially the result of lengthened periods of education and nonparticipation in the labor force. Many upper-income workers paid for part of their extended education with student loans that they repay with interest during their working years. If income distribution were analyzed on a lifetime basis, taking the repayment of student loans into account, the increase in income inequality would not seem so large.

3. I will argue in chapter 9 that the requirements for physical capital in an advancing economy have been offset by a decrease in the cost of forming capital with the same output capacity. Unfortunately, the cost of forming human capital by education will be seen to be *increasing*—at least insofar as the output of capital is measured in terms of years of education per student. The primary reason why educational costs take an increasing proportion of total output is the *increasing* cost of forming the higher and higher levels of human capital that are a necessary condition of affluence.

4. I relate educational expenditures to national income (NI) rather than GDP for two reasons. First, GDP differs from NI by depreciation of physical capital and the cost of final production represented by indirect taxes. Neither of these additions represent product or income available for expenditures on education (unless the physical capital stock were to be allowed to depreciate without replacement). Second, I am interested in

the portion of national income or tax rate that is necessary for the finance of education. In 1990, when the proportion of educational expenditures to NI was 8.4 percent, the proportion to GDP was 7.2 percent.

5. Current and projected enrollments are taken from *Digest of Educational Statistics* (1996).

6. There has been a continuing increase in the proportion of the population twenty-five years of age and older that has completed four or more years of high school simultaneously with the reduction in the proportion that actually has a high school diploma.

7. See Appendix Tables 8.1 and 8.2 for the historical record on enrollment and expenditure.

8. My analysis does not take into account expenditures by households and businesses that also are important factors in the growth of human capital. Expenditures for on-the-job training by employers—which may be as large as 2 percent of national income—are not included in my accounting, nor are student or parental expenditures for books or school transportation. Most important, opportunity costs for students are also not included as a cost of education.

9. I detail the formal relationships in the Appendix Note 8.2.

10. The real cost of education per student is increased by raising the teacher/student ratio and the relative compensation of teachers, or the cost of buildings, equipment, and administration. This does not necessarily entail an increase in the quality or productivity of the education received by the students. For physical capital, spending more on a building may not yield the owner the increased advantages sought by the increase in expenditures. But what accounting convention records is the cost of the change.

11. The formal derivation of the ratio components of the HCIR is presented in the Appendix Note 8.2.

12. By working in terms of demographic and relative cost ratios and such familiar ratios as teacher/student and instructional cost/total cost, the analytic framework used in this paper avoids the measurement problems created by the development of price deflators for long-time periods of analysis. Further, it lays bare such educational policy choices as class size and relative teacher compensation and such demographic constraints as the size of population cohorts and labor-force participation rates for the implementation of educational policy goals.

13. One of the analytic simplifications used in this chapter, as in the previous chapter on the relationship between the labor force and the retired population, is the assumed direct relationship between employment and output. Not all of national income goes to labor—the owners of physical capital and natural resources receive part. Some of the owners of those resources are not in the labor force. However, it is assumed that total national income, from which educational expenditures are financed, is *proportional* to the labor force. Thus, the participation rate of the population in the labor force directly determines the GDP available for the financing of education.

Changes in the age structure of the population that increase the participation rate increase GDP. Further, the increase in the participation rate of women has increased the national income available for educational expenditure. In earlier years when women stayed out of the labor force to work in the home, the imputed value of home production would have increased real national income, but it would not have been income available for expenditure on institutional education.

14. HCIR $\equiv$ E/Y $\equiv$ (cS)/(yN) = (S/N) x (c/y). To put some numbers to the equation, in 1990 the average cost per student year for all levels of education was $6,200 and national income per worker was $35,000—a ratio of 17 percent. In the same year the ratio of students/workers was .48—there was one student for every 2.08 workers. The multiplication of these two ratios produces the HCIR—the tax rate on national income

necessary to fund educational expenditures of 8.4 percent. This is the ratio for 1990 that appears in Text Graph 8.1.

15. An elegant formal proof of the necessary rise in the proportion of GDP taken by a service industry in which labor productivity is less rapid than labor productivity in the remainder of the economy may be found in Appendix 10 of Baumol and Wolff (1989).

16. Information for assembling these ratios is taken from Federal statistical agencies for census years. Values for these ratios are contained in Appendix Table 8.3 and the ratios are converted to indexes in Appendix Table 8.4. (Data sources are listed in Appendix Note 8.1.)

17. Since age cohorts overlap education levels it may be useful to note that a 69 percent enrollment ratio in public higher education for the twenty to twenty-four population cohort does not mean that 69 percent of that age group is enrolled. Some college students are in the fifteen-to-nineteen age cohort and some are older. Since we are interested in the ratio of students/population, the overstatement of the enrollment rate for a particular cohort is exactly offset by the understatement of the relative proportion of the population cohort from which enrollment is drawn.

18. The surprising decline in the elementary public school enrollment ratio in the 1910 to 1960 period can largely be explained by the increase in the proportion of the age cohort enrolled in (Roman Catholic) parochial schools. Similar but less powerful trends affect private sector enrollments at the secondary level.

19. There is no breakdown before 1940 in compensation figures for teachers between the elementary and secondary levels. Estimates for compensation levels in higher education prior to 1930 are taken from disparate sources and, for the period prior to 1930, are based on average salaries at a group of land-grant universities.

20. It must be remembered that national income per member of the labor force is different from the average wage. NI, for example, includes returns to capital and payments for Social Security and Medicare that the worker never sees in her paycheck.

21. In no sense should the figures presented on teacher compensation/national income per labor force member be construed as involving *equity* comparison of teachers' compensation with the compensation of other workers. On one hand teachers have different educational and demographic characteristics than the labor force as a whole. On the other they draw compensation for employment, as teachers, over fewer workdays per year than other members of the labor force. Further disaggregation and analysis would be necessary to make any judgments about disparate movements in compensation between teachers and other members of the labor force. I suspect that increasing opportunities for educated women in the labor force after 1970 were a contributor to any rises in the relative income of elementary and secondary teachers. The increase in part-time employment in the 1970s and 1980s increased the number of workers faster than income and slowed the increase in income per worker.

22. Total educational expenditure, by levels, is taken, as given, from public sources. (See Appendix note 8.1.) Estimates of teacher compensation represent the product of the total number of teachers and their reported average compensation. The ratio of total compensation to teacher compensation is the "overhead ratio." Thus, any errors in the total number of teachers or their compensation will be reflected in alterations of teacher/student ratios, teacher compensation/average income, or "overhead" ratios, but not in HCIR. The same overhead factor is used for both elementary and secondary education because the data aggregated for public school systems do not permit its breakdown.

23. Once again, no efficiency or equity conclusions can be directly drawn from the data on whether overhead or teacher compensation is too small or too large a part of educational expenditures. In other service sector industries, the ratio of capital/worker and capital expense per "production worker" has risen. Nevertheless, rising "overhead"

has been a significant factor in the increase of the education cost burden ratio until the big drop in the overhead ratio for all levels of education in the 1980s.

24. Since the age participation rates for the forty-five- to sixty-five-year-old male segment of the labor force have been declining over the four previous decades, it is unlikely that the overall participation rate will remain constant.

25. The classic work on returns to investment in education is Becker, 1964. Becker's estimates of the *private* rate of return for high school education for cohorts graduating in 1939, 1949, and 1959 were 16 percent, 20 percent, and 28 percent. (Becker, 1964, Table 14.) His estimates of the private rate of return for college graduates in the same cohorts were 14.5 percent, 13 percent, and 15 percent. Becker's estimate of the *social* rate of return were only slightly lower, since the addition of adjusted institutional expenditures was offset by the deletion of income taxes on income.

The rates of return presented in this paper are *social* rates of return. Becker's concept of private cost includes only the forgone earnings of students and tuition payments. It does not include public expenditures on education. His earnings estimates assume a growth rate for income on existing differentials and reduce income estimates for mortality, morbidity, and personal income tax. My cost estimates, on the other hand, are based on both forgone earnings and institutional expenditures. My income figures assume that current income differentials for different age cohorts will be constant and are not adjusted for mortality, morbidity, or personal income tax. There are a number of other adjustments. For example, Becker's data are based on white males and assume that students earn .25 of annual income while attending college and enroll for 4.5 rather than four years for degree completion.

26. The internal rate of return to investment in education is the discount rate that equates the present value of projected earnings *differences* over a working life and educational costs (including opportunity costs). My estimates of the social, internal rate of return are overstated by the nonallowance for mortality, morbidity, and nonparticipation in the labor force. They are also overstated to the degree that earnings differentials are directly correlated with the intelligence and motivation differences of workers who do and do not extend their education (Willis and Rosen, 1978).

27. Public higher-education institutional expenditures, per student, are approximately half the private level. Since income differentials for private and public college graduates were not available, the return estimates for private and public institution graduates could not be made separately. The internal rate of return estimates for public university graduates would be biased upward *if* graduates of private institutions have higher lifetime earnings.

28. While I provide a framework and data for the measurement of the returns from investment in human capital, there are a number of reasons why it would be difficult to make judgments about even a macroeconomic "equilibrium" level of educational expenditures for a society. A partial list would include the uncertainty of *ex ante* estimates of future returns, the equivalence of wage differentials and contributions to aggregate output, and the applicability of the "social time rate of preference" of neoclassical models.

I would concede, further, that many of the benefits of education to the individual come from the possibility of an increased quality of life at any income level. However, this would argue for treating expenditure on education as the purchase of a "consumer durable" and the evaluation of the distribution of the costs and benefits would need to take place with a different analytical apparatus than capital theory. None of these economists' qualifications, however, spares a society from the necessity of making public decisions about the level, sources, and allocation of educational expenditures—hence, the inclusion of some data on returns as well as costs.

CHAPTER 9

Explaining the Slowdown: Developing a Theory of the Mature Economy

> Good theory indicates how to carve a system at the joints. At each level, theory breaks a system down into a simple collection of subsystems that interact in a meaningful way.
>
> —Paul M. Romer (1996)

The opening chapter of Adam Smith's *Wealth of Nations,* dealing with the historical process of economic growth, is entitled "Of the Natural Progress of Opulence."[1] Smith theorized about natural progress *toward* opulence—not what would happen when an economy had *achieved* "opulence." That wasn't a pressing issue at the end of the eighteenth century! But now, in the United States and some other post-industrial economies, it is. As I have suggested in an earlier chapter, the United States has achieved a degree of economic *maturity* (to borrow a term from biology). The consequence of reaching a degree of maturity in output and demographic structure is that the rate of growth in per capita income—what Smith referred to as "the natural progress of opulence"—will slow down.

Chapter 2 described and explained how economic growth occurred in the American experience; it generalized about six characteristics of economic growth (specialization in production, technological change, increasing capitalization, a shift from household to market production, a shift of labor force from commodity production to the production of services, and change in the relationships between individuals and firms in the organization of economic activity). I illustrated the generalizations about growth with selected examples.

Chapter 3 quantified and explained the relative importance of productivity increase and participation rates in our twentieth-century experience. Chapter 4 explained the problems and biases involved in measuring aggregate economic activity in order to show that the decline in *measured* growth was overstated and that *unmeasured* changes also affect people's well-being.

Chapter 5 quantified and explained how productivity growth had been accelerated and decelerated by the structural change in the composition of output that accompanied growth. Chapter 6 quantified and explained the sources of the changes in the participation rate of the population in the labor force that resulted from the movement from household to market production, the movement of married women into the market labor force, and the changes in the age structure of the population.

Chapter 7 discussed the consequences of the demographic transition that has accompanied economic growth. The increase in the median age of the population first makes it easier and then makes it more difficult to maintain the aggregate saving rate and this contributes to acceleration and then deceleration in per capita growth. The effect of economic growth on demographic structure is necessary to the explanation of the growth slowdown because of the consequences for net saving and the incentive effects of inter-generational transfers.

Chapter 8 analyzed the effects of economic change on the formation of human capital and the increasing need for and costs of forming human capital through education. These chapters on the cybernetic consequences of economic growth are an integral part of the explanation on why growth in per capita income generally—and the disposable income of the working generation particularly—will slow down with economic and demographic maturity.

If, at this point, you have accepted the *evidence* of this book, you have an explanation of the natural progress toward economic maturity, an explanation of the relationship between the acceleration and deceleration of economic growth and structural change, a greater understanding of "the way it worked and why it won't."

To this point I have not presented a *complete* case for the inevitability of this process. So far, my explanation of why growth in per capita income will *inevitably* slow down is simply that the structural changes in output and demography that accompany modern economic growth have occurred and can't happen again. But optimists could still reject my forecast about "why it won't work"—why the growth rate will inevitably continue to decline. They might argue that there is still the possibility that the fundamental determinant of economic growth—increases in output per worker within sectors—*could* be accelerated in some or all of the sectors of the economy. A massive increase in saving and investment *could* accelerate capital growth. Technological change *could* be accelerated by more scientific research. The economy *could* be moved toward fuller and more efficient utilization of its labor and capital resources. The future *could* be different from the past.

Economists, in their optimistic and theoretical mode, might accept and even argue for all these possibilities. But economists, in their historical and empirical mode, are bound to be skeptical about hoped-for changes in the fundamental ways in which the human and natural worlds work. In the long run there isn't much percentage in betting that human nature will change from self-centered behavior, or that the observed "laws" of physics, chemistry, and biology will be repealed!

In this chapter I propose to go beyond the explanation of changes in output per worker—past, present, and future—based simply on the disaggregation of structural changes in the economy and the population. An explanation of the process of historical economic growth also needs to generalize about the determinants of productivity growth within sectors of the economy (as I have done in chapter 2). Thus, this chapter moves beyond explanation by disaggregation of measurable evidence to a more general and conjectural theory of the determinants of productivity growth *within* particular output sectors of the economy. After summarizing evidence and making some inferences from it, I will provide a modest and heuristic exposition and application of the standard conceptual framework of neoclassical microeconomics to explain why productivity growth within firms, industries, and sectors of the economy will also probably decline—to answer the optimists.

This chapter has four parts: Part I examines some macroeconomic evidence on saving, investment, and productivity growth and explains why I think that the conventional explanation of the slowdown in the growth in aggregate output per worker based on the slowdown in the rate of growth of aggregate physical capital is an incomplete and unsatisfactory explanation of the slowdown of economic growth. (I also note that concentrating on the wrong variables—particularly the NIA and GAAP restriction of "capital" to physical capital, while ignoring human capital, knowledge capital, and natural resource capital—leads to bad economic analysis and bad policy choices.)

In Part II, I summarize some of the implications of *measurable* phenomena about U.S. growth in output per worker that have previously been presented in chapter 5. I suggest that there is inconclusive microeconomic evidence to support the conventional wisdom that attributes a decline in the rate of growth of aggregate output per worker to the slowdown in the rate of growth of the physical capital stock per worker.

In Part III, I discuss how growth occurs to explain why I think that growth will slow even *within* the commodity-producing and distributing sectors where we have continued to have high productivity growth. In Part IV, I speculate on why we will be continue to be unable to get productivity growth—at least conventionally measured growth—in the education and health-care sectors, that will continue to expand in relative size.

The appendix to the chapter presents some further discussion of the shortcomings of neoclassical capital theory for the explanation of economic growth that will be of primary interest to readers concerned with the historical development of theory and methodology in economics. In the appendix I also present a "conjectural" explanation of the magnitude of changes in physical capital implied by changes in the output structure of the economy and their relationship to output per worker. While this chapter is more oriented than previous chapters toward other professional economists, I have tried to make it accessible to the noneconomist. It is important for noneconomists to understand the theoretical framework for the explanation of economic phenomena used by economists because, as Keynes once sagely observed, "Practical men, who believe themselves to be quite exempt from any intellectual influences, are usually the slaves of some defunct economist."[2] It is important to have a good theory of the slowdown–an explanation that fits and explains the facts.

PART I: CONVENTIONAL MACROECONOMIC EXPLANATIONS OF THE SLOWDOWN IN PRODUCTIVITY GROWTH

In popular and professional discussion of the growth slowdown, analysis and discussion of the issues has usually been structured by the concepts of neoclassical macroeconomic growth theory. The conventional explanation for the growth of an economy is the increase of the stock of (physical) capital. Using this model to explain the slowdown in the rate of growth of output per worker observed over the past several decades:

1. One can *theorize* that there has been a slowdown in the rate of growth of the (physical) capital stock per worker.
2. One can *infer* from *apriori* assumptions about the production function that diminishing marginal physical productivity is slowing growth in output from further additions to the growing (physical) capital stock per worker.
3. One can *speculate* that the slowdown in the rate of growth of aggregate output per worker results from the unexplained deceleration of technological change and/or its embodiment in new production methods.

A variety of these explanations has been used by neoclassical economists to explain the widely noted slowdown of productivity growth. If one's view of how the economy grows is restricted to the standard neoclassical macroeconomic growth model, there are three immediate possible explanations of the incontrovertible evidence that the *measured* rate of growth of aggregate output per worker in the American economy (and other mature industrial economies) has slowed over the past two decades: (1) slowing growth in capital per worker, (2) slowing growth in output per unit of capital from diminishing marginal productivity, or (3) unexplained (exogenously) slowing technological change.

THE CONVENTIONAL ARGUMENT

Popular arguments (erroneously) based on the model often start with a muddle! They assert that it is the *ratio* of investment (or saving) to GDP that is the determinant of the productivity growth rate of the economy. The saving or investment ratio has some applicability if one is talking about aggregate growth but is much less relevant to an explanation of increases in productivity—in output per worker or per worker hour.

To explain productivity growth one needs different information. The ratio of investment to GDP is inadequate because the causal relationship needs to be between changes in the *stock* of capital and changes in the number of workers. Changes in the *stock* of capital can't be inferred from the investment (or saving) ratio because (1) we don't know the depreciation rate to determine *net* investment and (2) the ratio of the net investment flow to GDP is different than the ratio of net investment flow to the capital stock.   Second, the number of workers is growing, so the rate of growth of capital per worker is the difference between the rate of growth of the capital stock and the rate of growth of workers.   To tell whether the capital stock per worker is growing, one needs quantitative measures of the rate of growth of the capital stock and the rate of growth of the labor force.   (The theoretical and measurement problems of the neoclassical model are discussed in Appendix Note 9.3.)

But, heroically ignoring these inconvenient problems (!), is it even true that changes in the ratio of saving or investment to GDP (by NIA definition they are equal) is associated with changes in the rate of growth of output per worker?

Consider the evidence in Text Table 9.1. The phenomenon to be explained by the conventional model is the slowdown in productivity—output per worker—after 1970.   Taking a longer view, note that productivity (the Δ triangle line) basically trends downward for the whole graph, covering the decades ending in 1930 and 1990.

Text Graph 9.1
Productivity Growth and the Aggregate Investment Ratio

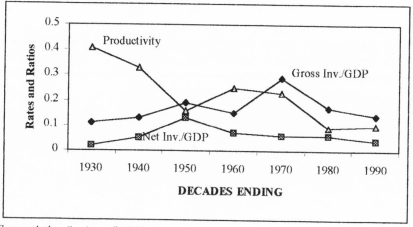

Source: Author. See Appendix Table 9.2

The conventional "decline in saving and investment" theory tries to explain the decline in the rate of productivity growth from 25 percent and 23 percent for the decades ending in 1960 and 1970 to 9 percent and 10 percent in the decades ending in 1980 and 1990. The misperception that the decline in the rate of economic growth is the consequence of profligacy results in frequent appeals to save and invest more as a nation. Certainly, as the popular adage suggests, "you can never be too rich or too thin," but, while saving is properly regarded as a virtuous activity, it should be borne in mind that it comes at the expense of a decrease in consumption.

Do you see any reduction in the ratio of gross investment to GDP (the ◆ line) in the last half-century? No. In fact, the gross investment/GDP ratio goes up and is crossed by the productivity growth line going down!

The popular model is erroneously presented, but *even if it were right*, the facts don't support it—wrong on the theory, wrong on the evidence! The ratio of gross investment to GDP (the diamond line, which is the highest line in the graph in 1990) reaches its decennial peak in 1970. It needed to because of all the new workers joining the labor force at the end of the 1960s! But in the decade following—the decade ending in 1980—the rate of growth of productivity (output per worker) was the lowest in the century. One certainly can't use the ratio of gross investment to GDP that reaches its highest point in 1970 to explain the steep drop and low rate of productivity growth in the following decade!

Yes, the ratio of *net* investment to GDP was low and declining after 1950, but it was also low when productivity growth was very high in the decades ending in 1950 and 1960. And net investment is, in part, an accounting artifact that depends upon an arbitrarily selected depreciation rate. Thus, the historical data do not exhibit any strong observable relationship between the ratio of saving to GDP and growth in output per worker—the popular (and erroneously presented) explanation of the slowdown in productivity growth.

The argument formulated and evidenced by Text Graph 9.1 doesn't use the appropriate variables for the conventional theory. The problem with using the saving ratio or investment ratio to explain productivity growth is that it doesn't give us the rate of growth of the capital stock per worker.

GROWTH IN CAPITAL AND GROWTH IN LABOR PRODUCTIVITY

Consider a *more correct* version of the "declining capital growth" model. What relationships can be observed between changes in the stock of physical capital per worker hour and changes in the flow of output per worker per worker hour? The economic theory is that the rate of growth of productivity (output per worker hour) ought to be directly affected by the rate of growth of the capital stock per worker. Productivity is the ratio of value added output to labor input. For reasons explained in chapters 4 and 5, I consider some of the measurement conventions that are used to calculate output unreliable. For reasons discussed in Appendix Note 9.1, I consider the measurement conventions for the capital stock unreliable. But, resolutely disregarding these data problems, what can we see in the evidence on the relationship between productivity growth and growth in capital per worker?

For the analysis of productivity, I restrict consideration to the industrial sectors of the economy, my Sectors I–VI. The output variable for these sectors is value added output in constant prices. The labor variable for these sectors is their labor force adjusted for average hours worked for the whole economy.

The capital stock variable is restricted to Equipment and Commercial and Industrial Structures for the whole economy (inventories, residential structures, and government capital are excluded).[3]   What is the relationship between changes in the rate of growth of productivity defined as the decennial rate of growth in output per worker hour [d(Q/N)] in the industrial sectors of the economy and decennial changes in the rate of growth of part of the estimated physical stock of capital?   The relationship between these variables for the decades ending between 1960 and 1990 is presented in Text Graph 9.2.

Text Graph 9.2
Changes in Capital Stock and Output per Worker Hour: Industrial Sectors (I–VI)

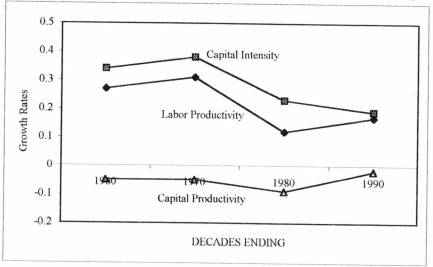

Source: Author. See Appendix Table 9.3.

In Text Graph 9.2 productivity growth (the ◆ line) and capital growth (the □ line) do appear to move together. Productivity growth is at 33 percent and 36 percent decennial rates in the decades ending in 1960 and 1970 and declines to the 17 percent and 19 percent range for the decades ending in 1980 and 1990.[4] These productivity growth rates coincide with decennial rates of growth of capital per worker hour of over 40 percent in the first two decades and 30 percent and 21 percent in the decades ending in 1980 and 1990. The parallel movement of productivity growth and capital growth seems to support the theory that capital growth affects productivity growth.

The third variable in the Text Graph 9.2, [d(Q/K)], is the rate of change of output to capital—it reflects the changes in output per dollar of capital. It is negative for the entire period.[5] The high rate of increase of capital stock per worker hour for the entire period since World War II has been accompanied by a negative rate of growth of capital productivity.

This would support the second argument of conventional analysis—productivity growth for capital is falling because of the diminishing marginal productivity of capital resulting from continuing increases in the capital/labor ratio. One could argue from the evidence that the slowing growth in capital productivity (more precisely the ratio of an output index to a capital stock index) is the *cause* of the decline in the rate of growth of capital per worker in the industrial (Sectors I–VI) part of the economy—investment is falling because it is becoming less productive and this is contributing to the decline in labor productivity in these sectors. I think this is correct, but I also think it is misleading in explaining causality as I will explain in Part III.

PART II: EXPLANATION OF THE OBSERVED GROWTH "SLOWDOWN" BY MICROECONOMIC DISAGGREGATION

Growth in U.S. GDP per worker and per worker hour has been slowing for the last half-century. As I have shown in chapter 5, the continuing slowdown in the *aggregate* rate of growth in output per worker hour has come primarily from structural change; sectors with more rapid productivity growth have decreased in relative size while sectors with slower (or unmeasured) growth have increased in size. Further, workers are no longer moving from lower to higher output sectors (and thereby increasing average output per worker), but the opposite. Within the industrial sector (Sectors I–VI) considered in the preceding Part II of this chapter, the relative share of employment has been increasing in the low-productivity Sector VI (trade), and decreasing in high productivity Sectors IV (manufacturing) and V (transportation, communication, and public utilities) that could be used to explain the slowdown in the rate of increase of productivity for the industrial sector.

Chapter 5 presents evidence that there is no secular decline in the growth rates of productivity *within* (admittedly) somewhat heterogeneous sectors of the economy. I only present evidence on growth rates by sector since the decade of the 1950s, but there is little observed secular decline in aggregate growth in per worker hour output prior to that—and the major growth slowdown in aggregate output per worker has come over the last quarter-century (Text Graph 1.2).

To generalize, there is little evidence of productivity slowdown—growth of output per worker—within sectors where measurement with our current GAAP and NIA concepts is meaningful. If there is no slowdown of productivity within sectors, then the explanations of productivity growth that cite declining capital growth, diminishing marginal physical productivity, or decelerating technological change are not operating within sectors. But, if these factors are not operating *within* sectors, where and how are these phenomena occurring?

It is possible, of course, for productivity growth rates within sectors to be relatively stable, over time, even though the aggregate growth rate of output per worker changes as a result of changes in the relative size of sectors. In fact, one would expect the high productivity growth sectors—like manufacturing—to decrease in their proportion of total employment as increases in output per worker hour permit fewer workers in those sectors to produce more output.

Further, differential productivity growth between sectors reduces the relative prices of manufactured goods and, thereby, decreases their relative weight in the measurement of total output. Thus, one would expect to see an expansion in the relative size of employment in the sectors in which productivity growth was slower—like services. This trend is further enhanced if those sectors produce goods and services that increase as a proportion of the population's consumption with the growth in affluence.[6] As a generalization, these changes are what one observes in the intra-sectoral growth rates and changes in sectoral distribution of the labor force presented in chapter 5.

The data presented in chapter 5 show large differences in the level and rate of growth of output per worker between sectors but do not show strong secular trends in rate of growth of productivity within sectors over the last century. Consequently, what needs to be developed in a theory of growth for a national economy is a microeconomic explanation of growth within sectors coupled with a macroeconomic explanation of changes in the relative size of sectors. Just looking at the aggregate rates of growth of the capital stock doesn't explain the decline in the aggregate rate of growth of productivity.

An aggregate theory of growth—such as neoclassical growth theory—that relates the aggregate capital stock to aggregate output contributes little to our understanding of the slowdown of growth resulting from structural change in the economy. Rather, what is needed for explanation of the growth slowdown is a taxonomic classification of the defining characteristics and distinguishing differences of production within sectors. This should then be followed by microeconomic explanations of growth within sectors that might include reference to declining rates of growth of their capital stocks, diminishing marginal productivity resulting from continuing increases in the capital/labor ratio, and/or the slowdown of technological and organizational change as part of the explanation of changes within sectors.

To use the biological analogy of the climax forest once again, neither the oak trees nor the cottonwood trees are growing more slowly than they did in the past, but the aggregate biomass of the total forest is growing more slowly because slower-growing oaks are replacing the more rapidly growing cottonwoods. It would be mistaken to proceed from the evidence that the aggregate forest is growing more slowly and try to explain the cause of the forest growing more slowly as a consequence of the reduction of sunlight or rain. If the slowdown in the growth of biomass in the forest ecosystem is due to change in the distribution of the species, one needs to explain why the cottonwoods grow biomass faster than the oaks grow biomass but then are replaced by them as the forest approaches maturity.

Contemporary explanations of the slowdown in growth in output per worker—following neoclassical growth theory—frequently allege that inadequate national saving and a consequent slowdown in capital formation is the primary explanation of the observed slowdown of the aggregate growth rate. However, it is not clear from the accounting measurements or the accounting concepts we use that there has been a decline in the ratio of saving to income

(GDP) or the rate of growth of the capital stock relative to labor force within sectors. Wrong on the facts?

But does economic theory even necessarily entail that a slowdown in aggregate physical capital formation would result in a slowing of aggregate growth? Counterintuitively, intra-sectoral growth rates in output per worker could be constant (or even increasing) despite a decline in the rate of growth of the aggregate stock of physical capital relative to the labor force or population. The constancy of intra-sectoral growth rates in output per worker, accompanied by declining growth in aggregate physical capital per worker, would be observed if there were a decline in the relative size of the sectors with higher physical capital/worker ratios and an increase in the size of the sectors with lower physical capital/worker ratios. As a generalization and simplification, that is what I observe in the process of American economic growth over the past century.

In the American experience of economic growth there was an initial acceleration in the increase of the aggregate physical capital/labor ratio. Historically, we observe an increase in the formation of physical capital/worker in the largest sector of the economy at the beginning of the twentieth century— Sector I (agriculture, forestry, and fisheries). Tractors, plows, and harvesters increased in number and size; investment in land clearing and subsequently irrigation increased the quantity and quality of acreage per worker; forestry workers obtained more and better mechanical equipment; fishermen got bigger boats; and so forth.

In Sector II (mining) there were large increases in capital per worker as the focus of the industry shifted, first, to deeper underground coal mines and subsequently petroleum drilling and strip-mining for coal. Sector III (construction) saw bulldozers replace shovels and power machinery replace hand tools.

In manufacturing (Sector IV) initial industrialization (steel mills, sawmills, petroleum refineries) increased the physical capital/labor ratios but modern industrialization (airplanes, electronics, pharmaceuticals) reduces the physical capital/labor ratio.

In Sector V (transportation, communication, public utilities) railroads and municipal utility systems start out being very physical capital intensive but technological change in construction and manufacturing reduces the costs of capital systems in water and gas distribution systems. Surface transportation moves from rail to road, which is less capital intensive (government-provided roads are not part of the capital stock of the sector).

In Sector VI (wholesale and retail distribution) there are initial increases in inventory/employee but then increases in annual sales/inventory and annual sales/fixed capital reduce the growth in the capital/worker ratio.

As I have explained in chapter 5, the financial services sector (Sector VII) includes both real estate management (including owner-occupied homes) and the management of financial assets by banks, insurance companies, and other financial services institutions. In real estate management there has been a substantial and continuing increase in the physical capital/worker ratio. But, in banks and insurance companies, the "capital assets" that are managed (money, stocks, bonds, and so on) are different from the physical capital (computers, leasehold improvements) of the asset managers. As banks close branches and the price of computers declines, the physical capital requirements, per employee, decline in this sector.

The big increase in employment in the economy of the past half-century has been in services (Sector VIII) and government (Sector IX). In the former (attorneys, barbers, cleaners, dentists, etc.) there are limited requirements for physical capital per employee. In the latter (postal workers, judges, teachers, policemen, etc.) the physical capital requirements per employee may or may not be relatively low or rising or falling, but it doesn't matter in terms of explaining GDP per employee in the Government Sector because the cost of capital is not included for production of governmental services!

Structural Change, Decreasing Capital/Labor, and Increasing Potential Output/Capital Ratios

If there has been a slow down in the rate of growth of the physical stock, it may be a natural consequence of structural change in the economy that has reduced the relative importance of sectors with higher physical capital requirements.   In assaying the need for aggregate capital formation, it is important to remember that the potential output/physical capital ratios for different types of physical capital and production can be markedly different.

For example, the ratio of the physical capital stock of the Southern Pacific Railroad embodied in the depreciated value of its track and engines to its annual output of revenue from the haulage of freight and passengers is very high. (Potential output/physical capital is low.)   The ratio of the value of the physical capital used by Microsoft to its annual sales is lower (because most of the productive capacity of Microsoft is embodied in knowledge and human capital, which does not appear on its balance sheet).

One implication of this disparity in the importance of physical capital is that as the relative importance of Microsoft in national output increases relative to Southern Pacific, the value of the aggregate stock of physical capital to annual output will decline. Observed structural change in the economy tends to increase the aggregate potential output/physical capital ratio. Labor costs/output are much larger at Microsoft than Southern Pacific, reflecting the greater importance of human capital at Microsoft. The gross capital formation rate will be reported as less at Microsoft because the costs of creating new knowledge capital (embodied in the software) will be accounted for as part of current costs of production. The human capital of the Microsoft employees is not carried on the corporate balance sheets and much of the returns to the human capital of the employees is received by them in their employee compensation.

Technological change increases the output/capital ratio by reducing the cost of capital per unit of output capacity within production sectors of the economy. Structural change—the increase in the relative size of high output/physical capital sectors (such as Microsoft) relative to low output/physical capital sectors (such as Southern Pacific)—also increases the aggregate output/physical capital ratio.

Both the technological and structural changes increase the output/physical capital ratios and decrease the physical capital/labor ratio necessary for a particular level of aggregate output.   This makes a reduction in measured saving and investment in physical capital possible. However, the technology of the expanding sector (Microsoft) will increase the demand for human and knowledge capital, which means an increase in the share of resources that must be allocated to increasing human capital (through education) and knowledge capital (through research and investment).

Even if there had been a slowing in the rate of growth of physical capital per worker over the past half-century (unproved), that may not have been the cause of the decline in the growth of output per worker if the physical capital needs of the economy were declining because of structural changes in the composition of output. But I am skeptical about the data—because there is no adequate conceptual framework for the collected quantitative data on the changes in the value of the various capital stocks that I do present.

What I observe resulting from the structural changes that have accompanied the development of the U.S. economy over the last century is a fall in the aggregate requirements for physical and natural resource capital relative to GDP, accompanied by a rise in the need for human and knowledge capital. Thus, my explanation of the historical process of economic growth emphasizes the effects of the changes in the relative sizes of output sectors that accompany growth on the need for physical capital and also distinguishes changes in the requirements for different kinds of capital. Human capital and knowledge capital become more important, and physical capital and natural resource capital become less important in the process of growth. Further, this structural change in output may have been accompanied by a rise in some sectors of the output/physical capital ratio from a fall in the price of capital goods relative to their potential output capacity, and fuller utilization of potential output capacity from the increase in size and efficiency of markets.

Economic theory and accounting practices have lagged behind the changes in the characteristics of the economy. For example, the production of physical capital is recognized explicitly in NIA procedures that distinguish saving and investment from consumption. In doing this NIA follows GAAP accounting principles. However, the formation of human capital by education and the creation of knowledge capital by research and development is not treated as saving and investment in the national accounts. Education is treated as part of consumption and/or government expenditure.   Private research and development is treated as a cost of production of goods and services, and public research and development is embedded in government expenditures. In either category the formation of human and knowledge capital is not explicitly recognized as capital formation in the national accounts. Yet, as I have shown (chapter 8), there has been a spectacular increase in the ratio of expenditures on human capital formation to GDP (educational expenditure/GDP).

Do our emphases in economic theory accounting concepts matter for analysis and policy? Yes! If we are focusing attention on physical capital while the requirements for physical capital are not growing as fast as the requirements for human and knowledge capital, we are looking for the wrong variable when we attribute the growth slowdown to inadequate saving and investment. We are calling for the wrong policy if we emphasize the need for an increase in national saving and investment to try to increase the rate of growth of output by increasing the rate of growth of physical capital.

PART III: THE WAY IT WORKED AND WHY IT WON'T: EXPLAINING PAST AND PREDICTING FUTURE INTRA-SECTORAL GROWTH IN PRODUCTIVITY

I have offered an explanation of why aggregate productivity growth has declined as a result of the natural changes that accompany economic growth in the output structure of the economy. I have not presented evidence or argued that productivity growth has slowed within sectors of the economy. So, the optimistic critic of my analysis might turn my argument to say, if productivity growth hasn't declined within sectors, why couldn't we increase it with more capital and increased technological change? I think we will be challenged to maintain constant productivity growth within sectors. I *conjecture*, in response to the optimists conjectures, that it will slow. In order to explain why I think intra-sectoral productivity growth is likely to decline in the future, it is important to understand how it worked in the past.

In the American past growth in output within firms and sectors of the economy came from capital growth and technological and organizational change. Technological change (discussed in chapter 2) involves changes in the way workers produce economic output. Technological change frequently results from specialization in production. Capital is almost always required for research and development and new technologies are embodied in machines or structures that require additional capital. *To specify a sequence, specialization results in technological change which requires increased capitalization.*

The result of technological change is the *potential* to produce more output per unit of labor and per unit of capital—productivity growth. My *conjecture* is that the slowdown of intra-sectoral productivity growth in commodity-producing and distributing sectors will result primarily from a slowdown in specialization that will then slow down technological change and reduce the opportunities for the profitable employment of capital. Causation runs from the slowdown of specialization to technological change to capital formation.

The Probable Future Decline of Intra-Sectoral Growth

In chapter 2, I described and explained the process of productivity change using the interaction of three ratios—capital/labor (capitalization), potential output/capital (productivity), and actual output/potential output (utilization) as the determinants of productivity growth. There are social limits to the first—increasing macroeconomic capitalization ultimately is limited by the increasing proportion of national income that must be allocated to gross investment to cover depreciation. But the microeconomic limit comes from declining returns to additional capital when technological change runs up against diminishing returns.

There is a natural limit to the output/capital ratio: Technically, one cannot get more energy out of matter than is there, one cannot decrease friction sufficiently to get perpetual motion, one cannot use genetic engineering to create characteristics that are not present in the gene pool. Finally, one cannot increase the ratio of potential output/actual output beyond one.

However, I speculate that the most important operative limit to growth is going to be the source of growth itself—specialization. The limiting factor for specialization will be the transactions costs that, ironically, increase as specialization replaces the operation of competitive markets with bilateral bargaining.

Specialization and Transactions Costs

Specialization has benefits. It also has costs. All of the transactions within and between organizations must be conducted and monitored, and agreements must be enforced and disagreements resolved. Specialization of employees within a firm must also be negotiated and coordinated. The transacting costs of specialization within firms and between firms increase with the extent of specialization and pose a constraint on the gains from specialization in addition to the constraints imposed by the size of the market.[7]

Text Graph 9.3, by construction, indicates that benefits increase—costs of production fall—(through specialization) with the extent of the market. It also indicates, however, that the increasing specialization of production leads to an increase in transactions costs, that eventually increase faster than the economies of specialization and pose a barrier to further cost reduction through specialization. In the graph, specialization leads to accelerating growth up to the point where the rate of increase in benefits from specialization is equal to the rate of increase in the transactions costs that are an accompaniment of specialization continue to grow, as do the transactions costs of specialization. But up to extent of specialization (5), gains are growing more rapidly than costs and increasing economic growth.

Text Graph 9.3
The Limits to Specialization from Decreasing Gains and Increasing Costs

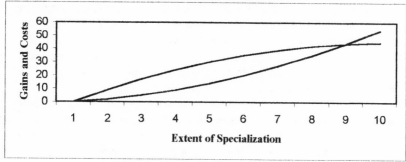

Source: Author. Values are illustrative.

After (5) costs are still less but increasing more rapidly and slowing growth until the extent of specialization reaches level (9). The decrease in the gains from specialization (slowing of growth) occurs before the end of growth.

It is possible that the position or slope of both lines could shift. For example, technological change might shift the gain line upward. A change in the legal structure might shift the cost line up or down—thereby changing the net benefits of specialization.

Barriers to Continuing Growth from Specialization

Individuals can gain from investing in the development of specialized skills. Firms can, similarly, gain from investing in the specialized training of their employees. Specialized suppliers and their customers can gain from investing labor and capital in the development of specialized equipment.

Specialization can lead to gains, but the size of the gains from specialization motivates the parties to increase the certainty of receiving a fair share of those benefits. This, in turn, leads to the increase in transaction costs. This is the "offensive" reason for the increase in transactions costs.

Specialization, ironically, also leads to the possibility that the parties to the specialization can be exploited in bargaining over their share of the gains because of their limited alternatives. This lack of alternatives—resulting from specialization—leads to the need to guarantee prospective specializers against the losses or failure to realize a "fair share" of the prospective gains from specialization. This is the "defensive" reason for the increase in transactions costs with the increase in specialization.

Consider the implications of the increase in specialization for the employment relationship. (I draw on the example of the nature of specialization discussed earlier in chapter 2.)   A General Electric (GE) engineer in the diesel locomotive division becomes very specialized in the design of a particular part. How much inducement should she be given to invest her time in an engineering education—what kind of return should she expect and what should be the certainty of those expectations?

When she joins GE the firm will invest the time of valuable employees on the personnel staff and within her division and department and work group to bring her into good working relationships with the specialized team she will join. The greater the extent of her specialized knowledge, the more she limits her opportunity to acquire different or broader engineering skills that would increase her attractiveness to alternative employers.

Or, if she decides to leave GE, what will be the cost to the firm in terms of lost production and disrupted working relationships? Realizing the costs to GE she could impose on the firm by leaving, will she try to benefit from her ability to inflict losses by pressing for higher compensation? What if another firm—supplier, customer, or competitor—tries to hire her away from GE to avoid the costs they would incur from developing her specialized skills over a period of time?

The protection of individuals from the "unfair" power advantage of firms has led to increasing social regulation and protection of individuals in their bargaining relationships with employers and increasing expenditures on legal and personnel departments by employers. Employees have the right to remedies against the firm for "unfair" practices and a legion of lawyers is ready to assist them in pressing those claims, while another legion of lawyers must be engaged to do battle against them. While the threat of legal action protects employees, it also increases the potential costs to firms from specialization and limits the extent to which firms have an interest in financing the specialization of their employees in the development of specialized skills and knowledge. The relationship is asymmetric because even if firms could bring suit for performance and damages when employers choose not to perform, the employees cannot be compelled to perform and they do not have the means to pay damages.

Consider another element of the employment relationship: The smooth operation of GE's operations over a period of time depends on its abilities to supply quantity and quality at a price. The International Brotherhood of Electrical Workers' (IBEW) Union knows this. It also knows that GE could absorb some higher wages, higher employment levels, or increased employee security without impairing the firm's ability to continue to attract needed capital. If the IBEW demands more wages or changes in working conditions, how much should GE give up before taking a strike? What if the IBEW brings pressure with increased (but contractually permitted) absenteeism? Once again, there is an asymetric relationship between employers and employees that militates against specialization.

Specialization also has important implications for the relationship between firms and their suppliers: GE makes the judgment that the computer control equipment in its diesel electric locomotives should be purchased from Minneapolis Honeywell rather than developed internally in the firm. To produce the computers Honeywell will have to make a substantial investment in the design of the computers and in some specialized equipment to make them.

Honeywell is induced by the possibility of future sales to GE to make the investment in the design of the specialized computers. There is a firm purchase contract with GE for fifty computers at $100,000 each, but Honeywell estimates that they will only be able to recover their investment in the development of this highly specialized component after the production and sale of 100 computers at that price. GE is unwilling to make a bigger commitment because it only has firm orders for 50 diesel engines. If GE does or doesn't make a subsequent order, what should both firms do?

One option for GE is to implicitly threaten to share the technology developed by Honeywell with another process computer manufacturer to bring pressure to bear on Honeywell on price after the first fifty they contracted for have been delivered. Or GE might bluff to produce them "in-house" even though it would cost more for GE than Honeywell to produce them internally.

One option for Honeywell is to plan to raise the price after the first fifty computers have been supplied when GE has orders for more engines. Honeywell might also let it be known that it is negotiating to supply the German manufacturer of locomotives—Siemens—which is competing for orders from American railroads with GE. All of these contingencies need to be considered and negotiated as transactions are arranged. The negotiation and monitoring costs result in the employment of expanding legions of lawyers for both firms—because the stakes are large and the pockets are deep.

Minneapolis Honeywell and GE come to a contractual agreement and Honeywell decides to finance the research and development and tooling-up costs with a new debt offering underwritten by investment banker Morgan Stanley and a new line of bank credit from commercial banker Citibank. What kind of information and loan covenants will be required by the investment and commercial banking firms who are putting in the necessary financing for the transaction? What transactions costs are added to the costs of financing the capital equipment?

The answer to all these hypothetical transactions and rhetorical questions is that the parties to joint production, to investment in knowledge, and to financial agreements must have implicit understandings and/or explicit contracts to specify and enforce their relationships.   As specialization in production and employment increases, the degree of interdependency lessens the alternatives in bargaining to all parties engaged in interdependent specialization and the lack of alternatives otherwise provided by the existence of competitive markets necessitates alternative guarantees to engage in specialization and interdependence.

The greater the increases in the gains from specialization, the larger the incentives of the cooperating and dependent parties to increase and/or protect their shares of the gains. The increasing size of the gains are, therefore, accompanied with the necessity of increasing the amounts of individual and company resources that have to be devoted to the negotiation, monitoring, and enforcement of contractual relationships.   Increasing the gains from specialization increases the potential gains and opportunity losses from specialization and, hence, increases the transactions costs involved in the completion, monitoring, and enforcement of contracts.

My argument, then, about the limits to economic growth from specialization is that specialization itself increases transactions costs. There have always been transactions costs involved in the organization of economic activity. For these to slow the rate of economic growth, it must be true that the transactions costs are increasing more rapidly than the gains from specialization. This means that to limit growth they take an increasing part of the potential additional gains from specialization and, thereby, limit the further increase in specialization that is a primary source of increases in output per worker.

What one would expect to observe from increasing specialization is an increase in the employees of firms who are purchasing, selling, and supervising relative to the employees engaged in production. One would expect to see increased costs for lawyers and accountants and the personnel providing the information for them to carry on their monitoring of the firm's activities. And that is precisely what is noted in the occupational distribution of employment and the rise in supervisory staff and overhead relative to production workers in firms.[8] Thus, my argument is that it is the same specialization that leads to growth in output per worker that will eventually retard it.

PART IV: CHANGES IN FINAL DEMAND, TECHNOLOGICAL CHANGE, AND ECONOMIC GROWTH

It will be noted that most of my description of the process of economic growth revolves around the gains from the specialization of production in commodity production, transportation, or distribution. (It was noted in chapter 5 that these were the sectors in which high measured productivity growth has occurred in the past.) Changes in these sectors increase output per worker as a result of increased specialization by the worker and the employment of larger and larger scale capital equipment. As the process continues a smaller and smaller part of the labor force is employed in the production and distribution of commodities and the production of capital goods. Thus, the process of growth leaves a larger and larger part of the labor force available for the production of services.

Most services offer less scope for the substitution of physical capital for labor. This appears to be particularly true for the two largest employers in the service sector—health care and education. Are there more limited possibilities for technological change in the service sector?

I would argue that there are because the heterogeneity of the humans who require the services doesn't allow the substitution of physical capital for human labor. Can one physician set more broken legs per hour? Possibly—with improved diagnostic equipment and better teams of paramedics working under her supervision. But she can't do it with a machine—there are limits to increasing capitalization if the capitalization can't be accompanied by increasing output per unit of capital. And decreasing time per patient assumes that there is going to be a steady stream of patients with uniformly broken legs to take advantage of the efficiencies afforded by specialization.[9] And doctors, being in the personal service business, are locationally restricted by the demands of their patients for attention. Specialization is limited by the extent of the market. Can one dentist fill more cavities per hour? Perhaps—with faster diagnostic procedures and drills, but the scope for the kind of increase in productivity we have seen in the production of food or energy is probably not there.

Can one first-grade teacher teach twenty, thirty, forty-five pupils per class to read? (successive 50% increases). Maybe, but it will take some very sophisticated preparation and equipment to give guidance and feedback to keep student learning on track. To respond to the numbers in my own question, in a class of forty-five students in class for six hours per day each pupil would get a total of eight individual minutes per day—seventy-five seconds per hour with no break between classes for students and no break between students for the teacher! I know teachers who walk on water but I don't know any who can do that!

Modern communication methods may increase the effectiveness of teachers' presentations of information to students. But sophisticated and mechanized presentations of information are not a substitute for the personal interaction between student and teacher, which is a very important element in the learning process in leading the student from what he does understand to what he doesn't.

The essence of mass production to reduce costs in the manufacturing sector of the economy is standardization and the elimination of individualization in the production of commodities. Mass production involves identical and interchangeable parts. The essence of service industries is that the customer is served as an individual. For this reason it is unlikely that we will see any substantial growth in productivity in the service industries. They are limited in increasing capital per worker because increasing capital will not be accompanied with increases in output per unit of capital. The absence of technological change and increased capitalization in the service sector will, therefore, continue to limit productivity growth relative to the industrial sector of the economy and increase the relative share of the labor force in service industries.

The specialization-driven, capital-using, cost-reducing technological change that has occurred in the process of modern economic growth has been concentrated largely in producing capital equipment for the commodity producing, transportation, communication, and manufacturing sectors of the economy. For the services producing sectors of the economy—health care, education, personal services—the scope for the use of physical capital and, therefore, the potential for reducing the capital and labor costs per unit of capacity of equipment are far more limited. This is because capital costs are a smaller proportion of total costs in the service sector and there is less scope for the replacement of human labor by machines.

To illustrate—the dentist's costs of physical capital equipment (drills and dental chairs) per patient served may fall but they form a very small part of his total costs. Further, better capital equipment is unlikely to offer very much scope for increasing the number of cavities drilled per hour, although it is possible that the quality of the dental work (measured in terms of longevity of repairs) may increase. At the same time, it is important to realize that the dentist's cost of human capital will be increasing as tuition costs for undergraduate college education and dental school rise relative to the cost of other goods. The dentist's opportunity cost of delaying entry into the work force while preparing to be a dentist increases, too, because of the increase in the labor income he has forgone by further education.

Increases in the cost of education itself will increase the cost of professional services. Better-equipped classrooms may be produced with lower capital costs per student, but capital costs of buildings and equipment are a small part of total educational costs.

Interactive computer technology and video have been proposed as revolutionary educational technologies that will allow an enormous increase in students per teacher. However, these technologies bear the same relationship to the student as the book, which has been available for 500 years.[10] Theoretically, students could currently go to libraries with minimum help and guidance for their acquisition of knowledge and intellectual skills but this does not occur because face-to-face motivation and guidance appears to be an integral part of education—at least for students who have not achieved a considerable maturity. Unless technological change or an increase in knowledge capital or the human capital of teachers increases the number of students who can be taught by one teacher, the scope for reductions in total cost per student are small.

In some service industries—hairdressers and upscale restaurants, for example—clients do not want an increase in customers per employee. They are paying for personal service and are willing to pay increasing amounts for more service and less customers per employee.

It could be pointed out that it is impossible to reduce the amount of labor time involved in a string quartet giving a concert performance or a band of actors giving a Shakespeare play. On the other hand, the recording of the performance on a videotape can make possible its enjoyment by millions and reduce the cost—per audience member—to a fraction of the cost of a live performance. Adopting the convention that a compact disc of a concert or videotape of a play was the equivalent of a live performance would be a way of achieving enormous increase in productivity in the entertainment component of final demand.

Similarly, it could also be noted that the incidence of dental caries can be efficiently reduced with the fluoridation of water and the incidence of communicable diseases that affect the demand for medical services can be reduced by preventive inoculation. Technological advance may involve dealing with the provision of the desired results in entirely new ways that are not measured as increases in output per unit of productive input.

Technological change can produce direct gains in productivity in some service industries. Financial services are a large subsector of the service sector. Within this part of the economy, banks (for example) have substantially increased the number of checks cleared or the amount of loans and deposits per employee and per dollar of fixed capital in buildings—largely by the introduction of computers coupled with sophisticated software and the falling costs of telecommunications technology.

There is scope for further productivity growth in the financial services industries. Much of the employment in real estate, insurance, and stock brokerage could be eliminated by continuing computerization of account maintenance and transactions in these industries. (However, the consequent reduction in asset management costs would lower fee charges per dollar of account balances and measured value-added output per employee in these industries.) As chapter 5 has shown, the difficulties of achieving growth in the service industries greatly limit the scope for increases in the aggregate economy because the service industries are now such a large part of it.

SUMMARY

My arguments in this chapter do *not* provide an *irrefutable* proof of the inevitability of a slowdown of growth in output per worker in a mature economy. Rather, I have tried to conjecture about what is likely to happen in a post-industrial economy to slow productivity growth within some sectors and continue to limit conventionally measured productivity in others.

My discussion of the evidence on savings rates and productivity growth in Part I is an attempt to dispel the neoclassical economic argument that the observed decline in aggregate economic growth in the United States could be explained simply as the result of an observed decline in the national savings rate and that it could be reversed by a higher rate of saving or higher rate of growth in physical capital alone. The conceptually unsatisfactory evidence on the rate of growth of capital stocks per worker presented in Part I of this chapter suggests that there may have been a decline in the rate of growth of physical capital per worker. But Part II shows that this evidence on declining capital growth could be explained as a consequence of the structural change in output in a mature economy.

The productivity of physical capital in the U.S. economy has always been strongly affected by its interaction with the stocks of human, knowledge, and natural resource capital. An explanation of changes in growth rates within sectors that implies a causal relationship between changes in the rate of growth of capital/worker and output/worker is incomplete without reference to all types of capital, the different requirements for different types of capital by the different sectors, and the interaction of different types of capital with each other.

My explanation in Part III of a probable slowdown in intra-sector productivity growth flows from an analysis and explanation of what caused growth within sectors in the past. Growth will slow because of the human limits to the specialization in production which has driven capital formation and technological change. The explanation of economic growth is also the basis for explanation of the slowing of growth in a post-industrial economy. We do not observe measured growth in the the education and health care parts of the service sector. My discussion in Part IV is a minimal attempt to explain why that is likely to continue. The implications of zero productivity growth in education or health care in an economy that will be demanding more of these services can take us back to some of the ethical questions about intergenerational transfers discussed earlier in chapters 7 and 8. How should we allocate and ration increasingly expensive medical care and education?

Finally, let me once again make a plea for informed discussion to be precise about the level of achievement, of "opulence," of wealth. Increases in efficiency or utilization decrease the possibilities for maintaining or increasing proportional growth rates. Analogies are often misleading but sometimes they are useful in illustrating the principles at issue. Using the analogy of the successful athlete, after the average speed of the mile run has increased from 10 to 12 to 14 to 15 mph (a four-minute mile is an average speed of 15 mph), it becomes increasing difficult to go on improving performance if performance is measured as acceleration. The increase from 10 to 12 mph was a 20 percent improvement. The same absolute acceleration from 12 to 14 mph was only a 17 percent improvement, and a heroic increase from 14 to 16 mph to shatter the four-minute mile would be only a 14 percent improvement. The same absolute increases in speed are declining percentage rates of growth in performance, but they are made with increasing physical difficulty—all of the obvious improvements have been made and actual performance seems closer and closer to the biological limits of the human body.

While our economy may still be some distance from achieving the four-minute mile, our success in incrementally increasing our growth rate is going to come more and more gradually, and with greater and greater sacrifices of current consumption—not because technology will cease to produce further increases in output per worker through reductions in the labor and capital requirements per unit of output, but because even absolute improvements will be smaller percentage increases.

It is impossible to *prove* that economic growth will continue to slow down, but this chapter has attempted to show why it probably will.

NOTES

1. Book III, Chapter 1.
2. Keynes (1935), p.383.
3. One of the major problems created by this assumption is that there is considerable physical capital in the service sector. Further, as specialization has

occurred, some of the ownership of physical capital has shifted to the service sector—industrial corporations lease buildings or equipment from the Financial Services Sector (VII) and the growth in value output is not reflected in Sectors I–VI but the growth of the capital stock is.

4. These productivity growth rates are above the rates presented for the same decades in Text Table 3.1 for growth per FTE worker because they are for Sectors I–VI, where productivity growth rates are substantially higher than for the whole economy. They are more comparable to the intra-sector growth rates presented in Text Table 5.2 but are per worker hour rather than per worker and are affected by the inter-sector shifts that affect the aggregate.

5. Mathematically, the rate of growth of productivity ($d(Q/N)$) is the sum of the rates of growth.

6. Baumol and Wolff (1989), Appendix 10.

7. Most economists are familiar with the Coase Theorem (Coase, 1960). The theorem has been variously interpreted but I take one of its core principles to be that mutually advantageous trades will take place unless the transaction costs are larger than the gains. Coase's presentation of the principle assumes given static situations in which the gains are known to the contracting parties. In the dynamic changes that take place in the process of specialization, the size of the gains are frequently uncertain while the costs of transacting are better estimated. I argue that the result is both to increase the share of resources (supervisors, accountants, lawyers) involved in monitoring the transactions and to stop the specialized exchanges from taking place at all.

8. Wallis and North (1986) have estimated that the share of GDP represented by the production of "transactions services" increased from 25 percent of the economy in 1900 to 50 percent by 1970.

9. There may be limited scope for increasing the number of legs that can be set by an orthopoedic surgeon. However, I am sure that there has been an enormous reduction in the number of broken legs sustained in skiing by improved boots, bindings, and the grooming of the slopes. How should this increase in safety be recorded in national output?

10. The lecture has been technologically obsolete since the invention of the printing press made it a less effective way of conveying information than the hand-copied book.

CHAPTER 10

Some Implications of the Slowdown in Economic Growth in the Mature Economy

> Natura non facit saltum (Nature does not make leaps).
> —Alfred Marshall, *Principles of Economics* (1896*)*

The growth rate of the American economy has slowed during the last half of the twentieth century. If the evidence and arguments of this book are correct, it will continue to slow in the twenty-first century. What are the implications of economic maturity and the consequent growth slowdown? Is this a problem?

A "problem" exists when an extant state of affairs is not what one would like it to be. Under that definition the slowing of growth in a mature economy is a problem. Of course Americans would like to be living better! And they would have higher measured per capita incomes at the end of the twentieth century if economic growth had not slowed in its last half.

But this state of affairs is just another version of the inevitable economic problem. A popular variant of economists' insistence on the inevitability of scarcity is that you can never be too thin or too rich! No matter how rich, a society will always have an economic problem as long as human wants exceed the capacity of the economic system to supply them. The economic problem exists by definition. I have argued in this book that the slowdown of growth in the American economy is a similarly unavoidable problem—it is the result of past success in achieving economic growth and the resulting structural changes that have accompanied and accelerated and then decelerated growth.

GROWTH AND THE AMERICAN DREAM

The central message of this book is that we should understand our current economic situation in terms of our stage of economic development and structure. It is unrealistic to yearn for the return of an earlier stage of economic development in which growth was easier. The fifty-year-old who tries to act like a twenty-year-old is advised, with disdain, to "act your age." Similar advice applies to a mature economy.

The slowdown (not end!) of growth makes choices harder. Economic growth has always been the American Dream for avoiding difficult choices. In the nineteenth century the western frontier was the "safety-valve," the escape from the social pressures of an industrializing society. The frontier (mythically, for most) offered new immigrants and native-born Americans the opportunity to acquire land by settlement and turn it into a productive capital asset. The frontier was the possibility of realizing the Jeffersonian idyll of a nation of independent small farmers and craftsmen who would be prosperous and independent by their own efforts.

The geographic frontier closed with the end of the nineteenth century. John F. Kennedy's rhetorical "New Frontier" at mid-century was a new incarnation of the old dream of pushing out the limits and giving every American an opportunity to prosper. Lyndon Johnson's "Great Society," to be built on the New Frontier, was an electoral promise to deliver the American Dream to all Americans. It promised unlimited educational opportunity for the young, generous Social Security and Medicare for the old, and plenty for all. This was all projected on the rising affluence anticipated from the rapid economic growth of mid-century.

Plenty for all was expected to be guaranteed by a rapidly growing economy that could painlessly redistribute income while not diminishing anyone's share in absolute terms. The government would be able to finance the transfers of the Great Society from slowly rising tax rates on a rapidly growing tax base. The dream started to come apart almost immediately. In addition to the stresses imposed by the Vietnam War and the global financial turbulence of the 1970s, the economic growth on which the Great Society was premised failed to materialize. One legacy of the Great Society was a high and increasing level of transfer payments and the creation of a permanent welfare class. It remains to be seen whether the welfare reforms of the 1990s really will end "welfare as we know it." They certainly won't end the transfers to the retired population.

After the political turbulence and economic stagnation of the 1970s, Ronald Reagan's "supply side economics" promised to return "morning in America" in the 1980s to bring back a higher rate of economic growth through tax cuts for the affluent and welfare cuts for the poor. The prophesied "supply side" response predicted increased labor-force participation and work intensity from both groups as the relative advantage of work to welfare or work to leisure increased. The prophecy proved fallacious. Older men continued to decrease their participation by retiring earlier, and married women increased theirs by entering the labor force after child-bearing. A forecast increase in saving from lower tax rates on the affluent failed to produce any substantial increase in savings but foreign capital did flow in to fund investment and the massive increase in the national debt.

Despite the seeming prosperity of the 1980s, per capita growth in GDP continued to slow and the "real" disposable incomes of labor force did not regain the levels of the late 1960s until the early 1990s.[1] One legacy of Reaganomics has been an increase in the ratio of the national debt to income that muted the Reaganomics reprise in the unsuccessful Bush and Dole campaigns of 1992 and 1996.   Another anxiety created by a complex of economic and demographic forces and fanned by political rhetoric was growing anxiety about the future of Social Security and Medicare and the contemporary system of public education.

Fortuitously, the slowdown in economic growth in the last quarter of the twentieth century could not have come at a better time, demographically. Indeed, the favorable demographic structure concealed some of the problems in the 1970s and 1980s that we now face at the turn of the century. As noted in chapters 7 and 8, the transfers necessary for the education of the young and the care of the old were moderated by favorable demographic structure. The United States was also lucky in the timing of the slowdown of growth because of the end of the "Cold War" after the collapse of the Berlin Wall in 1989. In the 1990s we got a "peace dividend" greater than just the reduction of federal defense spending. Our scientific talent and engineers were freed from research and development for weapons to efforts to improve the productivity the peacetime economy.

We can see in historical retrospect that the hopes of The Great Society for permanent rapid growth and the hopes of Reaganomics for a resumption of rapid growth were based on a limited understanding of the growth process and unlimited political rhetoric. At the end of the twentieth century, the rhetoric persists about the changes in government policies to reverse the slowing of growth but it carries more cynicism about government and less optimism about the American Dream of rapid growth to help us avoid hard choices.

CHOICES

We no longer have the choice of increasing growth—but it could be worse. We could have zero-growth or retrogression! We need to adjust our economic world view so we can respond   to our changed economic situation with appropriate social/economic policies.   Let me briefly refer to four policy issues: education, labor-force participation, immigration, and legal reform.

Education and Investment in Human Capital

As described and explained in chapter 2, productivity growth is the joint outcome of the interaction of the stocks of physical, human, knowledge, and natural resource capital.   Bearing this in mind, much of the contemporary emphasis on "saving" as the key to growth is misplaced if our concept of saving is limited to the acquisition of financial assets to be used for the formation of only one kind of capital—physical capital.

The growth of the stock of physical capital will have considerably less effect on economic output than the simultaneous growth of all four types of capital.

In addition, the large and rapidly growing service sectors of the economy are based much more on human and knowledge capital than physical and natural resource capital.

Arguments that tax increases to increase expenditures on education will reduce the incentives for working and saving may or may not be true—there is little strong evidence about the relationship between after-tax returns to work or saving. But the argument is couched in the wrong terms. Spending more on education ought to be viewed as allocating current productive capacity to educational investment. The likely outcome of no new taxes to support educational investment is really between more current consumption for the current working generation and less human capital embodied in the current younger generation to be drawn upon to support the current tax-paying generation in their retirement.

As presented in chapter 8, the mere *maintenance*—much less the growth of —the stock of human capital, is dependent on the human capital investment ratio—the HCIR. And herein lies a serious problem for our American emphasis on individualism. An individual's personal incentive to work and save and invest in stocks and bonds—financial claims to physical assets—comes from the existence of secure and liquid property rights to the flow of future income made possible by the creation of physical capital. If I buy the stock or bond of a corporation that invests in physical assets, I get the claim to a stream of future income from my investment and/or I can sell the claim to someone else if I want to use the money for my retirement. There is risk in holding individual stocks and bonds or other financial assets but the risk can be diversified or traded off for greater or lesser returns.

Investment in human capital is different than investment in physical capital. It is a social rather than an individual decision. Children cannot pay for their own education. College students have a limited ability to borrow for theirs and the tuition they pay covers only a small part of the costs of their education. Imperfect capital markets, the absence of indentures, increasing social returns to investment in education, and our historic commitment to the equality of opportunity are all reasons why education is *necessarily* a public rather than private investment decision.

Human capital formation is largely financed by taxation. The current working population has a more tenuous incentive to pay taxes to invest in the education of the succeeding generation than to consume or invest personally. To a substantial degree, we have to rely on the social benevolence of one generation to invest in the education of the next. Adam Smith cautioned that self-interest, rather than benevolence, motivated the decisions of the butcher and baker to supply their customers' needs. We need benevolence rather than narrow self-interest to provide education for the generation which follows us.

There is substantial dissatisfaction with the current effectiveness of the K-12 public schools, and one result is a vicious cycle of withdrawal of children and subsequent withdrawal of support for the public schools by the tax-paying middle classes. This will become an increasing problem if nothing is done.

Further, inadequate public elementary and secondary education limits the effectiveness of post-secondary education.

The future of America—not just the rate of economic growth—depends upon whether we can make the public schools effective. But it is a far more complex problem than just spending money. Inflation adjusted expenditures, per student, have been increased markedly over the last two decades—with declining effectiveness. A society can spend on public investment on education and yet achieve limited formation of useable human capital—just as it did with private investment in railroads and agriculture at the beginning of the twentieth century that yielded negative returns.

Education as the Fundamental Entitlement

The importance of the frontier in American history was its promise of opportunity. The "free land" of the frontier wasn't free to the homesteader—there was susbstantial income forgone while the homestead was being proved and substantial capital and sweat-equity produced by back-breaking work. The pioneer literally enacted the Lockean metaphor of mixing his labor with the land to acquire title.

The American Dream was the promise of the opportunity to acquire capital by the sweat of one's brow—capital that could make the citizen "better off" or at least independent. We need to think of the opportunity to acquire human capital through investment in education as the twenty-first-century counterpart of the nineteenth-century Homestead Act.

Note the parallel—the government gave the opportunity to acquire the land but the acquisition depended on work and short-term sacrifice by the individual. The Founding Fathers envisioned a nation in which "free" land offered opportunity for all to be independent participants in the nation's economy. The land was "free" but the opportunity cost—and all of the direct costs of making the "free" land a productive asset—were borne by the individual. This was the American embodiment of the political philosophy of "possessive individualism."

But consider further. The moral justification of private property arises from the exercise of human effort in its acquisition. But the moral justification of private property was conditional. John Locke's "proviso" about the continued justification of private property in land—the primary asset in the eighteenth century—was that the freedom to acquire it be open to all men—that "as good and plenty" remain for all. The continuing moral justification of private property in our century depends upon the freedom of all citizens to acquire the most important asset of our century—high quality education for all.

Human capital is as important to economic growth in the twenty-first century as natural resource capital was in the agricultural economy of the eighteenth century and physical capital was in the industrial economy of the nineteenth century. It is also as important politically because citizens without education—without considerable human capital—will be unable to participate as workers or citizens in our modern, post-industrial, information economy.

Policies to Increase Human Capital Formation

So what do we do about it? We have often heard the rhetorical question, "If we can send citizens into space, why can't we run the schools to prepare them to live on earth?" There are a number of answers to the question. We should start by remembering that we send a few astronauts into space every year and a few million school graduates into the working world. But, beyond that, the real costs of sending the astronauts into orbit were the research and development efforts of our best and brightest scientists. We didn't just fit some rockets to existing aircraft and blast them off!

Research and Development

First, we need to make some substantial investment in research and development into the education process itself so that we can increase efficiency in the production and improve the outcomes of educational expenditures. This translates into basic *research* into human cognitive processes in the acquisition of language and quantitative skills. It must be followed by further investment in the development of the pedagogical methods and hardware and software necessary to develop those skills for all students.

There is an interesting historical parallel here with the programs of the land grant universities in the nineteenth century. They were created with large endowments of public lands and tax supported to do basic and applied research in agriculture and industry and to help farmers and industry use that knowledge. Agricultural experiment stations did basic research in the laboratory and employed teams of agents to diffuse the knowledge to farmers. The agents literally went out into the fields to work with the farmers on the application of the new methods that originated in the research and development activities of the agricultural experiment stations of the land-grant universities.

It is my personal observation (as a faculty member at several universities and colleges) that there is relatively little research and development into cognitive processes and the development of educational methods that build on them. This is not surprising—it is not where the money or the prestige is in research (which is overwhelmingly funded directly or indirectly with public funds.)

The historical background of providing teachers and teaching methods for public elementary and secondary education is the "Normal School" or "Teachers' College" and the ethos of those institutions is craft training rather than scientific research and the diffusion and application of that research.[2] From these institutions comes the "craft" mentality in the education profession—a belief that education is *only* an art and not a science. This is the institutional source of the belief that the best way to learn to teach students more effectively is experience. There is limited acceptance of the notion that a basic set of scientific knowledge about the learning process could be developed and applied to improve the efficiency of the learning process.

Increasing the productivity of the learning process of students in the nation's schools is a much more complex challenge than increasing the productivity of the farmer in growing hybrid corn or the agricultural equipment manufacturer in building better tractors. In our post-industrial, knowledge-based society, it is also much more important than sending astronauts into orbit.

Private corporations have determined that it is a cost effective expenditure to educate their own employees—even when there is no guarantee that the employees will stay with them and not transfer to their competitors![3] Because the methods used by private corporations must be cost effective, they spend considerable amounts on the development of proprietary methods to increase the efficiency of in-house education and the hiring of experienced consultants to assure that the training of their employees is cost effective.

A nation has an advantage that private corporations do not have—the greater probability that a well-educated labor force will stay with it and not leave for a better offer from a competitor nation. A nation can invest in the education of the young and recoup the investment in the next generation by taxation of the higher incomes created by the investment in human capital.

I believe that the "slowdown" of economic growth can be mitigated—not reversed—by channeling national investment into the creation of knowledge capital to improve the educational process that creates human capital. The productivity of teachers—measured in terms of the number of students and learning per student—is the output of education. Increasing efficiency in the production of human capital is the most important challenge faced by our society—both for its effect on economic growth and for its role in preserving a society based on equal opportunity.

Production

We should educate and hire enough teachers and pay them for their contribution to social output.   Insist on performance by teachers and compensate them accordingly. In the twenty-first century we no longer have a captive labor force of highly capable women who become teachers because they are barred from other employment opportunities.   Further, in the long run a society can't count on running its most basic institution on idealism or altruism.

Pay for discipline and safety.   Make schools and neighborhoods safe for students and teachers. Education is difficult or impossible in schools without safety or discipline. Teachers with viable career alternatives will be reluctant to teach in schools without safety or discipline.   Parents will be dissatisfied with schools without safety and discipline.   If it takes a higher ratio of police and teachers per student to do the job—do it.   It will turn out to be less costly in the long run than poorly educating a population that can't participate in the labor force and ends up on welfare or in prison.

Capacity Utilization

Operate schools year round and considerably increase the length of the school day and the school year. A century ago, twelve-year-olds worked 60-hour weeks in field, mine, and factory. While that was not a desirable situation, surely nowadays they are physically and developmentally capable of spending thirty hours per week in school and doing ten hours of homework.

The productivity of teachers can be further increased by having them teach 240 rather than 180 days per year. That will decrease cost per student time unit of education and increase annual income per teacher. (Teachers who prefer to teach less time should be prepared to earn less pay than teachers who teach more time.[4])

Graduate students out of schools and into the workforce at an earlier age and provide for continuing education of persons on the job and in continuing education after they have left full-time school. Getting students into the labor force earlier will increase the effectiveness of their education and their earlier entrance into production will increase the tax base for the financing of education.

Allocation

Because funds for education are limited at the margin public authorities faced with the necessity of allocating funds between K-12 and post-secondary education should allocate it to the younger students. If they don't get a proper education in their formative years, they have very little chance of "making it" later. In American business practice, "Total Quality Management" has emphasized that it is far more efficient and profitable in the long run to set up the productive process to produce output up to acceptable quality specifications at every stage of the production line rather than fixing the product after it has been produced. There is an analogous problem in education. Students who didn't learn in elementary school have to learn before they can perform adequately in high school. Students who graduate from high school without being prepared for college require their more valuable time and resources getting the education in college that they should have acquired in high school.

At the margin older students can support themselves through loans or work if they have a good foundation and good prospects. But all citizens should have a fundamental right to a basic education that is satisfied before the benefits of higher education at the public expense are made available to the more privileged.

The Monopoly of Public Education

Some critics of the public education monopoly over public educational spending have likened it to the deadening bureaucracy of the late Soviet Union. That's probably overstated, but I believe that in the long run competition and accountability in the provision of educational services will have to be one component of policies to improve efficiency in education. Defenders of public education who insist on equal opportunity make a very important point —quity and efficiency are always competing social goals that must be balanced. But balancing is not the same as the preservation of the status quo.

Increasing Labor-Force Participation

As discussed in chapter 6, labor-force participation has increased substantially over the past three decades and has made a major contribution to the growth of per capita income. All of the increase in the participation rate has come from the increasing participation of married women. The participation rate of men—particularly in the fifty-five to sixty-four and post-sixty-five age groups—has declined.

Increasing the participation rate of older men will depend upon reducing the positive incentives for early retirement.[5] The Social Security system needs to be readjusted to increase the incentives to postpone retirement. It needs to be recognized that while getting older workers "off the payroll" may be advantageous for younger workers and employers, it decreases national income and increases transfer payments that have disincentive effects on employment.

All levels of government are notably more generous than is the private sector in their granting of retirement pensions after relatively shorter spans of service. Disability retirement programs are an easy target for collusion between employers, physicians, and employees. The expense of early retirement is borne by taxpayers and by younger workers who have less take-home pay because funds generated by current revenues in the private sector and taxation in the public sector are diverted to funding retired older workers rather than the current labor force. That is a statement of fact—not a value judgment.

I do not wish to impose my own value judgments here about the intergenerational distribution of income. However, a basic principle of our philosophy of "possessive individualism" is that wealth and consumption should be rewards for contribution. The lifetime pattern of consumption should be a matter for individual choice within the limits of that principle. If a worker voluntarily chooses to limit the span of his or her useful participation in the labor force, it should be done with a reduction in the compensation received over his or her lifetime. (I am not talking about cases of true disability, which can be handled through social insurance.) Retirement benefits do not come from the government—they come from the income of the current working population and, as I have explained in chapter 7, the increase in the incomes of the retired population can only be funded by a corresponding reduction in the consumption of the working population.

My argument here is based on both interpersonal and intergenerational equity. It is also made on the basis of increasing national income through increasing participation by delaying retirement. In a wealthy society, people can retire by personal choice—they no longer have to work until they are physically unable to toil as they did in the first half of the twentieth century.

America needs to preserve two principles, however, that are always in tension in the organization of production and compensation. The first is the individualistic principle that income is the reward for contribution and individuals' choices about their inter-temporal pattern of work and consumption should be constrained by that principle. The second is the social democratic (Rawlsian) principle that a society is a social compact in which the fundamental rules are framed to provide the least advantaged members of the society the highest level of income and security possible. This requires careful planning to ensure that the incentives to work are not reduced so much that the larger relative share of the least advantaged is smaller in absolute terms. Both of these principles are philosophically complex and their application in the rules that govern us are never easy.

Immigration Policy

Let me state, at the outset, that there are noneconomic considerations in immigration policy and my remarks are restricted to the effect of immigration on the growth in per capita personal income. I think it is a perfectly legitimate choice for a society to welcome refugees or immigrants on other grounds than economics, but a social decision to do this should be made on the basis of an understanding of the consequences. The composition of American immigration in the 1980s and 1990s has been totally different than it was a century ago and economic arguments couched in terms of historical parallels are totally misleading.

Most immigrants do come to this country seeking employment. Some don't find employment and end up on welfare. The latter obviously decrease per capita income. So do the former if they come without the level of human capital of other members of the labor force. If a society places a high priority on increasing per capita income, it makes economic sense to admit only immigrants who have a level of human capital equal to or greater than the average of the total population. If you were trying to improve the batting average of a baseball team, would you add players whose batting averages were lower than those of the rest of the team?

The economic interests of particular groups must always be considered in evaluating their arguments for public policy. Some employers have a strong economic interest in the continuance of immigration because they can employ immigrants at lower wages and benefits than they can employ native-born Americans. Some providers of public services to immigrants have a strong economic interest in the continuance of immigration.[6] But what is economically advantageous for one segment of the population is not always good economic policy.

Let me put this argument in strong terms—slave owners in pre–Civil War America had an economic interest in the continuation of slavery—because they could benefit from employing slaves. So do contemporary sweatshop owners and the upper-class employers of foreign maids, gardeners, and "nannies." The rest of the American population, on balance, does not benefit from immigrant labor. It may slightly reduce the cost of lettuce or the cost of garments made in the sweatshops employing immigrants below the minimum wage, but the alternative would have been importing the lettuce or the garments from abroad and exporting goods and services made by higher skilled labor.

In the nineteenth century the immigrants to the United States had a level of human capital comparable to or greater than the citizens who were already here. In fact, the immigrants came with the costs of education and upbringing already borne by their countries of provenience. At the beginning of the twentieth century, the economy had plenty of jobs for people with relatively low education as agricultural laborers or construction workers or unskilled factory workers or domestic service workers. At the end of the twentieth century, the economy has automated those jobs out of existence and there are not enough of them to provide employment for native-born citizens with low levels of education or other handicaps.

Some immigrants still come to the United States with a high level of education provided by their countries of provenience. They bring considerable economic advantage to the United States and we have an economic advantage in admitting them. There is currently substantial controversy about letting those workers in on employer-provided temporary visas. Most immigrants, however, come without the education that will allow them to produce in jobs at or above the average level of income, and—as a consequence, as a mathematical necessityey reduce the average level of per worker income.

However, the economic disadvantage of unskilled immigration does not end here. If all residents are guaranteed access to public services, and if poorer immigrants need a higher level of public services, they are a tax drain on the taxpaying members of the labor force.

The economic argument offered by the proponents of increased immigration for immigrants with less than average human capital are specious. They take into account only the current costs and taxes of these immigrants. Their studies may even show that working immigrants paying payroll and local taxes may be paying more in taxes than they receive in benefits, but that is because they are younger and employed. That is true for all workers in their age cohort. Over their lifetimes, however, the benefits received by immigrant workers with limited human capital will exceed their taxes and will decrease the net incomes of the native-born population.

There are arguments for welcoming unskilled and uneducated immigrants on humanitarian grounds. There are also arguments for admitting uneducated immigrants based on the political interests or economic self-interest of particular groups.   I am not aware of any adequately structured and appropriately evidenced economic arguments that immigrants with minimal education do not lower the rate of growth in per capita income and increase the level of transfer payments from the employed population.

Contemporary supporters of easing restrictions on immigration draw historical parallels. But we have a different economic situation than a century ago when the immigrant population had a higher human capital level than the resident population and there were no comprehensive social programs funded by taxation.   The humanitarian arguments are still valid today, but the economic arguments are not. Immigration policy poses harder social choices when the earning characteristics of the immigrant population, due to their lower human capital, change relative to the resident population. It makes the humanitarian choice more expensive.

The Civil Justice System

In chapter 9 I advanced the argument that the slowing of growth in productivity is coming about through the slowdown in specialization of production and that the cause of the slowdown was the increase in transactions costs. One source of the increasing transactions costs is the failure of our legal codes to facilitate transactions and another source is the way in which the tort system has evolved.

I have argued in previous books[7] that the system of secure property rights and enforceable property rights was a necessary condition for the success of our economic system.   However, I believe we have now reached a stage in our economic and social development where the uncertainties inherent in transactions between employees and firms and between firms and firms are inhibiting socially profitable specialization.

The following real-life example is not an argument—only an illustration. (For purposes of confidentiality, I conceal the names of companies involved.) A manufacturer of industrial bonding products has developed a metal bonding agent that can be used as a replacement for more expensive welding or rivets in the manufacture of truck bodies.   The manufacturer of truck bodies would achieve substantial efficiencies in manufacture if it were able to substitute the new technology for the old. The trucking companies who would benefit from reduced capital and maintenance costs would like to purchase the truck bodies fabricated with the new process.   The public doesn't know about the technologies involved but they would benefit from the effect on transportation costs.

Why doesn't it happen? Because statute law and tort practice offer no certainty to the transacting parties about liability should the industrial bond fail at some point in the future life of the truck; and tort law allows anyone who can claim injury to sue anyone and everyone in the specialized chain of production.

The legal counsel for the chemical manufacturer advises the company of the potential liabilities associated with the sale of the new product. This decreases the incentive for research and development of the product. It increases the cost that the chemical manufacturer would have to factor into its costs of production in the sale of the metal bonding product to the truck body fabricator.

The legal counsel for the truck body manufacturer advises management that the potential liabilities from its trucking company customers are uncertain and need to be factored into any decision to reduce production costs by shifting from rivets to metal bonds.

The legal counsel for the trucking companies advise management of the potential uncertainties of purchasing trucks incorporating the new technologies.

All of these uncertainties raise the potential cost that the supplier of the production chain has to factor into its selling price. All of these uncertainties lower the potential benefit from the adoption of the new technology for which the buyer of the new technology would be willing to pay. The first consequence is the reduction of specialization and technological change. The transactions costs are too large to permit mutually profitable exchange by parties specialized in the production of goods and services.

The second consequence, *even if the change is profitable in spite of all the uncertainties*, is still to increase the costs—ultimately to society—of all the lawyers and managers involved in negotiation and, potentially, in litigation of the liabilities involved.

The irony of our current situation is that the certainty of property rights and contracts historically was a powerful contributor to economic growth. Individuals knew if they developed land, built a factory, or invented a machine that the law and the courts would give them security in their use of the asset. They knew that if they made a contract with others, the contract would be enforced. These certainties increased the incentives for the creation of assets and the specialization of production.

Why doesn't this problem in economic organization get solved by passing new laws and changing tort liability to reduce the transactions costs? The simple economic answer is that the costs of changing the laws are large relative to the benefits to any particular participant in any production process. The simple political answer is that to change the laws to increase the certainty about the liabilities of the parties in the contracting process would decrease the employment and income of the legal profession. At the beginning of the twenty-first century, the interests of the legal profession in the current application of the law are as powerful a barrier to legal reform as they were when Charles Dickens was provoked to write about the protracted and financially ruinous proceedings in the London Court of Chancery in his novel, *Bleak House*, at the beginning of the industrial revolution. "The forensic wisdom of ages has interposed a million of obstacles to the transaction of the commonest business of life," he wrote in 1852.

I offer no solutions for this problem in this book.

Changing Our Conceptual Framework

Finally, let me move from social policy to social thought. There is a long tradition in our intellectual history of American "exceptionalism"—America as the "city on the hill," the "promised land," a "new world" in which the constraints of the old world on human opportunity no longer applied. In more recent times economists may have unintentionally contributed to this tradition by *ahistorical* analysis of economic growth as a *continuous* process rather than as a discrete process of historical change with natural bounds.

To the extent that economic thought has had an effect on the popular mind, economists may have unwittingly contributed to a popular belief that we could have constant or even accelerating economic growth. I say "unwittingly" because most economists, on reflection, would reject the notion that even a constant rate growth in productivity or per capita income could be maintained indefinitely.[8]

In their attempt to be more scientific, economists have also contributed to formulation of public policies through their attempts to measure "real income" and the "standard of living." When economists talk about real income, they know it is a short-hand term for some inflation-adjusted accounting artifact. But voters and policy makers and union negotiators believe (or pretend to believe) it is a "real something" rather than an intellectual construct.

The concept of a "real standard of living" comes out of economists' attempts to give a quantitative measure to a variable that is assumed to be important in economic models of labor supply decisions. It has progressed from economic theory to economic policy, however, as transfer recipients of welfare and social security benefits and public and private sector employees base their claims to income shares on index numbers constructed by economists.

As I have argued throughout this book, the measurement concepts we use to quantify economic performance become less and less reliable as we move beyond bread and clothing to the achievements of a post-industrial society in health care, habitation, and leisure activities. An objective index of a "standard of living" may be useful when measuring consumption of bread and coal, but it becomes much less reliable when valuing computers and appendectomies.

What are the implications of these comments for changing our conceptual framework? Economists need to admit that we have not resolved the paradox about the relative prices of diamonds and water that Adam Smith tried to solve two centuries ago by approximation and the concepts of "value in use" and "value in exchange." We need to admit that *everyman* is the measurer of his own "standard of living" and political leaders need to realize that the rights of any members of society to a particular standard of living entail the obligations of other members of society to adjust their own to provide it. Social relationships in an interdependent society must be viewed as interdependent and conditional rather than independent and absolute.

IN CONCLUSION

Economics, particularly historical economics, is about choices—the observation of how people made them and the explanation of the nature and effects of the choices on a people's history. For a long time Americans have been accustomed to thinking that the distributional choices—between rich and poor and between generations—could be made easier or avoided by increasing or at least maintaining high rates of economic growth. And economic growth (and demographic growth) did make choices easier.

Growth itself was *not* easy. American economic growth did not come without sacrifice—generations of Americans worked hard, were inventive, and saved to create physical and knowledge capital and human capital for their children. The abundance of natural resources, political and religious freedom, and economic opportunity attracted immigrants from their countries of provenience who were ambitious and enterprising and relatively well educated in comparison with their native-born contemporaries.

Our forebears were successful. Their achievements shifted the labor force from the grinding physical toil of field, forest, mine, and factory to the less physically demanding toil of offices, classrooms, and health-care facilities. The average work week dropped by half over the last century. The life expectancy of the population increased. Women escaped physical and social constraints on their productivity—and their freedom—in the move from household employment to the specialized labor force.

That was "the way it worked"—the way economic growth took place. But economic growth has slowed—not because we have abandoned the work ethic or the frugality of our ancestors—but because successive generations have moved the nation from a low level to a high level of productivity and labor-force participation. The structural changes in the economy as it moved from scarcity to abundance have occurred and thereby removed those opportunities for continuing the rapid rate of (at least, measured) growth. That is "why it doesn't work"—why growth has slowed. And increasingly in the next century, that is "why it won't work"—why growth will continue to slow.

NOTES

1. The increase in real wages between 1970 and 1990 is a matter of contention between political activists and between professional economists. Their change depends upon the sample group compared and the price index used to deflate nominal earnings.

2. This argument is made persuasively in Kenneth G. Wilson and Bennett Davis, *Redesigning Education* (New York: Henry Holt, 1995).

3. One estimate of corporate expenditures on education makes it equal to all the funds spent on post-secondary education in the nation's colleges and universities. (This figure includes wages paid to employees while they are learning—it is an opportunity cost not included in the national cost of post-secondary education.)

4. The long summer vacation of the current educational year is a throwback to an agricultural year when students and teachers were released for work in the fields to

reduce the opportunity cost of education. The opportunity cost of education is now too high to justify the vacations.

5. The nature of incentives for older workers is complex. On the employees' side compensation levels relative to retirement benefits must induce older workers to stay on the job. On the employers' side the increase of compensation levels with age and seniority creates an incentive to get rid of older workers.

6. In 1990 Proposition 187 was passed by the California voters to deny public education and public health benefits to illegal aliens. (The constitutionality is still in the courts.) The two largest contributors to the campaign to defeat the initiative were the California Teachers Association and the California Medical Association. Of course, neither group employed the illegal immigrants whom they taught or treated, but the incomes of members of both groups would have been reduced by the cutoff of funds to educate or treat the illegal immigrants.

7. See Bjork, 1969, 1979.

8. One exciting development in recent economic theory does raise the possibility of increasing returns to investment in capital when physical, knowledge, and human capital are appropriately defined (Romer, 1986).

Appendixes

APPENDIX 3: THE QUANTITATIVE RECORD OF U.S. GROWTH

(There are no appendixes for chapters 1, 2, and 10.)

Appendix Note 3.1. Sources and Presentation of Data Tables

Sources

All the reported decennial rates of growth in output relative to various demographic variables in Text Tables 3.1 and 3.2 and Appendix Tables 3.1–4 were derived from official U.S. Government statistics on output and employment.   Data for the decades ending 1970 to 1990 were taken from Appendix B of the *Economic Report of the President, 1994 (ERP, 1994)* (Washington, D.C., Government Printing Office, 1994). Earlier data were taken from U.S. Bureau of the Census. *Historical Statistics of the United States: Colonial Times to 1970* (Washington, D.C., Government Printing Office, 1975). To insure comparability, overlapping data from 1959 to 1970 were available from both sources.

From *Historical Statistics* population and employment data were taken from Series D 1-10 and D 11-25. Data on average hours came from D 803.   National income estimates came from F 1-5 and F 6-9.

Data for the 1960 to 1990 period came from the following tables of the *ERP, 1994*: Population, B-32; Labor Force, B-33, B-42, B-45; National Income Accounting (NIA): B-2, B-15, B-23.

Text Table III.3: Data for computation of decennial growth rates for various nations from 1870–1950 are adapted from Angus Maddison, *Phases of*

Capitalist Development (Oxford Univ. Press, New York, 1982), Table 3.1. They are based on 1913 prices.

International data for various growth rates from 1960 to 1990 in Text Table 3.3 comes from OECD, *National Accounts, 1960–1993*, Volume 1. (OECD, Paris, 1995), Part III and Part VIII. For most nations they are based on 1985 prices. Data for 1950 to 1960 come from OECD, *Statistics of National Accounts, 1950–1961* (OECD, Paris, 1964), volume indexes of Per Capita Gross National Product (1953 prices, unnumbered table). The source of data for Text Graphs 3.4 and Appendix Tables 3.4 is Sections VI and VII, ibid.

The slight differences in measured growth rates for the OECD figures and my figures for the United States for the decades of the 1970s and 1980s result from the use of different base years for the price indexes used to deflate current values and a slight difference in my figures on population. The biases introduced by alternative base years are discussed below.

Price Indexes and the "Bias" in Growth Calculation

"Real" Gross Domestic Product is a measure of the flow of production of final goods and services by an economy. All final goods and services are valued at their relative prices each year and then "deflated" to their value in a base year to control for changes in the general level of prices. The result is "real" GDP— "real" in the sense that the changes are in quantities measured in terms of their relative prices in the current year rather than in the changing prices of previous years.

U.S. real GDP from 1960 to 1990 was measured in terms of the prices of 1987. Real GDP from 1890 to 1960 was measured in terms of 1957 prices. As is well known by economists who construct indexes of output and prices, this procedure tends to understate growth rates as one goes back in time from the base year and overstate growth as one goes forward from the base year.

This "bias" in indexes occurs because the increases in output tend to be the greatest for goods with prices that have fallen relative to other prices over time. Thus, for example, when 1987 prices are used to value the output of computers in 1980, the relative importance of computers in 1980 GDP is understated (because they are valued in the lower 1987 prices) and the growth of GDP (in which computers are a component) appears to be slower from the vantage point of the present.

On the other hand, if one valued computers in their (higher) 1980 prices, their value in 1987 GDP would be more highly weighted and measured GDP growth would appear greater from the vantage point of the earlier year.

One illustration of the magnitude of differences in measured growth rates from using different years as a price base can be seen in the measurement of GDP growth between 1960 and 1970 using 1958 and 1987 prices. The measurement of change in the same quantities of goods in 1958 prices is 48 percent and in 1987 prices it is 46 percent. When growth is computed on a per capita basis, it means that the growth rate is 31 percent when the earlier base year index is used and 29 percent when the later base year is used.

I have used the later base. Since my purpose is to compare the lower growth rates of the decades ending in 1980 and 1990 with those ending in 1960 and earlier years, I have used the 1987 index for estimating "real" growth in those years because it "understates" the growth in earlier decades and, thereby, understates the decline in recent decades. Using the 1958 base year for the decades before 1960 reduces the growth rate of prior decades. Thus, the index years and methods I use understate the decline in economy growth—I choose the index base least favorable to my argument. The decline in recent "real" growth" could be presented as even greater by the use of the alternative index methods.

National Income Accounting Concepts

Growth rates of various components of output used in NIA are presented Appendix Table 3.1. National Income differs from Gross National Product primarily by the exclusion of depreciation and indirect business taxes. In every decade in the last century (except the decade ending in 1950), National Income grew more slowly than GDP. This indicates that an increasing proportion of total output was unavailable for consumption because it was being allocated to the depreciation of reproducible capital or to government tax revenues reflected in the cost of production of goods and services.

One of the expected consequences of a rising ratio for the value of the capital stock to annual output is an increasing share of output being devoted to the replacement of the capital stock. Another reason for the increasing proportion of depreciation in GDP is the declining economic life of modern capital assets— railroad engines may be depreciated over twenty years but computers are depreciated over twenty months. As "modern" capital assets increase relative to "traditional" capital assets, the total depreciation rate rises.

Disposable Income differs from National Income by federal, state, and local direct taxation less transfer payments back to the population and some other adjustments. It is a measure of the after-tax income that the population has available for Personal Consumption.

Personal Consumption Expenditure differs from Disposable Income by the amount of Personal Saving. The faster growth of Disposable Income than Personal Consumption Expenditure in the 1960s reflected an increase in the saving rate. The faster increase in Personal Consumption Expenditure than Disposable Income in the 1980s reflected the oft-cited decline in household saving.

Personal saving is often discussed as though people are continually deciding between consuming and saving their income. In reality, most Personal Saving is done contractually and is the difference between "saving" by the working-age population and "dis-saving" by the retired population. The employed population directs part of their compensation into building up the balance in their pension funds. Another large component of Saving takes place as home mortgages are amortized and the cash value builds up in life insurance policies.

Most dis-saving is done by the retired population, which draws down the annuity from their pension fund, sells their house, and devotes part of the proceeds to living expenses, or passes on life insurance payouts to heirs who spend it.   An important part of the change in the personal saving rate beween decades reflects a change in the proportion of the population that is dis-saving in retirement years rather than building up savings for retirement in employment years.

As the American labor force ages and retires earlier, a major problem facing the American population will be how to raise the saving rate for the employed population to compensate for the dis-saving rate of the retired population. (The mechanics and implications of saving are discussed in chapter 7.)

The measurements of gross output before 1960 are for Gross National rather than Gross Domestic Output.   Gross National is larger than Gross Domestic when the balance of net income over net outflow on foreign investments is positive.   Using one rather than the other makes no difference in calculated growth rates for the period after 1960.

I have used total population sixteen years and older rather than the frequently used noninstitutional population over sixteen.   The institutional population (prisons, mental institutions, permanent residents of health-care facilities) is a part of the population and consumes resources.   (2.5 percent of the male population between twenty and sixty-five was in prison or on parole or probation in 1990!)

At least some of the institutionalized population could be productive participants in society with better social organization.   If their proportion is increasing (as it is), their exclusion (current practice by the Department of Labor) makes growth rates of per capita output and income (slightly) higher. My inclusion (slightly) lowers measured rates (.3 percent for the 17 percent decennial growth rate in GDP per capita for the population in the decade ending in 1990).

There are two methods used by the Federal Government for estimating levels of employment in the economy—a survey based on information furnished by employers (Employment and Earnings) and a survey sample of households (Current Population Survey).   I have used the former in this chapter and in chapter 5 for employment estimates because it is also used for the estimation of GDP. It has the disadvantage of counting people holding more than one job and excludes self-employed entrepreneurs, farmers, domestic servants, and family employees.   I have remedied the exclusion of farmers by adding in an estimate of farmers based on the Current Population Survey.

On the other hand, in chapter 6, I have used the Current Population Survey to estimate population participation in the labor force by demographic groups.   The definition of "labor force" depends upon questionnaires and classification of persons not employed who are seeking work.   It should be noted that the participation ratio used in this chapter relates employment to working-age population rather than labor force to working-age population.

I have chosen to do this because employment and population can be directly identified, while the status of "participation in the labor force" depends upon definitions such as "seeking work" and "available for employment," that are not "hard" or directly observable.   There is another reason to do this: my use of employment/working-age population rather than labor force/working-age population catches the differences in unemployment that affect the ratio.

After 1950 the working-age population includes persons sixteen years of age and older. From 1870 to 1940 employed persons over fourteen years of age were included in the definition of the labor force. In the participation ratio used in this chapter, I have avoided changes in concept by using the ratio of actual employment to the sixteen to sixty-four age group.

There has been a long-term decline in average hours worked per week in private, nonagricultural employment. Using a forty-hour week as a standard "full time equivalent" (FTE) worker, an index of FTE employment was created by multiplication of employment times the ratio of average hours/40 (ERP, 1994) Table B42. This was then converted into a 2000-hour year.

Prior to 1960 average hours for all private nonagricultural workers were unavailable so the rate for 1950 and earlier was based on average hours in manufacturing employment (Series D803, *Historical Statistics*). This makes for a slight transitional discrepancy in the series. In 1960, for example, the average work week in all private sector employment was 97.3 percent of average hours worked by production workers. Thus, the estimates of average hours worked for the total labor force for 1950 and before may be slightly overstated. However, the seeming discontinuity between 1940 and 1950 comes in the same series and results from the "slack" in the economy in 1940 and the big reduction in participation by women workers (who are more likely to work part time) in 1950.

Commerce Department data on employment for the last decade are far more detailed than those used for the historical series presented in this book. For the current decade Commerce estimates by sector are available for: (1) total employed, (2) full-time equivalent workers, (3) persons engaged, and (4) total hours worked. (*Survey of Current Business*, Vol. 72/1, Jan. 1992, Vol. 77/8, Aug. 1997, Tables 6.8C and 6.9C, and Vol. 77/11 Nov. 1997, Table 12). Interestingly, growth rates of the labor force for these four alternative measures of the labor force (and consequently for GDP per worker and per worker hour) are remarkably similar.

Appendix Note 3.2. Ratio Disaggregation

My method of analyzing the relative importance of the various factors that affect the growth of output per capita is disaggregation of the determinants of output per worker and the participation rate of the population in the labor force and employment. I employ the following identities:

$Output/Population = (Output/Workers) \times (Workers/Population)$ *1.0*

$Output/Workers = (Output/Hours) \times (Hours/Workers)$ *1.1*

$Workers/Population = (Working\text{-}Age\ Population/Total\ Population) \times$

$(Workers/Working\text{-}Age\ Population)$ *1.2*

Thus, GDP per capita is the product of four ratios: (Output/Hours) x (Hours/Workers) x (Workers/Working-Age Population) x (Working-Age Population/Total Population).

These ratios are shown in Appendix Table 3.3. In Appendix Table 3.4 the ratios are indexed to 100 for 1990 and shown as index numbers for the census years prior to 1990. Appendix Table 3.4 is a table of index numbers based on the census year 1990 for the various determinants of GDP per capita. It will be noted, for example, that the index of GDP/Population for 1990 is 1.00 and for 1980 it is .85. The ratio .85 for GDP/Population for 1980 is also the product of the cross multiplication of all the other index numbers in the row for 1980.

Text Table 3.2 presents the decennial rates of change in the index numbers for the components of GDP/Population. For example, in 1980 GDP per capita was 85 percent of what it was in 1990. GDP/Population increased by 17 percent ([1.00/.85]-1) between 1980 and 1990. In the bottom left corner of the table, it will be noted that the decennial growth rate of GDP/Population is 17 percent. (Note that same 17 percent growth rate in both Text Graph 1.1 and Text Tables 3.1 and 3.2.)

The rate of change of the index of GDP/Population can be obtained as the sum of the rates of change of the indices of the four ratios: (1) GDP/Total Worker Hours, (2) Total Worker Hours/Employees, (3) Employees/Working-Age Cohort, and (4) Working-Age Cohort/Population (and cross products).

Appendix 3 Tables

Appendix Table 3.1
Decennial % Rates of Per Capita Growth in NIA Aggregates

Decade Ending	GDP/ Population	Nat. Inc./ Population	Disp.Inc./ Population	Pers.Cons.Exp./ Population
1900	20			
1910	29			
1920	1			
1930	13	9	19	
1940	15	11	6	12
1950	36	42	27	28
1960	15	13	13	15
1970	29	28	36	32
1980	18	16	21	21
1990	17	17	17	21

Source. Author. See Appendix Note 3.1.

Appendix Table 3.2
Decennial % Growth Rates in Various NIA Aggregates Relative to Various Demographic Groups for Decade Ending in 1990

IncomeAggregate		GNP	NI	DI
		30	29	29
Demographic Group				
Population	10	17	17	17
Working Age Population	9	18	19	17
Labor Force	17	11	11	10
Employment	20	8	8	7
Fte Employment	17	10	10	10

Source: Author. See Appendix Note 3.1.

Appendix Table 3.3
Ratio Determinants of GDP/Population (GDP in 1987$)

Decade Ending	GDP/ Pop.	GDP/ Hour	Annual Hours Per Worker	Workers/ Working Age Population	Work Age Pop/ Population
1890	3398	3.16	2946	0.62	0.59
1900	4092	3.75	2858	0.66	0.58
1910	5268	5.00	2550	0.67	0.62
1920	5334	6.28	2370	0.58	0.62
1930	6042	8.83	2105	0.51	0.63
1940	6946	11.74	1905	0.47	0.67
1950	9433	13.62	2025	0.54	0.64
1960	10890	17.02	1930	0.51	0.65
1970	14020	20.94	1855	0.57	0.63
1980	16561	22.76	1765	0.64	0.64
1990	19433	25.12	1725	0.70	0.64

Source: Author. See Appendix Notes 3.1, 3.2.

Appendix Table 3.4
Index Values for Ratio Determinants of Per Capita GDP (1990 = 1.00)

Decade Ending	GDP/ Pop.	GDP/ Hour	Annual Hrs Per Worker	Workers/ Working Age Pop.	Working Age Pop./ Pop.
1890	0.17	0.13	1.71	0.89	0.91
1900	0.21	0.15	1.66	0.94	0.90
1910	0.27	0.20	1.48	0.96	0.96
1920	0.27	0.25	1.37	0.83	0.97
1930	0.31	0.35	1.22	0.74	0.99
1940	0.36	0.47	1.10	0.67	1.04
1950	0.49	0.54	1.17	0.77	0.99
1960	0.56	0.68	1.12	0.74	1.01
1970	0.72	0.83	1.08	0.82	0.98
1980	0.85	0.91	1.02	0.92	1.00
1990	1.00	1.00	1.00	1.00	1.00

Source: Author. See Appendix Notes 3.1, 3.2.

APPENDIX 4: UNDERSTANDING THE MEASUREMENT OF ECONOMIC ACTIVITY

Appendix Note 4.1. National Income Accounting

The Concept of Income

NIA concepts for the definition and measurement of national output and income are intended to measure the concept of "income" articulated by economist Sir John Hicks in *Value and Capital* (Hicks, 1935). Simply stated, Hicksian "income" is the flow of goods and services that an individual could consume within a given time period without diminishing the stock of goods held at the beginning of the measurement period. The Hicksian concept of income has its intellectual origins in the double-entry accounting concepts developed by Italian merchants in the fifteenth century for the measurement of the activities of individual business enterprises.

In double-entry accounting the objective is to establish a value for the activities of an individual firm during a particular time period. The value is stated in terms of some "numeraire" (standard of measurement)—originally a precious metal like ounces of gold or silver and, later, in monetary units (which has its origin in an equivalent quantity of a precious metal).

The firm "produces" goods or services that are sold in the market for particular prices to produce a gross revenue during a period of time. The production may involve the alteration of raw materials—the grinding of grain into flour or the provision of services—carrying passengers or freight. Or it may involve only the purchase of goods from some parties and their sale to others—probably at different times and places and quantities.

The firm receives commodities, or money, or promises of future payment of money, from other firms or individuals. These comprise the firm's gross revenues. The firm delivers money, commodities, or promises to deliver to others at some future time. In the case of use of capital assets such as buildings or machinery, depreciation charges are imputed to represent a cost that the firm must (implicitly) pay to itself in order to maintain the value of its capital. These constitute the firm's costs of production.

The costs of production are subtracted from the firm's gross revenues to arrive at a net income. Net income is a measure of how the monetary or commodity value of the firm's assets would have increased during the year (if there had been no interim withdrawals), or how much of the firm's resources could be consumed or sold within the accounting time period without diminishing the starting value (balance sheet). It is a stock (as opposed to flow) value expressed in terms of a monetary numeraire, but the accounting change in the value of the firm's stock during a time interval is treated as a flow for that period.

NIA conventions modify the double-entry concept of a firm's net income. They treat the economic output of a nation as the sum of all of the payments received by the firms from final purchasers (interfirm transactions are excluded). The value of national product or income includes the value of all final purchases, and following double-entry accounting conventions is equal to the payments of wages, rents, interests, and profits paid to all the persons who receive them for their provision of services in the economic process of production. The citizens of the nation who receive the payments from the firm for services provided are the equivalent of the owners of the firm.

The intellectual antecedents of aggregating economic activities for the national income concept can be found in the work of Gregory King, a seventeenth-century English chronicler who actually tried to estimate the national product of England in his own time by multiplying the estimated number and estimated average wages of all the agricultural laborers, blacksmiths, and so forth, and summing their incomes. Adam Smith and the French Physiocrats in the eighteenth century elaborated the concepts without trying to collect data.

The modern concepts of NIA were developed, refined, and implemented by the privately funded U.S. National Bureau of Economic Research in the 1920s. They were adoped by most governments in the period from 1930 to 1960. The most important contributor to the intellectual development and actual implementation of the concepts, Simon Kuznets, received the Nobel Prize for Economics for this and other contributions to economics in 1975.

In the most basic conceptual version of NIA, the economy is divided functionally into "firms" and "households." Functionally, firms sell final output to households and purchase the use of the factors of production—land, labor, capital, and entrepreneurship—from households.

National product is a measure of the expenditures of households on "final products" purchased from the firms. National income is a measure of the purchase of factor services by firms from households. The measure excludes interfirm payments (except for capital goods) and treats any difference between firms' production and sales as an investment (or disinvestment) in inventories as a final sale of capital goods The NIA model is extensively elaborated to allow for flows to, from, and through the government, international markets, and financial intermediaries. National product and national income are equalized by accounting conventions.

NIA conventions like Generally Accepted Accounting Practices (GAAP) are founded on two bedrock principles: (1) The phenomena being measured must be observable; (2) they must be reported in the prices (measurement units) at which they are observed (or prices may be imputed if they are potentially observable). These two conventions are a basis for "hard" science.

The practical problems of data collection for the national accounts are enormous because so many different types of goods and services are produced by any society. Loaves of bread and tons of steel are heterogeneous in types and sizes. But even physically identical loaves of bread and tons of steel are delivered with varying transport and distribution costs at different times and places at different prices and are, therefore, economically heterogeneous.

Gallons of water and kilowatts of electricity might seem homogeneous but they have different costs of production and distribution. The sale of computers, air passenger miles, restaurant meals, heart bypass operations, musical concerts, housing services, legal counsel, and regulatory activities by a variety of governmental and nongovernmental bodies must all be aggregated at market or imputed prices to measure national output. The disparate transactions are aggregated by the simple convention of summing the prices received in final transactions when they are sold for "final" consumption (or investment, government purchase, or sale to foreign purchasers).

The diverse production of goods and services is valued by their reported (or imputed) market prices and aggregated to some current market value to measure Gross National Product (GNP). Of course not every transaction is reported. Elaborate sampling techniques and interpolations are used to come up with the quantity and price values.

Permutations of the GNP measure are "Net," "Domestic," and "Real." Gross and Net National Product differ from each other by the imputation for the amount of capital that is "consumed" or "depreciated" in the process of production. (Unfortunately, and I will discuss this further in Chapter 8, there are no generally agreed-on conventions for this depreciation imputation.)

National Product includes all production for which the citizens of a national state have responsibility. Domestic Product includes only transactions for final goods that take place within the geographic confines of some national state.

"Real" National Product differs from the nominal national product, which is actually observed by being revalued in the constant prices of some base year. Sophisticated index number theory is used to explain a number of conventions for price deflation.

Net National Product and National Income are equalized by accounting conventions. From National Income, further adjustments are made to obtain Personal Income and Disposable Income.

The Measurement of National Income at Market Prices

Why "market" prices? Several assumptions underlie the convention of using the observed prices and quantities of national output as the numerand for volume of output (or even "utility" or "welfare"). The first assumption is that the observed combination of goods and services produced and sold represents the currently most valuable combination of output that could be produced by a society with a given set of preferences and productive capacities. The observed output is the most valuable and becomes the standard of value because it has been chosen. "Revealed preference" becomes the basis for value.

As consumer, each society member is assumed to allocate her income among a variety of possible choices on the basis of getting the greatest satisfaction from that income. All producers are assumed to allocate their productive resources to the production of goods and by production techniques that will result in the greatest possible net income. Thus, if a worker is transferred from producing steel to producing health services, or from health services to police services, it is assumed that the value added in any of the employments reflects the amount that the worker is paid.

Further, each worker is assumed to labor up to that quantity and intensity of time at which the real purchasing power of an additional unit of labor is just equal to the value of the leisure foregone by working. Each provider of capital is assumed to provide the capital up to the point at which the return to the owner of the capital is equal to its value in current consumption. Thus, the national ouput actually observed and measured could be taken as a measure of "Pareto optimal" output—the most income that could be produced with given technology and relative values—under a number of restrictive conditions.

One of the theoretical differences between national income and total utility is that goods are assumed to exchange at the prices that reflect their marginal utility and workers are assumed to supply labor up the point where the marginal utility of the goods received in payment is just equal to the marginal utility of the leisure foregone. Thus, both consumers and workers get some "surplus" utility from their activities. Consumers would be willing to pay more for their goods than they actually do and workers would be willing to work for less than they actually do. Because of these consumer and producer "surpluses," changes in the market value of goods and services or the market value of factor payments are not a theoretically equivalent measure of the changes in total utility that the citizens of a nation derive from changes their economic activities.

Adjusting for Price Changes

The "nominal" (current market price) value of national output is the basis for all measurements of national output and economic growth. What is initially observed ("measured") is the sum of the quantitative values of a heterogeneous aggregate of goods and services valued at their current relative prices.

Nominal or current market value national product is then converted with some constant set of prices to a "real" (constant dollar) measure of output. This "real" or constant dollar measure is sought because the objective of the valuation and aggregation is to estimate the change in the volume of goods and services produced rather than changes in the market values of the goods that result from changes in their prices. It is the traditional problem of valuing the increase in the total quantity of apples and oranges when the two fruits change in number or volume at different rates, and it is a composite measure of number or volume change that is sought.

Estimating the "real" national output of a nation for a series of years starts with estimating the value of an aggregated quantity of goods and services produced in those years at their current prices and then revaluing those goods and services in the constant relative prices of some base year. Thus, the increase in real national output between 1994 and 1995 is the difference in the quantities of all goods and services produced in those years weighted by their prices in 1995 (A Paasche current weighted quantity index).

The use of 1994 prices (A LaSpeyres base weighted quantity index) would result in a different measured rate of growth of output. This creates no serious problems for international or intertemporal comparison of growth rates as long as the same types of indexes are used to "deflate" the periods or countries under comparison. As discussed in chapter 3, another set of issues arises from the use of currency exchange values or Purchasing Power Parity values to make international comparisons.

Appendix Note 4.2. Growth Accounting

Growth Accounting uses the same measures of economic output as NIA, but it can allow a greater understanding of the determinants of the growth of output that is measured by NIA and, particularly, growth in output per worker.

The measured increase in national product results from a number of factors. Consider some of them: The population and capital stock increase. The proportion of the population in the labor force increases. The proportion of the labor force that is employed increases, or they work more or fewer hours. The labor hours worked by more highly educated workers or more experienced workers increases.

The capital stock increases faster from investment or the depreciation rate of the capital stock decreases. The physical capital stock is employed more fully. The stock of intellectual capital increases. Or, finally, as a residual, output increases per unit of input for reasons that we can't otherwise identify so we call the unidentified residual the increase in productivity!

One of the useful contributions of growth accounting is to show, by disaggregation, that a large part of the increases in per capita national product can be explained by increases in the labor force and increases in the education of the labor force. Another revelation of growth accounting has been the relative unimportance of the sheer increase in the (arbitrarily estimated) constant dollar value of physical capital and the great contribution to growth in output made by the increased ouput per unit of capital resulting from technological and organizational change.

"Growth Accounting" is a technique used to analyze the sources of economic growth by disaggregation of inputs. The intellectual origin of the idea is found in the description of economic activity as a "production function."

The production function of an individual firm describes production as the result of combining "inputs" of labor time, capital services, raw materials, energy, and so forth, to produce "outputs" of bread, haircuts, police services, etc. (The production function concept is sometimes humorously referred to as the "sausage grinder" concept, where heterogeneous raw materials are fed in one end of the sausage grinder [production function] and sausages come out the other end.)

Growth Accounting starts from the simple production function relationship that increases in output come either from an increase in the quantity of inputs or an increase in the efficiency (or productivity) with which they are combined or utilized. For example, if there is a linear, homogeneous production function with a 10 percent increase in all inputs and a 15 percent increase in output, then it is inferred that there has been a 5 percent increase in productivity (from some unexplained process).

The production function of the national economy is aggregated from individual firms, as in NIA. Intermediate purchases of goods are excluded so that the ultimate basic inputs are labor and capital services and the only output is products and services purchased for final consumption or net investment.

The intellectual origins of the production function concept are to be found in classical and neo-classical economics. The extension and implementation of the concept to the analysis of changes in an aggregate production function were first made by Robert Solow (1956), who received a Nobel Prize for his work in 1978). The approach was subsequently applied with enormous detail to U.S. data by Edward Denison (1985), John Kendrick (1961), and legions of statisticians and economists at the Bureau of Economic Analysis of the U.S. Department of Commerce.

Measurement Problems for Growth Accounting

Growth Accounting attempts to move to the direct measurement of "physical quantities" of inputs of labor and capital and the "volume" of output of goods. There are four major measurement problems for Growth Accounting.

Quantification of Outputs. Valuation of final output follows the same conventions as NIA to measure real output and is subject to the same biases.

Quantification of Labor Inputs. Labor is quantified in terms of worker hours but different types of labor are given different weights. Following various forms of Adam Smith's and Karl Marx's labor theories of value, the first inclination is to try to identify labor inputs in a simple time dimension. However, the measurement of labor inputs has to deal with the observation that labor is paid at different rates and, therefore, must reflect different quantities of some inherent qualities or capacities that are valued by the employer. Systematic differences are noted between occupations and between workers of different age, sex, ethnic background, and educational level completed. Adopting the convention that workers' pay reflects the actual quantity (or quality adjusted quantity) of labor inputs supplied, it is inferred that if one worker is paid twice as much per hour as another, she must be supplying twice as many labor inputs. These additional labor inputs are explained as the result of embodied education and experience (and other sociological categories associated with education, experience, and employers' expectations).

One result of this convention is illustrated in the disaggregation of the slowdown of productivity growth (the important numerand of Growth Accounting) in the 1970s. The 1970s saw a big increase in the labor force and in the education (though not experience) level of the labor force. It was assumed that since workers with more education were paid more at various age levels, the imputed inputs of labor (education-adjusted labor) increased more rapidly than the actual number of labor hours.

The inputs of adjusted labor hours (adjusted for education) increased faster relative to the output of goods and services in the decade of the 1970s than they did in the 1960s, resulting in a decrease in the "residual," which is the measure of productivity in growth accounting. However, the conclusion, in growth accounting, that the growth of labor productivity slowed down depends upon the assumption that there were increases in the quantity of labor implied by the revaluation for education.

Capital Inputs. There is a different but equally complex set of problems involved in identifying some unit of measurement for capital inputs. To begin with, capital stocks are even more heterogeneous than humans. We aggregate hours of human labor even though we pay workers at different rates. It doesn't work to try to aggregate an hour of time worked by a mile of railroad track and/or an hour worked by a mainframe computer. The conventions adopted to deal with this involve tortuous assumptions and procedures. The capital stock is quantified by valuation in terms of the initial cost price of capital goods (like railway tracks and mainframe computers) and deflated by a price index of capital goods to create values in terms of constant dollars.

The sum of all capital purchases over a previous time period is then depreciated at an arbitrary rate to obtain a continually adjusted inventory value for a stock of capital goods whose quantity is estimated in constant value dollars. It is then assumed that the flow of services for this continually adjusted inventory of the capital stock is provided as a constant proportional input flow to the production of output.

Thus, one of the explanations given for the fall in productivity produced by Growth Accounting estimates in the 1970s was that the rise in energy prices had made much capital equipment obsolete and thereby increased depreciation and lowered the quantity of the capital inputs going into the economy. My methodological objection to this kind of explanation is that it introduces an arbitrary change in the accounting treatment of an input variable to explain the change in the output/input ratio.

The Production Function. The fourth problem for the measurement of growth accounting variables is the specification of the production function itself. When different input variables increase at different rates, how are the joint inputs related to outputs? They must be assigned weights for aggregation. A variety of ingenious relationships has been assumed and tested, but the relationships are not directly observable.

The Explanatory Value of Growth Accounting

The procedures followed by "Growth Accounting" for the estimation of labor and capital inputs are arbitrary. They have their roots in some logical and consistent economic and accounting concepts and convenient mathematical forms (which I will not explain here.) They do make it possible to disaggregate and quantify, under various assumptions, some measurement of the sources of productivity growth within the economy and within particular sectors of the economy.

Consider the application of Growth Accounting within a sector of the economy. In the 1970s there was a big increase in the growth of productivity of the commercial airline industry. Output could have been measured by changes in the inflation-adjusted revenues per employee or per dollar of balance sheet capital of the airlines. Or it could have been measured in terms of the passenger-revenue miles or freight-ton miles flown per employee hour, and so on. However, the explanation for the increase in productivity cannot be found without bringing in technological change to the production relationships. The employees were not "working harder" or longer. The airlines were not flying more miles or more passengers with the same type of airplanes.

More passenger or freight miles per employee or per dollar of capital were being flown because bigger, faster jets replaced slower, smaller piston-engine aircraft and the same size aircrews were able to fly bigger loads more miles. At the same time less frequent service intervals for jet engine than piston engine planes reduced the mechanical service personnel necessary for scheduled maintenance. On-line computers reduced the amount of clerical personnel necessary to deal with ticket sales and the monitoring of loads per passenger or freight mile provided (and also allowed fuller capacity utilization).

The airlines got more output per dollar of balance sheet capital because the big jets cost less per dollar of capacity—in constant dollar terms they cost less per unit of potential carrying capacity per year because of the technological improvements embodied in their design. But the capital was not valued in terms of its productive capacity but, rather, in terms of its constant dollar cost of production. The technological change occurred in the jet engine and airframe industries.

The airlines got more output per employee because the quantity of freight or passengers that could be handled by one employee with the use of larger, faster aircraft and computers for capacity scheduling had increased. Growth accounting shows large increases in labor productivity even though virtually all the increases in labor productivity are due to technological change in the design of aircraft and other equipment.

Growth Accounting is analytically useful when it is possible to identify both units of input and output measurements. When it is possible to quantify outputs such as barrels of oil or kilowatts of electricity or airline passenger seat miles flown and homogeneous and unchanging labor and capital inputs can be quantified, it is more revealing and diagnostically useful to measure and explain the sources and magnitudes of economic growth. But it is the essence of economic growth for technological change to increase output per labor hour and dollar of capital, and growth accounting is unable to capture those changes except as an "unexplained residual."

Unsolved Problems for Growth Accounting

Perhaps the greatest shortcoming for the current Growth Accounting techniques is the lack of applicability of the concept to the sectors of the economy providing personal services to the economy and particularly to services provided by the various levels of government. Since these presently constitute almost three–fourths of employment and output, this is a considerable shortcoming!

Government services, by and large, cannot be valued and analyzed since quantities of output (citizens protected by police, students educated by teachers, patients healed by health care professionals) are not measured and prices are not charged or imputed - the value of services is assumed to be equal to their cost.

Some application of the Growth Accounting concept is possible in the service and government sector. For example, commercial banks explicitly or implicitly charge the customers for the clearing of checks. The actual or imputed charges could be identified and matched with the bank labor and capital resources devoted to providing this service. The Federal Government does cost and price its provision of of Postal Services. But the scope for application of Growth Accounting in such large and expanding areas of employment and expenditure as health services, civil and criminal justice, national defense, police protection, and education are limited.

Conceptually, "Growth Accounting" is an elaboration of the NIA concept. It stands in somewhat the same position relative to National Income Accounting as Double Entry Financial Accounting does to Managerial or Cost Accounting. Growth Accounting explains causality by disaggregation. It has the same shortcomings in the identification of output as National Income Accounting and its disaggregation of inputs lacks conceptual simplicity and easy applicability.

Appendix Note 4.3.   An Alternative to Accounting Conventions: Measurement of Productivity by Changes in Relative Prices

One of the problems in using the production function technique of the estimation of productivity changes occurs when the total quantity of outputs and inputs is not known. However, there is an ingenious way to deal with the lack of data.

The importance of one relationship that has historically been used to measure productivity by economists comes from comparison of the simultaneous behavior of the prices of goods and the wages of labor used to produce the goods. This relationship has been employed to explain changes in "real wages" of labor. The concept formalized (from double-entry accounting and NIA) is the equality of amount paid for factor services and the amount received for the sale of ouput. Thus, by definition:

National Output = National Income   *4.0*

National Output = Output Quantity x Output Price   *4.1*

National Income = Input Quantity x Input Price　　　　　　*4.2*

Output Quantity x Output Price = Input Quantity x Input Price　　*4.3*

　　　and, by rearrangement,

Output Quantity/Input Quantity = Input Price/Output Price　　*4.4*

Thus, the increase in productivity (output per unit of input) is equal to the ratio of input to output prices. Thus, if total quantities of bread and labor hours can't be observed but it can be observed that the price of a loaf of bread has fallen relative to an hour's wage, the increase in the output of bread per labor hour can be inferred.

Of course, most outputs are produced by many inputs but those inputs can be weighted by the relative share of income they receive in the production of the output. For the economy as a whole, one measure of overall productivity growth is the change in the level of wages relative to the level of prices.

APPENDIX 5: STRUCTURAL CHANGE AND THE SLOWDOWN OF PRODUCTIVITY GROWTH

Appendix Note 5.1. Sources and Methods for Chapter 5 Text Tables and Graphs and Appendix 5 Tables

Sources

There are two separate series on employment and labor force that are widely used and cited but conceptually different. For nonagricultural employment I have employed data that comes from the monthly survey of establishments. This survey counts the number of persons currently on payrolls. It does not include farmers or the self-employed, domestic servants, or family or unpaid workers. It counts part-time workers and persons who may temporarily be on lay-off, and the same persons may be counted at more than one establishment.

The alternative series, which I have used only for the agricultural employment estimates (since these are not included in the former series), is based on a survey sample of households. In 1990 the establishment series reports about 110 million nonagricultural workers in comparison to the 114.7 million in the household series. In 1940 the figure is 32.5 versus 36.6 million nonagricultural workers.

I have used the establishment series rather than the household series because it is based more nearly on the system used to produce estimates of sector components of GDP.

Data Sources for Appendix 5 Tables

Appendix Table 5.1. Sectoral Shares of GDP. (Source for Text Graph 5.1) Sources: U.S. Bureau of the Census. *Historical Statistics of the United States: Colonial Times to 1970.* (Washington D.C., Government Printing Office, 1975), Series F250. 1950–1990: *Economic Report of the President, 1994 (ERP,1994).* (Washington, D.C., Government Printing Office, 1994). Table B-11.

Appendix Table 5.2. Sectoral Shares of Labor Force. (Source for Text Graph 5.2) Sources: Non-Agricultural Employment. U.S. Department of Labor, *Employment, Hours, and Earnings, U.S., 1909–1994. Bulletin 2445* (Washington D.C.: Government Printing Office, 1995). Agricultural Employment: *Historical Statistics,* Tables D 11-25 for the period up to 1970. For 1980 and 1990 agricultural employment data come from *(ERP, 1994). Ibid.* Table B-30.

Appendix Table 5.3. Sectoral GDP and GDP per worker. (Source for Text Table 5.2) Values were obtained by dividing the constant $ values for GDP by Sector by the number of workers in Labor Force by Sector. (Appendix Table 5.2). Sources: Constant $ estimates of GDP by Sector come from three sources: (a) Estimates in constant ($1958) for the decades 1950 and 1960 are taken from *Historical Statistics,* Series F130. (b) GNP in constant ($1972) for decades ending in 1960, 1970, and 1980 come from *Statistical Abstract (1984).* Table 738. (c) GDP in constant ($1987) for decades ending 1980 and 1990 are taken from *Statistical Abstract (1994).* Labor Force estimates are taken from the same sources as Appendix Table 5.2.

Appendix Table 5.4. Intra-Sectoral Growth Rates in GDP Output per Worker. Values were obtained by calculating the decennial change in output on the base of the starting year of the decade. Rates for the decade ending in 1960 were done on a 1958 price base. Rates for the decades ending in 1970 and 1980 were done on a 1972 price base. The rate for the decade ending 1990 was done on a 1987 price base. Text Table 5.2 is merely a simplification of the presentation of data from Appendix Table 5.4. Sources: Same as for Appendix Table 5.3.

Appendix Table 5.5. Contribution (Weighted) of Intra-Sectoral Growth to Total Growth in Output per Worker. The values in this table were obtained by weighting each intra-sector growth rate in output per worker (Text Table 5.2) with the proportion of the sector's labor force in the aggregate labor force (Appendix Table 5.2) and the Relative Sectoral Wage obtained by dividing the sectoral GDP per worker by the aggregate value (Text Table 5.1). Sources: same as for Appendix Table 5.3.

Text Graph 5.3. Sectoral Composition of Consumption Expenditures. 1910–1930; Historical Statistics, Series G416 and G470. 1960–1990 U.S. Department of Commerce, Survey of Current Business, July, 1961, Table 15, July, 1991, Table 2.4.

Derivation of Intra-Sectoral Growth

The formula for obtaining the contribution of each output sector for intra-sectoral growth and the total for intra-sectoral growth is derived as follows:

Assume:

$a_i \equiv$ *Proportion of total labor force in industry i* $\equiv N_i / \Sigma N_i$

$b_i \equiv$ *Relative output per worker in industry i* $\equiv Y_i / Y$

then

$Y_i \equiv$ *output of sector i* $\equiv a_i b_i$

$Y \equiv$ *Total output of i sectors* $\equiv \Sigma a_i b_i$

and

$\delta Y / \delta t = \Sigma a_i b_i [(\delta a_i / \delta t) + (\delta b_i / \delta t) + (\delta a_i / \delta t * \delta b_i / \delta t)]$

The contribution of the intersectoral shift of labor to the growth of total labor output in Appendix Table 5 is the difference between the aggregate rate of growth in GDP per worker and the sum of the weighted intra-sectoral growth rates. Text Table 5.5 is a simplification of the data.

Appendix 5 Tables

Appendix Table 5.1
Sectoral Shares of GDP (Current $)

Year	Agri	Min	Const	Mnfg.	Tr.&Pu	Trade	Fin Serv	Serv	Gov't
1890	0.14	0.02	0.06	0.19	0.11	0.17	0.13	0.13	0.05
1900	0.18	0.03	0.04	0.19	0.10	0.17	0.13	0.10	0.06
1910	0.19	0.03	0.04	0.18	0.11	0.16	0.13	0.09	0.05
1920	0.10	0.03	0.04	0.22	0.10	0.13	0.16	0.11	0.10
1930	0.09	0.02	0.03	0.23	0.11	0.16	0.13	0.11	0.11
1940	0.08	0.02	0.04	0.31	0.09	0.16	0.09	0.08	0.13
1950	0.07	0.02	0.05	0.32	0.09	0.17	0.09	0.09	0.11
1960	0.05	0.03	0.04	0.29	0.09	0.17	0.13	0.10	0.10
1970	0.03	0.02	0.05	0.24	0.09	0.16	0.14	0.12	0.14
1980	0.02	0.02	0.05	0.19	0.09	0.14	0.18	0.16	0.13
1990	0.02	0.02	0.04	0.19	0.09	0.16	0.18	0.18	0.12

Source: Author. See Appendix Note 5.1.

Appendix Table 5.2
Sectoral Shares of Labor Force

Year	Agri	Mining	Const	Mfg.	Tr.&Pu	Trade	Fin Serv	Services	Gov't
1890	0.42	0.02	0.05	0.19	0.07	0.10	0.01	0.12	0.04
1900	0.37	0.03	0.05	0.20	0.08	0.11	0.01	0.12	0.04
1910	0.30	0.03	0.05	0.22	0.09	0.12	0.02	0.13	0.05
1920	0.27	0.03	0.02	0.28	0.11	0.12	0.03	0.07	0.07
1930	0.26	0.03	0.03	0.24	0.09	0.15	0.03	0.09	0.08
1940	0.21	0.02	0.03	0.27	0.07	0.17	0.04	0.09	0.10
1950	0.14	0.02	0.05	0.29	0.08	0.18	0.04	0.10	0.12
1960	0.09	0.01	0.05	0.28	0.07	0.19	0.04	0.12	0.14
1970	0.05	0.01	0.05	0.26	0.06	0.20	0.05	0.16	0.17
1980	0.04	0.01	0.05	0.22	0.05	0.22	0.06	0.19	0.17
1990	0.03	0.01	0.05	0.17	0.05	0.23	0.06	0.25	0.16

Source: Author. See Appendix Note 5.1

Appendix Table 5.3
Sectoral GDP and GDP per Worker. GDP by Sector in $Billions:
Constant Dollars with Deflator Bases Noted

YEAR	Total	Agri	Min	Const	Mnfg	Tr&Pu	Trade	Fi Serv	Serv	Gov't
$58										
1950	355	20.4	10.7	16.2	105	30.8	60	41	33	36
1960	488	23.1	13.1	21.7	141	44.9	82	64	47	49
1970	722	26.2	17.2	23.6	217	77	126	96	69	70
$72										
1960	737	32	13.5	46.1	172	57.4	117	103	83.5	108
1970	1086	34	19	53.4	261	95	176	156	127	153
1980	1475	40	22	52	351	140	246	236	189	177
$87										
1980	3776	63	80	185	725	336	510	693	609	509
1990	4897	96	92	210	929	463	798	868	869	582

SECTORAL GDP PER WORKER

Constant $ annual GDP per worker

YEAR	Total	Agri	Min	Const	Mnfg	Tr&Pu	Trade	Fi Serv	Serv	Gov't
$58										
1950	6781	2849	11876	6853	6889	7635	6392	21716	6161	5974
1960	8182	4232	18399	7416	8395	11214	7199	24353	6370	5866
1970	9712	7566	27608	6577	11205	17054	8378	26337	5975	5576
$72										
1960	12356	5863	18961	15755	10241	14336	10271	39193	11317	12929
1970	14608	9818	30498	14883	13477	21041	11702	42798	10998	12187
1980	15730	11891	21422	11965	17303	27206	12112	45736	10565	10898
87$										
1980	40269	18728	77897	42568	35741	65293	25111	100K+	34041	31340
1990	43488	30132	100K+	41016	48700	79924	30961	100K+	31109	31796

Appendix Table 5.4
Intra-Sectoral Growth Rates in Output per Worker

Year	Total	Agric	Mining	Const	Mnfg	Tr&PU	Trade	F Serv	Servce	Gov't
$58										
1960	0.207	0.485	0.549	.0082	0.219	0.469	0.126	0.121	0.034	-0.018
1970	0.187	0.788	0.501	-0.113	0.335	0.521	0.164	0.081	-0.062	-0.049
$72										
1970	0.182	0.675	0.608	-0.055	0.316	0.468	0.139	0.092	-0.028	-0.057
1980	0.077	0.211	-0.298	-0.196	0.284	0.293	0.035	0.069	-0.039	-0.106
$87										
1990	0.080	0.609	0.666	-0.036	0.363	0.224	0.233	-0.037	-0.086	0.015

Source: Same as for Appendix Table 5.3.

Appendix Table 5.5
Contribution (Weighted) of Intra-Sectoral Growth to Total Growth in Output per Worker

	Total	Agric	Mining	Constr	Mnfg	Tr&Pu	Trade	Fi Serv	Servce	Gov't
$58										
1960	0.169	0.019	0.011	0.004	0.063	0.035	0.021	0.014	0.003	-0.002
1970	0.188	0.019	0.013	-0.005	0.089	0.043	0.028	0.011	-0.006	-0.005
$72										
1970	0.176	0.016	0.011	-0.002	0.084	0.039	0.023	0.012	-0.003	-0.006
1980	0.093	0.006	-0.007	-0.006	0.071	0.028	0.006	0.009	-0.004	-0.010
$87										
1990	0.132	0.012	0.013	-0.002	0.069	0.021	0.036	-0.006	-0.013	0.002

Source: Same as for Appendix Table 5.3.

APPENDIX 6: EMPLOYMENT AND ECONOMIC GROWTH

Appendix Note 6.1. Additional Sources for Text Graphs, Chapter 6

1. Text Graph 6.1. Sources: 1890–1940; U.S. Bureau of the Census. *Historical Statistics of the United States: Colonial Times to 1970.* (Washington, D.C., Government Printing Office, 1975), D29-41; 1950–2000; Sources listed for Appendix Table 6.1.

2. Text Graphs 6.2, 6.3 & 6. 4. 1890–1940; *Historical Statistics*, D29-41; 1950–2000: Sources listed for Appendix Table 6.2.

3. Text Graphs 6.5 & 6.6. Source: 1890–1930: *Historical Statistics*, A29, A119; 1940–1990: *Economic Report of the President, 1992*, (Washington D.C., Government Printing Office, 1992), B-32.

Appendix 6 Tables

Appendix Table 6.1
Labor Force Participation by Age, Sex, and Ethnicity

Year	1950	1960	1970	1980	1990	1995	2000
Group							
Men							
16–19	63	56	56	60	58	58	59
20–24	88	88	83	86	85	86	86
25–34	96	97	96	95	94	94	94
35–44	98	98	97	95	94	95	94
45–54	96	96	94	91	91	91	91
55–64	87	87	83	72	67	67	68
65+	46	33	27	19	16	15	14
Women							
16–19	41	39	44	53	55	57	60
20–24	46	46	58	69	74	76	88
25–34	34	36	45	65	75	79	82
35–44	39	43	51	66	77	81	85
45–54	38	50	54	60	71	75	76
55–64	27	37	43	41	44	47	49
65+	10	11	10	8	8	8	8

16+ participation rates by aggregates

	1950	1960	1970	1980	1990	1995	2000
Both Sexes	59.2	59.4	60.4	63.8	66.6	68.1	69
Men	86.4	83.3	79.7	77.4	76.4	76.3	75.9
Women	33.9	37.7	43.3	51.5	57.8	60.6	62.6
White men	83.4		80	78.2	77	76.9	76.6
White Women	36.5		42.6	51.2	57.7	60.7	63
Black Men			59.9	59.9	71.6	71.7	71.4
Black Women			48.7	53.1	58.9	61.1	62.5

Sources: 1950–1980: U.S. Department of Labor, Bureau of Labor Statistics, *Labor Force Statistics Derived from Current Population Survey, 1948–1987. Bulletin 2307.* (Washington, D.C., Government Printing Office, 1988), Tables A8-10. 1990–2000: U.S. Department of Labor, Bureau of Labor Statistics. *Outlook 2000, Bulletin 2352.* (Washington, D.C.: Government Printing Office, 1990. Table A1.

Appendix Table 6.2
Participation Rates by Age, Sex, and Marital Status

GROUP	1950	1960	1970	1980	1990
Single Men					
16–19	42	34	49	57	55
20–24	79	77	69	80	81
25–34	84	85	86	87	90
35–44	84	85	82	80	85
45–54	85	77	71	74	74
55–64	66	70	60	53	57
65+	28	24	21	20	16
Single Women					
16–19	26	26	39	49	52
20–24	75	73	71	72	75
25–34	85	80	81	84	81
35–44	84	80	73	78	81
45–54	78	81	72	70	72
55–64	63	67	64	54	52
65+	28	22	18	12	12
Single Men	Widowed, Divorced, Separated				
20–24	75	87	73	93	91
25–34	84	82	74	94	93
35–44	84	84	81	91	91
45–54	79	84	84	80	89
55–64	79	73	68	59	61
65+	30	18	16	13	12
Single Women	Widowed, Divorced, Separated				
16–19		37	46	51	54
20–24	45	55	60	68	66
25–34	62	56	65	77	77
35–44	65	67	68	76	82
45–54	62	68	69	71	77
55–64	40	51	55	50	51
65+	8	11	10	9	8
Married Men					
16–19	92	96	95	90	78
20–24	94	97	95	93	92
25–34	97	99	98	94	96
35–44	99	98	98	91	97
45–54	97	97	96	80	85
55–64	89	88	86	54	59
65+	48	37	30	13	18

Appendix Table 6.2 Continued

Married Women

16–19	24	25	36	48	50
20–24	28	30	47	60	66
25–34	24	30	39	59	70
35–44	28	36	47	62	74
45–54	29	40	44	56	71
55–64	17	24	36	37	44
65+	6	6	8	7	8

Sources: 1950–1980: *Labor Force Statistics Derived from Current Population Survey, 1948–1987, Bulletin 2307.*1990: *Statistical Abstract, 1995.* Table 636.

APPENDIX 7: TRANSFERS TO THE ELDER GENERATION: TAXES AND SAVINGS

Appendix Note 7.1. The Social Security Trust Fund and The Burden of the National Debt

The short- and long-term effects of government budget deficits and the resulting increases in the national debt are complex and contingent—politicians and people who should know better talk a great deal of nonsense about them! Let us consider the matter analytically.

If governmental deficits are run at a time when the economy is underemployed—when there is underutilization of the labor force and the physical capital stock—these deficits may increase the level of capacity utilization and increase GDP. That increase in GDP may lead to greater consumption and/or investment than would otherwise have occurred. If the economy is running at capacity, the government deficit cannot increase current production; increased current consumption or investment could only occur if there were to be a net inflow of foreign goods—which would have to be paid for in the future.

Government deficits are financed by the sale of government bonds. The bonds can be purchased by (1) the U.S. public (principally banks and insurance companies), (2) the Federal Reserve, (3) other governmental agencies (such as the Social Security Trust Fund), or (4) by foreigners.

If the bonds are purchased by the U.S. public, the public must either curtail current consumption or current investment spending to purchase the debt. (Most of this is actually accomplished by an increase in the holding of Treasury bonds by banks and pension funds.) If this happens, the government deficits offset private spending with public spending and there is no stimulating effect on total output. If private investment spending is reduced—"crowded-out"—there will be less capital stock to increase output in future generations.

If the bonds are purchased from the U.S. Treasury by the U.S. Federal Reserve, there is an increase in the money suppply. If there has been no increase in the production of goods, this will result in inflation of the price level and no consequent increase in production.

If foreign holders purchase the bonds, the United States can use the foreign investment to increase current consumption—particularly of foreign-produced goods. Or foreign funds could also be used to allow increased investment. The foreigners have to be paid back in the future. If the foreign purchase of U.S. bonds financed either current consumption or investment, the foreigners will have to be repaid—with interest—in the future. If foreign purchases of U.S. bonds made possible a higher level of investment, the foreigners may be repaid in the future from the higher output made possible by the investment. If the foreign funds financed consumption, future consumption (or investment) will have to be reduced in order to repay the foreigners.

If the bonds were purchased by the Social Security Trust Fund (SSTF), those purchases were possible because the SSTF was taking in more in payroll taxes than it was paying out in benefits, it was offsetting the deficit in the general Federal budget—a fiscally responsible policy.

If the SSTF accumulates Treasury bonds, it means that the Treasury will be repaying principal and interest to the SSTF in the future. That will mean that the Social Security Agency can collect less Social Security taxes in the future to pay Social Security benefits to the retired population because it can use interest and principal from the Trust Fund to do it.

However, it also means that future taxpayers will be paying more taxes to service and/or repay the debt. In either case the working population will be reducing its future consumption (or investment) to transfer income to the retired population. There is no way for future citizens to reduce the "burden" of the retired population in the future except by increasing the productive capacity of the economy that will provide the future incomes.

Consider the historical context of this discussion. Federal deficits were particularly large as a proportion of GDP in the 1980s. They had some stimulatory effect on the economy and made it possible for the generations living and working in the 1980s to consume more during their working lives. To the extent that the government deficits "crowded out" the formation of productive capital, subsequent generations will have a smaller stock of capital assets and, by assumption, less output. The smaller output (assumed from the smaller capital stock) creates the necessity of either increasing the tax rate (on the smaller future output) to finance intergenerational transfers or reducing the size of the intergenerational transfers to the older (or younger) generation. This is the way that one generation is burdened by its predecessor.

Part of the deficits of the 1980s were financed by an unprecedented inflow of foreign capital. The interest and repayment of foreign debt will reduce the output of future generations available for domestic consumption or investment.

Part of the deficits of the 1980s were acquired by the SSTF, which began running a deliberate surplus in the Old Age Survivors Insurance (OASI) account as a result of an increase in Social Security taxes in 1986.

It could be argued that government deficits resulted from government "investment" in roads and dams, or "investment" in the education of the labor force to create human capital, or investment in research and development to create knowledge capital. It would also be possible to argue that the government deficits were incurred for unnecessary defense expenditures or government bureaucracies, or transfer payments that financed current consumption.

What cannot be disputed is the principle that if there was a reduction in stocks of productive capital (reproducible, human, knowledge, or natural resource) resulting from government deficits, the "crowding out" of the potential capital formation reduces the future output that would have been available to service the interest on the debt. If that is the case, the interest on the Federal Debt held by the SSTF used to pay Social Security recipients will come from taxes on the future generation of workers paying income taxes to finance the interest on the debt from smaller incomes than they could have had from the benefit of increased capital formation. This is the real burden of the national debt—the reduction of the capital stock that would otherwise have increased productive capacity.

However, it is also true that if there were no government debt and no SSTF, it would still be necessary to tax the working generation to transfer income and consumption from the working generation to the retired generation and the amount would be exactly the same as it would be if done through a SSTF completely funded with government bonds. If government bonds existed but were not held in the SSTF, taxpayers would still have to service them and the transfer payments would go to the holders of the government debt—whomever they might be.

There are only two ways in which the burden of the support of future retired generations on future employed generations could be lessened: (1) an increase in the stocks of domestic capital by higher saving (and lower consumption) by the future retired population during their current period of employment (this increases the size of the future pie to be divided between generations); or (2) investment in the stocks or bonds of other populations (countries). The stream of investment income created by these foreign investments could be used to create a stream of foreign investment income to support the retired population without income taxes to service interest on the government bonds held by the SSTF or higher FICA taxes.

But this would have two disadvantages: the country would have to run a large deficit in its balance of trade to absorb the imports paid for with interest on overseas investment, and the domestic capital stock would be lower as a result of the foreign investment.

For a further analysis of the nature and consequences of the Social Security System, see Kevin Murphy and Finis Welch (1998).

Appendix Note 7.2. Derivation of Transfer Tax Rates

The "transfer tax rates" of Text Table 7.1 indicate the tax rate necessary to support the retired population at a particular fraction of the income ("replacement ratio") of the working population. This rate depends upon the ratio of workers to retirees which, in turn, depends upon the proportion of the working age population which is working ("employment ratio") and the ratio of the retired population to the total population ("retired ratio").

For derivation of the formula for transfer tax rates, I use the following notation:

$P \equiv$ *Population 16+*

$A \equiv$ *ratio of retired/total population, (ages 65+/16+)*

$1-a \equiv$ *working age population, (ages 16-64) population*

$Q \equiv$ *income*

$e \equiv$ *employment ratio $\equiv$ employed/working age population*

$r \equiv$ *ratio of average retirement income/average worker income*

$t \equiv$ *tax rate necessary to finance retirement incomes at ratio (r) to worker*

   incomes

Equalizing the tax rate on employee incomes with the revenues needed to fund retiree incomes at ratio (r)

$$t\{[e(1-a)P] \times [(Q/(e(1-a)P]\} = [aP \times r] \times [Q/(e(1-a)P] \qquad 7.0$$

which reduces to

$$t = \{[a/(e\ (1-a)]\ r\} \qquad 7.1$$

The Implied Benefit Ratio is the Ratio of Retirement Benefits/Employee Compensation generated by a particular tax rate.

From (7.1)$\{[a/(e\ (1-a)]\ r\}$, therefore, $r = t\ (e(1-a)/a$ 7.2

The implied benefit ratio generated by a given transfer tax rate on the income of employed workers is equal to the tax rate times the product of the ratio of (employees/working age population) times the ratio of the (working-age population/adult population) divided by the ratio (retirees/adult population).

Appendix Note 7.3. Derivation of Retirement Incomes and Replacement Ratios

I use the following notation:

"Replacement Ratio" $\equiv$ *C2/C1* $\equiv$ *Ratio of consumption per year in Retirement (C2) to the ratio of consumption in the last year before retirement (C1).*

C2 $\equiv$ *Annual Annuity Payment* $\equiv (K \times (r/(1-(1+r)^{-a}$

a $\equiv$ *length of annuity in years*

K $\equiv$ *Retirement Annuity Principal* $\equiv \sum_{i=1} Si(1+r)^{i\cdot}$

Si $\equiv sYi \equiv$ *Savings in Year i* $\equiv$ *Saving rate x income in i.*

s $\equiv$ *saving rate*

r $\equiv$ *interest rate*

C1 $\equiv$ *Pre-retirement Consumption* $\equiv C2 \equiv Yn(1-s)$

Yn $\equiv$ *Pre-retirement Income* $\equiv$ *Income x (growth rate + wage gradient)* $\equiv$ $Y(1+g)^i(1+w)^i$

g $\equiv$ *growth rate of income*

w $\equiv$ *wage gradient*

Appendix 7 Tables

Appendix Table 7.1
Historical Values for Retirement Tax Transfer Rates and Determinants of Implied Benefit Level

Year	Retired/Total Pop.	Wkg-Age/Total Population	Employed/ Working-Age	SS & Medicare Tax rate
1940	.09	.91	.47	.01
1950	.11	.89	.54	.02
1960	.14	.86	.51	.06
1970	.14	.86	.57	.096
1980	.15	.85	.64	.123
1990	.16	.84	.70	.153

Source: Demographic data same as Appendix Table 3.3. Social Security and Medicare Tax Rates, *Statistical Abstract, 1994, Table 633.*

Appendix Table 7.2
Determinants of Transfer Tax Burden of Retired Population and Implied Benefit Ratio

Year	Retired/ Total	Work age/ Total	Employed/ Work age	Retired/ Workers	Implied Benefit ratio	Actual Tax rate
1940	0.09	0.91	0.47	0.21	0.05	0.01
1950	0.11	0.89	0.54	0.23	0.09	0.02
1960	0.14	0.86	0.51	0.32	0.19	0.06
1970	0.14	0.86	0.57	0.29	0.34	0.096
1980	0.15	0.85	0.64	0.28	0.45	0.123
1990	0.16	0.84	0.7	0.27	0.56	0.153

Sources: Demographic data, same as Appendix Table 3.3. Actual Tax Rate from Appendix Table 7.2. Implied Benefit Ratio derived as per Appendix Note 7.2.

Appendix Table 7.3
Nominal and Real Rates of Return on Selected Asset Groups

Asset Category	Avg. annual nominal return 1926–1996	Avg. annual real return 1926–1996	Avg. annual nominal return 1946–1996	Avg. annual real return 1946–1996
Standard & Poor's 500 stocks	10.7%	7.6%	12.2%	7.9%
Small Company Stocks	12.6%	9.5%	13.9%	9.6%
Long-term corporate bonds	5.6%	2.5%	5.7%	1.4%
Long-term government bonds	5.1%	2%	5.2%	.9%
Intermediate-term government bonds	5.2%	2.1%	5.8%	1.5%
30-Day Treasury Bills	3.7%	.6%	4.8%	.5%
Inflation rate	3.1%		4.3%	

Source: Ibbotson Associates, cited in The Wall Street Journal, January 24, 1997.

APPENDIX 8: TRANSFERS TO EDUCATE THE YOUNGER GENERATION: ECONOMIC GROWTH AND THE INCREASING BURDEN OF EDUCATIONAL COSTS

Appendix Note 8.1 Sources and Methods for Text Tables and Text Graphs

Sources for Text Graphs

Text Graph 8.1. The Ratio of Educational Expenditures to National Income. The values for the graph are taken from Appendix Table 8.3.

Text Graph 8.2. Ratios of Students/Workers. The values for the graph are taken from Appendix Table 8.3.

Text Graph 8.3. Cost per Student Relative to Income per Worker. The values for the graph are taken from Appendix Table 8.3.

Text Table 8.1. Education Completion Levels. *Digest of Educational Statistics*, 1991, Tables 8,95.

Text Table 8.2. Relative Importance of Factors Determining Increases in Human Capital Investment Ratio. Increases in ratios are derived from Appendix Table 8.4.

Text Table 8.3. Social Rates of Return on Incremental Investment in Education. Computed by the author using mathematical formula for Internal Rate of Return. Educational Cost data based on Appendix Table 8.1. Incremental Earnings based on, *Digest of Educational Statistics*, Table 358.

Data Sources

Demographic Data. 1870–1970. *Historical Statistics*, Series A119-134. 1980–90: *Economic Report of the President*, Table B29. Projections for 2000: *Statistical Abstract*, Table 18.

Educational Enrollments. (Appendix Table 8.1) 1870–1970: *Historical Statistics*, H412-432. 1970–2000. *Digest of Educational Statistics*, Tables 3, 37, 160, 162. Updated with same publication for 1996. Projections for 2000: *Statistical Abstract*, Table 214.

Educational Expenditures. (Appendix Table 8.2) *Digest of Educational Statistics*.

National Income Data. 1870–1970. *Historical Statistics*, Series F1-F9. 1980–1990: *Economic Report of the President,1992*, B21.

Teacher Compensation and Teacher Student Ratios. (Text Graphs IV, V, VI) *Digest of Educational Statistics*, Tables 29,30,37. Tables 3, 4, 37, 59, 76. For higher education prior to 1940, American Association of University Professors, *Depression, Recovery, and Higher Education* (New York, McGraw Hill. 1937) 60.

Private School and College Enrollments. *Digest of Educational Statistics*, Tables 54, 57.

Earnings By Education, Age, and Sex. (Text Table 8.3) *ibid.*, Table 358.

Educational Attainment Levels. (Text Table 8.1) *ibid.*, Tables 8, 95.

Appendix Note 8.2. Derivation of the Human Capital Investment Ratio (HCIR)

Moving from heuristic treatment in the text to a more formal analytic framework, I disaggregate the components of the HCIR below. The following concepts and notation are employed (ratios are listed in lower case and quantities are given in uppercase letters):

A ≡ *total persons in a particular age group (cohort)*

B ≡ *total population in a census year*

$c \equiv$ *annual educational cost per student (E/S)*

$E \equiv$ *total educational expenditures*

$g \equiv$ *enrollment ratio of students in a cohort (Si/Ai)*

$i \equiv$ *educational level (e.g., Elementary, Secondary, Higher) and population cohort (e.g., ages 5–14) from which enrollment is drawn*

$N \equiv$ *labor force*

$m \equiv$ *teacher/student ratio*

$p \equiv$ *ratio of population/labor force (B/N)*

$o \equiv$ *indirect cost (overhead) ratio in education*

$r \equiv$ *relative size of a population cohort (Ai/B)*

$S \equiv$ *students*

$W \equiv$ *annual average teacher compensation*

$w \equiv$ *ratio of average teacher compensation to national income per labor force member (W/y)*

$Y \equiv$ *national income*

$y \equiv$ *national income per labor force member (Y/N).*

Using the concepts and notation above, the following relationships may be established:

$$E = \sum i(Si \times ci) \qquad\qquad 8.0$$

Total educational expenditures per year are the sum of the products of total students at each educational level and the educational cost per student year at that educational level.

$$S = \sum i Si \qquad\qquad 8.1$$

The total number of students is the sum of the students at each educational level.

$$Si = \sum gi \times ri \times B \qquad\qquad 8.1.1$$

The number of students in a particular educational level is the product of the enrollment ratio, the cohort ratio, and the population.

$$ci = mi \times Wi \times oi \qquad\qquad 8.2.1$$

The cost per student, at each educational level, is the product of the teacher/student ratio, average teacher compensation for that level, and the overhead cost ratio at that level.

$$Y = N \times y \qquad\qquad 8.3$$

National Income is the product of labor force size and average national income per labor force member.

$$HCIR \equiv E/Y \qquad\qquad 8.4$$

The human capital investment ratio is the ratio of educational expenditure to national income.

As noted above , the education cost burden ratio on an aggregated basis is:

$$HCIR \equiv (S \times c) / (N \times y) = [S/N] \times [c/y] \qquad\qquad 8.4.1$$

The human capital investment ratio (% of national income allocated to education) is the product of the ratio of students/labor force members (S/N) and the ratio of cost per student/income per labor force member (c/y).

Expanding 8.4.1 by disaggregation by educational level

$$HCIR \equiv \{\textstyle\sum_i [g_i \times r_i \times m_i \times o_i \times W_i \times B]\}/[N \times y] \qquad\qquad 8.4.2$$

which is transformed to

$$HCIR \equiv \{\textstyle\sum_i [g_i \times r_i \times m_i \times o_i \times (W_i/y) \times (B/N)]\} \qquad\qquad 8.4.3$$

or

$$HCIR \equiv \{\textstyle\sum_i [gi \times ri \times mi \times oi \times wi \times p]\} \qquad\qquad 8.4.4$$

Stated in terms of demographic and economic ratios, 8.4.4 posits that the education cost/national income ratio or the human capital investment ratio, (HCIR), necessary to finance education from national income is the multiplicative product of the six ratios (below) for each of the three levels of education:

1. (g) the enrollment ratio for the age cohort from which enrollment at an educational level is drawn.
2. (r) the age cohort/population ratio for the corresponding educational level.
3. (m) the teacher/student ratio.
4. (o) the total educational cost/teacher cost ratio.
5. (w) the ratio of average teacher compensation/ average labor force income (W/y).
6. (p) the ratio of population to labor force (the reciprocal of the participation rate (B/N).

Parallels Between Human Capital and Physical Capital Formation

There are important similarities and differences between the analytic framework used to explain the relative size of the investment flow into human capital (education) (HCIR) and the saving flow to form and maintain physical capital. In the national income accounts, investment in physical capital is financed by gross saving. Gross domestic saving, which is determined by the income and expenditure decisions of households, corporations, and governments, is currently about 12 percent of GNP. This saving ratio is a "burden"—a portion of output unavailable for consumption if physical capital per worker is to be maintained or increased. The formal relationship between ratio of gross saving/GNP (the saving rate), and the rate of growth of reproducible capital is a well-known feature of endogenous growth theory (Solow, 1956).

Following Solow:

$$s = (k + n + d)(K/Y)$$

The proportion of national income (s) that a nation must save in order to maintain or increase the capital stock per worker depends upon:

1. the rate of growth in the capital stock (k),
2. the labor force growth rate (n),
3. the depreciation rate of the extant physical capital stock (d),
4. the capital stock/output ratio (K/Y).

As an example for Solow's saving/physical capital model, with a desired rate of growth of capital per worker of 1 percent, a labor force growth rate of 1 percent, a depreciation rate of 4 percent, and a capital stock/annual output ratio of 2, the requisite gross saving rate would be 12 percent. The example for physical capital exhibits the relative quantitative importance of the depreciation and capital/output ratios in determining the gross saving rate necessary for maintaining or increasing the reproducible capital stock per worker.

I submit that there are useful analytic parallels between the determinants of the saving/income ratio (s) and the educational cost/income ratio (HCIR). The HCIR depends upon parallel factors:

1. (h), the desired rate of increase in human capital, is the counterpart of (k), the rate of growth of physical capital.
2. (H),the education level of the labor force, is the counterpart of (K), physical capital.
3. (n), the rate of growth of the labor force, is identical in both models.
4. (a), the rate at which the educational expense of labor force members is "amortized" over their working life is equivalent to the depreciation rate on reproducible capital, (d).
5. (H/Y), the aggregated capital cost of education/annual income ratio for the labor force, is analogous to the (K/Y), capital stock to output ratio.

Analogous to the Solow's equation for the saving rate for the physical capital stock:

$$HCIR = (h + n + a)(H/Y)$$

Consider, in turn, the determinants of these factors:

1. Increasing the growth of human capital (h) by educational expenditures entails an increase in the enrollment rates (S) and/or expenditures per student (c) at some or all levels of education.

2. Increasing the rate of growth of the labor force raises the ratio of the educational age cohort to the population (r) and the ratio of population/labor force (p)—both of which increase the HCIR.

3. The amortization factor (a) depends upon the length of average participation in the labor force. *Ceteris paribus*, an increase in education years decreases the available working years over which education expenditure is amortized and thereby increases the amortization rate. The amortization rate for human capital is the counterpart of the depreciation rate for reproducible capital. A working life of forty years entails an amortization rate of 1/40 or 2.5 percent per year.

There is an important difference between existing analytic frameworks for educational and reproducible capital in the measurement of stocks. The stock of reproducible capital is conventionally measured in terms of its constant dollar original cost of production, less accumulated depreciation, to estimate the aggregate capital stock and (K/Y) capital/income and (K/N) capital/labor ratios.

Educational capital conventionally is not measured in terms of its input cost but in output terms of average or median years of education per labor force or population member. (See Text Table 8.1 for measures of education completed.) Measuring educational capital by years of education measures the capital stock as time units of output rather than by measuring the factor cost of the educational capital.

Increasing the average or median years of schooling by increasing the proportion of the population completing college years would be more expensive than increasing the average years of education by increasing enrollment at the high school level. The cost per year of education has been rising over time, by levels, at the same time that student enrollment ratios have been rising at higher educational levels.

It bears emphasis that the cost of education would rise, relative to other sectors in the economy, even without changes in the average years of schooling per capita if productivity growth in the education sector were less than the rest of the economy (Baumol, 1989). As labor markets equalize factor income, slower growth in labor productivity in education increases cost per unit of educational output relative to the rest of GDP and, hence, relative expenditure on education even if the years of educational output were to remain unchanged. In fact, the long-run increases in teacher/student ratios, teacher compensation/average labor force compensation, and overhead ratios indicate an increase in real inputs per unit of educational capital output.

The counterpart of the (K/Y), value of physical capital stock/annual income variable, is the (H/Y), total education cost per worker/annual income per worker—in the human capital model. This depends upon the ratio of number and cost of total education years to annual worker income. Using the educational costs per student year of Appendix Table 8.3, and the age and completed education levels of Text Table 8.1, it is interesting to note that the ratio of educational capital to average worker income (the human capital/output ratio) is in the range of 2. (The 1990 cost of 8 years of elementary and 4.7 years of high school education [12.7 median school years completed in 1990 for the 25+ population] is about $70,000 while income per labor force member in the same year was some $35,000.)

Supplying some illustrative values to equation 5.0, a 1 percent rate of growth in human capital (h), a 1 percent growth in the labor force (n), a 2.5 percent amortization rate (a), and an educational capital/annual income ratio of 2 implies an educational cost burden rate (e) of 9 percent—close to the 1990 value of 8.6 percent (Text Graph 8.1).

To summarize, analogous to the model for the saving/income ratio (s) for the physical capital stock, HCIR—the educational cost/National Income ratio—increases with four factors: (H/Y) the ratio of total educational cost per worker/annual income per worker, (h) the annual rate of increase in the average (or median) level of education completed per labor force member, (n) the labor force growth rate, and (a) the amortization rate for human capital.

Appendix 8 Tables

Appendix Table 8.1
Educational Expenditures by Level and Type   (Millions of Current$)

| Year | Elementary and Secondary | | | Higher Education | | | |
	Public	Private	Total	Public	Private	Total	Yotal
1890	141		141	11	11	22	163
1900	215		215	18	18	36	251
1910	426		426	38	38	76	502
1920	1036		1036	100	100	200	1236
1930	2317	237	2554	334	341	675	2992
1940	2344	230	2574	402	273	675	3019
1950	5838	790	6628	1430	949	2379	9007
1960	15613	1413	17026	3904	2863	6767	23793
1970	40683	4400	45083	16234	8900	25134	70217
1980	104125	8200	112325	46559	23965	70524	182849
1990	218300	18500	236800	100300	55100	155400	392200

Source: National Center for Educational Statistics, U.S. Department of Education;   Office of Educational Research and Improvement *Digest of Educational Statistics, 1991* (Washington, D.C: U.S. Government Printing Office, 1991), Tables 29,30,37.

Appendix Table 8.2
Education Enrollments, 1890–2000 (Thousands of Students)

Year	Elementary		Secondary		Higher	
	Public	Private	Public	Private	Public	Private
1890	12520	1516	203	95	157	
1900	14984	1241	519	111	238	
1910	16899	1441	915	117	355	
1920	19378	1486	2200	214	598	
1930	21279	2310	4399	341	1101	
1940	18832	2153	6601	458	797	698
1950	19387	2708	5725	672	1355	1304
1960	26911	4640	8271	1035	2181	1459
1970	32577	4052	13332	1311	6428	2153
1980	27677	3992	13242	1339	9457	2640
1990	29742	4066	11284	1129	10912	3039
2000*	33032	4516	13507	1351	12220	3472

Sources: 1870–1970: . U.S. Department of Commerce, Bureau of the Census. *Historical Statistics of The United States: Colonial Times to 1970* (Washington, D.C, U.S. Government Printing Office, 1975), H412-432. 1970–2000: *Digest of Educational Statistics,* 1991. Ibid.,Tables 3, 37, 160, 162. Updated with same publication for 1996. Projections for 2000: *Statistical Abstract for the United States.* (Washington, D.C., U.S. Government Printing Office, 1991), Table 18.

Appendix Table 8.3
Ratio Determinants of Education Cost Burden. (By Level, Public Education Only)

Year	Enrollment / Age Cohort	Age Cohort/ Population	Teacher/ Student	Teacher Comp./ Worker Income	Overhead	Pop/ Labor Force	HCIR for Education Level
				Elementary			
1890	0.858	0.233	0.029	0.477	1.538	2.687	0.011
1900	0.881	0.224	0.027	0.648	1.569	2.608	0.014
1910	0.899	0.204	0.029	0.681	1.676	2.408	0.015
1920	0.877	0.209	0.030	0.458	1.753	2.541	0.011
1930	0.865	0.200	0.030	0.919	1.910	2.516	0.023
1940	0.837	0.171	0.031	0.942	1.857	2.485	0.019
1950	0.795	0.162	0.030	0.744	2.125	2.529	0.016
1960	0.762	0.198	0.031	0.812	2.277	2.554	0.022
1970	0.798	0.201	0.035	0.828	2.270	2.478	0.026
1980	0.795	0.153	0.043	0.757	3.048	2.131	0.025
1990	0.804	0.147	0.048	0.908	2.742	2.015	0.029
2000	0.836	0.182	0.048	0.908	2.742	2.222	0.041
				Secondary			
1890	0.031	0.104	0.028	0.477	1.538	2.687	0.000
1900	0.069	0.099	0.027	0.648	1.569	2.608	0.000
1910	0.102	0.098	0.036	0.681	1.676	2.408	0.001

Appendix Table 8.3 continued

1920	0.232	0.090	0.046	0.458	1.753	2.541	0.002
1930	0.383	0.094	0.049	0.919	1.910	2.516	0.008
1940	0.532	0.094	0.045	0.942	1.857	2.485	0.010
1950	0.540	0.070	0.056	0.744	2.125	2.529	0.009
1960	0.627	0.074	0.065	0.890	2.277	2.554	0.016
1970	0.702	0.094	0.071	0.875	2.270	2.478	0.023
1980	0.625	0.093	0.073	0.800	3.048	2.131	0.022
1990	0.641	0.070	0.087	0.943	2.742	2.015	0.020
2000	0.703	0.070	0.087	0.943	2.742	2.222	0.025
				Higher Ed			
1890	0.013	0.099	0.101	1.894	1.392	2.687	0.001
1900	0.016	0.096	0.101	2.591	1.154	2.608	0.001
1910	0.020	0.099	0.101	2.472	1.199	2.408	0.001
1920	0.033	0.087	0.082	1.262	1.701	2.541	0.001
1930	0.051	0.088	0.074	2.136	2.469	2.516	0.004
1940	0.069	0.088	0.098	1.895	1.768	2.485	0.005
1950	0.118	0.076	0.093	1.137	2.470	2.529	0.006
1960	0.202	0.061	0.105	1.180	2.443	2.554	0.009
1970	0.392	0.081	0.056	1.486	2.975	2.478	0.019
1980	0.438	0.095	0.058	1.269	3.233	2.131	0.021
1990	0.584	0.074	0.061	1.466	2.888	2.015	0.022
2000	0.679	0.073	0.061	1.466	2.888	2.222	0.028

Source: Author. See Appendix Note 8.1

Appendix Table 8.4
Index Numbers for Human Capital Investment Ratios (HCIR) Components. (1990 = 1.00)

Year	Enrollment/ Age Cohort	Age Cohort /Population	Teacher/ Student	Teacher Pay/ NI	Over–head	Pop./Lab. Force	Ed.Cost/ Nat. Inc./
				ELEMENTARY			
1890	1.067	1.585	0.591	0.526	0.561	1.333	0.393
1900	1.097	1.522	0.562	0.713	0.572	1.294	0.496
1910	1.118	1.389	0.601	0.750	0.611	1.195	0.511
1920	1.091	1.421	0.615	0.505	0.639	1.261	0.388
1930	1.076	1.362	0.623	1.012	0.696	1.249	0.803
1940	1.041	1.161	0.632	1.037	0.677	1.233	0.662
1950	0.988	1.101	0.628	0.820	0.775	1.255	0.545
1960	0.948	1.344	0.642	0.894	0.830	1.267	0.770
1970	0.993	1.365	0.715	0.912	0.828	1.230	0.900
1980	0.989	1.038	0.880	0.834	1.112	1.057	0.886
1990	1.000	1.000	1.000	1.000	1.000	1.000	1.000
2000	1.040	1.234	1.000	1.000	1.000	1.103	1.498
				SECONDARY			
1890	0.049	1.484	0.323	0.506	0.561	1.333	0.009

Appendix Table 8.4 continued

1900	0.108	1.412	0.314	0.687	0.572	1.294	0.024
1910	0.159	1.398	0.415	0.722	0.611	1.195	0.049
1920	0.361	1.284	0.535	0.486	0.639	1.261	0.097
1930	0.597	1.338	0.561	0.975	0.696	1.249	0.379
1940	0.830	1.345	0.525	0.999	0.677	1.233	0.489
1950	0.842	1.005	0.652	0.789	0.775	1.255	0.424
1960	0.977	1.057	0.750	0.943	0.830	1.267	0.769
1970	1.094	1.336	0.822	0.928	0.828	1.230	1.136
1980	0.974	1.330	0.838	0.849	1.112	1.057	1.083
1990	1.000	1.000	1.000	1.000	1.000	1.000	1.000
2000	1.097	1.000	1.000	1.000	1.000	1.103	1.210
			HIGHER ED				
1890	0.022	1.332	1.657	1.292	0.482	1.333	0.040
1900	0.028	1.294	1.660	1.767	0.400	1.294	0.055
1910	0.033	1.330	1.669	1.686	0.415	1.195	0.062
1920	0.056	1.171	1.349	0.861	0.589	1.261	0.056
1930	0.087	1.183	1.226	1.457	0.855	1.249	0.197
1940	0.118	1.185	1.620	1.293	0.612	1.233	0.220
1950	0.202	1.026	1.529	0.776	0.855	1.255	0.264
1960	0.346	0.814	1.723	0.805	0.846	1.267	0.419
1970	0.672	1.085	0.925	1.014	1.030	1.230	0.867
1980	0.750	1.275	0.960	0.866	1.120	1.057	0.942
1990	1.000	1.000	1.000	1.000	1.000	1.000	1.000
2000	1.163	0.977	1.000	1.000	1.000	1.103	1.254

Source: Author. Ratio values in Appendix Table 8.3.   Index values for each of the six components of the HCIR for each of the three educational levels was computed from the ratios for Appendix Table 8.3 using the ratio values for 1990 as a base of 1.

APPENDIX 9

Appendix Note 9.1. Measurement Problems with the Neoclassical Model

These (measurement) difficulties are conumdrums....The fact that two incommensurable collections of miscellaneous objects (the capital stock and net output) cannot in themselves provide the material for a quantitative analysis need not, of course, prevent us from making approximate statistical comparisons, depending on some broad element of judgement rather than strict calculation...their purpose should be to satisfy historical or social curiosity, a purpose for which perfect precision...is neither usual nor necessary. To say that (net GDP) is greater, but the price-level is lower, than ten years ago...is a proposition of a similar character to the statement that Queen Victoria was a better queen but not a happier woman than Queen Elizabeth–a proposition not without meaning and not without interest, but unsuitable as material for the differential calculus. Our precision will be a mock precision if we try to use such partly vague and non-quantitative concepts as the basis of a quantitative analysis.

J. M. Keynes (1935, p.35)

Measurement Concepts for Capital Stocks

Keynes raised the problem of measuring the variables of the neoclassical model more than half a century ago. One result was the development of an accounting system for national income and price indexes to convert output and capital series into "real" terms. However, the problems of measuring a flow of services from the capital stock and the rate of depreciation of the capital stock have not been satisfactorily solved in economic analysis.

While I have used an official governmental series for the physical capital stock in Appendix Table 9.1 and to provide evidence on the output/capital and capital labor series in Text Graphs 9.1 and 9.2, I regard these series as having limited validity. The following discussion explains why attempts to value the capital stock are not likely to be useful in explanations that seek to establish a direct causal relationship between investment and output.

An explanation of changes in the rate of economic growth that relies on changes in the flow of services from physical capital must have a careful specification of the variables being measured and a way to measure those variables. I have discussed the concepts that lay behind the dependent variable––the flow of quantity of goods and services represented by GDP. But what of the independent variable - the flow of services from physical capital?

Definitions. Repeating and expanding our definition of terms and measurement conventions: Capital is a "stock." Output is a "flow." Both can be valued in terms of their cost of production in current dollars. The increase, during a specified time period, in the accumulated stocks of physical capital possessed by a society is "net investment," which is the difference between two flows: "gross investment," the flow of current production into the creation of new capital stocks, and "depreciation," which is the flow of previously accumulated capital stocks out of productive use because of physical deterioration or economic obsolescence.

Economic growth, the time rate of growth of output, measures the rate of change in output rates between two time periods. The time rate of growth of the capital stock measures the net increase in the capital stock between two periods resulting from the difference between the positive flow of gross investment and the negative flow of depreciation. Conceptually, a society allocates the utilization of its productive resources during a current time period into the production of goods for consumption during the current time period or production of capital stocks for use in successive time periods.

Much of the original theorizing about capital was based on an analysis of grain seed–"eating the seed corn" was a common term for failure to save and form capital in the current time period. Grain seed forms an interesting example: the amount harvested (and available for consumption in the next time period) depends upon the amount left unconsumed from current stocks and, thus, available for sowing in the next time period. The productive power of grain had a further use in that it could be used to feed the human or animal labor available for producing grain in the next time period. The capital used for production and the production itself were measured in the same physical unit. A principal difference with modern capital theory is that the capital itself was totally consumed in the (annual) time period of production so there was no depreciation problem and no accounting for complementary inputs (plows, land improvements, etc.).

Application. The neoclassical model of the rate of growth of the (physical) capital stock depends upon the three factors:

1.   the share of current output devoted to capital formation (s) for saving
2.   the ratio between flow of current output and the current capital stock (y/K)
3.   the depreciation rate of the current capital stock (d).

To state the definitional relationships formally:

$\Delta K = sy - dK$

$\Delta K \equiv$ *the change in the capital stock between two time periods.*

$s \equiv$ *proportion of current production allocated to production of new capital.*

$y \equiv$ *the current flow rate of production.*

$d \equiv$ *rate of depreciation of the capital stock during the current time period.*

Dividing all the terms through by K yields : $\Delta K/K = s(y/K) - d$.

$\Delta K/K$ can also be defined as the time rate of change of K (the rate of growth of the capital stock $(\delta K/\delta t)$): so, defining $\delta K/\delta t \equiv k$, $k = s(y/K)-d$.

Derivation of the Growth Identity from the Definition of Saving, Net Investment, and the Equality of Saving and Investment in the National Accounts. These are the behavioral relationships between the rate of growth of output and the rate of growth of the capital stock over various periods. However, these behavioral relationships are not simple, direct, or constant.   The ratio of output/capital stock depends upon the extent of the utilization of the capital stock; for example, the kilowatt hours of electricity produced by a constant dollar of investment in an electric generator depends upon how many hours per year and/or at what speed the generator is operated. Without that specification, the output/capital ratio is variable and unspecified.

What determines the rate of depreciation—the rate at which the capital stock is diminished? It depends on arbitrary assumptions that are made to determine financial results and tax liability rather than actual net output.   Without the specification of an output/capital ratio or a means of quantifying depreciation, a capital stock and a flow of services from the capital stock cannot be empirically quantified.   And if economists can't quantify the variables in their theory the described relationships may be suggestive but they hardly qualify as natural laws of behavior for an economic system.

Explanation. Changes in the flow of value-added final output measured over discrete time periods—such as those disaggregated by sector in chapter 5—do not result primarily from net changes in the stock of capital within those time periods. Indeed, most of the change in potential output that is possible for an economy in any time period results from the economic decisions and actions taken in previous periods that create the stocks of capital available during the current period. These accumulated stocks are the primary determinant of the potential capital services flows and output flows during the current period. It is past–not current–economic activity that creates the stocks of capital which significantly determine the potential flow of output. A more detailed discussion of the problems of using the capital stock in growth models is made by Maurice F. G. Scott (1989). He makes the argument that gross investment, rather than the net capital stock, should be used to explain the rate of growth of output. I disagree.

Thus, one cannot move easily to compare and attribute causation from changes in the flows into the capital stock (gross investment) in one period to changes in the flow of output during the same period. Consider the income statement and balance sheet of an individual firm. The firm might record a significant increase in the value of a new issue of stock or bond financing. It would not necessarily be associated with the increase in gross revenues during the year although one would expect that the capital had been added in expectation of the growth of revenue in future years and that would have been the inducement for purchasers of bonds or shares in the firm by investors. The stock of capital that contributes to production in the current accounting period has been created by production in previous time periods and is utilized and used up at different rates in the process of production in the current time period.

Additions to the stock of accumulated physical capital are conventionally valued in terms of original (market or imputed) cost of production, which, in turn, reflects the opportunity cost of the consumption goods given up in the previous periods to produce the capital available in the current period. The opportunity cost of the capital goods depends upon the technology used in their production relative to the technology used in the production of consumption goods (relative cost), and the amount of productive capacity (quantity) used for the production of capital goods.

The valuation of a perpetual inventory of capital would theoretically make it possible to measure the current physical capital stock/output ratio for a society–a ratio of the value of a perpetual inventory stock of capital to the value of a flow of output from that capital during a particular accounting period. However, there are two problems here: (1) different kinds of out output have different capital stock/output ratios, and (2) the value of the capital stock/output ratio varies with changes in the level of utilization of the capital stock.

Conventional economic theory may postulate a direct relationship between changes in the rate of growth of the stock of physical capital and changes in the rate of growth of levels of output with respect to time. However, estimates of the changes in even the physical capital stock depend upon the use of arbitrary accounting conventions on depreciation and arbitrary assumptions about utilization. And estimates of the human capital, knowledge capital, and natural resource capital that are combined with physical capital in the production process are not accounted for.

Conceptually, one cannot use gross investment in previous accounting periods as the (lagged) independent variable for changes in the capital stock. Further, the statistical demonstration of a causal relationship between changes in output in the current period and changes in the capital stock in previous periods depend upon both the estimate of a changing inventory of capital and an estimate of the use rate of that capital.

The conceptual and data requirements of demonstrating a direct and stable relationship beween changes in the aggregate capital stock and changes in aggregate output are considerable—even before addressing the direction of causation! First, one would have to separate changes in the capital stock/output ratio from changes in the output mix and second, changes in the utilization rate of the capital stock have to be accounted for. Doing this for a national economy over historical time would be conceptually possible but arbitrary and empirically difficult. There are other conceptual problems as well. The first conceptual problem is deciding whether the capital/output relationship is gross or net. Does one, for example, compare the total output that is associated with a particular stock of capital or is the output of capital "net" value added after subtraction of payments to labor? One cannot just subtract the payments to labor on the grounds that they represent the "marginal product of labor" because the marginal product of labor is dependent on the capital available to enhance its productivity.

Economic Theory and Accounting Convention. There is a conceptual problem in deciding the appropriate depreciation rate for capital—the rates used for conventional accounting purposes are arbitrary with respect to the determination of physical capacity. What is the value of a computer that is completely functional but economically obsolete because it is slower, or has less memory than the machine that replaces it? The conventional accounting solution is to value capital equipment at cost or market—whichever is less. It would be theoretically possible to deal with the valuation of depreciation by periodically valuing existing capital equipment at its current market value. However, in many cases there are no markets for used capital equipment and if there were, the severance cost and/or transactions costs would severely diminish its value in the used goods market relative to its current value in use to the company.

There is a flow of services from the previously created capital. Part of the capital is consumed or diminished (1) by utilization in the production process of the current period, (2) by the deterioration from natural forces, (3) from technological obsolescence, or (4) from changes in the structure of demand.

As an example, the construction of the capital stock of railroad tracks in one decade increases the productivity of labor in the transportation sector of the economy in subsequent periods. The value of the investment in the track may (1) be worn out by usage (heavy loads cause metal fatigue), (2) deteriorate with time from the exposure to the weather, or (3) become less productive because rail traffic is shifted to the highways or (4) no longer be economically important on a particular railroad track because the coal mine formerly using the railroad has closed down from competition with petroleum.

Generally accepted conventions are not based on economic theory. A menu of alternative generally accepted accounting conventions (GAAP) has been formulated to standardize financial accounting for depreciation for public reporting and for tax purposes. A building may be depreciated over fifty years and a truck over five years. But, with proper maintenance, the building may have a useful life of 100 years and the truck be worn out by a high rate of utilization or be economically obsolete in two years. So there is no standard way to determine what reproducible capital passes out of productive use by depreciation. As a consequence, the reported estimates of the stock of reproducible capital made on the basis of original cost of production less accumulated depreciation do not form a consistent basis for estimating the size of the reproducible capital stock that makes a contribution to production during a current accounting period.

Economics has traditionally emphasized the importance of gross investment additions to capital in increasing the rate of current output. However, there is a time period disparity between the formation of capital and its use in production. Capital is formed by allocating labor and capital resources to the production of capital goods in prior periods so that the potential output in the current period is jointly determined by the stock of capital created in previous periods and the utilization of that capital during the current period.

It would be empirically simpler, in demonstrating the quantitative relationship betweeen changes in the stock of capital and changes in the level of output per worker, if one could directly estimate changes in the stock of capital in each production period and compare those with changes in the level of output. This could be done by a perpetual inventory method if the reduction in the stock of capital by depreciation could be as valued for the current accounting period by market transactions–the method used for the valuation of additions to the capital stock by gross investment. But it can't.

To illustrate the accounting problem in doing this; the farmer produces a crop of wheat with a particular market value. The value added (net output) depends upon accounting for changes in his capital stock. The fertilizer is quite straightforward–the consumption of fertilizer capital is measured as purchases plus changes in physical inventory. But how are changes in the machinery and barns measured in the capital stock? Changes in the accounting cost allocation change measured value added on an inverse one-for-one basis. Increasing the depreciation by $1 reduces the value of the inventory of the capital stock and net output by $1. Similar considerations apply to changes in the productive capacity of the land by grading, ditching, draining, fencing (and even past applications of fertilizer, pesticides, fungicides, etcetera,) if they have been capitalized.

Capital Theory and National Income Accounting

Classical economist David Ricardo and some of his neoclassical successors (e.g., Alfred Marshall and John Bates Clark) had the objective, in their economic analysis, of explaining the distribution of the income from a *given* production level with existing resources and technology rather than the determinants of the level and growth of production.

The categories of capital and labor also played a large part in the Marxian theory of the class conflict that would accompany economic development. While Marx attributed economic growth to capital formation and technological change, the emphasis in Marxian explanation was on the ownership of physical capital, on the changing proportions of fixed and circulating capital, and on the effects of capital accumulation on the functional distribution of income between capitalists and workers and the inevitable class conflict that this would produce.

These traditional concepts and categories of the factors of production are arbitrary–there is nothing unchangeable about them. One could relabel "land" as "natural capital" and further differentiate natural capital into undeveloped agricultural land, untapped mineral deposits, land whose value came from location, or merely combine land and other natural resources into a broader category of capital that included structures, land improvements, and even machines.

In contemporary accounting practice "capital" on the balance sheets of business enterprises is customarily broken down into "current assets" and "fixed assets." Current assets are subdivided further into such categories as inventories and accounts receivable and fixed assets are classified as site improvements, structures, and machines. Complementarily, in NIA, the calculation of gross investment is limited to business expenditures on plant, equipment, and inventory change and household additions to the residential housing stock. Inconsistently, expenditures by government on buildings and equipment are not included. Understandably, but contrary to the logic of current versus future consumption, expenditures by government and the private sector on education by educational institutions and businesses is not included and public and private expenditures on research and development that increase the stock of knowledge are not included in investment.

On the saving side (which matches gross investment after adjustment for international flows), government deficits or surpluses are part of the saving calculation, but taxes collected by government for capital formation in buildings and roads are not included in saving. Business saving includes retained corporate earnings and capital consumption allowances (depreciation). Corporate saving measures the flow to and from financial assets available to corporations for increasing their assets. It does not measure expenditure for the development of human capital or knowledge capital by corporations, or their consumption or diminution by pollution of natural capital.

Personal saving is estimated as the change in financial assets and the change in the stock of owner-occupied homes and consumer durables, less changes in mortgage debt and consumer credit. Thus, the measure of household saving includes the net flows into financial markets after adjustment for the self-financing of durable assets. Thus, the purchase of a car counts as saving and investment but the purchase of an education or acceptance of reduced compensation, while receiving on-the-job training, does not count.

Thus, our measures of saving and capital forming investment from GAAP and NIA concepts are incomplete. At a minimum there is no identification of government investment in (or depreciation of) reproducible capital. Some current business expenditures may create capital assets but be treated as part of the cost of goods produced and consumed during the current accounting period. Business and government expenditures on research and development are treated as part of the current cost of production rather than additions to the stock of knowledge. The large expenditures on institutional education of the population and the expenditures of business firms on increasing the knowledge and productivity of their employees are not identified as an investment in human capital.

Changes in the net stock of consumer durables may provide a stream of service from those durables, but then the measurement of that production is not included in the measurement of current production.   Neither neoclassical economic theory or currently used GAAP or NIA concepts are appropriate to an explanation of even the formation—much less the depreciation—of the stocks of capital that are a primary determinant of output and its changes over time.

A simply stated version of the neoclassical model is that capital is accumulated through producing capital goods. The production of capital goods can only take place when resources of existing capital and labor are used to produce capital goods rather than goods for current consumption. The addition of capital goods to the capital stock continues until the dimishing marginal physical productivity of capital drives the rate of return on further additions to the capital stock to a low level.

Diminishing marginal physical productivity of capital is expressed as the ratio of the increment of output to the incremental addition to the capital stock. There is a measurement problem here because physical units of output are not the same as the physical units of capital; the capital good—the electrical generator—is physically steel and copper while its output is electrical current. The diminishing marginal productivity must, therefore, be expressed in terms of the value of the flow of output of the capital good to the value of the flow of services from the capital good. The "low" ratio of the value of the flows is the lowest return that lenders will accept for a unit of future output to a unit of current output–a time rate of preference.

The Capital Stock and Neoclassical Growth Models

Most theorizing about growth by economists is structured by models of production and markets created to explain two other sets of phenomena—the determination of equilibrium prices and outputs, and the distribution of income between the factors of production. These models have limited application in explaining the nature and process of capital accumulation and technological and organizational change, which are the essence of economic growth.

The importance of physical capital in the theory of growth is a feature of classical economics. The theory of production and the theory of the growth of production in classical (Ricardian) economics is built on the theory of variable proportions. Simply stated, the classical model postulates that increasing inputs of a variable factor of production (such as labor or capital), while other inputs (such as labor or capital) are held fixed, will increase output—but at a diminishing rate. The extension of the Ricardian production function to a long-run macroeconomy assumes that as capital is increased relative to labor, total output and output per unit of labor will increase, but at a rate that steadily diminishes toward zero.

The historical origin of the classical model was Malthusian theorizing about agriculture. An important assumption of the Classical model is that *technology is held constant*. But, in explaining growth, of what use is a model where one assumes the constancy of the factor (technology) that one is trying to explain?

There is another characteristic of agriculture that conceals a problem in explanation. In agriculture the initial example of physical production was grain; grain was both an output and an input. It was an output that could be consumed or saved from output during one production period and directly used as an input in subsequent production periods in which it could also be consumed or used as an input to increase output the following year.

In the first elaboration of the relation of capital inputs and output in grain production, the yield of grain in a one-year production period depended upon the amount of seed held over from the previous year and sown in the new year (hence the allusions to consuming more than the net output of grain in one year as "eating the seed corn").

In this explanatory (and moral) tale, increasing the amount of seed corn withheld from consumption in one harvest and sown for the next increases the next harvest—but at a decreasing rate with increasing applications of seed. The rational farmer, varying only the capital input of seed, would plant seed up to the point where the net increase in the harvest in year two was just equal to the value to him of consuming the grain in year one relative to the value of the grain in year two—the time rate of preference. Abstention from current consumption was an important element in the model, and capital could only be used to increase production in year two by a deliberate decision to reduce consumption in year one. Further, in this simple model there is no difficulty in calculating net output after subtracting the initial seed—all the depreciation of the capital stock is done in one year—it is literally used up in the production process.

The classical model, however, lends itself to elaboration. Grain saved from year one can also be used to feed workers who clear new ground or build walls to exclude grazing livestock from the fields. Net output is again increased, but the increase in output from feeding the grain to agricultural workers to build physical capital comes over a number of years and the amount of depreciation of the initial capital in an annual production period becomes less determinate. Still, it seems obvious that devoting part of the production of one time period (saving and investment) to increase the production of subsequent periods is a process subject to diminishing returns.

Note, however, that the production process described in the example is static and the capital input of seed corn is only one possible input—nothing is assumed to vary the size of the harvest except the amount of grain saved from the previous harvest to increase yield per unit of land and labor. The inevitability of diminishing returns depends upon this assumption of constant technology and the exclusion from consideration of the complementarity of inputs. Most important, there is no possibility of reducing the cost of capital—the seed grain—relative to its seed grain output because it is measured in terms of itself—the output of seed capital is seed output!

In the "real" world diminishing returns to capital may be postponed indefinitely with the substitution of new capital goods or less expensive capital goods that actually increase the ratio of output/capital and output/labor. As an example, the improved tractor, which costs more (in constant dollars) than the old tractor but lasts longer and plows more acres per hour, has the effect of increasing the capital/labor ratio but also increasing the output/capital ratio. Further, it is possible that the cost of making tractors falls so much relative to their potential output that it decreases the capital/labor ratio but increases the potential output/capital ratio even more, hence, increasing the output/labor ratio.

What reduces the cost of the improved tractors or computers—making more of them! The increased production of capital goods reduces their price and, thereby, brings not diminishing but increasing returns in output per worker! The cost of capital with a given output potential is reduced by technological change in metallurgy or silicon chip technology, machine tools, engineering, and mass production techniques.

The classical model emphasizes that growth in output per worker must eventually come to an end because of the diminishing marginal physical productivity that necessarily occurs with the application of more and more capital per worker. But that is not what is observed in historical economic activity because the process of growth itself is continually increasing efficiency in the production of capital goods—which reduces the the ratio of their constant dollar cost per unit of production capacity and may even reduce their value per worker.

The neoclassical growth model adds to the classical model the growing burden of depreciation with the increase in the ratio of capital stock/output. It postulates that as an economy steadily increases the ratio of capital stock to output, the annual depreciation flow grows relative to the annual savings flow from any given output until, inevitably in the model, gross savings are equal to depreciation and net additions to the capital stock are zero. As the capital stock reaches a maximum, output/labor reaches a corresponding maximum. The asymptotic approach to this maximum is the slowing in the growth of output per worker–and this asymptotic behavior is inferred to be inevitable and to explain the inevitable decline in the rate of economic growth.

The Applicability of the Classical and Neoclassical Models to the Explanation of Growth

I find little explanatory power in the simple classical and neoclassical growth models. The rate of growth of the capital stock does not explain variations in the rate of growth of output. Further, one cannot move directly in explaining causation for the slowdown in economic growth from changes in the saving ratio (the ratio of Saving/GDP that can be observed) to changes in in the rate of capital growth. This is because (1) the growth in the the capital stock depends upon the depreciation rate, and (2) the marginal output/capital stock ratio is variable.

If, in the neoclassical model, economic growth were necessarily accompanied with an increasing ratio of capital to output, higher and higher gross savings rates would be necessary to compensate for the higher depreciation resulting from the higher ratio of capital to output. This, of course, would be a powerful argument for the inevitability of the slowdown of economic growth from the slowdown in the rate of growth of the stock of reproducible capital as depreciation takes an increasing share of gross investment—apart from any "diminishing returns" from increases in the output/capital ratio. But that is not what I observe has happened.

Appendix 9 Tables

Appendix Table 9.1
Constant $ Cost of Net Stock of Fixed Reproducible Tangible Wealth

Year	Private Total	Equipment	Residential	Government	Total
1930	2210	289	1050	399	2609
1940	1958	238	1001	584	2542
1950	2350	447	1194	1193	3543
1960	3418	655	1781	1330	4748
1970	5074	1070	2530	1883	6957
1980	7192	1709	3520	2123	9315
1990	9157	2202	4384	2539	11696

Source: U.S. Department of Commerce, *Survey of Current Business*, Sept. 1993, 73/9. Table 24.

This Appendix Table serves as the source of the capital stock variables used in Text Graphs 9.1 and 9.2. The labor and output variables used in those graphs come from the sectoral employment and output data presented in chapter 5 from sources presented in Appendix 5.

Appendix Table 9.2
Ratios of Gross and Net Investment to GDP and Productivity Growth

	GrossInvestment/GDP	Net Investment/GDP	Productivity Growth
1930	0.11	0.02	0.41
1940	0.13	0.05	0.33
1950	0.19	0.13	0.16
1960	0.15	0.07	0.25
1970	0.29	0.06	0.23
1980	0.17	0.06	0.09
1990	0.14	0.04	0.1

Sources: Gross and Net Investment and GDP: 1930–1960: *Historical Statistics,* Tables F-47, F144; 1960–1990 *ERP(1994)*, Tables B-1, B-14. Productivity Growth: *Author,* Text Table 3.1.

Appendix Table 9.3
Decennial Changes in Capitalization and Productivity:
Total Economy and Industrial Sector (I–VI) Only

Decade Ending	Total Economy			Industrial Sector (I–VI) Only		
	Labor Productivity d(Q/N)	Capitalization d(K/N)	CapitalProductivity d(Q/K)	Labor Productivity d(Q/N)	Capitalization d(K/N)	CapitalProductivity d(Q/K)
1940	0.21	-0.05	0.27			
1950	0.22	0.09	0.12			
1960	0.20	0.18	0.02	0.27	0.34	-0.05
1970	0.17	0.18	0.00	0.31	0.38	-0.05
1980	0.04	0.06	-0.02	0.12	0.23	-0.09
1990	0.08	0.05	0.03	0.17	0.19	-0.02

Source: Author. Capital Values from Appendix Table 1. Output and Employment Data from Appendix 5.

References

Arrow, Kenneth, "The Economic Implications of Learning by Learning by Doing," *Review of Economic Studies* (39) (1962): 155–73.

Barro, Robert J. *Macroeconomics*. New York: John Wiley, 1990.

Baumol, William, S. A. Batey Blackman, and E. N. Wolff, *Productivity and American Leadership: The Long View*. Cambridge: MIT Press, 1989.

Becker, Gary. *Human Capital: A Theoretical and Empirical Analysis with Special Reference to Education*. New York: Columbia University Press, 1964.

Bjork, Gordon. *Private Enterprise and Public Interest: The Development of American Capitalism*. New York: Prentice Hall, 1969.

_____. *Life, Liberty, and Property: The Economic and Politics of Land Use Planning and Environmental Controls*. Lexington, Mass.: D.C. Heath, 1979.

Blaug, Marc. "The Empirical Status of Human Capital Theory: A Slightly Jaundiced Survey." *Journal of Economic Literature* 14(3), (1976): 827–55.

Boskin, M. J., and L. J. Lau. "Capital, Technology, and Economic Growth," edited by Nathan Rosenberg et al., *Technology and the Wealth of Nations*. Palo Alto, CA: Stanford University Press, 1992: 17–55.

Chandler, Alfred D. Jr. *Scale and Scope: The Dynamics of Industrial Capitalism*. Cambridge: Harvard University Press, 1990.

Coase, Ronald. "The Problem of Social Cost," *Journal of Law and Economics* 3 (October 1960): 1–44.

Coatesworth, John, "Obstacles to Economic Growth in Nineteenth Century Mexico," *American Historical Review* 83.1 (1978): 84–85.

Daly, Herman, and John Cobb. *For the Common Good*. Boston: Beacon Press, 1994.

Denison, Edward F. *The Sources of Economic Growth in the United States and the Prospects Before Us*. New York: Committee for Economic Development, 1962.

_____. *Trends in American Economic Growth, 1929–1982*. Washington, D.C.: The Brookings Institution, 1985.

Easterlin, R. A. *Population, Labor Force, and Long Swings in Economic Growth: The American Experience*. New York: Columbia University Press, 1968.

_____. *Birth and Fortune*. New York: Basic Books, 1980.

Economic Report of the President, 1985–1997 Volumes. Washington, D.C.: Government Printing Office.

Fogel, Robert, "Nutrition and the Decline in Mortality since 1700: Some Prelimary Findings," *Long-Term Factors in American Economic Growth*. Edited by Stanley Engerman and Robert Gallman. Chicago: University of Chicago Press, 1986.

Franklin, Benjamin. "Proposal to the American Philosophical Society for promoting useful knowledge among the British Plantations in America—1743," In *Benjamin Franklin: The Autobiography and Other Writings*. New York: New American Library, 1961.

Gold, Bela. *Productivity, Technology, and Capital*. Lexington, Mass. Lexington Books, 1979.

Goldin, Claudia. *Understanding the Gender Gap: An Economic History of American Women*. New York: Oxford University Press, 1990.

Griliches, Zvi. "Hybrid Corn: An Exploration in the Economics of Technological Change," *Econometrica* 29 (Oct. 1957): 501–22.

Gruber, Jonathan, and David Wise. "Social Security and Retirement: An International Comparison," *American Economic Review* 88 (May 1998): 158–67.

Hempel, Carl G. *Aspects of Scientific Explanation and Other Essays on the Philosophy of Science*. New York: Free Press, 1965.

Hicks, John R. *Value and Capital*. Oxford: Oxford University Press, 1939.

Kendrick, J. W. *Productivity Trends in the United States*. Princeton: NBER, 1961

Keynes, John Maynard. *The General Theory of Employment, Interest, and Money*. London: Macmillan, 1935.

Kuznets, Simon.

———. *National Product Since 1869*. New York: NBER, 1946.

———. *National Income and Its Composition, 1919–1938*. New York: NBER, 1954.

———. *National Product Since 1869*. New York: NBER, 1961.

———. *Modern Economic Growth*. New Haven: Yale University Press, 1966.

———. *Population, Capital, and Growth*. London: Heinemann, 1973.

Landau, L. and N. Rosenberg. "Successful Commercialization in the Chemical Process Industries." In *Technology and the Wealth of Nations*, edited by Nathan Rosenberg et al., Palo Alto: Stanford University Press, 1992.

Lucas, Robert E. "On the Mechanics of Economic Development." *Journal of Monetary Economics* 22 (1988): 3–42.

Macpherson, C. B. *The Theory of Possessive Individualism*. Oxford: Oxford University Press, 1962.

Maddison, Angus. *Phases of Capitalist Development*. New York: Oxford University Press, 1982

Madrick, Jeffrey. *The End of Affluence*. New York: Random House, 1995.

Marshall, Alfred. *Principles of Economics*. London: Macmillan, 1890.

McClelland, Peter. *Causal Explanation and Model Building in History, Economics, and the New Economic History*. Ithaca: Cornell University Press, 1975.

Mowery, David. *Alliance Politics and Economics: Multinational Joint Ventures in Commercial Aircraft*. Cambridge, Mass.: Ballinger, 1985.

Murphy, Kevin, and Finis Welch, "Perspectives on the Social Security Crisis and Proposed Solutions." *American Economic Review* 88 (May, 1998): 158–67.

National Center for Educational Statistics. U.S. Department of Education. Office of Educational Research and Improvement: *Digest of Educational Statistics, 1991*. Washington, D.C.: Government Printing Office.

OECD. *National Accounts, 1960–1993*, Volume 1. Paris: OECD, 1995.

OECD. *Statistics of National Accounts, 1950–1961*. Paris: OECD, 1964.

Rawls, John. *A Theory of Justice*. Cambridge: Harvard University Press, 1971.

Romer, Paul M. "Increasing Returns and Long Run Growth." *Journal of Political Economy* 94 (1986): 1002–37.

Rosenberg, Nathan. "Technological Change in the Machine Tool Industry, 1840–1910."

Journal of Economic History (December 1963).
————. *Inside the Black Box: Technology and Economics*. Cambridge (UK): Cambridge University Press, 1982.
_____. *Exploring the Black Box: Technology, Economics, and History*.   Cambridge (UK): Cambridge University Press, 1994.
Rosenberg, Nathan, and L. E. Birdzell. *How the West Grew Rich*. New York: Basic Books, 1986.
Samuelson, Robert J. *The Good Life and its Discontents: The American Dream in the Age of Entitlement*. New York: Vintage Books, 1995.
Schor, Juliet. *The Overworked American: The Unexpected Decline of Leisure*. New York, Basic Books, 1991.
Smith, Adam. *An Inquiry into the Nature and Causes of the Wealth of Nations*. 1776. Reprint. Indianapolis: Liberty Classics Edition, 1981.
Solow, Robert M. "A Contribution to the Theory of Economic Growth." *Quarterly Journal of Economics* 70 (1956): 65–94.
U.S. Bureau of the Census. *Historical Statistics of the United States: Colonial Times to 1970*. Washington, D.C.: Government Printing Office, 1975.
_____, *Statistical Abstract*. Washington, D.C.: Government Printing Office, 1980–1995.
U.S. Department of Commerce, *Survey of Current Business*.   Volumes 70–78. Washington, D.C.: Government Printing Office.
U.S. Department of Labor. Bureau of Labor Statistics. *Labor Force Statistics Derived from Current Population Survey, 1948–1987. Bulletin 2307*.   Washington, D.C.: Government Printing Office, 1988.
————. *Outlook 2000. Bulletin 2352*. Washington, D.C.: Government Printing Office, 1990.
————. *Employment, Hours, and Earnings, U.S., 1909–1994*. Bulletin 2445. Washington, D.C.: Government Printing Office, 1995.
Wallis, John, and Douglass North. "Measuring the Transaction Sector in the American Economy." In *Long Term Factors in American Economic Growth*, edited by Stanley Engerman and Robert Gallman, Chicago: University of Chicago Press, 1986.
Willis, R. and S. Rosen, "Education and Self-Selection" *Journal of Political Economy* 87 (5), 1978
Wilson, Kenneth, and Bennett Davis. *Redesigning Education*. New York: Henry Holt, 1995.

Index

About the Author

GORDON C. BJORK is Jonathon B. Lovelace Professor of Economics, Claremont McKenna College and the Peter F. Drucker School of Management, The Claremont Graduate School. A former college president as well as consultant for various corporations and banking associations, Professor Bjork is the author of three earlier books on macroeconomic theory.

ISBN 0-275-96531-7

90000>

EAN

9 780275 965310